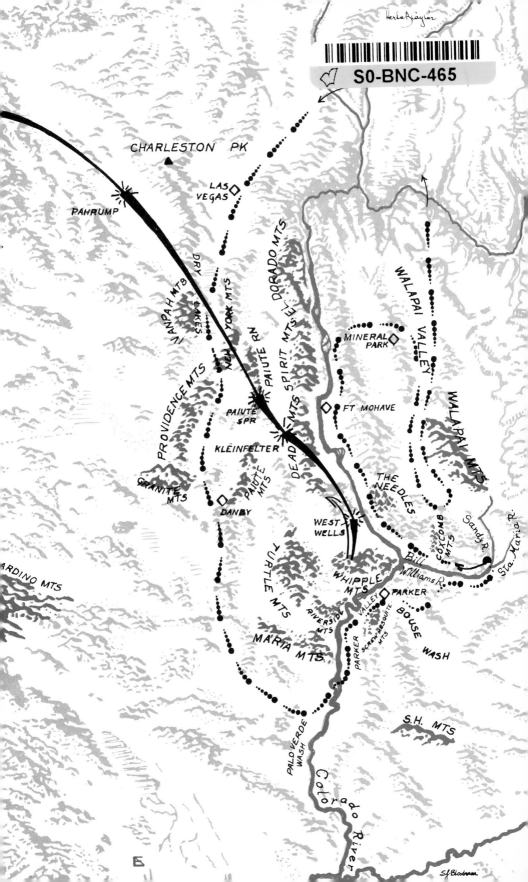

CHARLESTON PK

LAS VEGAS

PAHRUMP

DRY LAKES

ANPAH MTS

NEW YORK MTS

N PAIUTE RN

EL DORADO MTS

DEAD MTS

SPIRIT MTS

WALAPAI VALLEY

MINERAL PARK

FT MOHAVE

WALAPAI MTS

PROVIDENCE MTS

PAIUTE SPR

KLEINFELTER

GRANITE MTS

PAIUTE MTS

DANBY

THE NEEDLES

COXCOMB MTS

Sandy R.

Sta. Maria R.

WEST WELLS

Bill Williams R.

ARDINO MTS

TURTLE MTS

WHIPPLE MTS

PARKER

BOUSE WASH

RIVERSIDE MTS

PARKER VALLEY

SCREW MESQUITE MTS

MARIA MTS

S.H. MTS

PALO VERDE WASH

Colorado River

B

Sf Bloxham

THE CHEMEHUEVIS

THE CHEMEHUEVIS

CAROBETH LAIRD

MALKI MUSEUM PRESS

Printed in the United States of America
By Rubidoux Printing Company, Riverside, California

This book is based upon information furnished by George Laird and is dedicated to his memory and to the Chemehuevi tribe.

FOREWORD

IN the spring of 1971, Professor Lowell John Bean of California State University at Hayward took a group of anthropology students on a field trip to the Morongo Indian Reservation near Banning, California. Most of his students worked with Cahuilla informants at Morongo and Torres-Martinez reservations, but Bean sent a few students farther afield. Two of his students, Helen Hayworth and Joan Farnum, were assigned to Parker, Arizona, to conduct a general ethnographic survey among the Chemehuevi people.

While in Parker, Helen Hayworth and Joan Farnum located Indian informants who told them they should interview Mrs. Georgia Laird Culp, a tribal leader among the Chemehuevis and editor of the *Chemehuevi Newsletter*, who lived in Los Angeles with her mother, Carobeth Laird. Professor Bean was immediately intrigued by the latter name. While working with the unpublished papers of John Peabody Harrington at the Smithsonian Institution earlier that year, he had noted Carobeth Laird's name as co-author of a paper on the Chemehuevis. (Actually, the paper had been authored by Mrs. Laird.) He asked his students to arrange a meeting with Mrs. Laird, so that he could discuss the possibility of publishing the paper.

The results of their meeting were much more dramatic than Professor Bean could have foreseen. He learned that Carobeth Laird had once been married to Harrington, one of America's great linguists and ethnographers, and field ethnologist for the Bureau of American Ethnology for almost forty years. Mrs. Laird had been trained as a linguist by Harrington, had worked with him in the field from 1916 to 1920, and finally had left the anthropologist to marry her main Chemehuevi informant, George Laird. He also learned that she had recently completed the first full-length book ever written on the Chemehuevis—one of the least known Indian groups on the North American continent. She had worked alone, outside the world of academic scholarship, drawing primarily upon an immense amount of knowledge about the Chemehuevis acquired over the years from her late husband, George Laird. She had recently submitted the manuscript to an anthropologist representing a university press and had been told the book needed to be rewritten from a contemporary theoretical perspective. Bean, after examining the manuscript, recognized that Mrs. Laird's unique approach transcended the theoretical fads and fashions of anthropology. He began arranging for publication of this book by Malki Museum Press.

Two weeks later, Professor Bean invited Mrs. Laird to the annual fiesta held at Malki Museum on the Morongo Indian Reservation. Throughout the day, she sat in the shade of a palm-covered ramada, observing the festivities with interest and talking in Chemehuevi with Indian friends. The annual fiesta at Morongo is always attended by many linguists and anthropologists from universities and colleges throughout the state. Word spread quickly across the fiesta grounds that the former wife of John Peabody Harrington—a legendary and mysterious figure in the annals of American anthropology—was present at the fiesta. One by one scholars at the fiesta sought out Carobeth Laird under the ramada to question her about Harrington, about her knowledge of Chemehuevi, and to urge her to continue her own research. During the day, the editorial board of Malki Museum also met with Mrs. Laird and concluded arrangements for publishing this book. At the age of seventy-five Carobeth Laird returned to a life she had left fifty years earlier. She reentered the discipline of anthropology.

Carobeth Laird was born in Coleman, Texas on July 20, 1895, the daughter of Emma Cora Chaddock and James Harvey Tucker, who ran a printing shop in Coleman and published *The Coleman Voice*, later the *Coleman Democrat-Voice*. She remembers her childhood in Texas as "lonely, sickly, tense, introspective, and over-protected." Although precocious—she had learned to read by the age of five—she did not enter school until the age of nine.

The summer Carobeth turned fourteen, and for three successive summers thereafter, her parents made pilgrimages with her to Mexico: first to Saltillo, where her father had spent his childhood and adolescence; then on to San Luis Potosi; and finally, when her parents felt sufficiently acclimated, to Mexico City. It was in Mexico that Carobeth first discovered she had a facility for other languages. It was also in Mexico—at the age of sixteen—that she fell in love with an older man the family had met while traveling. The romance ended without marriage, leaving Carobeth with a daughter to support.

In February of 1913, the Tucker family moved to San Diego. Although Carobeth had gone to grade school in Texas and had attended two or three years of high school, she had not graduated. For the next two years she haunted the San Diego Public Library, bringing home "musty, outdated, inconceivably dull, and mostly incomprehensible tomes on paleontology, anthropology, and related subjects." It was an exciting period of her life: "You see, in the short time since we left that small, dreary Texas town where I was born, I had discovered *Evolution*, I had discovered *Science*, I had come to believe that there were those who spent their lives in pursuit of absolute truth, and I wanted above everything to belong to that elite band." In the summer of 1915, she persuaded the administration to permit her to enter San Diego Normal School to begin making up course deficiencies so that she might go on to college.

It was that summer in a class in linguistics that she met John Peabody Harrington, handsome, commanding in presence, suntanned from the field. He was thirty-one years old, unmarried. Since 1908 he had been studying the linguistics and ethnology of the Indians of the Southwest, particularly those of the Shoshonean, Yuman, and Chumashan linguistic stocks. For a young girl, already fascinated by scholarship, he seemed a romantic and dashing personality. Even his aloofness and distaste for "small talk" made him seem that much more attractive. As for Harrington, it appears in retrospect that much of his interest in Carobeth centered around the fact that he quickly discovered she had "one of the best linguistic ears"—or so he phrased it—that he had ever encountered.

It was a strange courtship—this romance between teacher and student—because Harrington was a strange man, who in time would become increasingly eccentric, so much so that one is never certain how many of the legends which cling to his name are apochryphal. Those legends are part of the currency of the discipline—exchanged when fellow anthropologists get together, since there is as yet no biography of the man.

Often called the "mystery man" of American anthropology, not a line concerning Harrington's spectacular career or achievements ever appeared in print during his lifetime in any of the many biographies devoted to men of science. He had few friends, a distaste for all publicity, and he moved his address whenever it became too well known to his associates.

Harrington was a man totally possessed with the belief that time was running out for the American Indian—so much so that he eventually gave up all social life, believing that time thus wasted was at the cost of his work as an ethnographer. His genius—and it is agreed that he had that—was committed to his obsession with data-gathering. For forty years, up to his death in 1961, Harrington was to labor in virtual anonymity, begrudging even the time spent writing an occasional paper, untiringly searching out the last survivors of Indian tribes on the verge of extinction. Increasingly, he became reclusive, refusing to cooperate with efforts to bring his name before the public. Even his superiors in the Bureau of American Ethnology often did not know his location in the field, since he rarely left a forwarding address. His unorthodox field methods, his scorn for bureaucracy, his secret codes for hiding the names of his informants from even his superiors, and his forgetfulness about data he had stored casually in warehouses during his wanderings created many problems for the Bureau. Even after his death, Harrington material was still turning up in various caches across the country.

Probably no ethnographer in history ever gathered so much field data as Harrington, nor was any linguist ever acquainted with so many American Indian languages over so wide a territory. During his lifetime, Harrington shipped tons of material to the Smithsonian Institution. His work on the Chumash alone filled sixty boxes. The monument of unpublished papers he left behind is being discovered today by a score of linguists and anthropologists who are making significant contributions to our knowledge of the American Indian.

This then was the man Carobeth Laird fell in love with in a classroom in San Diego in 1915. The following year, after he had been appointed field ethnologist to the Bureau of American Ethnology, they were married. For the next four years, Carobeth traveled with Harrington to Indian reservations and to remote remnants of Indian groups in isolated backwaters throughout the Southwest, acquiring the training for her own scholarship. It was a hard apprenticeship, spent in the field under conditions of stark deprivation, for Harrington rarely thought of comfort, and he drove his young wife as hard as he drove himself. It was scarcely a marriage; the one child of their union was placed with Carobeth's other child in the home of her parents.

Carobeth gradually discovered to her disillusionment that she could not make any sort of life with a man who was devoted to spending eighteen hours a day on research—a man who had no time to spare for the amenities of life itself.

In May of 1919, Harrington left for Santa Fe, New Mexico, from San Diego to put the finishing touches on a Tanoan study. He sent Carobeth to Parker, Arizona, to collect for him as quickly as possible some material on the Chemehuevi language. It was in a blacksmith shop in Parker that she met George Laird, working behind the forge. From then until Laird's death in 1940 she was not separated from this man who began his association with her as a Chemehuevi informant and three years later became her husband.

There is no reason to say more here about Harrington, or for that matter about George Laird. Carobeth has described her life with Harrington in her autobiographical work *Encounter with an Angry God* (Malki Museum Press, 1975). She tells about George Laird and their first meeting in the introduction to the book you are about to read. In fact, this book is a testament to a marriage of mind, spirit, and flesh between Carobeth and George Laird.

This book was produced at a time when Mrs. Laird was having difficulty with arthritis, and during part of its production she was confined to a hospital. Many of her notes were lost in an accident while the manuscript was being typeset, forcing her to rely solely on memory in double-checking much of the Chemehuevi orthography. During proofreading, Mrs. Laird worked under conditions of excruciating pain, and many corrections had to be made over the telephone from her hospital bedside and later from her home.

Despite her ill health, Carobeth Laird today is working actively to bring together all of the material she has gathered over the years on the Chemehuevis. She is regularly publishing articles on Chemehuevi culture in *The Journal of California Anthropology*, and she has begun work on a new book on Chemehuevi myth. In addition, she is collaborating with fellow scholars who are interested in the Chemehuevis.

Those of us who know and love Carobeth Laird respect her fierce integrity, her immense courage, which has brought her through triumphantly at a time in life when few continue to be productive, her gentle humor, and her deep love for the people about whom she has written here.

Harry W. Lawton
Riverside, California

ACKNOWLEDGEMENTS

IT has taken many years for *The Chemehuevis* to emerge final-ly in printed form, and there have been many moments when I wondered if, indeed, I should live to see its publication. First there was the problem of an unknown author without scholarly creden-tials finding a publisher. Even after Malki Museum Press accepted the manuscript, there were further delays. Malki is small and underfinanced, and *The Chemehuevis* presented a staggering array of expensive technical problems. Happily these problems were eventually solved. I wish to express my heartfelt thanks to Malki Museum Press and its Editorial Board for bringing to pass a life-long dream of mine which, quite frankly, I had nearly given up on.

So many dedicated people—all volunteers—were enlisted in the production of this work. Many of them have become cherished friends, but many others I do not know. So if I have inadvertently omitted any names, I trust I will be forgiven.

I wish to acknowledge my enduring gratitude to the following persons:

Georgia Laird Culp, the oldest daughter from my marriage to George Laird, who originally encouraged me to formulate my scat-tered Chemehuevi notes into a cohesive, if incomplete, manuscript.

Lowell John Bean, whose students "discovered" me and my manuscript on the Chemehuevis, and who immediately lobbied for publication of the manuscript with the Malki Editorial Board.

Harry W. Lawton, chairman of the Editorial Board, whose

dedication to *The Chemehuevis* and belief in it never wavered, even when the economics of producing it appeared at times beyond the reach of Malki Press; who set in motion the whole machinery for publication of the book; and who was chief technical advisor to the production staff.

Anne B. Jennings, who worked with me on original editing of the manuscript and who was the first to suggest to me that there might be some literary, as well as scholarly, merit to the work.

Robert C. Dickson, whose substantial loan made it possible for typesetting on the book to begin at a time when Malki Press was stymied for lack of funds.

Melanie Fisch and Herta B. Caylor, whose devoted labors made it possible for the book to be produced in its present format, rather than in some economical, quick-reproduction form. Melanie was not only the overall production manager, she was the volunteer typesetter of the difficult text, which is shot through with Chemehuevi words. She helped devise the orthography used to represent the Chemehuevi language and was responsible for the book's design, for the cover design, for layout and preparation of artwork within the text, for editing the index and the glossary, for text revision, and for proofreading supervision.

Working with Melanie as her assistant production manager, Herta Caylor was head proofreader and undertook the laborious tasks of preparing both the index and the appendix on the maps. In addition, it was Herta who engaged in the considerable research which produced the maps and who assembled a team of associates who collaborated on the mapmaking project. These maps have brought special joy to me, since they have come close to duplicating maps which George and I devised, but which were lost after his death.

Both Melanie and Herta, in their devotion to *The Chemehuevis*, spent far too much of their own substance. As for the time which they spent, I cannot begin to calculate that investment of theirs, nor, I suspect, can they. That *The Chemehuevis* has emerged the handsome work it has, is their responsibility. There have been many times I strongly felt that Melanie and Herta care even more about the book than I do myself.

The following names I have listed alphabetically, since so many of the volunteers participated in several phases of production:

Erika Aschmann, who prepared the base map for the Mythological and Hunting Song Territory map.

Robert and Katherine Bergmann, who contributed financial support for cartographic research.

Jeanne Binning, who performed bibliographic research and proofreading.

Steven John Bloxham, who revised the base map for the Mythological and Hunting Song Territory map, assisted in preparing map overlays, and helped with text revision and proofreading.

Jon Bosak, who helped to edit the manuscript and provided technical assistance with graphics and photographic processes.

William Bright, who gave technical advice on linguistics.

Dennis Casebier, who provided cartographic information on Chemehuevi territory.

James Caylor, who worked on editing and proofreading the index.

Ike Eastvold, who took the cover photograph of a double rainbow over Chemehuevi Valley.

Joann Edmunds, who conducted a library search for map preparation.

Amy W. Henderson, who helped with proofreading.

Margaret Langdon, who provided technical assistance on the alphabet design.

Lynn Mathews-Clark, who drew the Chemehuevi baskets and basket motifs used as text decorations.

Pamela Munro, who gave technical assistance on the glossary.

James J. Parsons, who donated early maps used in cartographic research.

Don Perceval, who donated technical assistance on the book design.

Jay Proetto, who helped proofread the index.

Charles Ray, who helped edit the index.

James Rothenberger, who conducted a library search for map preparation.

Adel Sartin, who prepared the base map for the Trails and Colorado River Region map.

Gerald A. Smith, who gave technical advice on the authenticity of the decorations.

Gregory L. Smith, who contributed to cartographic research.

Vernon Tegland of Rubidoux Printing Co., whose encouragement and technical knowledge has been a mainstay of Malki Museum Press since its beginning.

Philip J. Wilke, who contributed technical assistance with the cartography.

Weezy Wold, who donated the author's photograph.

CONTENTS

GEORGE LAIRD

INTRODUCTION

TOWARD the close of the 1860's, a German named Schmidt, together with a young Chemehuevi woman whom he had taken as his wife after the casual manner of that time and place, kept a stage relay station on the California desert, probably in the Chocolate Mountains. The Chemehuevi woman's name may or may not have been Pagɨnʔnasɨʔɨ,* Cloud Flower.[1] She was the late-begotten daughter of ʔAyarupagarɨmɨ, Black Turtle,[2] chief of a small band who lived across the Colorado River in Arizona. Not only was she wellborn, comely, and industrious, but also, as events proved, strong, brave, and resourceful. The couple prospered and were content. They had two children, toddlers, John and Anna.

White men, possibly guerrillas who turned to banditry in the aftermath of the Civil War, looted and burned the stage station, took the horses, and killed Schmidt. By what act of valor or cunning the young mother saved herself and her infants will never be known. What is known is that after she had buried her husband she started back east with her children to the Colorado River, back to her own people. Even the cradleboard must have been destroyed in the fire. Since the children were too young to walk far and too large to be carried together, the mother placed one under the scanty shade of a desert shrub, admonishing it not to stray or attempt to follow, and carried the other for as long a

---

* For pronunciation of Chemehuevi words, see Appendix B.

distance as she could cover, while still retaining in sight the sheltering bush. Then she deposited the child in her arms, warned it not to stray, marked the shrub well in her mind, and returned for the child that had been left behind. Since it was roughly a hundred miles to the River, and this method of travel involved walking every step of the distance three times, she was deliberately setting out to walk three hundred miles, probably without food and with only a canteen of water.

But rescuers were on the way. Two reporters from the *San Francisco Call*, travelling to the Colorado River to gather material for a series of feature articles, overtook the young mother and her children, crowded them into their buckboard, and took them to their destination, probably to join the Chemehuevi band living near the present site of Blythe, California.

Thompson Porter Laird had run away from his home in Tennessee at the age of twelve to join a westward-bound wagon train and had lived with Indians ever since. He was then in his mid-forties, a kindly, gangling, homely, rough-hewn sort of man, himself a quarter Cherokee: trapper, hunter, prospector, cook, laborer, and jack-of-all-trades. The Chemehuevis liked him and considered him almost one of the People. He found the young widow attractive and took her and her two children to live with him in or near the Indian settlement. There, in 1871, their first child was born. The Chemehuevis called him Wikontots*i*, Buzzard Head, because he was bald at birth; but Thompson Porter named him George and, as was proper and fitting, painstakingly entered his son's name and birthdate—March 3, 1871—in the Bible which was his prized possession, although he was by no means a religious man. (Thompson Porter called his wife María, and that is the only name by which her son remembered her.)

Three other children were born, Mary, Suzy, and Frances, and their names duly recorded in the Bible. George was past five when Frances was born, and he remembered the occasion well. His father was away working. His mother took the cradleboard, clean rags, a kettle of water, and a basin and went into a nearby thicket, telling the children not to follow her—and although she seldom or never disciplined them, they, as almost always, obeyed. Hidden in the thick brush (as George learned later), she braced her back against the trunk of a mesquite tree and brought forth her child.

At the time he knew only that she returned presently with a new baby sister neatly swaddled on the cradleboard and went about preparing a meal for her older children.

Then George turned six years old, and a great smallpox epidemic swept through the People like a devouring flame. All members of the family were sick, very sick indeed, except Thompson Porter Laird, who either had a very mild case or was immune as the consequence of a previous attack. The children were part white; they had a partial immunity in their genes, handed down from ancestors who had survived the plague house that once was Europe. George remembered how he looked out the window and cried because, in his delirium, he saw Sissy (Anna) cooking meat in the yard and she would not give him any, when in reality she lay inside the house in a coma. But it was María whom the fire consumed. Day and night Thompson Porter fought to hold his wife on the bed, while she struggled to get free, to run to the River and cool herself, as was the custom of her people. Early one morning he dozed in his chair, then fell into a sleep of exhaustion. When he awoke, she was gone. He found her dead, face down in the shallow water at the River's edge.

Frances lived out her year on a diet of flour gruel and mashed beans, then succumbed. John went with the Indians; the two remaining girls were farmed out with various Mexican families, and Thompson Porter took George with him on his new job as cook for a construction gang.

Early one morning Thompson Porter was splitting kindling, getting ready to make breakfast, and George was watching him, perched up on a packing case, kicking his hard, cold heels against the box in time to a little wordless song he had made up all by himself and repeated endlessly: ʔiilangalangalangalanga, ʔiilanga-langalangalanga. Suddenly violence boiled out of the bunkhouse, and a man was killed before their eyes.[3] Later Thompson Porter was subpoenaed to go to the county seat, San Bernardino, as a material witness. He left George with Anna, who was living with a man and woman named Martinez, and he himself rode away over the desert and mountain to a city which, although not at that time very big, was too big entirely for an old desert rat—so that he not only had his day in court as a witness, but was himself jailed—on a charge never made quite clear to his son (or probably to him either) connected with the making or selling or excessive drinking of whiskey. A whole year elapsed before he came back to the River to claim his boy.

The Martinez woman, called Panza de Agua because of her bloated belly, was probably ill and certainly cruel. Her husband was no less cruel. Anna was big enough to be of some use, but George was good for very little. So after the priest came up from Yuma, as he did periodically to "baptize the mavericks" and formalize marriages already consummated, and after the children had duly been made Catholics and George's soul was safe, his guardians set out deliberately to starve him. He was theoretically allowed one meal a day. But every afternoon the man would set him a task so far away from the house that he could not get back until after the others had eaten. Then, except for fragments of tortillas that Anna had hidden in her clothing, he went to sleep hungry. Talking in whispers at night, in their own language, the children decided that George must run away. On a night soon after, when by self-denial and theft Anna had managed to secure two or three tortillas, they tied the food and his few possessions in a bandana, which was tied in turn to the end of a stick suitable for balancing on his shoulder.

This young hobo had no idea of simply drifting about living off charity. When he came to the ranch of a Canadian couple named Brown, he applied for work and received food, clothing, shelter, and affection. Mrs. Brown also taught him the rudiments of reading and writing. There he stayed, treated like a son and doing whatever chores were assigned to him, until Thompson Porter Laird came riding along the River, inquiring at each small ranch and ranchería for his son.

For the next four or five years, father and son were much in each other's company. Thompson Porter told George tales of the half-remembered home in Tennessee—especially of the two grand-mothers, beautiful women with hair reaching below their knees. The Cherokee grandmother had hair that was crow-black—but the Scotchwoman! *Her* hair was finer and paler than cornsilk, almost white but with the sheen of gold. He also imparted bits of curious and useful knowledge that he had picked up through the years: to tender up a beaver so he'll be fit to eat, soak the meat in vinegar; to toughen up your hands for a job of pick and shovel work, bathe them in urine. And he inculcated in his son a code, simple but strict: commit no murder; don't lie; and *never* strike a woman.

By the time he was twelve, George had his own horse, his own rope and saddle, and was doing a man's work and earning almost a man's wages—fifty cents a day and found. About a year later his working career was interrupted by three months' attendance at a Protestant mission school. This constituted his only formal education, since a later brief promise of further schooling came to nothing. When he was sixteen a benevolent Government, desiring perhaps to test some theory of educability, offered to send three Chemehuevi boys and three Mohave boys to the Indian School at Phoenix, Arizona. George Laird was one of those selected. The three Chemehuevis were eager to go and had no difficulty securing parental and tribal consent, but the Mohaves were denied permission. Their elders, always conservative, refused to let the young men go away to a strange place out of sight of Monument Peak where they might die and their souls wander forever lost, and where, even if they lived, they would certainly be taught to commit obscenities—such as drinking milk and, by so doing, be reminded of their dead mothers. With admirable impartiality and impeccable logic, government authorities ruled that since the Mohaves would not take advantage of the offer, the Chemehuevis could not be permitted to do so.

However, when George Laird was sixteen, an opportunity for education of another sort, far more rare and valuable opened; if it seemed useless at the time in the white man's world, it proved eventually to be the means by which he broke out of the stagnation of Reservation life. He spent the whole winter taking care of a Chemehuevi man who was slowly and painfully dying of syphilis. More than a quarter of a century later George Laird could not surely recall this man's name, partly, no doubt, because he was disciplined not to remember the names of the dead; he thought it might have been ʔIluh or ʔIruh, from the Mohave *idho*, willow.[4] The dying man taught his young companion the pure Southern Chemehuevi dialect, which even then was becoming corrupted, and he would tolerate no slovenliness of grammar or pronunciation. Still more important, he filled the long, sleepless nights with tales of the Immortals, the pre-human Animals Who Were People, told with great style and elegance. Fortunately the time was winter, when such telling is permissible. These myths were already on their way to oblivion, and those which are included in this material (and which surely comprise only a fraction of the Chemehuevi oral literature) would have perished without this association between a dying wise man and a receptive, retentive youth.

When George Laird was growing up the old culture was dying but far from dead. In his youth he ran with the Runners and had proof that his cousin (or uncle?) Kaawɨ'a, Rat Penis, had the power of teleportation, being (so far as is known) the last of the Chemehuevis to travel in this ancient way. He spoke much with his grandfather, Black Turtle, whose life-span was so long that he was believed by both whites and Indians to have lived one hundred and fifty years, although this, of course, could not be substantiated. He attended funerals and Mourning Ceremonies (of which there were far too many in those days), where he joined in the singing of the old hereditary songs and heard descendants of the old High Chief sing fragments at least of the awesome and sacred Talking Song. He probably had personal contact with the three wise old men of Harimyiivɨ, to whom he credited the transmission of much of the ancient lore. He danced in the Ghost Dance, although he was not seriously impressed by its teaching. And all his life he retained a vivid memory of that night in Siwa'avaatsɨ, Chemehuevi Valley, when he lay by the fire listening to his grandfather in the company of 'Otawɨnɨrɨ, Sand Standing, and Nagaramaupa, Left the Mountain Sheep Behind, as those three spoke together in "real speech," the ancient dialect of Chiefs. This probably was the last time that there was anything like a convocation even of lesser Chemehuevi Chiefs. By the close of the nineteenth century the days of the mighty hunters had ended, the migratory habits of the People were much curtailed and their numbers greatly diminished; the old High Chiefs were dead and there were no successors.

George Laird could not escape a sense of frustration and was plagued all his life by attacks of melancholy, a deep inner sadness which he usually kept well hidden. He was a man of great kindness and self-control, abundantly supplied with the typical Chemehuevi sense of humor. He made his way not too badly in a world now dominated by the white man's culture. This way was a long series of hard and demanding jobs, performed always with good temper and a natural, easy rhythm. He worked as cowboy, prospector, miner, watchman, blacksmith, rough carpenter—almost anything. For awhile he ran his own freight line from Wickenburg to Prescott and became an employer of others. He had a spell of railroading, which he liked, but which, in the nature of things as they were, he could not make his career. It happened that there was a strike, and George was hired as a strike-breaker. I am not clear as to whether he worked as fireman or brakeman, but whichever it was, he enjoyed the movement, the new associations, and the sense of emerging into a new world of opportunity. Then the strike ended and with it, his job.

George had three or four marriages, traditionally casual "Chemehuevi-style" unions, terminated at will by one party or the other. Not infrequently an Indian Agent would urge upon him the desirability of legalizing the current arrangement, pointing out that, as an outstanding member of the Indian community, he should set an example to others. George always answered, "Piik^{y}ayu, piik^{y}ayutsin^{y}i"; then assuming an expression of utter imbecility, he would translate the phrase into broken English, "bye-m-bye"—and if he thought the white man looked stupid enough, he might even throw in "ugh."

In May of 1919, my husband, John Peabody Harrington, who was associated with the Bureau of American Ethnology in Washington, D.C., sent me to Parker, Arizona, to collect for him, as quickly as possible, some material on a Uto-Aztecan language, Chemehuevi. I went with tears because heat made me wretched, and I would have much preferred staying with my family in San Diego, or accompanying him to Santa Fe, New Mexico, where he intended to put the finishing touches on a Tanoan study. Nonetheless I went.

My first informant was a young woman, Ruby Eddy, who spoke English fluently but, as I discovered after two or three sessions, Chemehuevi rather carelessly. I asked if she could suggest some person who spoke in the old way. She replied that there were a few such, but that they never spoke to white people. There was, she went on, one "old fellow" who had no prejudice against whites, who spoke English, Spanish, Mohave, and excellent Chemehuevi. "But he works all the time," she added, "he wouldn't have time to help you." I resolved at least to contact this paragon.

Someone of whom I have no memory at all took me to the Agency blacksmith shop and introduced me to George Laird. He looked up from his work and saw me in the doorway, and I peered into the stifling gloom and saw his face illumined by the glow from the forge. We were not separated till death did us part. At the time of our meeting he was forty-eight, exactly twice my age.

Harrington was highly impressed by the quality of the material I sent him. In June, he suggested that I bring my informant with me to Santa Fe, where I could continue to work with him while helping with an analysis of Taoseño, and where Harrington in turn could check on the accuracy of my work. I explained the proposal to George. He said simply, "Yes, I will go with you."

I think his answer would have been the same even if he had not loved me. Although his life had had its interesting periods, had even been, in certain respects, remarkable ("for an Indian," was the qualifying phrase invariably added by Indian Agents and other whites), it had also been tethered to the Reservation and subject to the constrictions of a reservation-based environment. Leaving did not at any time improve his financial situation, but it opened the door for intellectual and spiritual advancement. As the restlessness of youth passed, he had resigned himself to living out the rest of his days in a rut; our meeting provided him with both opportunity and incentive to break free. Not without reason many who remained on the Reservation referred to me as "the white woman who took our George Laird away from us."

In October we three, George, Harrington, and I, went on from Santa Fe to Washington, D.C. And in the following May, George Laird and I drove cross-country to San Diego. There, in 1923, I obtained a divorce from Harrington, a man so obsessed by the drive to record dying languages that he was all but oblivious to human comings and goings—except, of course, as his work was affected thereby. In August of that year, George and I were married.

We made our home in the small back-country San Diego county community of Poway, returning to the Reservation only once for a brief visit when our first child, Frances Georgia, was about eighteen months old. Our acreage was too small to support a family, although we raised grapes and some poultry. George worked at whatever job he could get. For some years we continued intermittently to record what he knew of Chemehuevi language and lore. Naturally my ability to hear his speech improved, and as he opened his mind to the past, he recalled more and more of what he had heard and experienced in his youth. One of our more ambitious projects was to make tracings of Government topographical maps of the territory ranged over by the Chemehuevis and to locate on them Chemehuevi placenames. But there seemed to be little prospect of ever publishing our work, and gradually other interests, increasing family cares, and the mounting pressure of poverty turned us from it.

In April, 1940, George was employed, as he had been for some time, by the County of San Diego. He was working alone on a stretch of road known as "the Old Viejas Grade." He knew that his truck had defective brakes, but when a clod caught in the tailgate he simply set them and climbed back into the bed of the truck to remove the obstruction, neglecting to block his wheels. The brakes gave way and he was thrown out, breaking a leg in two places. For two hours he was alone there on the sunny hillside, surrounded by the fragrance of wild lilac and the hum of bees. He straightened out his leg as best he could and composed his thought, calling at intervals for help. Finally a sort of hermit whom we knew only as the "Bee Man" heard him, investigated, and found someone who called an ambulance. I was notified by telephone and waited at our gate for the ambulance to stop by on the way to the hospital. George's face was gray with pain but peaceful. He assured me that he was "all right" and handed me his worn and grimy coin purse, containing five dollars, all the money he had in the world. He died five days later of pneumonia.

A number of people of whom I had never heard came to his funeral. Little old mountain men and women, lonely women in sunbonnets and men in shabby clothes, wrung their gnarled hands and wept because Mr. Laird wouldn't stop by anymore to fix the pump or do some other chore that was too hard for them, or just to cheer them up and ask how they were. Surely there have been few men like him—so patient, so universally friendly, so unfailingly kind.

Always George Laird maintained that he would live a thousand years. He had a quality of agelessness, of eternality. He died on the thirteenth of April, 1940, aged sixty-nine years, one month and ten days; yet his life had spanned a thousand years and more of human development, from the end of the Stone Age to the beginning of the Atomic.

After his death I was, I think, for some years in a state of shock. I moved several times, and, partly through my own carelessness, much of our irreplaceable Chemehuevi material was lost, including the maps. Later the incompleteness of what was left deterred me from any effort to publish it. However, in 1969 our oldest daughter, Georgia Laird Culp, became deeply involved in the effort to reorganize the Chemehuevi tribe in order to assure for them an equitable distribution of the aboriginal claims money and the proper use of their Reservation. This brought me again, after almost fifty years, in touch with the People, and I began to see that incomplete information was preferable to none at all and determined to put in order what remained.

This, then, is very much George Laird's book. Virtually all the information it contains was furnished by him. Much of it is unverified or even unverifiable, and attempts at verification must be left to other students. But does this impair its value? Dreams, fantasies, and childhood memories are the stuff of which legend is formed; and legend is surely as important as fact in revealing the soul of an individual, a people, or an era.

I present this volume as a memorial to a remarkable man, in the hope that it will serve the interests of the People with whom he never ceased to identify himself. The information as given is incomplete and occasionally contradictory; but it is honestly recorded. I lay no claim to an erudition I do not possess. For example, animal and plant species are identified, if at all, by their popular or colloquial names, or sometimes by their Spanish names only, if the English equivalent was unknown to George Laird. Yet because of the deep intimacy between informant and recorder, I believe that this book provides a clearer view of the Chemehuevis and their culture than a more scholarly work would afford, and that it has, therefore, a peculiar value.

Carobeth Laird
Poway, California

THE CHEMEHUEVIS

CHAPTER I

IDENTITY, DISTRIBUTION, AND ORGANIZATION

THE word Chemehuevi is from the Mohave *tcamuweiva*, said by George Laird to mean "mixed with all." Whether this is the correct interpretation or not, I do not know, for I have not verified it with a Mohave informant; in any event it is, as will appear, eminently appropriate.

The Chemehuevis' name for themselves is tuumontcokowɨ (singular, tuumontcoko). George Laird gave no etymology for this word, but the derivation seems fairly obvious. The prefix tuu- must be for black (as in the personal name, tuuwɨnɨrɨ, Black Standing), montco means beard, and the final -ko- might be for kova, face. They are, then, the Black Beards or the Black Bearded Ones. But I have no idea whether they were so named because of their possibly having had more facial hair than certain other tribes, or because the term referred to a particular mode of painting the face for war, or harked back to some long forgotten episode or event. Tuumontcokowɨ is a true tribename, still remembered (in 1969) by a few persons. But now as in aboriginal times, the Chemehuevis generally refer to themselves as nɨwɨwɨ, the People. Now as then nɨʔɨkʷ nɨwɨ means I am a Person, a Chemehuevi, a particular and superior kind of person.

Chemehuevi men are almost invariably built "like the buffalo," with enormous, broad, and heavy shoulders tapering down to slender waist and thighs. Anciently a man was valued for his agility, keen eyesight, and skill as a hunter, and a woman for her

3

industry and comeliness. The young women are still beautiful and shy, the older women sturdy and wise. And all of them, men and women, away from the inhibiting presence of the white man, are incessant talkers.[1]

The Chemehuevi character is made up of polarities which are complementary rather than contradictory. They are loquacious yet capable of silence; gregarious yet so close to the earth that single families or even men alone might live and travel for long periods away from other human beings; proud, yet capable of a gentle self-ridicule. They are conservative to a degree, yet insatiably curious and ready to inquire into and even to adopt new ways: to visit all tribes, whether friends or enemies; to speak strange tongues, sing strange songs, and marry strange wives. In fact, outside marriages were so frequent that one wonders at the preservation of physical characteristics and tribal identity. But a person with a single drop of Chemehuevi blood was a Chemehuevi. A man might marry an Apache wife and go to live in Apache territory; he would still visit his relatives, and his sons would be Chemehuevis and inheritors of his Song.

The Chemehuevis strictly observed, and to a large extent still observe, their own taboos and held things not of this world in an appropriate reverence; yet their unquenchable and ironic sense of humor, their inherent lightness of approach, kept them from taking anything too seriously. They were nomads, at first through necessity, later by choice, yet capable of passionate attachment to specific places. Being alert and intelligent, they carefully observed and to a certain extent classified natural phenomena. Therefore, while they viewed the world with wonder and respect, to them it was bright and filled with adventure, not the dark and terrifying place it seemed to certain other tribes. Since their relationship with unseen forces tended to be one of cooperation rather than subservience, and since the most revered and important characters of myth were frequently also figures of fun, they had no need to build temples and invent cruel rites to placate dreadful gods. Even after they learned to plant crops, they continued to travel from place to place, gathering seeds and other foods in their seasons, following the great herds of game, paying visits to real cousins and courtesy cousins, related and unrelated tribes. Naturally, the material culture which they developed was limited for the most part to that which could be packed on the back, but that fact, as will be amply demonstrated, does not mean that they were culturally impoverished. Such articles as they did make, including weapons, baskets, cradles, carrying-nets, and articles of clothing both useful and ornamental, were things of beauty, fashioned with loving care; and the nonmaterial culture, that which was carried in the mind and transmitted by word of mouth, was of incalculable richness.

Originally the ancestors of the Chemehuevis lived by gathering and by hunting small game. There may have been a time when their existence was precarious in the extreme. With the perfecting of the bow and arrow and of the skill required to use them, their lives were greatly enriched. They made their hunting bows of willow backed with sinew. Their arrows (huuh) had well-shaped flint points and were carefully feathered, so that their flight would be straight. There were also war bows,[2] short and tremendously strong, with proportionately short and strong war arrows. On the trail, when families or groups of families travelled together, the men walked in front, each with his hunting bow in hand, alert for the sight of game; but even on peaceful expeditions, those who were warriors had their war bows and quivers filled with war arrows slung over their shoulders and were ready for instant battle should an enemy attack. The women, with infants and household possessions on their backs and the older children beside them, walked behind in a position of relative safety.

The People's improved weaponry and skill in battle earned them the respect of neighboring tribes and made them desirable allies. But the greatest effect of the invention of the sinew-backed bow was on their own lives. Once they had become hunters of big game, deer and mountain sheep, they had a plentiful supply of protein to supplement their immemorial diet of lizards, tortoises, jackrabbits and cottontails, as well as edible seeds of every variety, from the tiny ʔak*a*, so minute that its name was given to the finest mist (ʔakaʔɨwarɨ, ʔaka-rain), to the fat and savory pine nut (tɨvah), and including also wild berries, the fruit of the yucca and related plants (tcɨmp*i*), the heart of the mescal plant, tender shoots of cacti, and other items—so much in fact that a modern Chemehuevi remarked, "To the white man, the desert is a wasteland; to us it is a supermarket." Still later their food supply was further supple-

mented by the desultory practice of agriculture. There is no reason
to believe that the Chemehuevis were suffering from hunger at the
time of the arrival of the white man, although isolated families and
groups must surely have been the occasional victims of adverse
conditions and have felt the pangs of starvation.

More and better food did not serve to anchor the People in
one locality. On the contrary, it gave them greater freedom to
travel. Food caches were buried or sometimes hidden in caves.
Edible seeds were packed in storage baskets capped with suitably
shaped potsherds and sealed with greasewood gum. The heart of
the mescal plant (nantapik^{y}ovi) was boiled and pounded into a
large, flat slab (nantaw$ɨ$p$ɨ$ap$i$), and meat was pounded and dried
into similar slabs called tuku^{w}aw$ɨ$p$ɨ$ap$i$. These slabs were extremely
tough but would keep indefinitely and were nourishing. Possibly
the dried pulp of melons and squashes was also stored in this way.
Having prepared and concealed their surplus food as best they
could, a band was free to roam about, hunting, gathering, and visiting, secure in the knowledge that if times got hard they could return
home and find enough food to tide them over. The myth "How
Coyote Went to War Against Gila Monster" shows the way in which
a war could be started by the violation of a food cache.

Everything to do with the gathering and preparation of seeds
and fruits and with weaving belonged to the women's side. To the
men appertained all that had to do with game, especially big game
(except the packing of it into camp, when there were women
available for the task). The hunter, using his awl, sewed or laced
together buckskin clothes for himself and his family. In summer,
in the fierce heat of the lower deserts, everyone wore as little as
possible. The men went about in G-strings, the women wore little
aprons front and back, or sometimes frontal aprons only. But in
cold weather, if a man was a competent hunter, he and his wife
were well clothed.[3] A man's clothing is haagaru$^{?w}$ap$ɨ$, a woman's
dress, kwas$u$, and her apron, naw$i$. For a loved wife, a man would
make garments sewn along the edges with rare and valuable cowrie
shells[4] from the seacoast. For himself the man would also fashion
a peaked cap of buckskin, sewn round and round with quail crests,
known as kaitcox$o$, mountain hat.[5] The white people later called
this a war-bonnet, but it was simply a valued article of clothing
and perhaps a status symbol. Women wove for their own use hats

called sɨhɨgaitcoxo, woven mountain hat (sɨhɨvi, any material used for weaving), probably both ornamental and practical, certainly useful to protect the head from the sun while gathering. Also in ancient times men are said to have worn wonderfully beautiful feather capes. These were probably woven of yucca fiber, with feathers inserted in the manner used to ornament baskets but more thickly.

It is regrettable that so few of these artifacts[6] remain and that even the memory of them has largely vanished. However, the real wealth of the Chemehuevis never consisted of that which could be stored in the ground, worn on the person, or carried on the back. They had a threefold inheritance: their language, their myths, and their songs. The difficult and flexible language and the elegant body of mythology belonged to the People collectively; but the inherited songs each belonged to a specific group.

That California desert now named, somewhat ironically, the Mohave Desert might perhaps be considered Chemehuevi heartland. But at the coming of the white man the People were wandering over and claiming territory in portions of what subsequently became three states: California, Nevada, and Arizona. In California, they ranged freely to and beyond the Tehachapis. The San Bernardino Mountains[7] were a familiar hunting ground, well-sprinkled with Chemehuevi placenames. Death Valley was well known to them (as verified by a myth dealing with the journeys of Southern Fox), also Mt. Whitney. All the Panamint Range was considered sacred land, the Storied Land, where the great myths were said to begin and end. Chemehuevi trails and hunting ranges extended far up into Nevada. For as far back as tribal memory extended, they had had well established settlements in the many bends of the Colorado River and adjacent fertile valleys, on both the east and west sides. In Arizona, the territory claimed was less extensive, perhaps due to the occupancy by hostile tribes, but nonetheless the Chemehuevis definitely held land there, their range extending well up and to the north of Bill Williams Fork. However, when it is said that the Chemehuevis had a settlement in a certain place, it is to be by no means understood that there were Chemehuevis there all the time. As their range became constricted by encroaching aliens, settlements tended to be more continuously occupied; and always there were certain spots where groups wintered for a number of consecutive years or where, if situated near the River, they returned to plant and later to harvest crops. But even after the Chemehuevis were ostensibly under the control of Indian Agents, they went about their own business; they melted away and were not seen, and were seldom to be found in the spots where they were supposed to be. One of these early agents complained rather pathetically (in a letter written in the 1890's) that he was supposed to be in charge of a certain number of Indians but had not been able to locate one of them.

This scattered, wandering tribe or nation contained three subdivisions, each with its own name, although the term Tuumontcokowɨ included all.

Persons belonging to the northern branch were called Tantɨitsiwɨ, Northerners.[8] This word applied specifically to all the Chemehuevis living along the northern reaches of the Colorado River. Those who lived along the River farther south were Tantɨvaitsiwɨ, Southerners.[9] The dividing line between northern and southern territory was ?Ayatapagah, Mohave River (Fort Mohave), a place which no Chemehuevis ever occupied. The southernmost settlement of the Tantɨitsiwɨ was Wiyaan?nikʸatɨ, Adobe Hanging Like Tears, situated about four miles north of Fort Mohave. Southern territory extended to and included Wii?wirah, the Maria Mountains; south of this range no land was claimed by Chemehuevis. A certain half-joking antagonism existed between Northerners and Southerners. The Northerners called the Southerners by a somewhat derisive nickname, ?Angkanampawɨ (singular, ?Angkanampa), Red Feet. On seeing someone approaching, someone would ask, "Who is that fellow coming?" and another would answer, "It is a Red Foot." They also said that Southerners were lazy and ridiculed the Southerner's habit of "lying down and sticking his knees up" the moment he arrived on a visit. The Southerners, in turn, spoke with pride of their own height and of the lesser stature of the Tantɨitsiwɨ; and they said that Northerners spoke too fast and made excessive use of the particle -tsi-.

All Chemehuevis who inhabited territory well back from the River, either the high or low deserts or the desert mountains, were classified as Tɨɨranɨwɨwɨ, Desert People. Since they did not cultivate the river delta, they probably relied less on agriculture than other branches of the tribe, and I have reason to believe that there were also dialectic differences. Nonetheless, constant visits back and forth, shared war parties and hunting expeditions, as well as intermarriage (in which it was customary for the husband to live with or near his wife's parents) must have made for considerable tribal homogeneity.

After I had known George Laird for quite a long time and had questioned him several times without success about the possible existence of totemic clans, he astonished me by remarking, "The Chemehuevis owned land." This was his way of introducing the complex subject of hereditary songs and the territorial rights which ownership of these songs conveyed. Songs were individually inherited, passed from father to son; or if a woman was married to a non-Chemehuevi, a man who had no song (after the coming of the white man, it might well be to a non-Indian), the song passed from maternal grandfather to grandson.[10] The song defined a man's kinship and his hunting preserve; he was free to live or travel anywhere he pleased, but in theory at least, his hunting rights were limited to the land traversed by his song except when accompanied by others owning different ranges.

Unquestionably those owning the Mountain Sheep Song and the Deer Song constituted the most important hereditary song groups. Within the body of this material I do not have sufficient evidence to conclude that these groups were moieties—it may be that they were simply large and dominant clans, comprised of a number of subdivisions. However, on several occasions George Laird stated that everyone was either a Mountain Sheep or a Deer. At another time he said that these two groups owned all the land and when they hunted "invited outsiders to go along with them"—these outsiders being perhaps visitors from other tribes or men who had married into the tribe. Each of these songs was divided into various versions, and each version was associated with a definite territory. The subdivisions of the Mountain Sheep Song appear to have been more numerous than those of the Deer Song (certainly the total amount of land covered was greater), but the latter may have had several subsidiary songs bearing different titles associated with it. The Salt Song seems to have been allied with the Deer Song, but was itself very long, ranging over a vast amount of territory. Persons now living (1969) say that it had two separate branches. George Laird himself owned by inheritance both the

Deer Song and the Salt Song. Although he had learned only snatches of each, he knew enough of the routes to be sure that the Salt Song travelled over Deer territory.

The ancient division into moieties, if such it was, had pretty well broken down by the time George was old enough to take an interest in such things and to remember what he heard. But he stated positively that even in the closing decades of the nineteenth century there were still some groups of as many as twenty-five or thirty men inheriting the same song and hunting range. When a Chemehuevi asked, "How does that song go?" he did not refer exclusively to its words and tune; primarily he meant, "What is the route it travels?" Each landmark and watering place was mentioned in order, by recognizable allusion or description if not by name, so that a man's song constituted an oral map of his territory.[11] Also the song described the hunter's equipment and the way in which these accoutrements moved in response to the swift and rhythmic movements of his body; and along with the character and "feel" of the land it conveyed a poignant sympathy for the animal hunted and a sense of the relationship between the hunter and the hunted. From the songs and from the Chemehuevis' attitude toward them one learns that the connection between a man, his song, and his mountain (or his land, as the case might be) was sacred and unbreakable, and that the animal he pursued was included in this sacred unity.

The Chemehuevis did not consider themselves to be descended from the mountain sheep or the deer, and there was no prohibition against the eating of either animal by either group, although certain parts of an animal were taboo to the hunter who had killed it. Even in mythological times, When the Animals Were People, the mountain sheep and the deer appear as game animals, hunted by the Immortals of that pre-human era. Kwanantsitsi, Red-Tailed Hawk, is represented as having killed two female mountain sheep so that he might use their eyes to replace the eyes of his young wives who had been blinded, and he also went clothed in buckskin from the deer that he had killed. Tɨvatsi, Wolf, tosses the loin of a mountain sheep to his feckless brother, Cɨnawavi, Coyote, telling him to "make himself a loin" to replace the loin that Bear had torn off. Only one myth in this collection personifies Mountain Sheep and Deer, as it recounts the conversation between Naxa, Mountain

Sheep, Tcagwara, Chuckwalla, and Tɨhiya, Deer, at the time when each chose his future habitat.[12]

In still another respect the mountain sheep and the deer differ from all other animals: they are the only animals who were not shamans in the mythic period, yet appear as shamans' familiars[13] in this present time. This no doubt leads to a certain confusion in our attempt to reconstruct the correlation between song and hunting range, because the shamans also had their songs. Prior to the turn of the century one old man laid claim to all the game in both the Providence and the Granite Mountains, each of which was formerly covered by a distinct version of the Mountain Sheep Song whose legitimate owners were now all dead. This individual lived most of his life, much of the time without human companionship, beside a spring between the two ranges, where he irrigated a small field. He was a mountain sheep shaman and was said to be able, by his shamanistic power, to protect "his" game (both mountain sheep and deer) from all would-be hunters. Curiously, this old man had a Mohave name, pronounced by the Chemehuevis either as ʔIlyaalyiʔivya or Yaariʔivʸa; and still more curiously, he was said to be a Deer by inheritance.

George Laird's memories of hereditary songs and song groups were necessarily incomplete and fragmented, sometimes confused and contradictory, but still of great importance. I can only record as best I can what he told me.

Mountain Sheep Song

The Mountain Sheep Song (Nagahuvʷiyavɨ[14]), with its variants, covered territory lying west of the Colorado River. The southernmost hunting ranges were said to lie in "strips" including the land from the top of one mountain range, through the intervening valley, to the top of the next, a distance described as cuukutɨɨravɨ, one "Indian mile," literally, one desert. (Later cuukutɨɨravɨ came generally to mean simply one mile, that is, one white man's mile—a much shorter and more precise distance than the term had originally indicated.) Each strip extended, or at least was said to extend, to the ocean, but since none of these songs is on record it is impossible to say whether any of them actually traced the route to the coast. In the southern hunting ranges, the single exception to this strip-shape was the Mountain Sheep Song of Whipple Mountain, which started somewhere in the Whipple Mountains (Wiyaatuᵂa), travelled down to the River and returned to its point of origin. Further north all subdivisions of the Mountain Sheep Song were in "blocks" similar to the one covering the Whipple Mountain range rather than in "strips." One variant embraced the New York Mountains,[15] another the Providence Mountains (Timpisagwagatsitcɨ), another the Granite Mountains (Toyongkaririɨ). The subdivision might be specifically indicated by prepounding the name of the territory covered by the song: Wiyaatuᵂanagahuvᵂiyavɨ, Mountain Sheep Song of Whipple Mountain; Wiyaatuᵂanagahuvᵂiyagantɨ, one who has or owns this song, that is to say, a member of the Whipple Mountain division (clan or subclan) of the Mountain Sheep people.

A Mountain Sheep man spoke of the range his group owned as "my mountain." Certain Chemehuevi nouns have a special form used only with the possessive case of a noun or with some form of possessive pronoun, and only when there is an intimate relationship between the possessor and the thing possessed. Many but not all of these words are names of body parts. Thus we have pɨhɨvɨ, fur, hair, or body hair, but pungkutsi pɨhɨʔah, the dog's hair; tcopivɨ, hair of head, but nɨɨni tcopivɨʔah or tcopivɨʔaanɨ, my hair; wɨnʔnapɨ, flint, but huu wɨnʔnawa, the arrow's flint, the flint which is now an integral part of the arrow; and kaivʸa, mountain, but nɨɨni kaiʸa or kaiʸanɨ, my mountain. In this way the structure of the language itself confirms the nature of the relation of a man to his mountain.

Manavisoʔotsɨ, Thorn Baby, was among the last owners of the Whipple Mountain range. A descendant of his, Pagɨɨnampa, Fish Foot, whose English name was Pete Chile, lived on well into the twentieth century and knew all, or nearly all, of this version of the Mountain Sheep Song. George Laird knew him well and heard him sing many times. He was able to recall and sing for me two fragments of the song as Pete Chile sang it.

These brief snatches give no clue to the route of the song; but they reveal it as a song of movement, associated with the hunter and the game he hunts as well as with the terrain over which he travels: a song which has, for all its rhythmic motion, a wild and wailing character. The first remembered fragment pictures the various erratic motions of the hunter's canteen or waterbag which are induced as he runs or leaps swiftly from one rocky formation to another in pursuit of game. The waterbag is called kaipipovɨ, translated by George Laird as "mountain canteen." He described pipovɨ as a "round gut" which all ruminant animals have, probably the paunch or rumen. The pipovɨ of the mountain sheep is cleaned and put away to dry when the animal is butchered. Later, in preparation for another hunt, it is soaked till soft, filled with water, and its mouth tied tightly with a buckskin thong. Fastened to the hunter's belt, it is carried easily and kept with him no matter what else has to be abandoned; and it serves both as water container and emergency ration, for in time of hunger it can be boiled and eaten. Wayuk^{w}agaiv^{y}a is a future tense of wayuk^{w}a-gaig^{y}ah, swings (or is swinging or going along swinging) back and forth like a pendulum, and pantungk^{w}agaiv^{y}a is similarly derived from pantungk^{w}agaig^{y}ah, bounces up and down like a ball tied to a string. The following conveys some idea of this portion of the song:

Ka'ipipoo'vɨɨ'tsini'	My mountain canteen
wa'yuk^{w}aa'gaiv^{y}a'	will go swinging like a pendulum
wayuk' (or *wa'yuk^{w}aa'*)	swing like a pendulum
ka'ipipoo'vɨɨ'tsin'	my mountain canteen
pantu'ngk^{w}aa'ga'iv^{y}a'	will go bouncing up and down
pa'ntungk^{w}aa'gaiv^{y}a'	will go bouncing up and down
ka'ipipoo'vɨɨ'tsin'	my mountain canteen

The second fragment of this song is based upon the tradition that in each flock of mountain sheep there is a single white one, the killing of which would bring bad luck. This white sheep is called kaitos*a*, mountain white. In the song, it is a white lamb that is mentioned, tosamɨntcats*i*. The first and third lines are elisions of the phrase tosamɨntcatsi⁷ung^w*a*, that invisible white lamb. Yaga- is the root of the verb meaning to cry and is used both of human or animal distress: of the crying of a child or of an adult, or of the bleating of a lamb. The element -pa- in yagapagaiv^{y}a is unexplained. In listening to this song, one feels that the hunter has killed, or thinks that he may have killed the white lamb's mother; and although he no longer sees it, he hears it crying and has a poignant sense of its loneliness as it wanders lost and hopeless in the rocky wilderness:

Tosa'mɨntca'tcung^wa'   That unseen white lamb
yaga'paga'iv^ya'   will go along crying
tosa'mɨntca'tcung^wa'   that unseen white lamb
yaga'paga'iv   will go along crying

In this song as in all others there is endless repetition, varied by shifting accent, the interjection of syllables (usually ha), vowel lengthening, consonantal change and/or elision; final unvoiced vowels become fully voiced, voiced and lengthened, or clipped completely. The rendition of a song, while adhering to a basic pattern, must have varied in accordance with the style of the individual singer.

The ritual use of the Mountain Sheep Song may have been confined to funerals or Crying Ceremonies (Yagapɨ[16]) held for persons who had belonged to that group. So far as George Laird knew, it was not sung to secure good fortune in hunting. When sung ritually, the singer could only be one who owned the song legitimately. But when sung for pleasure, to entertain the people, it might also be led by one who had "borrowed" it, that is, had learned it merely by hearing it sung and had no hereditary right to it.

Deer Song

It is said of the Deer Song (Tɨhiyahuv^wiyavɨ[17]) that "it roamed about in rolling, hilly country east of the Colorado River." The large wash which runs from Parker, Arizona, to Bouse, called by the Chemehuevis Tɨhiya?ɨgatɨah, Deer Entrance, or Deer Entering Place, was in Deer Song territory, and the song also ranged over the region just north of Bill Williams Fork. If we knew the route of this song we should certainly be able to pinpoint more exactly the eastern range of the Chemehuevis, the country which was known to them and over which they claimed the right to hunt, though some of it was actually occupied by other tribes. Ranking next in importance to the Mountain Sheep Song, it must have had variants and have been divided among groups of related families. But George Laird, although himself a Deer, knew less about these divisions than he knew about those of the Mountain Sheep Song.

A man who was a Deer would designate the territory over which his song travelled as "my land," not "my mountain"; but here again a word-form would be used indicating the intimacy and inalienability of the relationship: tɨvipɨ means land; but one would say nɨɨni tɨviwa or tɨviwanɨ, my land.

ʔAyarupagarɨmɨ, Black Turtle, George Laird's grandfather and chief of a band of people living east of the River, was a notable Deer Singer, and Yaariʔivʸa, the mountain sheep shaman, was also known to have owned the Deer Song. ʔAtatuʔᵂatsɨ, Young Crow, who lived in Chemehuevi Valley, must have belonged to the Deer Song group, for his brother (name not remembered), who resided near Wickenburg and had an Apache wife, owned and sang the song. In the late 1880's, while this brother was visiting in Chemehuevi Valley, a son of ʔAtatuʔᵂatsɨ died, and his uncle sang a portion of his version of the Deer Song at the funeral. Then the uncle returned to the Hassayampa and lived there till he himself died, his Deer Song dying with him. George Laird had no memory at all of the song as sung by his grandfather, although he had heard him sing, but he recalled one brief fragment of the Deer Song as he heard it at the funeral of ʔOpitcokotsɨ, Mesquite Bean Pounder, oldest son of ʔAtatuʔᵂatsɨ.[18] This was as follows:

Paatcaa'witsi'ya	(Where) water seeps
yɨwaa'rukʷa'ituʷa'	through a valley
paatcaa' witsi'	water seeps
yɨwaa'rukʷa'i	through a valley

Even from this single group of two word-phrases repeated, the mournfully beautiful quality of the song is apparent. Tcawitsi-, George Laird said, was not a word in common use. It is evidently the root of a rare or obsolete verb applied to the seepage of water (paa-); yɨwaavɨ means valley. This excerpt hints at a grassy meadow where deer would delight to graze.

The Deer Song was used, like all hereditary songs, on occasions of mourning, but it definitely had another ritual use. When a hunting party had failed to secure deer, a member who owned the Deer Song would be asked to sing, and the others, regardless of song group affiliation, would join in. They would continue to sing and dance all night, and during the night, as they were "singing the Deer," one or more of the hunters would faint. This was an indication of the number of deer that would be killed next day—a clear intertwining of the life of the hunter with the life of the hunted. The fainting men could not be revived immediately, but all would be fully recovered in time for the hunt. In the morning, all the hunters would go out, very sleepy but confident, and would secure the expected number of deer. A very long time ago a woman who was a deer shaman would sing in this way for and with the hunters.

The use of the Deer Song on occasions when the People came together simply to feast or to be entertained was non-ritualistic. At such times the singing might be led either by a Deer Singer or by one who had "borrowed" or knew how to "imitate" the song. Huv^{W}iyari$^?$agah means borrows a song (ti$^?$agah, borrows), and huv^{W}iyanitagah, imitates a song, "mocks" a song as the mockingbird mocks various sounds. The terms are interchangeable. One or the other is applied to the singing of a song, no matter how skillfully, by one who does not have the hereditary right to it. The translation of nita- as to mock, that is, to imitate without understanding, as a bird might, implies that only the owner of a song could truly understand it.

Salt Song

$^?$Asi- in the Salt Song ($^?$Asihuv^{W}iyav$i$[19]) is from the Mohave $^?ath^?i$, salt. The Chemehuevi word for salt is $^?$asomp$i$; therefore, in pure Chemehuevi the name of the song would be $^?$Asohuv^{W}iyav$i$, but this form is never used. The entire song is composed of Mohave words, pronounced and combined in such a manner as to be unintelligible to Mohaves.[20] This playing with words, especially with foreign words, and the fact that the song ranged boldly into enemy territory delighted the Chemehuevi sense of humor; coupled with its sheer birdsong gaiety, all this made the Salt Song peculiarly appropriate for use on festive occasions. Yet it was a genuine hereditary song and as such was used in the solemn ritual singing commemorating the demise of one of its owners.

George Laird inherited the Salt Song along with the Deer Song, connecting it in thought very strongly with his mother. I believe that certain other Salt Song owners were also Deer, and the song definitely traversed Deer territory for part of its course. This encourages the surmise that it was a subsidiary of the Deer Song and that the Salt Song group or clan may have belonged to the Deer moiety.

The Salt Song tells of the wandering of a flock of birds

consisting of many different species (collectively witci?itsiwɨ, though each variety had its own name). This flock was comprised of every sort of land bird that inhabits the Colorado River Valley. The song starts up Bill Williams Fork, perhaps forty-five miles from the Colorado, follows the Bill Williams down to the River, then goes upstream to a point above Fort Mohave; thence it goes east across the mountains, reaches the vicinity of Mineral Park, and proceeds on into Walapai Valley; then travels north again to cross the Colorado River and start out southwest on the Nevada side, coming down to Las Vegas. The Salt Song then follows the valley of the Dry Lakes on down by New York Mountain, thence down through the hills till it strikes the valley where Danby is situated, then goes across from Danby behind the hill where there is a rock salt mine and proceeds southeast from that point until it reaches the Palo Verde Wash below Blythe. It goes north again on the California side, crossing the River about three miles from Blythe intake and so into Parker Valley in Arizona; then it goes up through that valley to within some three miles of Parker, up the wash (Tɨhiya?ɨgatɨah, Deer Entrance) that runs from Parker to Bouse for about ten miles, then northeast over rolling hills until it strikes the Bill Williams, and continues up Bill Williams to the starting point.

The Song travels all night, arriving at Las Vegas about midnight, at Parker towards morning, and back home to the place of origin by sunrise. If the night on which it is sung is very short, the Salt Song—as the other hereditary songs—may be shortened so that it will not outlast the night. But it is important that this cutting be properly done, by one who knows both song and terrain thoroughly.

The Song must reach the right place at the right time, because towards morning, in the vicinity of Blythe, the Birds begin to drop out of the company. When each Bird (a single Bird represents an entire species) recognizes the place that will be his home, he says, "I stay here." Having in ancient times found their respective places, as narrated in the Salt Song, the birds multiplied, and now the whole river valley is filled with birds of various kinds.

Although George Laird recalled so clearly the route of the Salt Song, he could sing for me only the following brief phrases:

ʔAna'si'pakaiyoo' kaiyoo'   The sun is rising, look!
waiyo ʔongo haniyanga'   [not translated]
tcomaruripanga'i   (there are) many ants

The first line is based on Mohave *ʔanya ʔitcpak kíyuk*, the sun is rising (literally, emerging, coming out, as an animal emerges from its hole or den), look! In Chemehuevi, which employs the same idiom, this would be tavamawisiy punik^{y}aing$u$! The Mohave word for sun (tava-) is *ʔanya*, and *kíyuk* is the equivalent of Chemehuevi punik^{y}aing$u$, look! The last phrase is from Mohave *tcamadhulya ʔapalya*, in Chemehuevi *ʔavaʔatsasiyavi*, many ants. It is said to refer to there being many ants in the vicinity of Fort Mohave.[21]

A person who had hereditary right to the Salt Song but wished to acquire it in a more private and personal way than simply by listening to his relatives could learn it by visiting a sacred cave, located near where the Santa Maria and the Sandy flow together to form Bill Williams Fork. This will be discussed in detail in the following chapter.

Other Songs

Two other songs definitely associated with hereditary hunting territories were Kakarahuv^{w}iyav$i$, Quail Song, and Tavamuhuu-huv^{w}iyav$i$, Day Owl Song (tava-, sun, day; muhuump$i$ts$i$, large owl species). George Laird asserted that these songs differed from the Mountain Sheep and Deer songs only in that each belonged to a single group of related persons and neither was "split up" into different versions covering different ranges. Since both the quail and the "day owl"[22] are ground birds of the Colorado River Valley, they must have been in the company of Birds whose habitats are accounted for by the Salt Song, and this suggests a connection with the Deer Song-Salt Song complex. A man named ʔIluh inherited the Quail Song from his father and also claimed the Day Owl Song from his mother (possibly by default of another heir). The name ʔIluh (or ʔIruh) is a corruption of Mohave *idho*, willow. The father of ʔIluh died about 1880. He was called Wangkasiigwas$i$, Cow Tail. Others who had the Quail Song were Wikunt$i$pa, Buzzard Mouth, and his cousin, K$i$mamoʔo, Different Hand. Tuhug^{w}ant$i$sagwagar$i$mi, Green Enemy, was a younger brother of Wikunt$i$pa and a "rattlesnake doctor." He probably knew the

Quail Song, although he never sang it. The Quail Song is remembered now by name only, and the Day Owl Song is probably also lost.

Yet another song which might be placed in the category of hereditary hunting range songs was the Skunk Song, Poniyahuv^wi-yav*i*. George Laird was unsure of this. The song was definitely inherited, but it may have been a shaman's song, unassociated with hunting rights. Shamans also passed their songs on to sons, daughters, and grandchildren.

It is easy to see how new song groups might have been formed in a time when the tribe was expanding, numerically and territorially. The shaman's song might have become disassociated from shamanistic powers and its route adapted to the family hunting grounds; or foreign songs might have been adopted and adapted as needed. For example, the Chemehuevis had an inordinate admiration for the Cahuilla Bird Song and sang it at social gatherings. It might have formed the nucleus for a new group or subdivision if the native culture had continued to develop normally.

The ritual use of hereditary songs formed an important part of the rites for the dead; their social use was a celebration of life and was fully as important. The telling of myths was taboo except in wintertime, when the snakes are dormant, but songs could be sung at any time and were a favorite form of entertainment for a summer's night. To the end of his life George Laird remembered with great pleasure warm and moonlit nights in a patch of ripe melons when the People feasted and sang the whole night through. The man who led the singing on such an occasion would most probably be an owner of the song, but he might be a borrower, if his borrowing or imitating was sufficiently skillful and accurate.

Let us reconstruct as best we can such a scene of song and feasting. The place is Chemehuevi Valley, a site long occupied by the People and called in their own tongue Siwa?avaats*i*, Place of Hardpan Mortars. Here there are numerous though scattered brush houses and well-cultivated fields. And here also are the graves of many Chemehuevis, for the time is in the late 1880's, and many have perished in the great epidemics. The ancient culture is rapidly breaking up before the impact of an onrushing white civilization; it is being carried away like driftwood in the current. But the building of Parker Dam is still many years in the future, and no one dreams that the day is coming when this dear and fertile strip of land will be inundated. At this time the People, though decimated and saddened, cling to the old ways. They have come together to sing and dance and eat, to take pleasure in each other's company even as they did when the earth was younger, when hunters roamed freely over many mountains and through many valleys, filled with the sheer exuberance of life, leaping and playing games as they went on their way. The irrigation ditch which skirts this particular field is already old, fringed with willows like a natural stream. The sweet scent of water and willows, ripe and over-ripe melons, is laid against the pungent background of miles upon miles of creosote bush and the more immediate pungency of a wandering skunk, whose favorite melon patch is now invaded by humans. The night air is very warm, but it feels pleasantly cool to those whose blood has been thinned by the fierce daytime heat. On this night, the moonlight is so bright that it reveals the tattoo marks on the women's faces: some of the younger ones wear only a single dot, like a Hindu caste mark, in the middle of their foreheads, but most of them also have lines radiating like cats' whiskers from the corners of their mouths and running vertically down their chins. These women wear full-skirted dresses of dark calico and headbands. Their children, boys and girls alike, wear shifts made out of floursacks, and the smaller toddlers tumble naked at their mothers' feet. The young men who are now in the white man's employ, running his cattle, breaking his horses, digging in his crude mines, have short hair and wear dungarees and work shirts; but some of the untamed ones, like the conservative old men, wear only their G-strings, and their long hair, the badge of manhood, hangs about shoulders glistening with sweat. Perhaps it is one of these old men who is requested to lead the singing. For such a gathering, the Salt Song is a great favorite and many people know it, but if some notable singer of the Deer or Mountain Sheep or Quail is present, his song may be the one selected. It may be that such a singer is very ancient, that his sons and grandsons are already dead or have not cared to learn from him, and that this is one of the last times his particular song will be heard. The women, too, own these songs, and their voices ring out strong and true. But a woman would not be asked to lead, for she would be less familiar with the terrain which the song traverses, and she would not know the shortcuts from one place to another which must be used if it becomes necessary to shorten it. In the mind of the leader the whole route is clearly etched, for since early youth he has travelled and hunted and fought over this mountain or this land which is peculiarly his. The song begins, and the People listen intently, joining in the dance but dropping out from time to time to sit on the ground and cram their mouths with the sweet, juicy flesh of the melons while they murmur bits of gossip to each other. Children play among the vines, and couples slip away into the brush to make love. All too soon coyotes salute the false dawn, then day breaks, the song returns to its starting place, the Sun emerges from his lair, and the People disperse, some to sleep briefly and others to go immediately about their daily tasks.

We have no evidence that the Mountain Sheep and Deer moieties (or large clans) were exogamous, but the smaller subdivisions were strictly so. A man would not marry a woman of his immediate Song Group, that is, one whose family had inherited the same version of a song, because they would be known kinfolk. A single person was a rare phenomenon, for marriage was not only pleasant and convenient, it was a virtual necessity. A woman desperately needed a man to hunt for her and her children, and a man needed a woman to gather and grind for him. But under ordinary circumstances, no stigma attached to the dissolution of a union.

There were two methods of contracting marriage with a young girl who had not left her parents' home. The more formal way was employed when a man wanted a girl who was generally industrious, a skilled basketweaver, a good seed-gatherer, and therefore of considerable value to her family. In this case, the suitor would approach the girl's father; if the father was satisfied that the young man was of desirable character and an able hunter, he and his relatives would proceed to subject him to the smoke test. If he was able to endure strong smoke without shedding tears,[23] he got the girl. The other way of getting married was for the suitor to take a male cousin with him on a visit to the girl's family. During the night the cousin would go over to the young woman and lie down beside her to talk the matter over. If she was agreeable, the cousin would yield his place to the bridegroom, and in the morning the family awoke to find the marriage consummated.

Either way, it was customary for the young married man to stay for awhile at least with his wife's family, perhaps for a few days, a few months, or, not infrequently, permanently. Or after a time he might take his wife to visit his own family, returning eventually to make his home with or near hers. The wife had a strong sense of her marital rights, and should the husband have a love affair with an unmarried woman, she would be properly furious. This was a frequent cause of feuds. If the girl's relatives wanted the man, they would fight against the wife's relatives; or if the husband's people thought the girl was desirable, they might help him spirit her away.

These marriage customs resulted in the formation of bands, loosely but not exclusively matrilocal. Such a band was called a nɨwɨavi.[24] Every band, no matter how small, had a spokesman. If it consisted of more than two or three families, it would be under the leadership of a lesser chief, called in Spanish *un capitán chiquito*, in Chemehuevi simply tog^wa^intɨmɨ, chief—or if it were necessary to state clearly that the man was not a High Chief, one might say mi'ʸaupitog^wa^intɨmɨ, little chief. Allegiance to the chief was based on residence, not on inheritance, and residence was purely a matter of choice, having nothing to do with the location of a family's hereditary hunting territory. Once when I pressed George Laird for some connection between hereditary grouping and allegiance to a chief, he answered rather impatiently, "If I live in San Diego, I'm under the mayor of San Diego, and if I move to Los Angeles, I'm under the mayor of Los Angeles." The people of a nɨwɨavi planted and harvested their crops together, travelled together on gathering or hunting expeditions, and if necessary, fought together. For hunting it was especially desirable that men owning various ranges should be available, for this would give the hunting party a wider territory in which to look for game. It was not requisite to have a Deer along in order to kill deer or a Mountain Sheep in order to hunt mountain sheep; but it was obligatory to have a hunter in the party who owned the mountain or land where the hunt was conducted.

The Chemehuevis recognized the fact that with them irrigation was a learned art[25] and that therefore there must have been a time when they depended solely on the overflow of the River to irrigate their corn, beans, melons, and pumpkins. They had absolutely no tribal memory[26] of a time when they had not also planted wheat (ʔatsitа) in the floodplain. In late September or October, in each little occupied bend of the River, the People sowed their wheat. Then the whole nɨwɨavɨ, or at least the greater part of it, went roaming in the hills, gathering pine nuts and seeds, camping and hunting in various places until March or April. Upon their return, if the Mohaves or other enemies had not raided their fields, they found the wheat still green and the grain in its delicious, milky stage. This they ate as it was, right from the field, until it ripened in late May; then they harvested what remained, for the high water would come in June, inundating all the fertile land. When the Chemehuevis were allies of the Maricopas, the two tribes probably shared the use of their fields.

Each nɨwɨavɨ took its name from the place where the People returned to plant their crops, or from whatever place they considered to be their headquarters. For example, ʔOtawɨnɨrɨ, Sand Standing, was chief of a small band located on the Arizona side of the River, across from Chemehuevi Valley. Their place was called Kwayantuʷatɨ, and they were known as Kwayantuʷatɨtsiwɨ, inhabitants of Kwayantuʷatɨ.[27] Another place on the River, Harimyiivɨ, notable because it was always free from frost, was located below Chemehuevi Valley and occupied by a small band under a lesser chief named Tuuwɨnɨrɨ, Black Standing. Tuuwɨnɨrɨ, who could see but not hear, never left Harimyiivɨ. After he became too feeble to act as chief, he was succeeded by another man of about the same age who could hear but not see. This man (whose Chemehuevi name was not recalled) roamed about in the normal Chemehuevi way in spite of his infirmity. George Laird's own nɨwɨavɨ lived six or seven miles down-river from Chemehuevi Valley, on the California side. Another bend in the River, situated on the Nevada side, was called Wiyaanʔnikʸaatɨ, and its inhabitants were Wiyaanʔnikʸaatɨtsiwɨ. There were enough of them to have a chief.[28] This place was about two miles down the road from the

Hardyville ferry at the point where the road to Paiute Hill left the main road. All the little valleys from there on up the Colorado had Chemehuevi names and were occupied by clusters of families.

There was an aura of almost priestly dignity about the chiefs, even the lesser chiefs. They and their families, like the High Chiefs and their families, were privileged to wear the turquoise and to eat quail-beans (kakaramurih, black-eyed peas); and also like the High Chiefs, the lesser chiefs were able to speak together in the Chief's Language (Tɨvitsiˀampagapɨ, Real Speech). On a memorable night in the year 1891, ˀAyarupagarɨmɨ, ˀOtawɨnɨrɨ, and another chief from the vicinity of Banning, named Nagaramaup*a*, Left the Mountain Sheep Behind (and, incidentally, said to have been the biggest liar among the Chemehuevis), were together in Chemehuevi Valley. They sat by the fire and talked all night long in the dialect reserved for chiefs, and George Laird kept silent and listened, spellbound. First one would speak for half an hour or an hour at a time, then with great dignity another would take his turn. This dialect was known as a "short way" of talking. In so far as he was able to remember, George Laird thought that the words were clipped short with final vowels omitted, or perhaps even stripped down to the bare roots, and they were declaimed or chanted with a strong accent. This manner of speaking is unintelligible to ordinary folk.

The function of the High Chiefs was not, as will be seen, wholly or even primarily political. High chieftancy was a sacred office, bound up with the most profound religious beliefs of the People.

High Chiefs had regional jurisdiction. The Tantɨitsiwɨ had a High Chief living somewhere in the vicinity of El Dorado and Cottonwood Island. One of the last High Chiefs of the Tɨɨranɨwɨwɨ was Tukupɨr*a*, whose band travelled about near Daggett. He had lesser chiefs under his control. His jurisdiction probably included the Desert Chemehuevis of Providence Mountain, and he was in every way the equal of "the Big Chief down by the River," that is, the High Chief of the Southern Chemehuevis. Tukupɨr*a* was generally respected. The white people called him Captain Tuku-pɨr*a*. In Spanish the High Chief of a region was referred to as *el Capitán Grande*; in Chemehuevi he was spoken of as Tɨvitsitog^(wa)intɨ-mɨ or Haˀɨtɨtog^(wa)intɨmɨ, Real Chief or Genuine Chief, when it was necessary to distinguish him from a lesser chief.

And now we come to the last and most sacred of the hereditary songs, which differed in several very important ways from the hereditary songs previously discussed. The Talking Song, ⁊Ampagahuvʷiyav*i*, also known as the Crying Song, Yagahuvʷiyav*i*, was the exclusive hereditary property of the High Chief and his close relatives. It was called ⁊Ampagahuvʷiyav*i* because certain portions of it, either at the beginning or the end, were declaimed or recited in Real Speech, the Chief's Language. Its second appellation derived from the fact that it was sung only at funerals or Mourning Ceremonies (Yagap*i*), which will be more fully discussed in the following chapter. It was not connected with any territorial hunting rights, for the territory over which it ranged was not of this world. Since its use was purely ritualistic, it might never be borrowed or imitated; it must be sung by one of its legitimate owners or not at all. There were, even among the Southern Chemehuevis, several slightly divergent versions, including dreamed versions, but these differences did not indicate different family groupings. We may conclude then that possession of this song was an indication of Chief's blood rather than of clan.

George Laird was only able to remember one phrase from the Talking Song:

⁊Ampaar*i*⁊aamay⁊	On top of the voice
⁊ampaar*i*⁊aamayu⁊	On top of the voice
⁊ampaar*i*⁊aamayu	On top of the voice

This was repeated for a very long time, with doubled a's very long and wailing and with minor variations at the end of each line. It derives from ⁊amp*a*, a rare or obsolete form of the word for voice (possibly the form used in Chief's Language?), and t*i*⁊amay*u*, top. Kaivʸay t*i*⁊amay*u* means top of the mountain, the mountain's top; but it would be misleading to translate this phrase from the Talking Song as top of the voice, because by analogy with the English idiom that would indicate shouting—which would be, in Chemehuevi, ⁊ampagavaigʸah.

The old High Chief of the Southern Chemehuevis (whose name George Laird did not know, but to whom he referred, always with great respect, as "the Old Chief" or "the Big Chief down by the River") was the great Talking Singer of his people. He died in 1875. His son, ⁊Aapanap*i*, White Clay Lightning Flash, was shot by a white man[29] some five years later at the beginning of the trouble which interrupted the building of the old Blythe Intake. Tugumpayaaʔoʷasiʸakarɨmɨ, Yellow Sky, whose English name was Charley Snyder and who was also known by the Chemehuevi name of Totsaarɨmɨ, was related in some way to the old High Chief and learned the Talking Song directly from him. He died of thirst in the desert during World War I, his son and grandson having predeceased him. (Tugumpayaaʔoʷasiʸakarɨmɨ had started to go over the mountains from Needles to Chemehuevi Valley. While he was camped at a place called ʔOpinʸawɨtɨmʔma,[30] Closed Itself with Mesquite, his horse got away from him. He started to follow the horse, then having gone too far to return to his campsite, tried to reach Tukumumuuntsitɨnah, At the Base of the Mountain Lion, where springs are located at the foot of a high cliff. Being a little lame, he could not travel well on foot, and so he died.) Pisoʔorɨmpa, Baby Mouth, was cousin both to the High Chief and to Tugumpayaaʔoʷasiʸakarɨmɨ. He had a dreamed version of the Talking Song (which he had of course heard many times), differing radically in accent and melody from the original but with virtually the same words. George Laird heard Pisoʔorɨmpa sing several times at Cries (Mourning Ceremonies), and the phrase of the song which stuck in his mind came from this dreamed version. Pisoʔorɨmpa was survived by two daughters and a son. The latter was called Tcɨgaʔuruʷantɨ, Walks Like a Duck, and was about forty-five years old in 1920. Although he was the senior inheritor of the Talking Song he knew only a few stanzas of his father's version, and up to the time when George Laird last heard of him had not been spiritually impelled to become a Talking Singer. George Laird expressed the opinion that the song might yet "come to him"; but if so, he would have to dream it, for there was no living person left to teach it to him.

The Cry and the Gathering were the two occasions upon which the People came together from far and near. When preparations for either event were well enough in hand so that a date might be set, the knotted string was sent out. In this string, called tapitcapɨ, "the knotted," knots were tied equal in number to the nights that would elapse before the occasion to which the people were being summoned. Each night that he spent on the road the messenger (called tapitcapɨyawitsɨ, "bringer of the knotted string") would untie a knot. When he arrived at a settlement there would be great excitement; the people would exclaim, "Tapitcap nayaak^aing*u*, the knotted string is brought!"

The Gathering was called Suupaaru?^wap*i* (from a root form suupaaru?^wa- meaning to gather; a person would say masuupaa-ru?^wavaan*i*, I shall gather up anything—clothing, leaves, trash, for example—with my hands, but would have to say Suupaaru?^wap*i*-vaantu^wavaan*i*, I shall go to—i.e., towards—the Gathering), and another name for it was Nagarip*i*.[31] These assemblies used to be held quite frequently. The persons who wished a certain matter to be brought up would consult with each other, listen to various suggestions, and select an appropriate time and a place (the home of one of those initiating the Gathering) where there would be plenty of food. The High Chief, T*i*vitsitog^waint*i*m*i*, would be present to address the people. So great was his dignity that sometimes he would not speak directly to those assembled, but would have a spokesman (?ampagangk*i*av*i*) to speak for him. This spokesman knew what was in the mind of the Chief and conveyed his thought to the People.

When the succession to the chieftancy was in doubt, or when the Chief was unsatisfactory and needed to be replaced, the People would take the opportunity to decide this matter when they were gathered together ostensibly for some other purpose.

George Laird stated emphatically that it was the duty of the High Chief to set a good example and to teach his people a moral code, long since lost. He also said that the High Chief guided the people in the ways of peace and that when it became necessary for them to go to war a special War Chief would be appointed. This is not borne out by the myth "How Coyote Went to War Against Gila Monster." In this myth both Coyote and Gila Monster are High Chiefs with lesser chiefs under them (Coyote with many, Gila Monster with one), yet both lead their people in war as well as in peace. (Typically, Coyote is a poor peace-time Chief, selfish and improvident, but proves to be a splendid strategist in time of war.) Perhaps even in ancient times there was no inflexible custom in this regard; much may have depended upon the temperament and abilities of individual chiefs.

Among the T*i*iran*i*w*i*w*i* around 1850 there was a leader described as a "bad chief" because he led his people in depredations that could only eventuate in disaster for all. So ingrained in George Laird's concept of a High Chief were the qualities of wisdom and restraint that he felt sure this man must have been a mere lesser chief under one of Tukupɨra's predecessors. Sometimes, he commented, High Chiefs could not control their subordinates, just had to let them go and do as they pleased. He felt that this "bad chief" was not justified in going on the warpath however great the provocation, which in this case was very great indeed. The trouble started when a band of Desert Chemehuevis were camped seed-gathering somewhere between Providence and Soda Lake Mountains. While the men were away hunting and the women peacefully gathering seeds, immigrants came upon and massacred the unprotected women and children. Shortly afterwards men of this band were camped at Kwiyavaah, Snake Water, a place situated some forty or fifty miles from the present town of Barstow. Two white men came along in a buggy carrying money for a payroll, octagonal fifty dollar gold pieces as well as ten and twenty dollar gold pieces, stored in a stout canvas sack. Two Chemehuevis attacked and killed them. They knew nothing of the value of the money. While one went back to the spring for something that had been left behind, the other dropped the gold pieces down a crack in a rock so that they might have the use of the sack. Afterward, having tasted blood, the band ranged as far as Paiute Springs, probably even to Tehachapi, harassing wagon trains, and committing depredations on white settlers, vainly trying to stem the westward-flowing tide. The chief who led them claimed he could not be killed because he wore a shirt which was a talisman. It is true that he engaged in many fights without even being wounded. But one night he dreamed of falling over a cliff, and the next day he was killed in a battle with a company of immigrants. This broke up the marauding band. While they were still active they were accompanied by a lame Tantɨvaitsɨ. A hunting party including this Southerner came upon some white men and attacked them. One of the white men was Tom Halleck, a Texan, who told how he fired a shot at the Indians and saw a lame man run straight up the mountain with incredible agility in spite of his infirmity. He could do this, George Laird said, because he was a Mountain Sheep. The ability came to him naturally because of his hereditary right to the song and also because "he had dreamed it"–that is, he was both a Mountain Sheep by inheritance and a mountain sheep shaman.

I am impressed by the recurrence in these notes of phrases such as "The People met and talked it over," "They got together and talked it over," or "They talked it over and decided." It is clear that the last word remained always with the People. A charismatic or strongwilled Chief might mislead his followers for a time, or a man might become Chief who was weak and ineffectual, but nothing could interrupt for long the tribe's exercise of an informal but effective democracy. Eventually, the unwise or unworthy Chief would be replaced by one who would act in accordance with tradition and with the will of the People. Nonetheless, the Chief's power, while he remained Chief, was very real. In such a society as this, custom and taboo operated as powerful enforcement agencies for the unwritten law.

It was unheard of for a woman to succeed to the chieftaincy. But the voices of women were heard equally with those of men at the Gatherings and on other occasions when the People met "to talk things over."

CHAPTER II

SHAMANISM AND
THE SUPERNATURAL

THE Chemehuevi word for shaman is puh^wagant*i*.[1] Since -gant*i*
signifies having (as in the placename N*i*vagant*i*, Having Snow,
or in kani^yagant*i*, having or owning a house), the term must mean
one who possesses puh^wa-, the power to "doctor," to heal or to
harm by spiritual means. George Laird translated puh^wagant*i* as doctor and considered healing to be the primary function of a shaman.

The Chemehuevi shaman required no feathered headdress, no
regalia of any kind, no eagle feathers or down, no sacred bundle,
no collection of healing herbs.[2] His one indispensable piece of
equipment was his por*o* (or poor*o*), a rod shaped like a shepherd's
crook.[3] This was an archetypal object of great power, known in
many ages and to many cultures. It was the rod of Aaron and of
the Egyptian priests, the magic wand, the scepter of authority. In
the myth "How Wolf and Coyote Went Away," it is said that with
a single twist of his por*o* Wolf tunneled through a great mountain
and that Coyote used his por*o* to hook the wind down from its
high level so that it might sweep across the surface of the earth. In
that ancient, storied time, When the Animals Were People, after all
Wolf's or Coyote's warriors had been killed in battle, slaughtered
by malevolent beings, or had died of thirst, they were revived by
the touch of a por*o* in the hands of Wolf or of some other
pre-human shaman. The por*o* was peculiarly the shaman's badge of
office; it is not to be confused with p*ii*r*i*, a crooked stick upon
which an old man might lean in his infirmity.

Every shaman had at least one familiar, a spirit-animal who was his helper and was invisible to any eyes but his. This familiar was known as a tutuguuv*i*. Shamanistic powers were indissolubly bound up with the possession of a tutuguuv*i* and of the song by which it could be summoned. The home of all tutuguuviw*i* with the exception of paatsats*i*, bat, was in a place located vaguely to the northwest of the Colorado Desert. This place was known as Hauwawangk*i*gar*i*, Bone-Gray Peaks (haungkar*i*, the color of an old bone which has bleached gray, not white; wawangk*i*gar*i* [from wawangk*i*gagah], several or many objects standing up serrated "like the blade of a saw, but tall." A single peak would be kwitcuvar*i* or kwitcuvakat*i*). Hauwawangk*i*gar*i* may have been entirely mythological but was more probably, like N*i*vagant*i*, the sacred mountain, an actual place to which mythological beliefs became attached. As the shaman performed his healing office, as he sang and danced, his song traced the route by which the familiar was travelling from its mysterious home. Sometimes the shaman had a scout or runner, whose duty it was to go back and forth between the shaman and his familiar, reporting on the latter's progress. This scout (howar*i*) would not have to be an animal that is very swift, because the familiar travels slowly, going "as the song goes," and arriving towards morning. It is unclear to me whether the scout belonged to another class of supernatural beings or whether it was a life-form visible to all but capable of travelling back and forth between the realm of ordinary perception and the spiritual world. There was a shaman named ʔOompos*i*[4] who had the dragonfly, wiwʔwingngkurats*i*, as his scout; one of his familiars was tukumumuunts*i*, mountain lion, but he also had nax*a*, mountain sheep, and possibly several others. ʔOompos*i* was a notable shaman of whom we shall hear more later. He was still remembered by name by persons living on the Colorado River Reservation in 1969.

The mouse and the packrat were especially desirable as familiars because they were able to "steal the disease away." Any carnivorous mammal or bird (but not snake) was classified as tukuᵂar*i*kawagant*i* (plural tukuᵂar*i*kawagam*i*), flesh eater, and to have such a tutuguuv*i* was not an unmixed blessing. There was always the possibility that it might feed on a person, thus causing sickness rather than curing it. A shaman who possessed a flesh eater as his helper was considered potentially dangerous; when in his dreams he had communion with his familiar, he became niwirikaganti, person eater or cannibal. It was said that a shaman (not ?Oomposi) who had the mountain lion as his familiar once had such a cannibalistic experience when he was a member of a hunting party out after mountain sheep. A few of the hunters awoke in the night and saw this man sitting up eating a rib. Since they had killed no game, they became suspicious and asked what kind of meat he was eating. He explained that his tutuguuvi had brought him the rib. After further questioning, he admitted that his familiar had told him it was a rib belonging to a man whom they all knew, a man who had some relatives among the hunters. These relatives persuaded the shaman to return to the village to repair any possible damage. They found the man whose rib had been eaten dying. The shaman cured him by confessing his acts publicly, in his song. George Laird explained that it was not the actual, physical rib which had been eaten, but an other-world counterpart which was the spiritual essence of the rib.

All the tutuguuviwi were spirit-animals whose forerunners in the time When the Animals Were People had been themselves shamans, with the exception of the mountain sheep and the deer. As previously noted, even in pre-human times these animals usually appeared as game hunted by the Immortals, yet their spiritual counterparts reappear in this present time as shamans' familiars. George Laird himself commented on this. Like shamans owning other familiars, mountain sheep and deer shamans were those who had dreamed repeatedly of the song and the spirit-animal and had been instructed in these dreams, both by the song and the familiar, what ills they would be able to cure and how they should go about their healing work. But it must be emphasized that the songs of mountain sheep and deer shamans were of necessity quite distinct from the hereditary songs bearing the names of these animals and associated with specific hunting ranges. The songs of deer and mountain sheep shamans traversed no earthly hunting grounds, for they must summon the deer familiar (tihiyatutuguuvi) or the mountain sheep familiar (nagatutuguuvi) from the home they shared with other spirit-animals among the Bone-Gray Peaks. Deer and mountain sheep familiars made good helpers, for they were always beneficent, never malignant like the carnivores.

Of all the tutuguuviw*i*, only paatsats*i*, bat, made his home on Par*i*ʔas*i*kaiv*ʸa*, Ice Mountain (pa- for paa-, water; t*i*ʔas*i*p*i*, that which is frozen, from t*i*ʔas*i*agah, freezing [intransitive]; kaiv*ʸa*, mountain), an unidentified but probably not wholly mythical mountain said to be of solid ice—possibly a mountain where there are ice caves. The bat familiar, like his counterpart in mythic times, had the power of producing intense cold; therefore, he conferred the power to heal burns upon the shaman whose helper he was. In the myth "How Bat Killed Rattlesnake," Bat caused all the children in the camp of Coyote's people to burn their hands so that he might "test his power" by healing them. In this present time, and yet very long ago, probably before the advent of the white man, a party of Chemehuevis travelled over toward the coast to visit some tribe that was having Fire Ceremonies, which the Chemehuevis themselves never held. A young Chemehuevi looked on for awhile, then walked into the midst of the big fire and sat down. All the spectators could see him melting away, being consumed, and they could hear the fire sizzling as it does when it comes in contact with something wet. After a time the young man arose and walked out of the fire, intact. His companions asked him how he had accomplished it. "We saw you sizzling there," they said. "That was not I," he replied, "that was a big chunk of ice." During the ceremony he had suddenly acquired the bat as his familiar, a marked exception to the general rule that it takes a long while and much dreaming to gain shamanistic powers.

Woman shamans were not uncommon. Such a woman would be called mamauʔ puh*ʷ*agant*i* (mamauʔuvu*ʷ*agant*i* would be an impossible word because it describes an impossible situation—the possession of a woman as a familiar). Munuukw*a*, Round Like a Ball, was a shaman, and so was her sister, Pagaarayuningk*i*, Kicker Against the River Bank to Make it Cave In. Munuukw*a* was Joe Valenzuela's wife and was called Maria Valenzuela. Pagaarayuningk*i* was commonly known as Taasi.[5] She had several familiars, of which the most powerful was the largest of all rattlesnakes, called in Mohave *haikwiira*.[6] George Laird did not know what Maria's familiar was, but Taasi's was stronger. It injured Maria without Taasi's having willed it to do so. Taasi tried unsuccessfully to cure her. The Santa Fe Railway doctor said Maria had a tumor and could be cured by going to Los Angeles for an operation. Her husband wanted to send her, but she was afraid and would not go. She chose to die among her own people, under the care and treatment of her remorseful sister.

The kind of shaman one is, that is, the familiar with which he is allied, is usually indicated by prefixing the name of the spirit-animal, as in nagavu^wagant*i*, mountain sheep shaman. But kwiyavu^wagant*i*, "snake doctor," does not imply that the shaman has the rattlesnake as his familiar, but that his peculiar skill lies in the curing of snakebite. Also huv^wu^wagant*i*, always translated "wound doctor" but literally "arrow (or bullet) doctor" (huuh, arrow; but ʔ*i*aruʔ^wats*i*, wound), indicates one who is able to heal wounds. It must be that snake doctors and wound doctors have familiars, but they do not summon them when treating because time is of the essence. It appears that having survived the bite of a rattlesnake had something to do with becoming a snake doctor. At one time George Laird remarked that a snake doctor could cure toothache as well as snakebite, and again he stated that if a person had been bitten by a rattlesnake on the hand or foot and had recovered, he could take away the pain of toothache by laying the hand or foot, as the case might be, against the afflicted cheek.

Jim Haikur*i*mp*a*'s mother was huv^wu^wagant*i*, and from her Jim Haikur*i*mp*a* inherited a song for curing bullet or arrow wounds, as well as the Skunk Song, which (as previously noted) may or may not have been a shaman's song. Jim Haikur*i*mp*a*'s mother, "Doctor" Billy Eddy's mother, and George Laird's mother were cousins. Of these three women, only George Laird's mother was not a shaman. "Doctor" Billy Eddy's mother evidently passed on her song and shamanistic power to her son.[7]

The shaman's duty was to heal, and he was rated "good" or "bad" according to his healing ability; but a really "bad" or dangerous shaman was one who was not merely inept but malevolent, producing illness rather than curing it. The curative rite must have been awesome and not infrequently accompanied by psychic phenomena. It is said that certain shamans exhibited pebbles or similar small objects as proof that the disease had been extracted from the patient's body, but I feel that intentional trickery was almost nonexistent, that the shaman's commitment to his calling was sincere, and his emotional involvement even greater than that of the spectators. There was one shaman whose clothes always fell off while he was performing his office. This man was a Tantɨitsɪ, a Northerner. George Laird thought that he was either Tumiingu, who came from up around El Dorado Canyon or possibly Las Vegas, or ʔɨwarɨngkova, Rain Face, who also came from that part of the country. George Laird did not know the English name of either man (Tumiingu surely derives from Spanish *Domingo*), nor did he know what their familiars were. Another shaman whose work was marked by a peculiar manifestation was Yampavin^yuk^wɪ, Mockingbird Runner. When his patient was too far gone for his ministrations, when the case was hopeless, he would find himself juggling two skulls. Everyone present would see the skulls. The English name of Yampavin^yuk^wɪ was Johnny Moss. He met his death in Dagget at the hands of some Mexicans who killed him with "a pick or an axe."

The culmination of the shaman's work was the public revelation of the evil intent or malevolent thought which was at the root of the illness and the exposure of the person responsible. Toward morning, when the night-long singing and ritual dancing had brought the familiar from his home in the Bone-Gray Peaks, when the very air was pregnant with mystery and power, the shaman's song would reveal the hidden evil; and not infrequently this would bring about the confession of the guilty party and so complete the cure. This public "telling" was an integral part of the healing ritual. However, in the myth "How the Pleiades Came to Be," the shaman who cures Coyote's ailing daughter by exposing her father's incestuous relations with her first prudently sends Coyote on a fool's errand to fetch a jug of water from the ocean—any effort to secure a confession from that reprobate would probably have proved fruitless.

To become a shaman was a mystical, arduous, and lonely experience. It generally involved several years of spending much time by one's self, meditating upon mysterious, demanding, unshared dreams. If a person went to a magic cave to learn an hereditary song, he had only to hear it once; but a shaman's song, whether or not it was first heard in a cave, had to be dreamed repeatedly. Sometimes an individual felt impelled to choose this way of life, consciously seeking to acquire a familiar and to open his mind to dreams; to others, the power came unsought and often undesired. Once having become a full-fledged shaman, the responsibilities were heavy. The medicine man was expected to heal; if his familiar was dangerous, he was expected to keep it under control and not to injure people, voluntarily or involuntarily. For this reason, there were persons who were unavowed shamans. Having acquired song and familiar, perhaps unwillingly, they refrained from practicing their profession. Especially those who had undesirable familiars tried to keep their status secret. Such an individual might be suspected, but nothing could be proved unless in some emergency he summoned his tutuguuvi by singing. Sometimes a shaman preserved this secrecy all his life; but usually when some dearly loved relative fell ill he would betray his power by curing him or attempting to do so. After that he would be publicly known as a "doctor," would undertake the cure of others, and his familiar would become known. Tuuk^watsi, Stretched, Herbert Chapo's wife, was suspected of being a shaman because of her power to will disaster or illness by use of the mangasuyaganuh (may that one . . .) formula. She would see a man going along and think to herself, "May he fall down!" The man would promptly fall down, then get up and go on his way without knowing what had caused him to fall. She could also cause sickness or trouble to absent persons, to ones whom she did not see; but she could not or did not will people to die.

The bond between shaman and familiar was very intimate. The shaman often partook in some way or other of the character of the familiar and in rare instances was able to assume the form of his spirit-animal. We have already mentioned how the possessors of carnivorous familiars might become in a sense cannibals, eaters of the essence though not the material substance of human flesh. The case of the lame Southerner[8] who, in spite of his lameness, exhibited the agility of a mountain sheep has also been noted. The redoubtable ʔOomposi, who had the mountain sheep among his familiars, could create a mountain sheep out of a certain kind of bush (either sianupi or tavaapi, George Laird was not sure which). This semblance of a mountain sheep was so exact in every detail that the hungry hunters could kill and eat it; but afterwards all would be sick, because it was really the bush that they had eaten. There was also a certain man, a Tïïraniwi, Desert Chemehuevi, described as "some sort of Paiute," who would go along uprooting trees, large stumps, and yuccas when he was alone. If anyone happened to observe him, he would explain that the trees and stumps were rotten and that he was "just trying his strength." But they were not rotten. After he had pulled them up, one could see the big roots lying exposed. This man's name was not recalled, but he was identified as Henry Hall's wife's uncle. He was papawa-pu^waganti, that is, papaway tutugu^wanti, one having the bear as his familiar. He could exercise the strength of a bear in his human form, and he could also on occasion turn himself into a bear. But while almost all "bear doctors" were said to be able to cure anything, this man had small success as a healer.[9]

Sacred Caves

Sacred caves have been mentioned in connection with the acquisition of hereditary songs[10] and also of shamanistic songs and powers. They were places of great power and mystery. George Laird spoke of the cave itself as an entity, withholding or bestowing its gifts; but he also spoke of the spirits of the cave. These, he insisted, were not tutuguuviwi, spirit-animal familiars; they were not ʔinipiwi, the minor demons or "devils" such as animate whirlwinds; and certainly they were not nauguviwi, spirits of the dead. They constituted a fourth order of supernatural beings, whose name he did not know or could not recall. In the course of their wide-flung wanderings, the Chemehuevis may have encountered several such magically inhabited caves, but George Laird knew of only two.

Kwin^yaváh was associated with the Salt Song only. Located in Arizona, near the confluence of the Santa Maria and Sandy washes, it was in Apache territory, and the name has an Apache ring to it. The suppliant—someone, I understand, who already owned the song by right of inheritance although he might not be able to sing it, at least not to his own satisfaction—would enter the cave and make it a present of a piece of buckskin, a pair of moccasins, some tobacco, or anything he wished to give. This could be a small token gift, not necessarily something of much intrinsic value, more of a courtesy present than a sacrifice. Having presented his offering, the seeker would talk to the cave and make his request, then he would remain there all night. Sometime during the night he would hear the Salt Song being sung and would find himself singing along with the voice or voices in the cave. The version which he learned in this way would not vary at all from that sung by his relatives. One undertaking such an expedition to the cave might say, Kwin^yavaavantu^wavan*i*, I am going to Kwin^yaváh, literally, I shall towards Kwin^yaváh.

There was another cave, far up in the mountains of Nevada, which was truly great in every sense of the word: great in size, running far back into the mountain, and great in potency.[11] George Laird did not remember the name of this cave, but he had heard that from it one might get any song or gain control over any tutuguuv*i* that one desired. It was in this cave that the shaman ʔOompos*i* acquired his various songs, powers, and familiars. This cave was also notable in that it had a will of its own and would reject those whom it did not like. The unwanted intruder would—as he thought—keep on walking deeper into the cave, but without his knowledge he would be turned around and would find himself coming out the way that he had gone in. A Las Vegas white man, Hi Stewart,[12] grew up with the Indians (probably Northern Chemehuevis and/or Paiutes) and spoke their language well. He declared his intention of going in to see the cave. His Indian friends doubted that he could. He tried repeatedly but kept coming right out again. In Kwin^yaváh one hears noises; in this great cave one hears no sounds (presumably the songs are learned in dreams), but sees footprints, small like the prints of three- or four-year-old children. Formerly they were all of moccasined feet, but a man who visited the cave in more recent times, after the Chemehuevis had completely adopted the white man's way of dressing, reported that now all the spirits wore little shoes!

The Jimson Weed

The root of the jimson weed, when chewed or made into a decoction and drunk, was capable of producing dreams and visions, but so far as George Laird knew, was never used by would-be shamans for the purpose of acquiring a familiar. There was a ceremonial and correct way to secure the root. One would approach the plant (momomp*i*), address it respectfully as "old woman," apologize for disturbing it, and explain fully just what revelation was desired. A frequent request would be for a dream to reveal the name of an enemy who was bringing about misfortune by supernatural means, but most often and most successfully the root was used to locate lost or mislaid objects.[13] (Perhaps the mind-expanding effect of the drug unlocked the subconscious.) After having talked to the plant, the suppliant would gently uncover the root and take only the "east root," the prong pointing eastward. A single root is tɨnavɨ, but a root with branches is tɨrɨnavɨ; the "east root" would be described as tasɨantɨ marukʷatu tɨrɨnavɨ, literally, dawn there-visible-under-towards root branch.

Demons

Demons, ʔɨnɨpiwɨ (singular ʔɨnɨpi), were disliked but not feared to an extent that would protect them from disrespectful treatment. An ʔɨnɨpi is seen principally as animating a whirlwind, turunniʔʸarɨ. When a whirlwind passed close by where there were people, they would exclaim, "ʔɨnɨpiʔikʷa, it is a devil!" and encourage the children to run out and beat it with sticks. Then the adults would comment, "Turunniʔʸarɨ kwikwipagah, they (three or more) are clubbing the whirlwind." Sometimes by their violent activities the children would succeed in setting up so many cross-currents that the whirlwind subsided. Then the remark would be, "Turunniʔʸarɨ mayɨwaʔaingkɨtsɨ, they killed the whirlwind" (not "they killed the demon"). Not infrequently after its "death" the whirlwind would re-form a short distance away as several small eddies coalesced into one; whereupon the spectators would say, "Turunniʔʸar suʷatavoʷaatsɨ, the whirlwind came to life" (suʷapɨ, breath; tavoʷaatsɨ, got well, recovered health).

The smoketree is called ʔɨnɨpimahavɨ, demon bush.

Spirits of the Dead

The spirits of the dead are nauguviwɨ (singular nauguvɨ or nauxu). Leaving the body at the time of death, the spirit travels far to the north to Naugurɨvipɨ, Spirit Land, a pleasant place where the crops are always abundant. The departed souls do not take with them the hereditary songs by which their relationships and hunting ranges were defined in life; in their new abode, the clans are distinguished by the color of the corn which they possess.

Apparitions of the dead were considered to be omens of approaching death, because it was known that the spirit of a dead person would sometimes return to conduct the soul of a close relative. A young woman who was at the point of death saw her dead father patiently waiting for her outside the door of the house. She told the people gathered around that he had brought a white horse for her to ride. Although the shaman continued his treatment, she was soon dead.

It is said that once very long ago a young man whose wife had died after only a few months of marriage chewed the root of the jimson weed while keeping vigil at her grave. On the fourth night after the burial, he saw her arise, shake the dust from her long, loose hair, and start towards the north. He called to her, but she paid him no heed. He then followed, keeping her in sight but never overtaking her, never exchanging a word with her. They travelled thus for many days. Arriving at Naugurivipɨ, the young man was courteously received by the Chief of that land, although it was made plain to him that he had come where the living had no right to be. He asked to be allowed to take his wife home with him, and the Chief granted his request on one condition: that he should not sleep at all until he reached his own house. The young couple started on the long journey back to the land of the living, but this time the man led the way, and his wife followed. At night they rested; the woman slept, but the man did not close his eyes. At length they came in sight of their own house. Because the night was very hot, they lay down outside, the wife's head pillowed on her husband's arm. The weary young man slept long and deeply. When he awoke, he found himself embracing a log. Perhaps if he had taken his wife inside the house, he might have kept her.

The Rites of Death

The rites of death were and are sacred and of immense importance. The funeral was of necessity held without much preparation, but was followed, perhaps as long as six months or a year later, by the Yagapɨ, the Cry or Mourning Ceremony. On both these occasions the man's own song was sung and also the Talking Song, if possible; but since the Talking Song could never be sung except by a member of the High Chief's family and, when used ritually, no hereditary song could be sung except by a legitimate owner, there must have been times when it was impossible to fulfill these requirements at a funeral—and this, no doubt, was the reason, or one of the reasons, for holding a later Cry, at which time the proper singers[14] would be available as well as numerous other mourners. (For it must be remembered that the Chemehuevis were great travellers. Families sometimes travelled alone or in small groups, and deaths must often have occurred during these periods of isolation.) At the time of the funeral, women relatives of the deceased cut their hair (the closer the relationship, the shorter the bob), some property was burned, and there was ritual singing. Not much more could be done, considering the short time which must elapse between death and burial.[15]

For the Yagapɨ, extensive and elaborate preparations were made. A date was selected, three months, six months, or even a year after the funeral. If there had been several deaths fairly close together, the bereaved families might choose to cooperate in providing for a single Mourning Ceremony. September was often the month chosen because food would be plentiful at that time. The relatives would have planted much more than usual to provide for the occasion. Eagle feathers braided into bands and also the whole skins of eagles cured with the feathers on them were used ceremonially at the Cry, and time was needed to acquire these. First an eagle's nest must be located, then the young had to be captured and raised to maturity.[16] The Chemehuevis did not catch and keep eagles when no Mourning Ceremony was in prospect, but sometimes they bought them from other tribes, usually the Walapais, who did make a practice of keeping them. No special ritual was connected with the killing of the eagles. The eagle's skin with feathers was called mɨng tcaku$^{?w}$in^{y}akatɨ, which sounds as if it meant "skinned eagle," but applies to the prepared skin, not to the body of the bird. During the Cry, it was worn by one of the mourners giving the ceremony (yagatɨgaarɨ, mourner; plural yagatɨgaakarɨmɨ) or by one leading the singing,[17] or it might simply be exhibited on the wall of the takaganɨ, the "flat house" or shed built especially for the occasion.

When the date of the Cry had been set, the knotted string was sent out, as described in the preceding chapter. In ancient times, as the people journeyed along toward the site of the Cry, the men would keep a sharp lookout for suitable building material. One might find a sohorah, a post with a natural U-shaped notch at the top. Others would gather bundles of brush suitable for thatching.

Then when all were assembled, they would work together, and the takagan*i* (also known as havagan*i*, shade house) would be erected in no time. First they would put up the four notched posts, then the flat roof; then they would add another "roof" sloping downwards on the west side, thatched part or even all of the way to the ground, to shield against the afternoon sun. They would make a very large flat house[18] to contain all the goods that were to be burnt or given away. In later times, the mourners who were giving the Cry prepared the takagan*i* in advance.

At the Cry the ritual songs were sung, including always and pre-eminently the Talking Song, sung by the High Chief himself or a member of his family.[19] Valuable goods, which had been purchased by those giving the ceremony, were given away, and horses, some of which had also been bought especially for this purpose, were slaughtered or given away. All of the possessions of the deceased which had not been burnt at the time of the funeral were now burnt, along with other articles belonging to his close friends. Items which the deceased had not seen might be given away; but everything which he had ever seen, with the possible exception of a horse, was destroyed. The Circle Dance was danced, with the fire at the center of the circle. Last of all to go into the fire were the eagle skins and the braided eagle feathers. These were very sacred and were never used in conjunction with Gatherings.

The Cry was an unrestrained expression of communal and personal grief and a tremendous catharsis. Afterwards the living went about their business (as the dead presumably was going about his). The name of the deceased was, under ordinary circumstances, mentioned no more, and if reference to him was absolutely necessary, it was made in a circuitous way.

The Scalp Dance and the Ghost Dance

The Scalp Dance and the Ghost Dance were both known as N*i*kap*i*, Circle Dance. With the exception of the description given in the myth "How Wolf and Coyote Went Away" (see Note 2, this chapter), there is very little in this material about the Scalp Dance. There is every reason to suppose that the description in the myth is accurate and that the song is a version of an authentic Scalp Dance song—the whole picture being, of course, transferred to mythological time and furnished with mythological characters.

Nonetheless the Scalp Dance is not to be thought of as belonging to a remote past. Although it has not been danced within living memory, it was surely not so long ago that it (as the Cry still does) served as a great catharsis for the emotions. I was assured (in 1969) that an ancient Dancing Place (Nïkatïah) may still be seen, "with the pile of rocks in the center where they stuck the pole with the Mohave's scalp on it." Because of long-standing friction between the two tribes, "Mohave" was often equated with "enemy."

However, the Ghost Dance[20] was familiar to George Laird; he had himself participated in it and spoke of it at length.

First the pipe came down from the north. After it had progressed from one settlement to another, after all the Southern Chemehuevis had smoked it, they sent it on to another tribe. About a year later, in 1890, the first Ghost Dance songs arrived, and the People began to dance. Kuyuutï was the name of the man who brought the Ghost Dance from Chemehuevi Valley to Needles. He was the son of a woman called ʔOotca, who was half Mohave.

The Ghost Dance teaching in the form that reached the Chemehuevis, was, as George Laird recalled it, that the world was soon to be destroyed by fire and only those who had danced in the Ghost Dance would survive, dancing on top of the flames until the time of renewal should come. This suggests a strong Mormon influence upon those responsible for bringing the Ghost Dance south.

In primitive times, there had been no place for eschatology in Chemehuevi belief. Time had been circular. The seasons revolved in their accustomed way as the Immortal Ones had decreed, and only a few of them were counted and briefly remembered. When the first Mexican settlers (*mestizos*) came, blending almost imperceptibly with the native population, this order was only slightly disturbed; and perhaps it was even less disturbed by the advent of mountain men, trappers, and desert rats such as Ben Paddock and Thompson Porter Laird, who took Chemehuevi wives and lived in most respects as Indians. Now towards the close of the nineteenth century with the influx of white settlers and the assertion of Governmental authority, the curtailment of hunting ranges, the frightful smallpox epidemics, the inroads of alcoholism and syphilis, and the consequent inevitable erosion of the age-old "system of sentiments," time had become suddenly, frighteningly linear. The preaching of the Ghost Dance at once expressed and alleviated the sense of impending doom. Like the Scalp Dance, which would be danced no more, the Ghost Dance provided both emotional release and an opportunity for sociability, sorely lacking now that the last of the High Chiefs was dead and the great Gatherings a thing of the past. Many Chemehuevis who, like George Laird, retained the old, wholesome, light-hearted attitude towards things of the spirit, danced it "for fun," purely or principally for social reasons. But others accepted it with complete seriousness.

After the Ghost Dance had continued for about a year, a man announced that "someone" would speak from above, from the sky. All listened, and many heard this voice. There were among the dancers members of many tribes, including the Chemehuevis, the Havasupais, the Walapais; certain northern tribes (Tantɨitsiwɨ) were also represented, among them the Paranʔnɨgiwɨ and Sivitsiwɨ.[21] Of all this company, each man who heard the voice heard it speaking in his own tongue. Among the Chemehuevis who had this Pentecostal experience were ʔOtawɨnɨrɨ, Sand Standing; Tcawiih; Kaiwaɨkatɨ, Swift Mountain Runner; and Nagaramaupa, Left the Mountain Sheep Behind.

To some, perhaps to many, Ghost Dance songs became substitutes for hereditary songs, and in this way the Ghost Dance joined other influences contributing to cultural change. Thus ʔAtatuʔʷatsɨ, Young Crow, and his oldest son, ʔOpitcokotsɨ, Mesquite Bean Pounder, who were Deer and should have become Deer Singers, chose the songs of the Ghost Dance instead.

Ocean Woman

Ocean Woman, Hutsipamamauʔu, was, so far as I know, the only one of the Immortals, the mythological personages, to whom invocations were addressed. Chemehuevi myths, obviously symbolic and psychological, were not presented as inflexible dogma. Although the framework of a myth was fixed, the skillful narrator was free to fill in and to embroider the details, and the more outrageous he made the exploits of his heroes, especially Coyote, the better he pleased his hearers. Eventually Wolf and Coyote were represented as having fulfilled their roles as assistant creators of and pattern-setters (potential and actual, respectively) for mankind. They then departed from this earth which is now the habitation of humans, and all the host of Animals Who Were

People also departed. But there are other supernatural beings, such as the spirits inhabiting caves, the demons animating whirlwinds, and whatever it is that gives the jimson weed power, who were never animal or partly animal in form and therefore continue on, coexistent with human beings. Ocean Woman, although she is supreme among all mythological or supernatural beings, since she is the prime creator of all things and the personification of the mysterious Ocean,[22] also belongs in the category of those who can be helpful to mortals. The nearest approaches to petitionary prayers in Chemehuevi religion were the requests previously described addressed to caves and to the jimson weed and the invocations offered to Ocean Woman. On the occasion of a child's losing a baby tooth it was (and still is, among those adhering to the old ways) customary to take him by the hand and lead him away from the house. Then the discarded tooth was ceremoniously thrown away, while Ocean Woman (respectfully addressed as Hutsipam'aa'ipitsi, Old Ocean Woman) was asked to replace it with a "good, big one." There were doubtless many other occasions when it was appropriate to make requests of Ocean Woman. Considering these practices, one can scarcely doubt that the belief in an intervening deity was altogether alien to Chemehuevi thought. The help of a supernatural being was not to be despised, and properly phrased requests were in order; steps should also have been taken if possible to circumvent the curse of an enemy skilled in occult matters; but a Chemehuevi, a Person, neither groveled to nor pleaded with man or god.

It is thought-provoking to learn that the Chemehuevis, who surely had been desert dwellers for centuries, had the sea goddess as their Magna Mater. The virtual taboo on the eating of fish (anciently a genuine taboo and still so real that many Chemehuevis would prefer starvation) may not be unconnected with this fact. The obvious explanation is that Chemehuevis find fish distasteful, and the obvious way of accounting for this distaste would be that fish are not tïïravatci, a product of the desert. But neither are corn and melons native to the desert, yet they have long been included in the Chemehuevi diet. I would suggest that the primary (and long-forgotten) origin of the taboo might be that fish were once considered to be the property of Ocean Woman, and that an ancient thought of profanation might have developed into a deeply implanted aversion. It may possibly be relevant that among the rather small list of men's names included in this material three begin with the word for "fish": Fish Vagina, Fish Intestines, and Fish Foot.

The Bear Cult

Generally confined to circumpolar regions, the Bear Cult was present in vestigial form among the Chemehuevis. As evidence, we have first the relationship between Wolf and Coyote on the one hand and the Bear People on the other;[23] second, the presence of bear shamans in the days when shamanism flourished, together with the high esteem in which they were held; and third, the long-standing truce or treaty of peace existing between all Chemehuevis and all bears. If a Chemehuevi travelling in the mountains should happen to meet a bear, he had only to address him as "Niwaani, my friend" (compare niwaantsini, my cousin), and the bear would immediately abandon all hostile intent.

The Runners

The Runners[24] were a group of young men who may have been the last remnant of an ancient cult or guild. In aboriginal times, a pool of highly trained swift runners would have been useful to High Chiefs needing to exchange messages of peace or war, or perhaps to bear the knotted string on occasions of great importance. In the last two decades of the nineteenth century they ran simply for the joy of running in each other's company, taking the old trails well back from the River, well out of enemy territory, and making use of short cuts which slower travellers would have done well to avoid because of the distance between watering places. Since none of these youths (or at least none of those whom George Laird sometimes accompanied[25]) "carried the poro" or owned a familiar or had any shamanistic pretensions, an account of them could scarcely be included in a chapter dealing with the supernatural, had it not been for the extraordinary ability of one of them—an ability which must at least be classed as supranormal.

These young men were all, more or less imprecisely, cousins. They addressed one another as "cousin," or by the words which mean either "brother" or "cousin," and all of them were lean,

strong, beautiful, and remarkably swift. Only one was a true
Runner, a Runner indeed. He had his "secret way of travelling,
which was the old way." His name was Kaawɨ̓a, Rat Penis. He was
a young man of quiet and gentle demeanor, never boisterous or
high-spirited as others of the group occasionally were, and among
them he had only one intimate, his first cousin (or brother[26]),
Pagɨɨwɨxɨ, Fish Vagina. They called each other by the reciprocal
nickname of Kamuutɨ (from Spanish *camote*, sweet potato). But
that is as near as Kaawɨ̓a came to a joke. He would just sit quietly
and listen to the others, smiling gently at rare intervals. When he
travelled in company with his companions, he ran as they did, but
when he went alone, he used his secret method. This was possibly
a way of teleportation, but of it only this was known for certain:
that it enabled him to arrive at his destination with no lapse of
time. This, George Laird insisted, was not done by the use of
magic—"It was something altogether different, it was the old way."

Early one morning, George Laird said, they were all in the
vicinity of Muuviᵞa, Cottonwood Island, in Nevada. The sun had
not yet risen. Kaawɨ̓a stood up and announced, "I am going to
Yuma"—that is, to the Chemehuevi settlement at the mouth of the
Gila, near Fort Yuma. "We'll all go," his companions said. But
when he answered, "No," quietly and firmly, they did not argue
the point, for they knew what he had in his mind to do. They
watched him run away from the camp in a long, easy lope and
disappear over a sand dune, just as the rays of the rising sun struck
across it. The young men were silent for awhile. Then one
suggested, "Let's track him." They followed his tracks up to and
over the crest of the dune to the point where they had lost sight of
him. The tracks continued on, but now they were different. They
looked as if he had been "just staggering along," taking giant steps,
his feet touching the ground at long, irregular intervals, leaving
prints that became further and further apart and lighter and lighter
on the sand. Silently, by mutual consent, the other Runners
continued on down-river. When at length they reached the village
at the mouth of the Gila, they inquired, "Did Kaawɨ̓a come
here?" "Yes," the people answered, "he arrived on such and such
a day (the day that he had left them) just as the sun was rising."

No one ever saw Kaawɨ̓a travel in his special way. If he
happened to sight a party ahead of him, he would join them,

running in the usual way, and go along with them at whatever rate they were travelling. No, George Laird said, he had no tutuguuv*i*, no supernatural helper; what he had was the ancient knowledge. He was not interested in women and was close to no human being, with the exception of Pag*ɨ*w*ɨ*x*i*.[27] Kaaw*ɨ*ʔ*a* died of smallpox while still young, possibly under twenty, never having known woman nor communicated his secret; contaminated at last by the white man's disease but never by his culture.

The main branches of the Chemehuevis never felt the iron hand of Spanish conquest and therefore never became *esclavos de la Mision*[28] (slaves of the Mission), although some related California bands had that unhappy experience. Their introduction to Christianity was gradual and non-violent. It is quite probable that most of the women who married Mexican settlers, who learned to speak Spanish more fluently than their own tongue, and whose children were brought up as Catholics, did not feel the weight of the new religion too heavily.[29] In George Laird's youth, earnest Protestant missionaries, learning that C*ɨ*nawav*i*, Mythic Coyote, was the "Way Shower" for mankind, tried to equate him with Christ Jesus rather than Old Adam! This tickled the Chemehuevi sense of humor and helped to keep Christianity in perspective.

And always, though perhaps now with decreasing frequency, archetypal symbols have continued to break through into con-sciousness. People still at times dream dreams touched with mystery and power, although such dreams may be unwelcome, and may even be told peremptorily to "go away."

Back in the days of the Ghost Dance, George Laird's half-brother, John Smith, wished to become a Ghost Dance singer. He dreamed repeatedly and spent a great deal of time roaming about in solitary places, meditating upon his dreams. At first all went well; his dreams were in line with his ambition. Presently they changed, and he began to receive instructions on how to heal the sick; and finally he perceived that the spirit instructing him was the poro itself! Since John Smith was not the type of man who would wish to adapt himself to the heavy responsibilities of a medicine man, he broke up the whole mystical process by telling his dreams, and thus ended up neither shaman nor Ghost Dance singer.

George Laird found this experience of his half-brother somewhat amusing. On the surface he himself seemed quite removed from any tendency toward the supernatural. Two things, however, lead me to believe that he was at least touched by shamanistic power.

One was his natural ability to heal. Often in the early years of our marriage he would come home from work to find me exhausted by my efforts to cope with a sick and fretful infant. He would then wrap the baby in a receiving blanket, bringing forward one side and then the other in such a way that the child's arms were held firmly in a straightened position (he called this process "papoosing"), then he would take the snugly bound bundle up and walk back and forth, sometimes singing under his breath any snatch of song that came to mind. Presently the child would fall asleep, to awaken, more often than not, well and happy. When in his later years he became interested in Christian Science, he said, "This is what I have always practiced without knowing it," indicating that without benefit of theory or dogma he had known instinctively how to achieve that inner quietness and concentration of thought which is conducive to healing.

The second evidence of inherited "power" was a dream recurring at intervals through most of his life. This I believe to have been the sort of dream that, accepted and meditated upon, would have led to the acquisition of a familiar, but it inspired George with such intense terror that he never opened himself to it. In the face of physical danger he was a man of courage and resourcefulness, but this dream left him sweating and shaken. After considerable persuasion, he attempted to tell me about it. There was, he said, a Place, not anywhere that he recognized and not describable except that it was very frightening and there were big rocks all around. The really horrible thing was that in this Place he saw Something "with a face like a sheep." (It will be recalled that Yaariʔivʸa, who was, like George, a Deer, was also a mountain sheep shaman.)

At the present time small fundamentalist churches have proliferated on the Colorado River Reservation. Their impact has not been favorable, even granting that religion is a form of psychotherapy and has offered an alternative to alcoholism and suicide to a people who were for a long period without hope. The end result of this brand of religiosity has been further cultural depletion and loss of racial pride. A narrow, intolerant teaching has made many of the People ashamed of their pagan or "heathen" heritage. It is encouraging that there are those who remember in part the old ways and the old teachings, who still make mention of Ocean Woman, who view the earth with awe, and worship its wonder in their hearts.

Now in this period of tribal reorganization, the young people's interest and pride in their Indian heritage is awakening; they are becoming eager to listen and to learn, and this stimulates their elders to remember and to speak. In the general renaissance in everything from basketry to mythology, much that is of value will still be remembered and preserved. Perhaps in time there will be those who will open their hearts to the old dreams of power and magic!

CHAPTER III

KINSHIP AND PERSONAL RELATIONSHIPS

O N the morning that I first met George Laird, he had work in hand at the blacksmith shop which had to be finished, but he took time out to introduce me to a woman who, he said, was competent to help me. I approached her armed with immense naïveté and an elaborate questionnaire on kinship terms. It seems incredible that after three years' fieldwork with the Indians of California I should have been as ignorant and insensitive as I actually was. I met with evasion, embarrassed giggles, and at best reluctant answers. Years later I asked George, "What did Annie say about me?" He laughed. "She said that you tried to make her commit obscenities by mentioning her dead relatives."

After the immense and thorough communal catharsis of the Cry, the dead are spoken of no more, unless dire insult is intended to the living.[1] If reference to a known person's dead relative is absolutely necessary, polite and elaborate circumlocutions are employed—and even these must not be voiced in the presence of the survivor. The sense of relationship is very strong. If the word for "father" is requested, it is difficult to conceive of an answer except in the context of "your father" or "my father." Perhaps if I had made clear to my informant that my father was still living and had asked, "How would I speak of him in Chemehuevi?" my question would have been less offensive, but to ask bluntly, "How do you say father?" constituted a gross breach of etiquette.

Fortunately, George Laird had a mind that was extraordinarily capable of abstract thought. He was able to divorce the concept of a systematized table of relationship terms from any emotional context. Nowadays, the need for tracing bloodlines and proving tribal membership is hastening the abandonment of the old taboo upon the mention of dead relatives. Judging from the general simplification that has taken place in the language during the last fifty years, however, it is quite unlikely that even a willing informant could furnish as many kinship terms as George Laird remembered.

The Chemehuevi kinship system seems to contain internal evidence of a primitive symmetry which has been broken down somewhat through the substitution of new terms, some of them borrowed from other languages. Existing side by side with terms which specifically describe age, sex, and exact relationship are others which are highly generalized. For example, it will be seen that there are five separate terms for sibling, in addition to another set of terms derived from personal pronouns, and still another term which means simply "sibling" without distinction of age or sex.

Single relationship terms are normally used with possessive pronouns: nɨɨni muwa, muwani, or more emphatically nɨɨni muwani, my father. But all these simple terms may add -akaavi, which means someone's. For example, one may say muwaakaavi, someone's father, or ʔantamuwakaavi,[2] some man's brother-in-law, just as one would say kaniʸakaavi, someone's house. A still less definite indication of relationship results from the use of the postfix -vi (a common termination of both animate and inanimate nouns), which added to a relationship term has the force of an indefinite article. The use of -vi is restricted within the kinship system to certain words discussed in detail below: muwa and ʔantamuwa; piya; yɨɨpiya, nɨmpiya, hutsimpiya, and musimpiya; hiwa; ʔɨsaaviwa; ʔontokʷavɨ (which drops -vɨ before -vi but retains it before -akaavi: ʔontokʷavi, a male cousin, but ʔontokʷavɨakaavi, someone's male cousin); kuma, hohoguma, and naingkuma; piwa; hohoviwa, and naimpiwa.

Collective terms are formed by prefixing na- or nana- and adding the plural -wɨ to simple terms, and indicate a reciprocal relationship between two or more individuals. These are used for reference only, never in the vocative or in any form of direct address. They may not be employed with possessive pronouns.

The myths have shown us that siblings, especially siblings of the same sex, tend to be regarded as replicas of each other, mere divisions of a single entity. Perhaps this accounts for the use of the same terms for "siblings" and "cousins." The implied reasoning might run something like this: my uncle is not my father, but he is the same as my father; therefore, my uncle's son is to me as my father's son. This would account for the feeling that sexual relationships between cousins were just as incestuous as between brother and sister. George Laird told of an incident of illicit relationship between a woman and her second cousin (probably a first cousin once removed). The man moved into the house with his cousin and her husband. Shortly thereafter, the wife began to treat her husband coldly, and finally she and her cousin forced him to sleep outside. Even after this treatment, he was shocked and distressed when the guilty pair eloped. He said he had not connected his wife's unkindness with any involvement with the other man, for he had considered them "the same as brother and sister." George Laird said that this took place "not very long ago." In aboriginal times, he said, the force of public opinion would have prevented the elopement.

Parent-Child Category

The Parent-Child Category contains the following single terms:

Muwa, father; muwani, my father, is said by a child of either sex.

Piya, mother; piyani, my mother.

Hiwa, (1) parent; (2) relative. This vague term is useful when it becomes necessary to refer to someone's deceased relative. Hiwani, my relative, may be used in direct address when the relationship is remote or obscure; when the meaning is "parent," hiwa is used in the singular for reference only and never in direct address. However, when speaking to both parents together it would be natural to say hiwawɨni, my parents. If one uses the expression hiwani, in conversation, the listener may ask, "Haganiʔyami, how (related) to you?" The speaker then replies with a more specific relationship term.

Tuwa, man's son.

Patcɨ, man's daughter.

Pipiso?ʷa, woman's child of either sex. A man says tuwanɨ, my son, or patcɨnɨ, my daughter, but a woman does not use these terms. She says simply pipiso?ʷanɨ, my child, my offspring, indicating sex if necessary by using the word for "boy" or "girl," or, if the child has reached maturity, by prefixing taw?wa-, man, or mamau?u-, woman. A woman who has had a child is spoken of as pipiso?ʷagantɨ, child having. The word for mother is clearly related to pipiso?ʷa, woman's child; piso?otsɨ, infant (less than four months old); and pipiso?otsɨ, child of approximately four months to six years. After six years, the male child is ?aipatsɨ, boy, until he becomes ?aivʸatsɨ, adolescent boy or youth. An adolescent girl or young woman is naintsɨ.

In the Parent-Child Category we find the following collectives:

Naawawɨ, father and child of either sex; nanaawawɨ, father and two or more children. Muwa is not the basis for any collective form.

Naviyawɨ (na-, reciprocal or reflexive prepound, plus piya-, plus plural termination -wɨ), mother and child; nanaviyawɨ, mother and two or more children. The personal name of the husband may be prefixed to these terms—as, for example, in the myth "How Wildcat Brothers Recovered Their Hunting Song," Tavahukʷana-naviyawɨ indicates Sun Spider (Tavahukʷampɨ) and his wife and children, Sun Spider and family.

Grandparent-Grandchild Category

The single terms in the Grandparent-Grandchild Category are:

Kɨnu, father's father; father's father's brother; father's mother's brother.

Hutsɨ, father's mother; father's mother's sister; father's father's sister.

Toxo, mother's father; mother's father's brother; mother's mother's brother.

Kaxu, mother's mother; mother's mother's sister; mother's father's sister. Kɨnunɨ, hutsinʸɨ, togonɨ, and kagunɨ are said by a person of either sex.

All junior reciprocals in this class are formed by the addition of the diminutive -ts*i*:

> K*i*nuts*i*, man's son's child; man's brother's son's child; man's sister's son's child. A man addresses his son's child of either sex, his brother's son's child, or his sister's son's child as k*i*nutsin*ʸi*, and the junior relative (male or female) replies with k*i*nun*i*. In every case, the sex of the older relative is clear, that of the younger is ambiguous.
>
> Hutsits*i*, woman's son's child; woman's sister's son's child; woman's brother's son's child.
>
> Togots*i*, man's daughter's child; man's brother's daughter's child; man's sister's daughter's child.
>
> Kaguts*i*, woman's daughter's child; woman's sister's daughter's child; woman's brother's daughter's child.

The Grandparent-Grandchild Category has remarkably few collectives. Those that do occur derive from the grandmother (or great-aunt) terms only and lack forms indicating three or more persons (senior and two or more junior relatives):

> Nahutsiw*i*, paternal grandmother and grandchild; great-aunt on the father's side and great-nephew or great-niece.
>
> Nagaguw*i*, maternal grandmother and grandchild; great-aunt on the mother's side and great-nephew or great-niece.

To include two or more grandchildren (or great-nephews and -nieces), one would have to say: mamauʔ (or personal name) hutsitsiw*i*waʔ*a* (waʔ*a* for -waʔi-, and), woman and son's children, etc.; or mamauʔ kagutsiw*i*waʔ*a*, woman and daughter's children, etc. And to indicate the collective of grandfather or great-uncle and junior relatives it would be necessary to say: tawʔwats (or personal name) k*i*nutsiwaʔ*a*, man and son's child, etc.; tawʔwats k*i*nutsiw*i*waʔ*a*, man and son's children, etc.; tawʔwats togotsi-w*i*waʔ*a*, man and daughter's children, etc.

In discussing this category, George Laird stated emphatically that all words including brother or sister of the senior relative also included that relative's male or female cousin. Thus k*i*nun*i* would actually mean my father's father, my father's father's brother, and my father's father's male cousin; but if asked more specifically as to the relationship one could say haʔit*i*k*i*nun*i*, my real k*i*n*u*, which would narrow the field to father's father or father's father's brother. If literally and consistently applied, this practice would spread the net of consanguinity very far indeed. Since a man could not marry into his immediate song group, and since the practice of exogamy would have made him cousin in one degree or another with most of the members of other song groups, he would have been left with virtually no one to choose as a wife. However, I doubt that the prohibition was actually carried further than to first cousins and first cousins once removed. The practice of neither mentioning the name nor the relationship term referring to a dead relative would have mitigated against the tracing of direct or collateral lines of descent past a certain point.

To refer to a direct or collateral ancestor or ancestress more remote than a grandparent the words for "younger brother" or "younger sister" are used. Thus tcak^{a}i$^{\gamma}$in^{y}i, my direct or collateral ancestor more remote than grandfather or great-uncle, literally, my younger brother. To this the proper response would be pavin^{y}i, my great-grandson, my great-great-nephew. And on the female side we would have mani$^{\gamma}$in^{y}i, my direct or collateral ancestress more remote than grandmother, literally, my younger sister; to which the proper reply is patcin^{y}i, my older sister, said by a very old woman when addressing her great-granddaughter or great-great-niece. This form of address connotes care and affection for the aged and implies the reversal of roles which has now taken place, the older relative having become helpless and perhaps lacking in judgment, while the younger relative must be strong and protective. If there were a special kinship term for such an aged person as a great-grandparent, it would inevitably suggest the imminence of death and be a reminder of those already dead. Collectives in the sibling class, as noted below, apply only to siblings and cousins, not to a relationship where there is a gap of two or more generations.

Sibling Category

The single terms in the Sibling Category are:
Pavi, older brother; older male cousin.
Patci, older sister; older female cousin.
Tcak^{a}i$^{\gamma}$i, younger brother; younger male cousin.
Nami$^{\gamma}$i, younger sister; younger female cousin.
Yïpiya, man's sister. Only a male may say yïpiyani, my

sister (regardless of age). The preceding pairs of terms distinguish between "older" and "younger" but may be used by members of either sex. Since yɨɨpiya ends in -piya, it may take the endings -vɨ and -akaavɨ, as described above.

Kwituyawɨ, half-sibling with a common father. This word apparently derives from kwitumpɨ, anus, and yawig^yah, carries in hands or arms. Half-siblings with a common mother are considered full siblings, and in ordinary conversation half-siblings with a common father are frequently addressed by the appropriate terms for full brother or sister.

Collectives in this category are as follows:

Naaviwɨ (an irregular form in which the first v is elided) or navaviwɨ, two brothers, two male cousins; nanavaviwɨ, three or more brothers, three or more male cousins.

Navatsiwɨ,[3] two sisters, two female cousins; nanavatsiwɨ, three or more sisters, three or more female cousins.

Nayɨɨpiyawɨ, brother and sister; nanayɨɨpiyawɨ, a group of two or more pairs, each consisting of a brother and a sister. This form beginning in nana- is not in common use and would never be understood as referring to one brother and several sisters or to several brothers and sisters of the same family. A man having more than one sister might be described as yɨɨpiyawɨgantɨ, sisters having.

Nagw^aitunayawiwɨ, two half-siblings with a common father. There is no derivative beginning with nana-, but the simple plural may be used, kwituyawiwɨ, two or more half-siblings with a common father.

There are additional sibling terms derived from nama, two adjoining or two close together (as in nam kani^yagantɨ, two adjoining houses, two houses close together). Like the collectives, these derivatives may not be used with possessive pronouns. These terms are as follows:

Namangkutcatsɨ, a twin; namangkutcatsiwɨ, twins, one pair of twins. One never says "my twin," but addresses the twin by the proper term for older or younger brother or sister, even though the difference in age may be a matter of moments.

Namantɨmɨ, two siblings, without regard for age or sex; nanamantɨmɨ or nanamantɨmɨwɨ, three or more siblings.

There is also a set of sibling terms derived from personal pronouns and meaning primarily "a part of one"—a concept curiously reminiscent of the English expression, "one's own flesh and blood." When used to indicate an actual part of the body (such as one's arm or leg), these substantives are inanimate and take no plural endings; but applied to siblings they take a dual form in -mɨ and a triplural in -mɨwɨ. They are used for reference only, never in direct address or in conjunction with possessive pronouns, either free or postfixed. These terms and their derivations are as follows:

Nɨwantɨ (nɨʔɨ, I), my sibling; nɨmiwantɨ (nɨmɨ, we two or more, exclusive of the person or persons addressed), a sibling of us two or more; tamiwantɨ (tamɨ, you and I, we two including the person addressed), a sibling of you and me; tawawantɨ (tawa, I and you two or more, we three or more including the person or persons addressed), a sibling of us three or more. The plurals would be nɨwantɨmɨ, my two siblings; nɨwantɨmɨwɨ, my three or more siblings, etc.

ʔɨmiwantɨ (ʔɨmɨ, you, singular), your sibling; mɨmiwantɨ, (mɨmɨ, you two or more), sibling of you two or more.

ʔIngʸawantɨ (ʔingʸa, this animate), sibling of this one; ʔimɨwantɨ (ʔimɨ, these animate), a sibling of these two or more persons.

Mangawantɨ (manga, that one animate visible), sibling of that visible person; mamɨwantɨ (mamɨ, those animate visible), a sibling of those visible persons.

ʔUngʷawantɨ (ʔungʷa, that one animate invisible), sibling of that invisible person; ʔumɨwantɨ (ʔumɨ, those animate invisible), a sibling of those invisible persons.

Uncle/Aunt-Nephew/Niece Category

The Uncle/Aunt-Nephew/Niece Category is rather complex and asymmetrical. It appears that the archaic pattern was more symmetrical and that changes have crept in through substitution of words for the ancient, more regular forms. Apparently Chemehuevis have always delighted in all sorts of play with words. This is the category as George Laird knew it:

Kuu$^?u$, father's older brother or father's older male cousin; kuu$^?$un$i$, my father's older brother, etc., is used by either male or female.

Hai, father's younger brother or father's younger male cousin; step-father. This seems to be a loanword. Although George Laird usually pronounced it (as he was careful to pronounce all Chemehuevi words when standing alone) with final aspiration (haih), the i is not long and ai is treated as an ordinary diphthong in compounds: hain$^y i$, haits$i$, etc. If it was a word of Chemehuevi origin it would be pronounced hah except in compounds.

Pah$a$ (pah in ordinary conversation but páha- when followed by another syllable), father's sister or father's female cousin. This word is a homonym for mortar; pa-han$i$ means (1) my mortar, (2) my father's sister, etc. Perhaps this usage arose through the function of the father's sister or female cousin as an industrious grinder! Since the junior reciprocal is musits$i$, it would appear that the original term was mus$i$; but no such word occurs as a kinship term.

Like pah$a$, all the following senior terms in this category have completely irregular junior reciprocals.

Kok^{wa}i, mother's older brother or mother's older male cousin.

Sin$a$, mother's younger brother or mother's younger male cousin.

Mawɨ$^?$ɨ, mother's older sister or mother's older female cousin.

Nɨmpiy$a$, mother's younger sister or mother's younger female cousin. Since this word contains the element piy$a$, mother, it may derive in some way from the ancient practice of sisters or first cousins sharing a common husband. By analogy with hai, one might expect nɨmpiy$a$ to also mean step-mother—but there is no word for step-mother.

$^?$ɨsaaviw$a$, father's brother or mother's brother. This general term is the equivalent of English "uncle," except that it does not include aunt's husband, who would not be considered a relative.

Kuu⁷uts*i*, man's younger brother's or man's younger male cousin's child; regularly formed from kuu⁷*u*, for which it is the reciprocal.

Haits*i*, man's older brother's or man's older male cousin's child; also man's step-child.

Musits*i*, woman's brother's or woman's male cousin's child. As noted above, this is the reciprocal of pah*a*; the older woman says musitsin*ʸi*, my brother's child, my male cousin's child, and the junior relative of either sex responds with pahan*i*.

⁷Aiv*ʸ*ay*a*, man's sister's or man's female cousin's son. This is the first term listed in this category to distinguish sex of the junior relative. It obviously derives from ⁷aiv*ʸ*ats*i*, adolescent boy or youth, and bears no linguistic relationship to kok*ʷᵃi*, for which it is the reciprocal. In the myths, Wolf, Mountain Lion, and Mythic Coyote addressed the members of their respective bands of warriors or hunters as ⁷aiv*ʸ*ayawin*i*, my nephews. Used in this way, the term does not denote actual relationship but is loosely equivalent to the English expression, "my lads."[4]

Naintsi*ʸa*, man's sister's or man's female cousin's daughter. The word derives from naints*i*, adolescent girl or young woman and is the reciprocal of sɨn*a*.

Tuu⁷*ʷ*ats*i* (compare tuw*a*, man's son; ⁷atatu⁷*ʷ*ats*i*, young crow, from ⁷atapɨts*i*, crow; kamuwaants*i*, young jackrabbit, from kamɨ, jackrabbit; and tavo*ʷ*aats*i*, young cottontail, from tavuts*i*, cottontail rabbit), woman's sister's or woman's female cousin's child of either sex. This is the junior reciprocal of both mawɨ⁷ɨ and nɨmpiy*a*.

Kuu⁷uts*i*, haits*i*, and musits*i* are reciprocals for ⁷ɨsaaviw*a*.

Since there is no generalized term meaning man's nephew or niece, collectives in this category are:

Nahaiwɨ or nahaitsiwɨ, man and older brother's child, man and older male cousin's child, step-father and step-child; nanahaiwɨ or nanahaitsiwɨ, man and two or more children of older brother, man and two or more children of older male cousin, step-father and two or more step-children. These collective forms are notable in that they may derive either from the term for senior or junior relative, rather than from one or the other.

Navaawɨ (from pah*a*, which becomes a single strongly stressed syllable, -vaa-), woman and brother's child or woman and male cousin's child; nanavahawɨ, woman and two or more children of brother or of male cousin. Na²aiv^yayawɨ, man and sister's son or man and female cousin's son; nana²aiv^yayawɨ, man and two or more sons of sister or of female cousin. Only collectives formed from the term for junior relative are employed here.

Nanɨmpiyawɨ, woman and older sister's child or woman and older female cousin's child; nananɨmpiyawɨ, woman and two or more children of older sister or of older female cousin.

Na²ɨsaaviwɨ, uncle and nephew or uncle and niece; na²ɨsaaviwawɨ or nana²ɨsaaviwawɨ, uncle and two or more nephews, nieces, or nephew(s) and niece(s). Only nana²ɨsaaviwawɨ derives regularly from ²ɨsaaviw*a*.

Cousin Category

In considering the Cousin Category, it is important to remember that one's cousin is "the same as" one's sibling, and that one's sibling—especially of the same sex—is almost "the same as" one's self. The terms for cousin, which are identical with the terms for sibling, are not thought of as words with dual meanings; the relationships which they indicate are essentially one, although if necessary, more meticulous definitions may be given. These sibling/cousin terms, together with the more generalized cousin terms, serve to define the extended family and to foster the ties within that group. In 1969 an elderly woman, Mary Hill, who is the daughter of George Laird's half-brother John Smith (variously known as Bishop Smith, Chemehuevi-ized as Piisop*i*, Junito, or Johnito), referred to Georgia Laird Culp as nami²in^y*i*, my younger sister, my little sister.

The cousin/sibling terms are, as previously noted:

Pav*i*, older brother or older male cousin, reciprocal tcak^ai²*i*, younger brother; and between females, patc*i*, older sister or older female cousin, reciprocal nami²*i*.

The collectives also apply to both cousins and siblings: naaviw*i* or navaviw*i*, two brothers or two male cousins, triplural nanavaviw*i*; navatsiw*i*, two sisters or two female cousins, triplural nanavatsiw*i*.

Words applying exclusively to cousins are:

ʔOntok^waav*i*, male cousin. The etymology is obscure; ʔonto- may possibly be the same element as ʔanta- in ʔantamuw*a*, man's brother-in-law or cousin-in-law.

Niwaants*i* (diminutive of niwah, friend), cousin of either sex.

Haʔit*i*niwaants*i*, "real cousin," first cousin of either sex.

From these are derived the collectives:

Naʔontok^waav*i*w*i*, two male cousins, or two cousins, one man and one woman, but never two female cousins; nanaʔontok^waav*i*w*i*, three or more cousins, at least one of whom is male.

Naniwaantsiw*i*, two cousins without discrimination as to sex; nananiwaantsiw*i*, three or more cousins.

Haʔit*i*naniwaantsiw*i*, two first cousins; haʔit*i*nananiwaantsi-w*i*, three or more first cousins.

Another term in common use is naʔᵃitcikaavaw*i*, two cousins. This collective derives from a Mohave word for cousins which the Chemehuevis pronounce ʔitcikaav*a*, but do not use "except in talking to the Mohaves."

If one wishes to clear up any confusion resulting from the use of a term which means both sibling and cousin, he may ask a question that will elicit an unambiguous answer. For example, if two persons are referred to as naaviw*i*, one may ask, Nahaganiʔ^yaa-w*i*, how (are) they to each other? The answer will be, Haʔit*i*na-mant*i*m*i* (haʔit*i*- for emphasis only, since namant*i*m*i* never applies to cousins), real siblings, or naniwaantsiw*i*, cousins, as the case may be.

It is interesting to note that although cross and parallel nephews and nieces are rigidly distinguished, cross and parallel cousins are entirely undifferentiated.

Relationships By Marriage

Relationships by marriage involve a complex terminology. In the Spouse Category we have:

Kuma, husband.

Hohoguma (hohovɨ, bone), "bone-husband," husband who was formerly the husband of a deceased sister or cousin.

Piwa (containing the element pi-, as in piya, mother, pipisoʔotsɨ, child, etc., plus -wa as in hiwa, relative), wife.

Hohoviwa, bone-wife, wife who was formerly the wife of a deceased brother or cousin.

Collectives in this category are:

Nagumawɨ, husband and wife; but nanagumawɨ means two or more married couples, never a man with two or more wives.

Hohonagumawɨ, husband and wife, one of whom was formerly the spouse of a deceased sibling or cousin.

Nahontsiwɨ (with -hontsi- compare hutsɨ, father's sister, etc.), two co-spouses or two consecutive spouses; husbands of two sisters or cousins; wives of two brothers or cousins. The triplural nanahontsiwɨ means three or more co-spouses or consecutive spouses, spouses of three or more siblings or cousins. George Laird was very sure that nahontsiwɨ applied to co-spouses as well as to consecutive spouses—actually he thought of co-spouses as the primary sense of the word; he was certain that it meant two husbands of one woman as well as two wives of one man. Yet within his memory, polyandry had never been practiced and polygamy very rarely. The myths he knew told of two sisters sharing a single husband, but not of a woman having more than one husband at a time. Considering, however, that a man's brother or male first cousin was "the same as" himself, it seems not impossible that situations may have arisen in which it became necessary or desirable for brothers or cousins to share a wife. In aboriginal times, it was not only proper but obligatory for a man to marry the widow of his deceased brother or cousin.

Step-parent/Step-child Category

Relationship terms in the Step-parent and Step-child Category consist solely of the word hai and its derivatives, which have already been listed:

Hai, step-father, also father's younger brother or younger male cousin; reciprocal haits*i*, step-child or child of father's older brother, etc.

Nahaiw*i* or nahaitsiw*i*, step-father and step-child, man and older brother's or older male cousin's child; nanahaiw*i* or nanahaitsiw*i*, man and two or more step-children or children of older brother or older male cousin.

It is perfectly natural that the same word (with its reciprocals and collectives) should be applied to both relationships here described, for in most cases it would be the younger brother who survived and undertook the duty of caring for his deceased brother's wife and children. This practice was not the Biblical levirate in its strict sense. It was not the man's duty to "raise up seed" for his brother, but quite simply to provide for those who no longer had a man to hunt for them. There appears to be no word for step-mother. This too is natural, for when a marriage was broken by death or separation the children remained with the mother; and if she should die, their care devolved upon her female relatives.

Parent-in-law Category

The Parent-in-law Category is as follows:

Yah^{a}ig^{y}ap*i*ts*i* (-p*i*ts*i* indicating respect, as in maa$^?$*i*p*i*ts*i*, old woman), parent-in-law. The wife of a son or the husband of a daughter addresses either father-in-law or mother-in-law as yah^{a}ig^{y}ap*i*tsin^y*i*, my parent-in-law.

Mon*a*, son-in-law. The final vowel of mona- is nasalizing, and therefore the plural form may be either monam*i* or monaw*i*.[5]

Hutsimpiy*a*, daughter-in-law (compare hutsits*i*, woman's son's child; the word appears to express the concept "mother of woman's son's child").

Collectives are formed from both senior and junior terms:

Nayaig^{y}ap*i*tsiw*i* (yah^{a}i- becoming -yai- when occupying the position of principal stress), parent-in-law and child-in-law; but nanayah^{a}ig^{y}ap*i*tsiw*i*, parent-in-law and two or more children-in-law.

Namonam*i* or namonaw*i*, parent-in-law and son-in-law. No form was given in nana-.

Nahutsimpiyaw*i*, parent-in-law and daughter-in-law; nana-hutsimpiyaw*i*, parent-in-law and two or more daughters-in-law.

Sibling-in-law Category

In the Sibling-in-law Category, I do not know whether the term translated man's brother-in-law refers both to the man's sister's husband and to his wife's brother or only to one of these relatives, but I believe the reference is to both. The term translated woman's brother-in-law definitely indicates the woman's husband's brother, for he is her potential husband, but I believe it also refers to her sister's husband. This would follow logically from the close sense of identity between siblings of the same sex. These relationship terms are as follows:

?Antamuw*a*, man's brother-in-law or man's male cousin by marriage—that is, the husband of a man's female cousin. The word is formed from ?anta- (compare ?onto- in ?ontok^{w}aav*i*, male cousin) plus muw*a*, father.

Musimpiy*a*, woman's sister-in-law or female cousin by marriage. This word is formed from musi- (the root of musits*i*, woman's brother's or woman's male cousin's child) plus piy*a*, mother, and obviously means "mother of one's musits*i*."

Naingkum*a*, woman's brother-in-law or woman's male cousin by marriage. The element nai- (although here nasalizing) used in forming this term and the following term is said to derive from naig^{y}ah, gets revenge, takes vengeance; so naingkuman*i* would mean "my vengeance husband." Since it was the clear duty of a man to avenge the death of his brother (or cousin) and to take the widow into his household and care for her children, the husband's brother was inevitably thought of as a potential or vengeance husband; and if the husband who was slain had no brother, it is not improbable that the widow's sister's husband would assume responsibility. Polygamy under these circumstances would have been normal. A myth which has not been included in this volume because the English version given to me by George Laird has been lost, concludes with the following episode: Muuhumpɨtsi, Great Horned Owl, is suffering with a painful illness, secretly induced by his wife. Sensing the approach of death, he tells her to take their son and go to his cousin, Kwanantsitsi, Red-Tailed Hawk, who is a good hunter and will provide for them.

Naimpiwa, "vengeance wife," man's sister-in-law or wife of man's cousin.

ʔUnyih (from the Mohave; in this word, the termination is treated as if it were a word of Chemehuevi origin—ʔunyiinʸi, my sister-in-law—but palatalized n occurs in Chemehuevi only after i), woman's sister-in-law or wife of woman's cousin.

Collective forms are:

Naʔantamuwawɨ, two brothers-in-law or two male cousins by marriage; nanaʔantamuwawɨ, three or more brothers-in-law or male cousins by marriage.

Namusimpiyawɨ, two sisters-in-law or two female cousins by marriage; nanamusimpiyawɨ, three or more sisters-in-law or female cousins by marriage.

Nanaingkumawɨ, man and sister-in-law or man and female cousin by marriage. There is no form in nana- and no collective formed from naimpiwa.

Naʔunyiiwɨ, two sisters-in-law or two female cousins by marriage; nanaʔunyiiwɨ, three or more sisters-in-law or female cousins by marriage.

Nahontsiwɨ, man and wife's sister's husband or man and female cousin's husband, woman and husband's brother's wife or woman and male cousin's wife; nanahontsiwɨ, man and husbands of wife's two or more sisters or female cousins, woman and wives of husband's two or more brothers or cousins. This relationship term, which has no simple or non-collective form, has already been mentioned under its alternative meaning of co-spouses or consecutive spouses.

Spouses of uncles and aunts, nephews and nieces, grandchildren, and collateral grandparents are not designated by special terms because they are not classed as relatives.

Deceased Relatives

As indicated at the beginning of this chapter, the designation of deceased relatives is a matter of great delicacy. When the relative is dead or, in the case of a relationship by marriage, the connecting relative has died or a separation has taken place, the suffix -gaipɨ is added to the simple (non-collective) relationship term.[6] Used in connection with animate nouns, -gaipɨ means either deceased or former; with nouns designating inanimate objects it means old, worn-out, or no longer serviceable. But relationship terms with this suffix must be employed with extreme care. To curse and revile an enemy, one mentions to his face a list of his dead relatives: muwagaipɨʔɨmi, your dead father; kɨnugᵂaipɨʔɨmi, your dead father's father; kagugᵂaipɨʔɨmi, your dead mother's mother; and so on. This constitutes the deadliest insult and greatest provocation that can be offered. However, there are ways in which it is possible to mention a deceased relative without giving offense. If in the course of a conversation it becomes desirable to state that a certain person had lived for awhile in such and such a locality, or was notable for something, or had performed an heroic exploit, he may be referred to, though the reference would seldom or never be made in the presence of the bereaved individual. In making this polite reference to a dead parent, the specific terms muwagaipɨ and piyagaipɨ must be replaced by hiwagaipɨ, deceased parent; if necessary, sex is defined by saying tawʔwahiwagaipɨʔɨngᵂa, his dead man-parent, or mamauʔuhiwagaipɨʔɨngᵂa, his dead woman-parent. I understand that in making clear his hereditary right to a song a person may properly trace his ancestry and in so doing mention dead ancestors, but I do not know precisely how this would be done.

Usually when -gaipɨ is added to terms indicating relatives by marriage, it would be understood to mean "former" rather than "deceased." If a woman has left her husband, her mother or father might properly refer to him as monangkaipɨni, my former son-in-law, and he in turn could say yahᵈigʸapɨtsigʸaipɨwini, my former parents-in-law. Under such circumstances, no offense would be given. Still, the inevitable association of all words ending in -gaipɨ with the concept of death tends to place a restraint upon this usage, and the usual practice would be to drop the relationship term altogether.

The personal names of Chemehuevis were (and are) varied, imaginative, and sometimes of deep significance. The mention of names of persons now deceased is subject to the same restriction as that applying to relationship terms referring to such persons. As has been stated, this taboo is gradually losing its force, but around the turn of the century it was still potent. For this reason, the names of quite close relatives frequently dropped from memory very quickly. George Laird did not know his own mother's Chemehuevi name. She died when he was six, his father referred to her always as María, and the Chemehuevis were too courteous to mention her in his presence. However, if an individual was noted as a singer, a chief, a shaman, or the performer of great exploits, his name was remembered and mentioned. The powerful shaman, ?Oomposɨ, is remembered by name, although the name of another shaman, the one who could turn himself into a bear, seems to have been forgotten, while the man and his feats are still recalled.

It would appear from the limited number of names included in the material which follows that those ending in -wɨnɨrɨ, standing, or -?uruᵂantɨ, walking, going, are masculine, as are also those containing references to parts of the human anatomy. Several names of women terminate in -sɨ?ɨ, flower (independent form, sɨ?ipɨ), evidencing an appreciation of feminine beauty; while -vu?i (for pu?ᵂi-, eye) as an ending for masculine names emphasizes the importance of keen eyesight to a hunter. Both men and women bear the names of animals or personal names in which reference to an animal is incorporated. When color is mentioned in the name of a person, the independent form of the word (ending in -karɨ or -garɨ) is used as a postpound, plus the animate termination -mɨ, as in ?Ayarupagarɨmɨ, Black Turtle; but as a prefix only the root form occurs: for example, ?Angkasɨ?ɨ, Red Flower (?angkarɨ, red). Finally, it should be noted that personal names are often irregularly formed, and not a few seem to have no particular meaning or derivation.

In identifying Chemehuevis by families, it is necessary to bear in mind that although many English surnames were acquired by intermarriage with non-Indians, others were simply bestowed or taken arbitrarily and do not imply non-Indian descent.

George Laird did not recall the name of the "Old Chief." According to information given me in 1972, it was:

Wigintiravi, Bare Vagina (wigimpi, vagina; tiiravi, desert; tiiraganti, translated as bare, means literally, having desert). This was the Chemehuevi name of the chief who was referred to in documents as *Pan Coyer*, which is the Mohave equivalent of Wigintiravi. But the information was relayed to me that Wigintiravi did not actually sign the treaty ("put his thumb-mark on the paper") with the Mohave chief, *Irataba*, at the end of the Yuman wars. "Another man did it for him."

Among the members of the family of the man whom George Laird considered to be the last truly functioning High Chief of the Southern Chemehuevis were:

ʔAapanapi, White Clay Lightning Flash (ʔavi or ʔaavi, white clay; panapi, lightning flash or, as recently translated, simply "light"). A son of the High Chief. He was killed by a white man named Calloway during the trouble which attended the building of the Old Blythe Intake.[7]

Pisoʔorimpa, Baby Mouth (pisoʔotsi, infant; timpa, mouth). A cousin of the old High Chief and co-inheritor of the Talking Song, of which he had a dreamed version. In 1919, two of the three daughters of Pisoʔorimpa still survived. One was the wife of "Doctor" Billy Eddy and the other of Herbert Chapo. Although women never officiated as singers of the Talking Song, the right to it passed through them to their male descendants. Therefore, the sons of these daughters of Pisoʔorimpa could sing the Talking Song—*if* they were interested in so doing, *if* they could find anyone to teach it to them, or *if* they were able to dream it.

Tugumpayaaʔoʷasiʸakarimi (occasionally also recorded as Tugumpaʔoʷasiʸakarimi), Yellow Sky (tugumpa, sky; -yaa-, unexplained; ʔoʷasiʸakarimi, pale yellow). He was also called by the shorter name of Totsaarimi, for which no etymology was offered. His English name was Charlie

Snyder. Tugumpayaaʔoᵂasiʸakarɨmɨ was either a close collateral relative or direct descendant of the High Chief. He had learned the Talking Song directly from him and sang it with great exactness.

Tcɨgaʔuruᵂantɨ, Duck Walker, Walks Like a Duck (tcɨxa, duck; ʔuruᵂagah, travels, goes, walks). This man was the son of Pisoʔorɨmpa but knew only a few phrases of his father's song.[8]

The family of Herbert Chapo was connected with the High Chief by marriage only. George Laird recalled the following names of persons belonging to or in some way connected with this family:

Pooʔᵂavi, Louse. He was Herbert Chapo's father. In the mythology Pooʔᵂavi had the form of a seductive woman; after her union with Coyote she laid the eggs from which the human race was hatched—but this evidently did not make the name exclusively feminine in the present era.

Kwitutcapɨatsɨ, Spread Anus (kwitumpɨ, anus; compare kwitcapɨ, excrement). Herbert Chapo.

Tuukwatsɨ, Stretched (cp. tuukwarɨ, anything that stretches; said, e.g., of a rubber band). Herbert Chapo's wife. As mentioned in Chapter II (page 37), she was suspected of having secret shamanistic powers.

Kanahiʸutsɨ (George Laird gave no etymology but commented that the name sounded as though it might be of non-Chemehuevi origin). An older brother of Herbert Chapo.

Piviisa (no etymology). Another of Herbert Chapo's brothers.

Povisatsɨ (species of small bird resembling but not identical with the bird called by the Chemehuevis "knee-pounder"). This was the name of a woman mentioned as in some way connected with the Chapo family.

Still another family group was the following:

Wikuntɨpa, Buzzard Mouth (tɨmpa, mouth, appears here as -tɨpa, probably for reasons of euphony—the juxtaposition of two nasalized consonants, nt and mp, would have an awkward sound).

Tuhug^wantɨsagwagarɨmɨ, Green Enemy (sagwagarɨ, blue or green). The younger brother of Wikuntɨpa. He was known as a rattlesnake shaman, one who had power to cure snakebite.

Kɨmamo²o, Different Hand (kɨma-, different, other; mo²o-pɨ, hand). The name did not imply that he had a different sort of hand, but that all his life he used his hand to work for other people, not for himself. He owned the Quail Song, which now is extinct. His cousins, Wikuntɨpa and Tuhug^wantɨsagwagarɨmɨ, also had hereditary rights to this song, although Tuhug^wantɨsagwagarɨmɨ was never heard to sing it. Wikuntɨpa and Kɨmamo²o addressed each other as niwaantsin^yi, my cousin; or less formally as ²ontok^waavɨ (without the possessive -ni), male cousin. Kɨmamo²o was the father of two daughters, Antonia and Luisa. Antonia's Chemehuevi name is not recalled.

Tutukɨwaay²yuni (no etymology). Luisa, daughter of Kɨmamo²o, further identified as "Lubeck's woman."

Other Quail Song owners were:

²Iluh or ²Iruh (from Mohave ²Idho, willow). ²Iluh also had the Day Owl Song, inherited through his mother.

Wangkasiigwasɨ, Cowtail (wangkasih, cow; kwasɨ, tail). Father of ²Iluh and owner of the Quail Song only.

The Deer Song also has now been forgotten. Among those who had the hereditary right to it were:

²Atatu²^watsɨ, Young Crow (²atapɨtsɨ, crow). He lived in Chemehuevi Valley.

²Opitcokotsɨ, Mesquite Bean Pounder (²opimpɨ, mesquite). He was the oldest son of ²Atatu²^watsɨ. When he died, his uncle, whose Chemehuevi name is unrecorded, came to Chemehuevi Valley to sing the Deer Song at his funeral. This uncle, brother of ²Atatu²^watsɨ, lived near Wickenburg with his Apache wife and must have been a notable Deer Singer. But ²Atatu^watsɨ and ²Opitcokotsɨ gave up their heritage and became Ghost Dance singers instead.

Kiipisɨ (no etymology). Second son of ²Atatu²^watsɨ. He had no interest in spiritual things and became neither Deer nor Ghost Dance singer.

ʔApatí (probably of Apache origin). Youngest son of ʔAtatuʔᵂatsi. He died before reaching maturity and therefore had no opportunity to learn the Deer Song from his uncle.

ʔAyarupagarimi, Black Turtle (ʔaya, desert tortoise or land turtle, a creature close to the hearts of all Chemehuevis and prominent in mythology; tupagari, black). He was famous as a Deer Singer, his song starting up around Bill Williams Fork in what was said to be the ancestral home of his people. He was also a lesser chief of some renown, as has been previously noted. He lived frequently among the Mohaves, probably with one or more Mohave wives, and his name was translated into Mohave as *Kapet Kwiniʔilya* (as George Laird pronounced it). A daughter of pure Chemehuevi descent, remembered by George Laird by the non-Indian name of María, became the wife successively of two non-Indians: Schmidt and Thompson Porter Laird (see Introduction). By the first husband she had two children, John and Anna (who later used the anglicized form of the name, Smith), and by the second three who survived, George, Mary, and Suzy (in this material, the Indian names of Anna, Mary, and Suzy are not recorded, and neither is the purely Chemehuevi name which must have been given John). From these five children, many Chemehuevis now living have sprung, and all these descendants would be Deer according to the ancient classification.

Piisopi (Bishop) is one of the names or nicknames by which John Smith is remembered. This name was bestowed upon him because of his matrimonial habits, said to resemble those of a Mormon bishop. He is also referred to as Johnito (John plus the Spanish diminutive *-ito*, sometimes pronounced Junito). Some of his descendants are under the impression that Piisopi, Johnito, and John Smith refer to three separate individuals, but this is not the case.

Wikontotsi, Buzzard Head (wiku or wikumpitsi, buzzard; totsi, head). George Laird. He was so called because he was bald at birth. He is also remembered to this day as

Wipusi^yavɨ, Lard, because lard was the nearest the Chemehuevis could come to pronouncing his surname.
Other descendants of ʔAyarupagarɨmɨ were:
Kaawɨʔɨ, Rat Penis (kaatsɨ, rat; wɨʔapɨ, penis). He was the
Runner who knew the ancient secret of teleportation.
Pagɨɨwɨxɨ, Fish Vagina (pagɨɨtsɨ, fish; wɨgɨmpɨ is probably
the independent form of wɨgɨ-, vagina). Brother or
cousin of Kaawɨʔa, and his only close friend and
associate. As has been noted, the relationship terms for
older and younger brother and older and younger male
cousin are the same. George Laird did not remember
whether these two ever addressed each other as ni-
waantsin^yɨ, my cousin, or ʔontok^waavɨ, male cousin,
which would have clearly defined the relationship. He
was under the impression that they were cousins to the
other members of the group—yet if they were, as he
sometimes stated, sons and not grandsons of ʔAyarupagarɨmɨ, this would have made them his uncles. Kaawɨʔa
and Pagɨɨwɨxɨ reciprocally called each other by the joking
and affectionate nickname of Kamuutɨ, Sweet Potato,
from Spanish *camote* (see page 48).
Another man who probably had the Deer Song by inheritance
and members of his family were:
Yaariʔiv^ya (from the Mohave name pronounced by George
Laird ʔIlyaalyiʔiv^ya). It seems to have been not uncommon for Chemehuevis to have Mohave, Apache, or other
foreign (even non-Indian) names. Yaariʔiv^ya was a
Tɨɨranɨwɨ, a Desert Chemehuevi, living between the
Providence Mountains and the Granite Mountains and
claiming to protect all the game on those ranges by his
shamanistic power. George Laird thought he was a Deer
by birth, but a mountain sheep shaman.
ʔAngkasɨʔɨ, Red Flower (ʔangkagarɨ, red; sɨʔipɨ, flower) is
described as "Guico's woman" and a daughter-in-law of
Yaariʔiv^ya. Yaariʔiv^ya must therefore have had a son
known as Guico.
Pasaatsɨ (no etymology). The sister of ʔAngkasɨʔɨ and first
wife of John Smith.
Toopoxɨ, Has Black Lumps (the verb form is tuupog^{wa}i-

g^yah; tuu- and too- are often interchangeable when o is an adjacent vowel). Another sister of ꞏAngkasɨ'ɨ.

Among those mentioned as owning the Mountain Sheep Song were:

Pagɨɨnampa, Fish Foot (nampa, foot). This was the Chemehuevi name of the man referred to frequently by George Laird as Pete Chile, but whose name appears on the oldest Reservation rolls as Chile Pete.

Manavisoꞏotsi, Thorn Baby (manavɨ, thorn; pisoꞏotsi, infant). He was one of the last owners of the Whipple Mountain hunting range, that is, of Wiyaatu^wanaga-huv^wiyavɨ, Mountain Sheep Song of Whipple Mountain, and was a relative of Pagɨɨnampa.

As has been noted, the Skunk Song may have been either a song attached to a hunting range or a shaman's song; at any rate, it was hereditary. Mentioned in connection with this song was:

Haikurɨmpa, White Man Mouth (haiku, white man, probably a loanword from the Mohave; tɨmpa, mouth). George Laird always spoke of this man as Jim Haiku-rɨmpa. From his mother he had inherited the Skunk Song and also a song for curing wounds. His mother, "Doctor" Billy Eddy's mother, and George Laird's mother were cousins, which also connects Jim Haiku-rɨmpa with the family of ꞏAyarupagarɨmɨ. Of the three female cousins, only George Laird's mother was not a shaman.

Besides ꞏAyarupagarɨmɨ, other lesser chiefs whose names were recalled were:

Tuuwɨnɨrɨ, Black Standing (tupagarɨ, black, frequently as prefix tuu- or too-; wɨnɨrɨ, stander, standing, one who stands, form of wɨnɨgah, standing). The deaf chief of the band residing at Harimyiivɨ (see page 23).

ꞏOtawɨnɨrɨ, Sand Standing (ꞏotavɨ, fine sand). Chief of a band on the Arizona side of the Colorado River. ꞏOta-wɨnɨrɨ figures prominently in George Laird's reminiscences. ꞏOtawɨnɨrɨ, ꞏAyarupagarɨmɨ, and Nagaramaupa were the three who spoke together in Chief's Language on a memorable night in 1891.

Nagaramaupa (also recorded as Nagaaramaupa), given as

equivalent to nagay tamaup*a*, Left the Mountain Sheep Behind (nax*a*, mountain sheep; tamaupats*i*, left behind or that which was left behind—here, as in Toopox*i*, a proper name is formed from the root of a verb). Since Nagaramaup*a* is described as "the biggest liar among the Chemehuevis," one wonders if his name might not have derived from a claim to have outrun a mountain sheep.

Grandsons of Nagaramaup*a* were:

Huk^{w}ivu^2*i*, Charcoal Eye (huk^{w}i-, charcoal). He is further identified as "Victoria's son." He died in 1891, the great year of the Ghost Dance.

Kwiyavu^2*i*, Snake Eye (kwiyats*i*, rattlesnake). Billy Calloway.[9] He lived in the vicinity of Indio or Banning.

^{2}Otawɨnɨrɨ and Nagaramaup*a* were among those Chemehuevis who heard a voice from on high speaking to each in his own tongue one night during the Ghost Dance. Others mentioned in connection with the Ghost Dance were:

Kaiwaɨkat*i*, Mountain Runner (explained as deriving from kaiv^{y}agwaɨngkat*i*; George Laird equated kwaɨngkat*i* with Spanish *ligero*, one who is very swift and agile in running over rough territory). He also heard the voice at the Ghost Dance.

Tcawiih (no etymology). Another who heard the voice.

Kuyuut*i* (probably from coyote—compare kamuut*i* from *camote* and Tumiingu from *Domingo*). He was the man who brought the Ghost Dance from Chemehuevi Valley to Needles.

^{2}Ootc*a* (a foreign name, no etymology). Mother of Kuyuut*i*. She was half Chemehuevi, half Mohave.

Two members of the Tobin family were:

Wagatamuh^{w}aratɨm*i*, Bitter Frog (wagat*a*, frog; muh^{w}arat*i*, bitter). This was the man known by the English name of Mike Tobin, but George Laird commented that he and his sister were full-blooded Chemehuevis. In 1969, Stella Smith Mike gave his name as Wahat or Wahatats, and said that it was "just a name," with no meaning; but other Chemehuevis remembered that he was Frog. Mike Tobin, George Laird, Ben Paddock, and Bill Fisher all worked together for some time at the Indian School at

Fort Mohave. Mike Tobin was the youngest of the four and the one who survived the longest. He died in the autumn of 1969. In his lifetime, he was not more notable than his contemporaries; but because he was the last of his generation, and with him an era and a culture passed, six tribes came together to give him a funeral and a Cry worthy of a chief (see Note 15, Chapter II).

ʔAkasiʔɨ, Palmita Flower (ʔaka, palmita, also the minute seed borne by this plant). Mike Tobin's sister.

Besides Jim Haikurɨmpa, who was a "wound doctor," the following shamans were named:

ʔɨwarɨngkova, Rain Face (ʔɨwarɨ, rain; kova, face). A Northern shaman.

Tumiingu (Chemehuevi pronunciation of Domingo). Also a Northern shaman, mentioned in connection with ʔɨwarɨngkova.

ʔOomposɨ (no etymology). A very famous shaman whose powers and exploits have been described in Chapter II. He is still remembered by name along the Colorado River.

Yampavinʸukʷi, Mockingbird Runner (yampa, mockingbird; nukʷi, runner). Johnny Moss. He was murdered by Mexicans at the town of Daggett.

Additional personal names were:

Tukupɨra (George Laird gave no etymology, but possibly tuku, wildcat, may be the first element). He was a widely known High Chief of the Desert Chemehuevis, respected both by Indians and whites (see page 24).

Pagɨɨsagwᵃivɨ, Fish Intestines (sagwᵃivɨ, intestines).

Tɨmpimoʔo, Stone Hand or Money Hand (the primary meaning of tɨmpɨ is stone, but it is also used of money). Son of Pagɨɨsagwᵃivɨ.

Tɨrapukʷipɨ, Desert Blower (tɨɨravɨ, desert—possibly the first syllable of the name should be Tɨɨ-, but I have given it as recorded with single ɨ, since personal names are frequently irregularly formed; pukʷigʸah means blowing with the mouth, but for "wind blowing" one must say nɨagah, so this name does not refer to the wind blowing across the desert.

Samikwitutsi (no etymology, but kwitu- is probably for anus, a common element in masculine names).

Nivasi²i, Snow Flower (nivavi, snow). Wife of Samikwitutsi.

Pahoomparigatsi, Hail Gatherer (pahompa, hail, but oo in the name). Personal name of a woman, not identified.

Pagin²nasi²i, Cloud Flower (pagin²nava, cloud). This was given by George Laird merely as an example of a feminine name, but some persons now living believe it may have been the name of his mother as well as of a woman who lived much later.

Timpici²i, Stone Flower (s becomes c between i and i). Annie Eddy Laird's sister.

George Laird frequently spoke of two non-Chemehuevi chiefs:

²Ierateiva. *Irataba*, the famous Mohave chief.

²Aasukit. A lesser chief mentioned in a derogatory manner in the phrase "²Aasukit's gang." This was reputed to be a marauding band, predominantly Apache but including some Chemehuevis as well as members of other tribes.

Chemehuevi names are still bestowed and still in use; also many names of deceased persons are still to be obtained, now that the old taboo against mentioning the dead is breaking down. I add here a few names given to me in 1969 and subsequently. Some of these differ phonetically from the old Southern Chemehuevi which George Laird spoke, The names of members of the Snyder family which were given to me by Wendell Goodman, Sr. are particularly important, since this family was related to the High Chief. Mr. Goodman's Chemehuevi name is Sawatosarimi, White Arrowweed (see Note 8, this chapter). Among the names obtained from him and others were:

Paati (no etymology given). Sam Snyder. He was Wendell Goodman's uncle and inherited the Talking Song. The Snyders were born in Chemehuevi Valley; now they are scattered as far as Wyoming.

²Irinapiwinih (napiw, old man, offered as partial etymology). Also given as name of Sam Snyder. He and Wendell Goodman's step-father used to sing the Salt Song together.

²Ayatsi, Turtle (²aya plus termination -tsi). Personal name of a Paiute woman. It will be recalled that George Laird

said that all Northerners (Northern Chemehuevis and related tribes) make inordinate use of -ts*i*.

ˀOntok^war*i*m*i*. Mary Hill, the oldest daughter of John Smith. Stella Smith Mike said this referred to the somewhat lighter color of Mrs. Hill's hair; ˀontok^war*i* has the form of a word designating color, but was not among the color names obtained from George Laird. Mrs. Mike (whose dialect is Northern, perhaps mixed with Paiute) pronounced the third syllable -ka-, but as said by Mr. Goodman and Mrs. Hill herself -k^wa- was very distinct.

ˀ*I*p*i*nits*i*. Chemehuevi name of Bill Fisher, George Laird's contemporary. The name was furnished by Stella Smith Mike, who said she could give no etymology.

Vin^y*a*, Ben (Paddock). Modern Chemehuevi pronunciation of Ben and seemingly the only name remembered for Ben Paddock, who was George Laird's contemporary and the son by a lesser chief's daughter of the white soldier and trapper called Ben Paddock. Both Stella Smith Mike and Gertrude Hanks Leivas pronounced the word with initial v. In all other Chemehuevi loanwords that I have recorded, p substitutes for initial v—as in Piigis*i*, (Las) Vegas. Final *a* was brought out in the expression "Vin^y*a*n kwaik^y," which Mrs. Mike translated as "I am talking about Ben."

Siiw*i*nt*i*ˀip*i*. Henry Hanks. Obtained from Mrs. Mike, who gave no etymology. Siiw*i*nt*i*ˀip*i* was the uncle of a man who returned to Chemehuevi Valley after ten years in prison and kept his money in buckskin bags hanging from the roof of his earth house. This man was some sort of relative of Mrs. Mike's mother, thus forming a link between her family and the Hanks family.

Matavi^y*um*i*, Having Ticks (matav*i*, tick, also said to mean flea). Mary Molino gave this as the name of a man now deceased. She said that Matavi^yum or Matavi^yuts was also the name of a dog.

The following instances illustrate the manner in which personal names may still be acquired:

Watsamamauˀ*u* or Watsamaaˀ*i*p*i*ts*i*, Bee Woman or Old Bee

Woman (watsav*i*, bee; mamau*ʔu*, woman; maaʔɨpɨts*i*, old woman, always a term of respect). Gertrude Hanks Leivas called my daughter, Georgia Laird Culp, Bee Woman "because she is always busy and sometimes she stings." Mary Hill gave the word its more honorific form. Because Mrs. Hill is the daughter of George Laird's half-brother and much older than Georgia Culp, she is Georgia's patc*i*, big sister, older sister, and addresses her as namiʔin*ʸi*, my little (younger) sister. If either form of this name happens to catch the fancy of those who still speak Chemehuevi, it will no doubt stick; otherwise it will soon be forgotten.

Witsiʔitsits*i*, Little Bird, Baby Bird (witciʔitsits*i* is the diminutive of witciʔits*i*, a bird of any one of a number of small, twittering species; or simply, more loosely, bird). This is sometimes applied to Rachel Hanks. Rachel's aunt, Mary Molino, says that when Rachel was a baby she was nicknamed Tweety or Tweety Bird, and this was rendered into Chemehuevi as Witsiʔitsits*i*. But young Rachel, when she was about eight years old, gave the following dreamed or fantasied explanation: when she was very small (she said) she saw a baby bird sitting in a tree trying to fly, and she climbed out on the branch beside it and flapped her arms and cheeped; therefore, she also became Witsiʔitsits*i*, Baby Bird.

CHAPTER IV

THE NATURAL WORLD

TO a Chemehuevi, the line between natural and supernatural was not firmly drawn. As he wandered over the face of the earth, hunting or simply travelling, any creature he encountered, from bear or mountain lion to tiniest insect, which deviated in the slightest from its normal behavior might well be his friendly—or not-so-friendly—neighborhood shaman going about mysterious business in his (or her) alternate form. Even so, while reasonably cautious, he was less fearful than certain other so-called primitives, and his urge to investigate recognized no barriers between the natural world and the spiritual. The following story is an example.

When George Laird was twelve years old, he went to work for three white miners. They made their headquarters in an isolated house, a one-room shack with lean-to, beside a well in the desert. Every day they went up into the waterless foothills to work their claim. George cooked and cared for the livestock and each evening unloaded the ore from the wagon. Most of his working hours he spent driving the patient mule around and around in an endless circle to power the *arrastre* (the men called it a 'raster) in which specimens of ore were ground. He was wildly excited about his first real job, seething with curiosity about the primitive mining and assay operations, and inclined to look up to the men and to believe whatever they said; while they, seeing his shy and decently quiet exterior, no doubt considered him as dumb and stubborn as the beast he drove.

On Christmas Eve the men broke out the whiskey they had stashed away and got roaring drunk, and George listened with interest to the tales that slipped from their loosened tongues. It seemed that each man had at least one murder in his past and walked in fear of an avenging spirit. As the night grew older and the men drunker, it was quite a natural development for one of them to point to the window and howl that the ghost had come for him. George looked up and saw the ghost plainly: a dark, shadowy, emaciated face with a sort of white cowl around it. All three men yelled and threw things, piled wood on the fire, and grabbed for their bottles. Then the ghost disappeared, the men drank themselves into a stupor, and George went to his lean-to and slept the sleep of the innocent.

In the morning he awoke obsessed by the question: does a ghost leave tracks? The men were still snoring. George slipped outside and inspected the ground under the window, and indeed there were the marks of feet which had stood and shuffled in the sand, then staggered away. "I'll track him," George thought,[1] still not doubting that he was tracking a spirit. Just a few yards away, in the bed of a small, dry wash, he found the body of a Mexican, one hand still clutching a ragged piece of canvas around his head, the other stretched out and clawing at the sand. Then he knew that there had been no ghost. A man nearly dead of thirst and exposure had come to the window, had come so near to water and shelter only to be frightened away by the figures leaping and shouting in the firelight (perhaps thinking in his delirium that he looked into Hell itself!), and had stumbled on to his death.

At that moment of discovery George Laird accepted the dictum of the Chemehuevis: haiku katc mugu?ʷatɨmɨ, the white man has no sense, no sensibility, no proper understanding (literally, no semen).

After the Mexican was buried the miners, somewhat sheepish but unregenerate, finished off the whiskey and plotted a claim-jumping expedition for New Year's Eve. They told George he was to come along with them. He said nothing, but the first time he was left alone he got on his horse and rode away. Thompson Porter Laird hadn't raised his boy to be a claim-jumper—and for the time being he was tired of white men and their ways.

His canteen was empty when he reached the only water

between them and the River. It was a well, and the wooden cover had been carelessly replaced. When he drew up the bucket, the bloated body of a snake lay across it. The memory of the Mexican face-down in the sand provided an antidote to squeamishness. He drank deeply, filled his canteen, watered his horse, and returned to the People.

This adventure illustrates two ways in which the Chemehuevis related to their environment: inquisitiveness and the tough ability to survive its challenge. There was another—sheer delight—which George Laird retained to a remarkable degree. One day while we were working together in Parker he arrived very late. He explained that he had been unavoidably delayed in accomplishing his Agency chores. Just before sunrise, he said, as he drove his wagon along the River Road, there had been rabbits playing in front of him, and he had had to stop to watch them. He described how they raced and dodged and leap-frogged undeterred by his presence, and how he could not bear to interrupt their play. (Later I understood what deep racial memories this scene must have stirred in him, memories of the days when the young men in their exuberance leaped and raced and wrestled on the way to some rendezvous of hunters or warriors.) Even now, many Chemehuevis are quietly enraptured by the sight of an animal in its native state, a stone, a shrub, or some natural formation of strength and beauty. All nature, including those aspects which are quite unassociated with magic, has a numinous quality. It is inconceivable that such a people could ever have been bored in aboriginal times, no matter what long and lonely periods intervened between the great excitements of Gatherings, Cries, war parties, Scalp Dances, and communal hunts. Only after the white man's culture was superimposed, with its rigid concepts of time and work, its denigration of native language, custom, and belief, and its rejection of all that had seemed natural and beautiful, did the collective heart of this people fall victim to boredom, alienation, frustration, and despair.

By the beginning of the twentieth century the old Chemehuevi world view, with its knowledge derived from observation, rich traditions, and associated sentiments, was well on the way to dissolution. In this chapter we shall try to reconstruct what we can of it from the surviving fragments of George Laird's memories.

Water, Earth, and Sky

Water, earth, and sky comprised the world. Of these, water
was the primary element. In the creation myths (as recorded in
Chapter VI), we see how Hutsipamamau⁷*u*, Ocean Woman, made
the earth out of the particles of dead skin from her own body
which she rolled up and sprinkled upon the ocean and how, by her
immense labors, she stretched out the land until it was large
enough to be habitable. The earth, then, was thought of not only
as encircled by water, but as actually floating upon the primeval
sea. The word for water is paah (actually paa-, but when standing
alone the long a is followed by an aspiration); as the first member
of compounds (and occasionally in other positions) the word
appears as pa-. Various bodies of water are described as follows:

Hutsip*a*, ocean. No etymology was given for this word, but
it is tempting to connect the first part with huts*i*,
father's mother—perhaps the ocean was once thought of
as Grandmother Water! The ocean is also called Nar*i*-
wiin^y apah (na-, reflexive particle; t*i*wiin^y agah, tells a
myth; pah, water), Immortal (literally, Self-Mythologizing) Water.

Pagar*i*r*i* (pa plus kar*i*r*i*, sitting, sitter, from kar*i*gah, sits),
lake, literally, water sitting. But the Primeval Lake of
fresh water from which Tavuts*i*, Cottontail Rabbit,
caused to be formed all lakes, springs, tanks, and other
watering places from which men drink was also personified as Nar*i*wiin^y apah.

Pagah (-gah unexplained), river. George Laird thought
that this would apply to any large river, but as
commonly used it meant only the Colorado River.

Huwip*i* (from huwig^y ah, flowing; also given sometimes as
huwip*i*) is the term for any stream, wash, or arroyo.
Any tributary of the Colorado would be huwip*i*, no
matter how much water it carried.

Pik^y avo⁷*o* (no etymology; -vo⁷*o* possibly for -vu⁷*i*, eye) is
applied to any natural tank in the rocks where water
accumulates (Spanish *tinaja*).

There was no specific term for spring in my notes. The various
springs were named, and the element pa- or paa- frequently but

not always appeared in these names—as, for example, in the placename Sɨʔapivʸaatsɨ, Sage Water.

Land, earth, or soil is called tɨvipɨ. This is a very generalized term. It also means country and loosely, by extension, world—although a word indicating world or universe would hardly be in accord with Chemehuevi thought. An earth house (one built in the old manner, or in modern times made out of adobe brick) is called tɨvikʸanɨ (kanɨ, house), while tuhugʷantɨrɨvipɨ (tuhugʷantɨ, enemy) means enemy country, enemy territory. Tɨwiinʸarɨvipɨ means Sacred Land, Storied Land. It is vaguely located to the north and is said to include the whole Panamint Range; but this term is never personified, never preceded by the reflexive na-. Earth's formations are:

Kaivʸa, mountain. The form indicating intimate association with someone is kaiʸa (as in kaiʸanɨ, my mountain, said by a man whose song travels over that specific mountain), and the root kai-, appears in many compounds, such as kaitcoxo, mountain hat, and kaipipovɨ, mountain "canteen." Individual mountains were not personified, but the expression Narɨwiinʸakaivʸa, Immortal Mountain, expresses an idea of great power and mystery.

Kaampɨ, a long, low-lying hill or chain of hills. A single hill is kaangkarɨrɨ, hill sitting, sitting hill.

Yagah, a pass between two overlapping mountain ranges.

Tɨɨravɨ (tɨɨ- possibly for tɨ- of tɨvipɨ), desert. This is a general term for any desert land and also means the space between one desert mountain range and the next. Formerly cuukutɨɨravɨ, one desert, one "Indian mile," indicated the distance from the top of one range, through the intervening desert, to the top of the next range; now the expression means one (white man's) mile. Although tɨɨravɨ is never personified or treated as an animate noun, it indicates a concept of immense importance to Chemehuevi thought. The desert was the homeland, not only of the Desert Chemehuevis but of all branches of the tribe. Anything which originates in the desert, especially anything fit for human consumption, such as meat or seed, is known as tɨɨravatcɨ.

Yɨwaavɨ, valley. This would be a river valley or any valley not described as desert.

Hopak^ai, hollow or dell.

Pasa, field.

Since the environment was minutely and lovingly observed, there doubtless were (and still are) other such descriptive terms in common use.

The following are among Chemehuevi mineralogical terms:

ʔAsompɨ (also recorded as ʔasompi), salt.

ʔO^wavi, rock salt.

Hukumpa, dust.

ʔOtavi, fine sand.

Siwampɨ, coarse sand.

ʔAavi, white clay.

Siwaʔaavɨ (obviously a combination of siwampɨ and ʔaavi), hardpan.

Wiyavɨ or turumpɨ, adobe.

ʔO^wasi^yapi (from ʔo^wasi^yakarɨ, pale yellow), a stone used in pottery making. It turns red when fired and makes the red line in the design.²

Tɨmpi, rock, stone. This is a generalized term; a large rock formation or a stone that one picked up to throw would be tɨmpi. The syllable tɨ- (compare tɨvipɨ and tɨɨravi) is nasalizing when it means stone; tɨngkanʔni (from tɨmpi and kani, house) means a cave in the rock.

Toyompɨ, boulder.

Tcungk^wapɨ, granite.

Tuntug^wiv^yi, lava; malpais.

Wɨnʔnapi (wɨnʔnawa if attached to arrow), flint.

Si^yapɨ, schist.

Tookovaronumpɨ (too- for tuu-, black; kova, face; -ro- for -tu-, particle indicating to make or to cause; -numpɨ, instrument or material used—as in pananumpɨ, lamp), black paint, literally, material used for blackening the face.

ʔOmpi, red paint. Deposits of black and red paint occur together in a place worked as a manganese mine during World War I; George Laird worked there shortly before we met.

Sagwamuvinʔn^yangkavɨ (sagwagarɨ, blue or green; muvi-nʔn^yangka, nose ring or nose pendant, in turn deriving from muv*i*, nose, and nangk*a*, which means both ear and earring; -v*i*, termination), turquoise, literally, blue nose pendant material. There was a turquoise mine situated north of New York Mountain.

The sky is called tugump*a*. Like t*i*vip*i*, earth, this is an inanimate noun. There was a land on top of the sky to which mythological beings had access.[3] This locality was designated by the phrase tugumpay (for tugumpay*a*, objective or possessive of tugump*a*) ʔiv^yaʔan*a*, sky here visible on top of, which is precisely the same construction as kani ʔiv^yaʔan*a*, on top of this house. This suggests the concept of the sky as a solid roof for the world in which we live. The heavenly bodies were said to sit (in the sky) or to travel west across it. The names for sun and moon are animate in form, as are those of all constellations and single named stars; but as noted below the generalized word for star is inanimate. There must have been a time when the face of the sky was as familiar to the Chemehuevis as the face of their beloved desert; but most of their astronomical lore, together with the rich body of accompanying mythology, vanished quickly after contact with the white man. Here I record the little that George Laird was able to dredge up from his boyhood memories:

Tavap*i*ts*i* (tava-, sun, in compounds—also tavi- or simply ta-; -p*i*ts*i*, honorific postfix), Sun. In the myths, the Sun is an animate being, and he is male,[4] but ordinarily I would say that this usage was simply poetic. So far as I know, unlike Ocean Woman, the Sun was never addressed or invoked, nor were offerings made to him. The phenomenon which as a child I heard described as "the sun drawing water," as well as the rays which are sometimes seen extending across the sky at sunrise or sunset are called Tavap*i*tsi montc*o*, Sun's beard, also Tavap*i*tsi montcoʔa uk^wa (-uk^wa is an inanimate pronominal form, but is also used as a connective—the expression probably should be translated as "it is the Sun's beard"). Of the reddish glow that is very rarely seen around the sun at its rising or setting it is said, Tavap*i*ts kutsik^yig^yah, the Sun is burning [transitive], implying that the Sun is burning trash or making some sort of bonfire. Sunlight is called tavip*i*, said to derive from tavig^{y}ah, throws [transitive], and translated simply as that which is thrown—the implication being that light is what the Sun throws out from himself; but, as noted above, tavi- not infrequently means sun in compounds. When it is a hot day they say, taru$^{?w}$ig^{y}ah, it is hot, in contradistinction to citu$^{?w}$ig^{y}ah, it is cold; these are expressions used of the weather. Anything (stone, water, or any substance) which has been heated by the sun is called tagutuutsitci, but if it has been heated by fire it is called kutuutsitci (tava-, sun, but ta-, by solar heat; kuna, fire, ku-, by fire). Tavahuk^{w}ampi is always translated Sun Spider (huk^{w}ampi, black widow spider), while Tavamuhuumpitsi is just as invariably translated Day Owl. Tavahuk^{w}ampi lives in the Land on Top of the Sky and is associated with the guardianship of the "sky-hole"; in this material Tavamuhuumpitsi appears only in connection with the Day Owl Song.

Mi^{y}arogopitsi (no etymology was given for this word, but it is tempting to think that there might be a connection between mi^{y}a- and mi$^{?y}$aupi, little, especially since mi$^{?y}$aupitog^{wa}intimi indicates a lesser chief; -rogo- might mean maternal grandfather—it is worth recalling that Sun Spider was the maternal grandfather of Wildcat; -pitsi is either an archaic diminutive of -pitsi or simply the termination -pi- plus a second termination, probably animate and/or diminutive, -tsi), Moon. In the myth "How Cottontail Rabbit Conquered the Sun" the Moon, emerging first from the place where the Sun would later come out, is surrounded by innumerable crows (?atapitsiwi); so it seems that in Chemehuevi mythology, as in Greek, the Moon had a distinctive bird, the black crow instead of the white dove! When the new moon appears in the sky the Chemehuevis say, Mi^{y}arogopits kakari, Moon sat down or Moon sitting, implying that the Moon has now arrived and taken its place in the sky. As the moon waxes it is said, Mi^{y}arogopits nanawa$^{?a}$ig^{y}ah, Moon goes (away from speaker) towards growing; and as it wanes, Mi^{y}arogopits ya$^{?a}$iwa$^{?a}$ig^{y}ah, Moon goes (away from speaker) towards dying. Even fifty years ago another expression was also in common use for the waxing moon: Mi^yarogopits putcawa^{?a}ig^yah, Moon goes (away from speaker) towards fullness; but this is an adaptation of the English and Spanish idiom and does not accord with Chemehuevi symbolism. The full moon is Mi^yarogopits tog^{wa}intɨrawaagantu^wa, Moon at half-center—half-center implying mid-center, the very center, or in Spanish *el mero medio*. Mi^yarogopits ya?a, Moon died, is said either of the dark of the moon or of an eclipse; and ya?a is also used of the death of the Sun when it is eclipsed. A ring either around the sun or the moon is designated as nɨkatɨah, circle-dance place (nɨkapɨ, circle-dance such as is danced as part of a Mourning Ceremony, is also the name of the Scalp Dance and the Ghost Dance; -tɨah, place).

Puutsivɨ, star. This is the general term for star or planet. Since puutsivɨ is inanimate, it has no plural form; of the multitude of stars, one says, ?ava?an puutsivɨagah, there are many stars. If the motion of the planets was observed and commented upon, this fact is not recorded in my material. Of the stars moving across the sky it was said, puutsiv ?ɨgatu^warɨ, stars going west, more literally, stars (or star) going towards the entrance—that is, towards the place where they, together with the Sun and Moon, enter in after their journey. When a person travelled by day, he took his direction from the sun; by night he was guided by the stars, for they "follow the Sun." He did not fix his course by the North Star, for which George Laird knew no Chemehuevi name. The morning star is called tasɨantɨpuutsivɨ, dawn star, and any star or planet conspicuous by its size is spoken of as hokontɨpuutsivɨ, large star. Of a falling star, the Chemehuevis say puutsiv wɨ?ig^yah, which means either "star falls" or "star shoots" (compare tuguwɨ?ig^yah, shoots [arrows] at the sky, and wɨ?ikutsɨ, fell down).

Nagawɨ, Mountain Sheep (plural). Orion's Belt, called in Spanish *Las Tres Reyes*. The Mountain Sheep in the middle was the largest, and he had been shot by a blind man on the earth. Nagawɨ and the following five names of stars or groups of stars were tied together in some tremendous ancient tale which George Laird had never heard in its entirety.

Huu Wisiʔʸah, (huuᵂa, possessive of huuh, arrow; wisiʸavɨ, feather or feathers, but wisiʔʸah if attached to bird or arrow), Arrow's Feathers. These are the three stars in Orion's Sword which are named in Spanish *Las Tres Marías*. The arrow referred to is the one with which the blind man shot the Mountain Sheep.

Huu Wɨnʔnawa (wɨnʔnapɨ, flint, wɨnʔnawa if attached to arrow), Arrow's Flint. The cluster of stars that marks Orion's head.

Tɨhoᵂagantɨmɨ, Ambushers. Betelgeuse and Rigel. These were the ambushers in the great hunt for the Mountain Sheep.

Muhᵂintɨ, Leader (the leader in the hunt). Aldebaran.

Tɨrɨnapɨgantɨ, Follower. Sirius. This follower was the father of the Mountain Sheep who was shot.

Soniyawɨ, Nests (an animate plural form derived from the inanimate noun soniyavɨ, a soft, fur-lined nest or den such as a rabbit makes). The Pleiades. The Chemehuevis distinguish six stars in this group: Mythic Coyote's wife, his son, three daughters, and a shaman. The story of the events which led to their departure for the sky is briefly sketched in Chapter VI.

Naugupoh (nauxu, spirit, soul, ghost; pooh, trail or road), Ghost Trail. The Milky Way.

Kamɨmugᵂigʸarɨtɨah (kamɨ, jackrabbit; mugᵂigʸarɨgah, rabbit sits, as distinct from karɨgah, (a person) sits; -tɨah, place), Jackrabbit Sitting Place. This is the name of an unidentified group of three or four dim stars. The jackrabbit referred to here, and in the name of the following group of stars, is that one which Wildcat wounded and pursued all the way to the Land on Top of the Sky. In ancient times there must have been many episodes from many myths poetically bound up with the night sky—the myths identified the stars and constellations, and the starry heavens reminded men of the myths.

Kamɨnuk^{w}itavipag^{a}ipɨ (nuk^{w}i-, to run; tavi-, to throw; pag^{a}i-, to progress, to go along; -pɨ is a frequently appearing terminal syllable, usually inanimate), Where the Jackrabbit Made Tracks as He Leaped, or more literally, Jackrabbit Went Along Run-Throwing. This designates three or four pairs of dim stars leading upward from the group called Kamɨmug^{w}ig^{y}arɨtɨah.

ʔIsagawɨ (no etymology given; the plural form suggests that it referred to animate beings). This is an unidentified constellation said to rise (emerge) just before the sun at the beginning of spring. It was one of those signs for which the old men watched in their pre-dawn vigils in the days when Chemehuevis read the seasons in the stars and not on the white man's calendar.

Tcɨg Kasatok^{w}avin^{y}akatɨ (tcɨxa, duck; kas$a$, wing; tok^{w}avin^{y}akatɨ, that which is shot off or broken off), Broken-Winged Duck. An unidentified group of stars, the story of which is no longer remembered.

Times and Seasons

Times and seasons were established by correlating the changes in the heavens with the changes on the face of the earth. The year was seen to consist of four distinct seasons, and this was proper because it conformed to the pattern of fours set by Mythic Coyote. But each season contained only three months, instead of four as might have been expected. The charming story (briefly narrated in Chapter VI) of Coyote's conflict with Burrowing Owl over this matter gave an appropriate explanation and acknowledged the occurrence in nature of patterns of three as well as of four.

Taking its name from the winter season, the year is called toov$i$. In fact, cuukutomo, one winter, is freely interchangeable with cuukutoov$i$, one year. This usage probably derived from the practice of counting back how many winters had been spent in one place and thus loosely dating fairly recent events. In aboriginal times no effort was made to record the passage of years with any accuracy or to remember very far back. ʔAwats too^{w}agantɨ, several years being, was the expression for an indeterminate period of time.

The year began with spring, and the observations which determined this date were of the greatest importance. Certain venerable men knew what stars or constellations would mark the advent of spring by emerging just before the sun rose. As the season was felt to be approaching, these old men would come out from the shelter of their earth houses and stand naked in the pre-dawn chill to watch the sky. They would consult gravely with one another. Of a looked-for star they would say: katcus mawʔwisiwaʔa, it has not yet emerged, or mawʔwisitcaʔaka, it has emerged; and of a constellation or group of stars, katcus mayaangawaʔa, they have not yet emerged, or mayaangakutcaʔa-ka, they have emerged. Of all these various harbingers of spring, ʔIsagawɨ is the only one which George Laird remembered. This sky-watch was a true rite of spring. In ancient times the wise men who watched had good buckskin clothing, blankets of rabbit skin, capes woven of yucca fiber and thickly set with feathers; later they had clothes and blankets from the trading post. But it was requisite that they stand naked in the cold. Later the young men worked perforce by the white man's time. They learned to read the printed calendar and to denigrate the old, deliberate ways. When there were no longer youths eager to receive the ancient lore and a whole people waiting to learn that spring was at hand, the old men stopped their futile watching, and their knowledge perished with them.

Spring is tamana and the all-important beginning of spring is called tamawɨʔatsɨ. Tatca is summer and tatcawɨʔatsɨ, the beginning of summer. But yɨvana, autumn, forms yɨvanawɨʔatsɨ, the beginning of autumn, retaining the ending -na- which must be dropped in the term for the beginning of spring. From tomo, winter, toowɨʔatsɨ, the beginning of winter, is irregularly derived.

Tog^{wa}itomo, half-winter, mid-winter, and tog^{wa}itatca, half- or mid-summer, are said of the winter and summer solstices respectively. Apparently there was no term for equinox.

Possibly by the turn of the century mɨantsɨ, month, had largely replaced mi^{y}arogopitsɨ, moon, as a measurement of time. Yet mɨantsɨ almost certainly derived from English month. The months, or moons, do not appear to have had names, and the year was not said to consist of a certain number of months. The terms tamamɨantsɨ, spring month, tatcamɨantsɨ, summer month, yɨvana-mɨantsɨ, autumn month, and tomomɨantsɨ, winter month, were in use, but these months were not designated as first, second, or third month of the season. The solstices were determined by stellar observation, but the moons slipped by without accurate count, and there was no thought of determining the number of days in a year. It was enough that the observation of sun, moon, and stars gave a quiet and orderly sense of rotating seasons. There could be no question of tying this observation to a non-existent mathematical system, and the Chemehuevis possessed no device for measuring time more complex than the knotted string—and as previously mentioned, this was only used when people were being summoned from great distances. After the partial assimilation of white culture, saandipɨ,[5] from English Sunday, came into use to indicate week, as in pah^aikusaandipɨ, three weeks; or cuukusandin wɨɨkavɨh (wɨɨka-, from work), I worked one week.

Tavayu, day, is comparable to an English adverbial form as an indication of time. Although it is the only permissible form when used alone, it may not be used with prepounded numerals. Thus one would say tavay ʔuru^wagah, travels in the day, travels by day; but cuukutavα, one day, or more rarely (at least in modern times) cuukutavapɨtsɨ, one sun. With -tavα the short form of the numeral (without -ku-) may be used, although it is not permissible with any of the words for night, week, or year. Cuutavα means one day, all day, or the whole day, and cuukutavα means exactly the same: cuutavan wɨɨkavɨh or cuukutavan wɨɨkavɨh, I worked one day, I worked the whole day through.

The word for night has two substantive forms, tug^wavɨ and tug^wanu, as well as tug^wavayu, comparable to tavayu, and used in such expressions as tug^wavay ʔuru^wagah, travels at night, travels all night. The prefix tu- indicates blackness, darkness.

Day and night are divided into the following periods:

Tavimawisitsɨ (from tavimawʔwisɨ, the sun emerged [from its den or hole], the sun rose; here we have tavi-, sun, instead of tava-; compare tavipɨ, sunlight, said to derive from tavig^yah, throws), sunrise.

Tavavaʔapɨ (-vaʔapɨ from paʔagah, is high; the free adjective is paʔantɨ), high sun. This is said of the time of day when the sun is two or three hours high.

ʔɨitcuku, morning, forenoon, any time between sunrise and noon.

Tog^{wa}itavayu, half day. Noon.

Tawɨʔikutsi (wɨʔiku, dropped or fell; here the prefix is simply ta-, never tava- nor tavi-), sun dropped. This indicates the time immediately past noon, when the sun has just crossed the meridian.

Wɨsɨpapɨ, cool, cool of the day. All forms of wɨsɨpagah, is cool, refer only to the coolness of late afternoon. But sɨpanguntsi, became cool, may be said of food or anything else which has cooled off after having been warm or hot and, with the prefix ta-, applied to weather: tasɨpanguntsaʔᵃukʷa, it has become cooler, may be said at any time of the day.

ʔɨgapɨ (from ʔɨgagah, enters, goes in, applied here to the going down of the sun), sunset or late afternoon. This designates the same time of day as wɨsɨpapɨ.

Taviyɨʔakᵃitsi or tavapɨts yɨʔakᵃitsi, sun disappeared. Sunset or, more accurately, the moments immediately after sunset. (Here one would expect taviʔɨganguntsi, but instead of "the sun went in" this latter expression means "went in out of the sun": taviʔɨgangumpaani, I shall go in out of the sun, is the exact equivalent of havaʔɨgangumpaani, I shall enter the shade—although it sounds as if it should mean "I shall enter the sun.")

ʔOnosɨatugʷanu (tugʷanu, night; ʔono-, unexplained; -sɨa-, possibly as in tasɨantɨ, dawn), the first half of the night, the period between sunset and midnight.

Togʷᵃitugʷanu, half-night. Midnight.

Togʷᵃitugʷanu ʔugʷaavaʔanguntsi (togʷᵃitugʷanuʷa, objective of togʷᵃitugʷanu; the verb used is the same as in kaivʸay ʔugʷaavaʔanguntsi, went over the mountain), went over midnight, crossed half-night. This is the time just past the middle of the night.

Cɨnaʔarasɨapɨ (cɨnaʔavi, coyote), coyote dawn. False dawn. This is the time when the coyotes begin to howl.[6]

Tasɨatugʷanu, dawn-night. The period of darkness between false dawn and true dawn.

Tasɨapɨ or tasɨantɨ (tasɨagah, dawns), true dawn.

Navuniwatuʔʷatsi (na-, reflexive; puni-, to see; compare -tuʔʷatsi with ʔatatuʔʷatsi, young crow), became visible. This is the beginning of full daylight.

Directions

Directions are mentioned in pairs: north/south, east/west. Only four directions were named. For zenith the Chemehuevis simply say tugump*a*, sky, or tugumpay ʔivʸaʔan*a*, on top of this sky; nadir would be tɨvip*ɨ* ʔitcuk*ʷa*, under this earth.[7]

The north/south pair of directions derive their names from the earth and its contours:

Tantɨh (ta-, directional prefix; -ntɨh for -ntɨi-), north. Tantɨitu*ʷa* means to the north, towards the north. Tɨh, up (that is, up the hill, upstream) may loosely be used to indicate north. Thus one may say, tɨinguʔ*u*, go up! go north! But to be explicit one would have to say, tantɨinguʔ*u*, go north!

Tantɨvah (tɨvah for tɨvai-), south; tantɨvaitu*ʷa*, to the south, towards the south; tantɨvainguʔ*u*, go south! Tɨvah indicates downhill, downtrail, downstream and, loosely, south, but is not definitely directional without the prefix ta-.

East/west is the sacred or ceremonial pair of directions. In ancient times a sick person was always placed with his head towards the west; then the shaman danced first to the east, turned and danced to the west, and kept turning to east and west and back again all the while he was performing his healing ritual. The terms for this pair of directions derive from the sky and differ in form and usage from those indicating north and south.

Tasɨantɨ maruk*ʷ*atu*ʷa* (tasɨantɨ*a*, possessive or objective of tasɨantɨ, dawn; ma-, there or that inanimate visible; -ruk*ʷ*a-, under; -tu*ʷa*, towards) or tavapɨtsi maruk*ʷ*atu*ʷa*, towards under the dawn (roughly paraphrased, towards [the region] under the dawn) or towards under the sun. East. Neither phrase may be used without -tu*ʷa*, and neither may be employed as a verb. To give the command, go east! one has to say tasɨantɨ (or tavapɨtsi) maruk*ʷ*atu ʔuru*ʷ*akwaʔinguʔ*u*, go (travel) towards the east!

ʔɨgatu*ʷa* (ʔɨga-, root of ʔɨgagah, enters, with all its derivatives, applies to entering a house, to an animal entering its hole or den, and to the sun, moon, and stars going into their place beneath the earth; -tu^{w}a, towards, is indispensible to this directional term), towards the entrance, towards the entering (place). West. ʔɨgatu ʔuru^{w}akwaʔinguʔu, go west!

Meteorological Phenomena

Meteorological phenomena fascinated a people who roamed under the open sky in all seasons. The Chemehuevis appreciated the beauty and drama of these phenomena and described them in terms both accurate and poetic. The mythological Wolf and Coyote saga terminates in the great tale of "How Wolf and Coyote Went Away," which is replete with glorious weather symbolism forming the basis for many of the following terms.[8]

Various forms of precipitation are classified as follows:

ʔɨwarɨ, rain. The verb ʔɨwagah, raining, falls as rain, is used of the precipitation of rain, hail, or snow, but not of dew or frost.

Tatcannɨwarɨ (tatca, summer),[9] summer rain, describes rain accompanied by thunder and lightning. It is applied to this type of rainstorm occurring at any season of the year.

ʔAkaʔɨwarɨ (ʔaka, a minute, edible seed, also the plant which produces it, called in Spanish palmita), palmita rain. This term describes a very fine, mist-like rain.

Pahompa (pa-, water; the o in -ho- is not only nasalizing but pronounced as a strong and distinctly nasal vowel),[10] hail. When falling, hail is called pahonnɨwarɨ, hail-rain, and one may also say pahonnɨwagah, (it) hail-rains, (it) is raining hail. Pahoavitcɨ or pahompahavitcɨ (havitcɨ, lying, that which lies, from havig^{y}ah, lying) is said of hail lying on the ground.

Nɨvavɨ, snow. The terms for falling snow and snow lying on the ground are formed in the same way as those descriptive of hail: nɨvaʔɨwarɨ, falling snow, literally, snow-rain; nɨvaʔɨwagah, (it) is snowing; nɨvaavitcɨ, snow lying (on the ground).

Huʔunɨvavɨ (huʔu-, unexplained), frost. Of frost lying on the ground one says huʔunɨvaavitcɨ, but there is no word for the formation of frost.

Panook^{w}aiy$u$ (nook^{w}aiy$u$, is carried, passive of noog^{w}ah, carries on back), water is carried. Dew, the moisture that is borne on grass and shrubs.

Clouds, cloudy conditions, and vapor are spoken of as follows:

Pagɨn?nav$a$, cloud. So far as George Laird knew, various kinds of clouds were not named. The popular woman's name, Pagɨn?nasɨ?i, Cloud Flower, seems to convey a thought of the majestic beauty of cumulus clouds.

?ɨwapu?^{w}ik^{y}aiy$u$ (?ɨwa-, rain; pu?^{w}i-, possibly eye; -kaiy$u$, passive termination as in panook^{w}aiy$u$), is cloudy, and ?ɨwapu?^{w}aats$i$, became cloudy, became overcast, are expressions used of a cloudy sky. No derivation of pagɨn?nav$a$ is used in this connection.

Koso^{w}av$i$, steam, vapor. When vapor rises from the earth, one says tɨvip koso^{w}agah, the earth steams.

When there is a storm in the desert, thunder rumbles and crashes; beneath dark clouds the rain thrusts forward like an advancing army, accompanied by the glare and crackle of lightning; while away from the immediate center of the storm, rainbows arch over valleys or hang their transparent arcs of glory across rugged cliffs. This is the tremendous spectacle dramatized by the Chemehuevis in the great myth previously mentioned.[11] Many of the terms used to describe the phenomena associated with storms are warlike terms, recalling Wolf's and Coyote's final battle with the Bears.

Thunder is an act, not a thing nor a person, and is described by active verb forms:

Tɨmɨmɨ?agah, (it) thunders, is an onomatopoetic word applied to the deep, prolonged rumbling of thunder.

?ɨwar yagagah, rain cries, rain weeps, rain cries out (as if in grief or pain), describes the sharp crack or crash of thunder.

The word for a lightning flash, or perhaps for any sudden flash of light, is panapɨ—as in the proper name, ?Aapanapɨ, White Clay Lightning Flash. The root pana- occurs in pananumpɨ, lamp, torch, and in panakaiy$u$, has been lit up or illuminated, which would be said of a room in which a lamp had just been lit. There are several terms to describe various types of lightning:

Panayɨmpɨ?ig^{y}ah, light vibrates, light is vibrating, is used of

the repeated glow of lightning in the sky when the lightning flash itself is not seen. This is said of heat lightning.
Panatcɨmpɨʔigʸah indicates a shade of difference. Both
yɨmpɨʔigʸah and tcɨmpɨʔigʸah describe a vibrating movement of light, but the latter implies more vigor and
brightness.

ʔɨwar tonagah, rain thrusts, rain stabs, and ʔɨwar panatonagah, rain light-thrusts, are expressions used when bolts
of lightning are seen repeatedly; ʔɨwar tonatsɨ and ʔɨwar
panatonatsɨ indicate single lightning flashes. Where lightning has struck and melted the sand, fragments of a
white, opaque, glassy substance (described by George
Laird as somewhat resembling gypsum, but very hard)
may be found. The Chemehuevis believed that this had
broken off the lightning bolt—that it was, as it were, the
point of the lance with which the rain thrust. This substance is called tutupɨ. A man named Samikwitutsɨ
found a piece of it in a mesquite tree which lightning
had split. It is very dangerous to carry tutupɨ on one's
person, for it attracts lightning and could cause its possessor to be struck.

The colors of the rainbow are not named in any particular
order, or at least they were not so listed in former times. The
rainbow is described as poʔokʷatɨ, variegated, streaked, but the
indigo/violet portion of the spectrum seems to have exerted the
strongest claim upon the Chemehuevi imagination. Curiously, pa-
roogʷaatsiwɨ, water-purple, is applied both to an indigo-hued rainstorm and to the bright and glorious colors of the rainbow. The
rainbow is described as paroogʷaatsiwɨʔikʸaiyu, water-purple has
been streaked (across the sky), and one of its names is paroogʷaa-
wɨnɨrɨ, water-purple standing. The primary and secondary rainbows are distinguished by names derived from the great myth:

Tɨvatsi haagaruʔʷagaipɨ (Tɨvatsiʸa, Wolf's; haagaruʔʷapɨ,
clothing; -gaipɨ, former, worn-out, cast-off or discarded),
Wolf's former clothing, and Tɨvatsi naroʔogʷaipɨ, Wolf's
former shirt, are terms designating the primary rainbow.
The word naroʔo, shirt, seems also to be applicable to
armor that protects literally, like the "stone shirts" of
Gila Monster and Turtle mentioned in the myth "How

Coyote Went to War Against Gila Monster," or magically, like the shirt worn by the Tɨɨranɨwɨ chief.[12]

Cɨnawavi haagaruʔʷagaipɨ (Cɨnawaviʸa, Mythic Coyote's), Mythic Coyote's former clothes, and Cɨnawavi naroʔo-gʷaipɨ, are names for the secondary rainbow (in the myth, it was the marvelous brilliance of his Brother's warclothes which provoked Coyote's jealousy).

Wind is called nɨarɨ; nɨagah, wind blows, is used only of the wind and is never interchangeable with pukʷigʸah, blows (with the mouth of a bellows). In the myth "How Dove's Son Escaped from Wind Woman," the wind is personified as Nɨarɨmamauʔu, who represents all that is lustful, possessive, and insatiable in woman. Other terms for the movement of the air are:

Paɨnarɨ, breeze. This is said of a breeze so gentle as to be barely perceptible; paɨnagah, the breeze blows gently.

Hukunɨarɨ (hukumpa, dust), dust wind; hukunɨagah, the dust wind is blowing (said of a sand storm).

Turunniʔʸarɨ, whirlwind. Whirlwinds were supposed to be animated by "devils," that is, by ʔinɨpiwɨ, a minor order of demons.[13]

Colors

Colors were not associated with points of the compass. The only color association which George Laird mentioned was the connection of various colors of corn with the clans of the dead. In this context it is worth noting that the root of at least one Chemehuevi color name, sagwa-, blue or green, is virtually identical with the Tewa word for this color.[14] This implies a rather long, if tenuous, contact with peoples who had cultivated corn much longer than the Chemehuevis, and to whom it was generally more sacred.

In form, Chemehuevi color names are verbal derivatives. The verb -kagah (-gagah, ngkagah) means is a certain color and does not occur independently. The substantive derivative in -rɨ, usually given as the equivalent for the color name in English, means being such a color or that which is such a color. Roots are prepounded with adjectival force. The following are the colors recalled by George Laird:

Sagwagarɨ, blue or green; sagwagagah, is blue or green, being blue or green. This is the color of turquoise. The root of the word is sagwa-.

ʔAngkarɨ (ʔangkagah,[15] ʔangka-), red.

Tosagarɨ (tosagagah, tosa-), white.

Tupagarɨ, black; tupagagah, is black. In compounds the root appears variously as tupa-, tuu-, and tu-, sometimes with o substituted for u. Dark (as the night is dark) is tupunuᵂantɨ.

Toogᵂaagarɨ (too-, black), purple; toogᵂaagah (compare ʔangkagah, being red), is purple; root toogᵂa-. This describes a purple flower and also, as noted above, appears in some of the words applied to the rainbow.

Torosakarɨ (to-, black; -rosa-, white, but here followed by k, instead of g as in tosagarɨ), gray, literally, black-white; torosakagah, is gray; root torosa-.

Haungkarɨ (haungkagah, hau-), gray, bone-gray. This describes the color of an old bone which has bleached gray rather than white. It was first mentioned in connection with the placename Hauwawangkɨgarɨ, Bone-Gray Peaks, the home of the shamans' spirit-animal familiars.

Tupasiʸakarɨ (tupa-, black; -siʸa-, an element appearing in color names to indicate a light or pale shade), brown, literally, light black, but never applied to a grayish color; tupasiʸakagah, is brown; root tupasiʸa-.

Hɨvɨngkarɨ (hɨvɨngkagah, hɨvɨ-), bright yellow. This would be said of a bright yellow flower or the yolk of an egg.

ʔOᵂakarɨ (ʔoᵂakagah, ʔoᵂa-; compare ʔoᵂavɨ, rock salt), cream-colored, buff. This word is used to describe the skin color of a white person who is rather fair but not florid; such a person would be called ʔoᵂakarɨmɨ.

ʔOᵂasiʸakarɨ (ʔoᵂasiʸakagah, ʔoᵂasiʸa-), light yellow, pale yellow. This word never indicates a paler buff than ʔoᵂakarɨ but always carries the idea of a yellowish tinge, lighter than hɨvɨngkarɨ. Compare ʔoᵂasiʸapɨ, the stone which furnishes coloring for the designs on pottery.[16]

ʔAngkasiʸakarɨ (ʔangkasiʸakagah, ʔangkasiʸa-), pink, literally, light red.

Poʔokᵂatɨ (from poʔokᵂaiyu, is marked or streaked, has been written upon, which is related to poʔogᵂah, marks [transitive]; poʔo- does not appear as a descriptive prepound), variegated (variegated corn, for example), piebald, streaked, or striped.[17] Rocks which bear markings or carvings are called tutuguuvoꞎopɨ, marked by tutuguuviwɨ, animal familiars.

Taste, Flavor, or Texture

Taste, flavor, or texture (the "feel" of a substance in the mouth) is expressed by the verb -kamagah (-gamagah), tastes (intransitive), has flavor, preceded by the word which describes the specific taste. The root kama- occurs initially only in the phrases:

Kamaiyɨraꞎᵃukᵂa (literally, does it taste?), does it taste salty? is it salty enough? is it properly seasoned with salt?

Kamasɨꞎigʸah, it is too salty. This might be said of over-salted beans or of sea water.

Simply to state "it is salty" one has to say:

ꞎOᵂasopiʸagamagah. This incorporates both the word for rock salt (ꞎoᵂavɨ) and for salt (ꞎasompɨ or ꞎasompɨ).

Similar expressions are:

Pihʸagamagah (pihʸavɨ, sweet substance, such as sugar, syrup, or honey), tastes sweet; pihʸagamayɨraꞎᵃukᵂa, is it sweet enough?

Kutusikʸamagah (ku-, with fire; compare kutsikʸigʸah, burns [transitive] —food or trash, for example; kutuutsigʸah, becomes hot from fire; kutuutsitcɨ, that which has been heated by the fire), has a burnt taste.

Mohᵂagamagah (muhᵂavɨ, or mohᵂavɨ, bitter substance—in the white man's world, quinine, for instance; but muhᵂaratɨ, bitter), tastes bitter.

Paꞎigʸamagah (pagɨɨtsɨ, fish; in this derivative both g and ts are omitted, forming a rare triphthong), has a fishy taste. To the Chemehuevis this was not pleasant.

Tumpigʸamagah (tumpitcɨ, that which is puckery, Spanish *agaroso*), has a puckery taste. This applies to certain screw mesquite beans, also to the twigs, leaves, and bark of the small species of willow known as kanavɨ.

Wikʸamagah (compare wiwavɨ, oil or grease), has an oily, greasy taste.

Wikʸigʸamagah (wikʸivɨ, jellied substance, such as meat broth which has cooled and jelled), has a jelly-like "taste" or texture in the mouth. This would now be said of okra or tapioca, formerly of *chia*[18] or manav*i* (literally, thorn), the new branch just budded out from a cholla cactus when cooked for food.

Plants

Plants furnished food, medicine, and building material. Words designating trees and various types of vegetation, plants, and plant parts and derivatives are inanimate in form and therefore the same in singular and plural. Plants were not as a rule personified, although in the story "How Cottontail Rabbit Conquered the Sun" the bushes and shrubs replied to questions; and, as previously remarked, when taking the "east root" of the jimson weed one addressed the plant as "old woman."

Naturally the Chemehuevis were most familiar with the plant life of high and low deserts, but these wide-ranging people were also well-acquainted with whatever grew in the mountains and foothills, around streams and waterholes, and in the River floodplain.

The word kukwap*i* is a very loose term covering everything from a supply of firewood (or, in modern times, lumber) to a stand of timber; kukwagant*i*, having wood, could mean a person who has wood or a forested mountain range. In the heyday of the hunters, Chemehuevis must have had names for various species of conifers and oaks, but in what remains of the material furnished by George Laird I find only the name for pine nut and for one large species of pine tree—no word at all for oak or acorn, though acorns were gathered for food when the Chemehuevis travelled into oak tree country.

Another generalized term is mahav*i*, brush, also translated as bush when applied to a single plant. Brush was the principal building material for a people who spent most of their time on the move, who had neither the tools nor the inclination to construct permanent dwellings or houses of assembly. From the materials at hand, the Chemehuevis built four types of houses. The word for house is kan*i*, and kan*i* also means the nest of a bird.

The construction and purpose of the takagan*i* or havagan*i*, flat house or shade house, have already been described in connection with the Mourning Ceremony.[19]

The tcuupik^yan*i* (tcup*i*, anything brought to a point, such as a bunch of grass tied together at one end), the pointed "wigwam" type of house, was the easiest and quickest to erect because the poles which supported it were not driven into the ground but just leaned together at the top. These poles could be quickly cut from willows (sagah) or cottonwoods (soovimp*i*), if either of these trees was available. The tcuupik^{y}an*i* was thatched with brush with the butt ends up so that it would shed water. One pictures a house of this sort being built quickly by a family on the move, for protection against a threatened rainstorm. It should be emphasized that, although the Chemehuevis made much use of this pointed frame, they never covered it with skins, only brush.

The samarók^{wa}*i* or samarók^{wa}ik^{y}an*i* was more carefully constructed, roomier, and altogether more suitable for a shelter intended to last for weeks or even months. Samarók^{wa}*i* is an obvious loanword, and quite possibly the whole concept was originally borrowed from the Walapais or Apaches, both of whom had houses of this type. To make this house, willow saplings were cut down and driven into the earth in a circle, then opposite saplings were twisted together at the top. If the wild grapevine (ʔiyaa-vimp*i*) was available, it came in very handy, probably to tie the saplings together. A samarók^{wa}*i* was about six feet high, not too high for a person to reach up and tie the saplings. It might be thatched with any kind of brush, but sage (murunav*i* or si*ʔ*ap*i*) and arrowweed (sawap*i*) were preferred.[20]

Brush was also essential to the construction of the earth house, tivik^{y}an*i*.[21] To build this house, George Laird said, they first put up four posts. I am inclined to think that he meant four posts to each side, for he went on to say that the next step was to put a layer of brush on each side of the posts and finally to fill in between the two thatched walls with earth. The front wall of such a house would be about three feet thick. These houses were not built communally or for communal use. They were built for old people[22] or by families with the firm intention of wintering in one locality who wanted a little more comfort than that afforded by a brush hut.

It is not to be assumed that the terms kukwap*i* and mahav*i* correspond with any degree of accuracy to the white man's categories of "trees" and "shrubs." A group of large old willows would probably be kukwap*i*, and that is certainly what the wood obtained from them would be called; but a thicket of young willows might be referred to as mahav*i*. Each tree, shrub, bush, or other plant was individually named. Sometimes the name of a plant was identical with the fruit, seed, or other food which it produced, sometimes closely related, sometimes entirely different. My material is far too fragmentary to attempt anything as elaborate as a section on ethnobotany; yet the tree and plant names and other botanical terms included in the following list throw considerable light on the relationship of the Chemehuevis to the growing things found within their environment—or rather within the various environments through which they formerly ranged:

Yuvimp*i*, a large but unidentified species of pine.

Soovimp*i*, cottonwood. Poles from cottonwood trees were used in house construction.

Sagah, willow. This is the species of willow which furnished the framework of the samarók^{wa}ik^{y}an*i*, also for the konoh,[23] cradleboard, and was used to make the sinew-backed hunting bow.

Kanav*i*, the small species of willow called in Spanish *saucillo*. Its twigs, leaves, and bark were notable for their astringent or "puckery" quality. Willow (probably of both species) supplied the basic material for basketry. Anything used for weaving or prepared for weaving is s*i*h*i*v*i*. The basketry hats worn by women were called s*i*h*i*gaitcoxo, woven mountain hats. These were the feminine counterparts of the kaitcoxo worn by men, fashioned of buckskin and ornamented with quail crests. I do not know if the women's s*i*h*i*gaitcoxo were also ornamented with feathers, but in view of the use of feathers in basketry and of the tradition of feathered capes it is not unlikely.

ʔAaparik^{y}*i*, ironwood.

ʔAtsitak^{a}*i*, a species of *palo verde*.

ʔOpimp*i*, mesquite. The seed (not the entire bean) of the mesquite is called kak*i*mp*i*, and the same name is applied to the hard, flattish seed characteristic of a certain kind of *palo verde*. To prepare them for eating, mesquite beans were parched (kammagah, parches) by shaking them in a basket with hot coals. Many other edible seeds were treated in this way.

Kwiyarampɨ, screw mesquite. The screw mesquite bean or fruit of the kwiyarampɨ is called kwiyara.

ʔɨnɨpimahavɨ, "devil bush." Smoketree. It will be remembered that ʔɨnɨpɨ is a demon of the sort that animates whirlwinds, which children are encouraged to "kill" with sticks or clubs.

Murunavɨ, a species of sage.

Sɨʔapɨ, another kind of sage. Both murunavɨ and sɨʔapɨ furnished good material for thatching houses; possibly the seed of both species was edible, but I do not think that either is the plant called *chia* in Spanish.

Sawapɨ, arrowweed. This was desirable thatching material and was also used in making arrows.[24]

Pagampɨ, carrizo. This reed was used to make the shafts of arrows. According to George Laird, reeds were straightened by use of an arrow straightening stone, a stone with a carefully shaped groove. This stone was heated in the fire, then the reeds were drawn one at a time through the groove.

Saimpivɨ, tule. Four-holed flutes tuned with a strip of buckskin were made from tule.

Sɨʔanupɨ, described only as "a kind of bush."

Tavaapɨ, a bush mentioned in connection with sɨʔanupɨ. It was out of one or the other of these bushes that the gifted ʔOomposɨ, as we have already seen, could create the semblance of a mountain sheep.

Yatampɨ, creosote bush, commonly called greasewood. This was and is one of the great medicinal plants of the Chemehuevis. It is classified as navuᵂaganumpɨ, medicine, literally, self-curing material—that is, a substance which ordinary folk apply to themselves or to others. But the genuine art of healing belongs to the shaman and involves the use of other than material means.

ʔAka, the plant known in Spanish as *palmita*. This plant bears delicious edible seed, also called ʔaka, so tiny that their name was appropriated to describe a barely perceptible mist: ʔakaʔɨwarɨ, *palmita* rain.

ʔIyaavimpɨ, the wild grape vine, useful in house construction. The grapes which it bears are called ʔiyaavɨ.

Three varieties of plant, which George Laird always spoke of as "three kinds of yucca," bear the fruit called tcɨmpɨ, which he translated as yucca date. Tcɨmpɨ were an important food item, and journeys were made so that the women could gather them when ripe. They were sometimes roasted. The three plants which bear yucca dates are:

ʔUuvimpɨ.[25]

Kaayuvimpɨ. Compare kaiv^ya, mountain, and kaampɨ, a chain of low-lying hills.[26]

Sovarampɨ. The possible etymology is interesting. Soovarantɨ signifies "mean" in the sense of vicious or dangerous and would be said of a vicious dog. This was no doubt the word used to describe the mythological characters, Yucca Date Worm Girls, in the story "How Bat Killed Rattlesnake."[27] Besides their fruit, yucca plants furnished fiber for string and for weaving. Sometimes women's aprons were made of the material woven from this fiber, and it furnished the base for the exquisite feathered capes which are now scarcely a memory.

Other important plants known to the Chemehuevis are:

Nantapɨ, mescal plant. The word nanta is given as meaning mescal, probably referring to the edible portions. The sharp points were cut off, and the remainder of the plant was roasted. Then the leaves were pulled off one by one, and it was eaten like a giant artichoke, the tough and stringy parts being discarded. The heart (called pik^yovi or nantapik^yovi) was either eaten at once or pounded out with a pestle to form a cake several feet in circumference. When dried, it is flexible but very tough. That is why the Chemehuevis say that a man taking a bite off a plug of tobacco appears to be eating nantawɨpɨapɨ. (A slab of dried meat similarly prepared for storage is called tuku^wawɨpɨapɨ).

Pagoosovɨ, *guatamote* plant.

Monompɨ, bunchgrass, Spanish *zacaton*.

Momompɨ, jimson weed. The root of this plant produced visions and hallucinations.[28]

Tcupani, the herb called in Spanish *yerba del manso*.

Máskwawi (not a native Chemehuevi word), a plant with

slender, juicy, green leaves, bright pinkish-lavender flowers, and large black seeds. The seeds were probably edible, and the plant itself was used for greens.

Tu?u, Indian asparagus. This also, I believe, is edible.

Hu?upɨ, squawberries. I do not know whether this applies to the berries only or whether it also means the bush that bears them. Squawberries ripen early in the spring.

Tɨvah, pine nuts. Again, I do not know whether this is also the term for piñon tree.

?Antsɨ, an edible seed described only as "grass seed." Perhaps ?antsɨ is the name both of a species of grass and its seed. Compare ?akɑ.

Three additional botanical terms are:

Manavɨ, thorn. This is also the term for the new branch just budding out from the cholla;[29] this is edible and has a jelly-like texture when cooked.

Sɨ?ipɨ, flower.

Tɨnavɨ, root. This is said of a single root which does not have branches or of a single prong or branch of a root; the duplicated form, tɨrɨnavɨ, means a pronged root, a root with branches.

Among the cultivated plants which George Laird frequently mentioned by their Chemehuevi names are:

?Atsitɑ, wheat.

Murih, beans.

Hawivɨ, corn.

Animals

Animals are regarded by the Chemehuevis in a way which I find particularly congenial. This attitude is not sentimental, although it is both interested and respectful. Animals of every sort are fellow creatures, not as in the Judeo-Christian culture inferior beings created for man's pleasure and subject to man's whims—co-existence rather than dominion would express the Chemehuevi concept. In aboriginal times everything edible (with the exception of fish, as noted before) was eaten, with gusto and without regret; but wanton cruelty and wanton destruction were, I firmly believe, completely foreign to the thought of the People. It is to be remembered that the pre-human Immortals (the gods, if you will) were Animals Who Were People. These Forerunners, these Ancient Ones whose bodies shimmered as it were between animal and human forms, these denizens of the elder dream-world, have long since taken their final departure; yet they remain as the visible animals of this everyday world. Cinawav*i*, Mythic Coyote, super-trickster and pattern-setter for mankind, is not cina*?*av*i*, raiding fields and howling on the hills before dawn—and yet, in a certain mystical sense, he is. This is true of every animal, from the largest mammal to the smallest insect. Therefore there are no "varmints" or "pests." When George Laird first went on a picnic with my family, they were amazed if not horrified by his treatment of the ants. He searched around the place where we intended to eat our lunch, located each ant hill, and scattered crumbs close to it so that the ants could share our feast without molesting us. To my parents this represented an utterly alien mode of thought.

In the following list of animal names, plurals are given where I am sure of them. In Chemehuevi as George Laird spoke it, many if not all names for animals had dual and triplural forms, as well as the plural forms indicating two or more. I believe only these simple plurals remain in modern Chemehuevi, and they are all that I have attempted to show. I have included in the list a few names supplied, or re-supplied, by Chemehuevis now living.

Some of the mammals known to the Chemehuevis are:

Tivats*i* (plural tivatsiw*i*), wolf.

Cina*?*av*i* (plural cina*?*aviw*i*), coyote. The coyote is especially close to the Chemehuevi heart. To this day people regard him with affection and like to hear his voice. These two great predators, Wolf and Coyote, in their pre-human phase are perhaps the most important characters in Chemehuevi mythology, fit pattern-setters for the bold and skillful hunters and warriors of aboriginal times. Mythic Wolf, the omniscient, powerful, and supposedly elder brother of Mythic Coyote, was known simply as Tivats*i*, but Mythic Coyote, as has already been remarked several times, had his own distinctive name, Cinawav*i*, differing in this respect from most of the other animals who were formerly people. Wolves were more prevalent in the northern ranges of the Chemehuevis and coyotes in the southern; and in the great culminating myth of the Wolf and Coyote saga[30] it is said that Wolf "went north," and Coyote followed far behind. The esteem in which coyotes are held evidently did not prevent them from having been occasionally eaten in times of great hunger, for it is said that the loin of a coyote tastes exactly like the loin of a mountain sheep.

Yɨpatsɨ (plural yɨpatsiwɨ), fox, probably specifically the California gray fox. Tantɨvaiyɨpatsɨ, Southern Fox, is a popular mythological hero, an inveterate traveller (like all Southern Chemehuevis), visiting relatives north and south and having adventures along the way. I cannot say whether there was a species of fox called "southern fox" or whether, like cɨnawavɨ, tantɨvaiyɨpatsɨ was the exclusive name of a mythic character.

Pungkutsɨ[31] (plural pungkutsiwɨ), dog, pet. The dog was the only animal domesticated by the Chemehuevis. In the material furnished by George Laird there were no myths about the dog, but I am told that there is a story still extant about the time when the Dogs could talk. The People take great pride in their dogs and treat them virtually as members of the family.

Tuku, wildcat.

Tukumumuuntsɨ (plural tukumumuuntsiwɨ), mountain lion. The deep, rumbling sound of the latter part of this word suggests that it may be onomatopoetic. Tukumumuuntsɨ is another one of the great predators who was present with Ocean Woman at the time of the creation of the earth, but has no distinctive mythological name. All the ferae, together with flesh-eating birds such as the hawk, are classed as tukuʷarɨkawagamɨ (singular tukuʷarɨkawagantɨ), flesh-eaters, but snakes are not included in this category.

Tukupukutsɨ (plural tukupukutsiwɨ), domestic cat, literally, pet wildcat. This is the old name for the housecat; nowadays people say puusɨ, from English pussy.

Tɨhiya[32] (plural tɨhiyawɨ), deer.

Naxa (plural nagawɨ), mountain sheep, bighorn. The word for lamb is mɨntcatsɨ, and there was probably also a separate term for fawn, although I do not have it on record. The mountain sheep and the deer were the big game animals.[33] They were the animals most important to the Chemehuevi life-style as it had evolved prior to the coming of the white man. Sometime in the remote past of this people, improved hunting skills and improved weaponry brought these marvelous beasts increasingly within the range of the ordinary hunter. Then sinew became plentifully available to back the hunting bows; then there was buckskin for winter clothing, storage bags, and numerous other purposes, and meat in sufficient quantity to dry and store. Finally some ingenious member of the hunting aristocracy must have noticed that the spreading antlers of the mule deer were of the right size, shape, and resilience to make a yet more powerful bow adapted to the use of warriors.[34] From these vast improvements in daily life and tribal status sprang a sense of mystical identification with the animals involved, leading to the development of the principal hereditary songs,[35] new enrichment of mythological material, and the concept of the deer and the mountain sheep as powerful animal familiars, shamans' helpers, although they had not been among those who "carried the poro" in their pre-human incarnation.

Wangkasi (plural wangkasiwi), cow; from Spanish vaca, probably by way of some other language. This word is linguistically interesting because of the substitution of w instead of p for the original initial v.

Kami (plural kamiwi), jackrabbit, hare; kamu^waantsi, young jackrabbit.

Tavutsi (plural tavutsiwi), cottontail rabbit; tavo^waatsi, young cottontail rabbit. The two species are considered to be very closely related. They are the small game animals. In the times of the great hunters they ranked next to the big game animals, the deer and the mountain sheep; and in very primitive times they must have been of paramount importance to survival. Always they have provided food, and blankets made from their skins have furnished protection from the cold. The Chemehuevis had special words to describe their habits. For example, karɨgah means sitting as a person sits, but mug^wig^yarɨgah, sitting as a rabbit sits. It is said that each rabbit (jackrabbit or cottontail) has a certain place where he sits under a bush. This is called mug^wig^yarɨtɨah, rabbit sitting place, or, more briefly, mug^wivɨ. Or one may be specific and say, for instance, kamɨmug^wig^yarɨtɨah, jackrabbit sitting place. In the summer the rabbit goes into his hole, called (in the case of the jackrabbit) kamɨtaroso. The element mug^wi- suggests that there may have been a general term (possibly mug^wivi or mug^witsi) inclusive of both species, just as witciʔitsi is applied to a bird of any one of several small species. Both Kamɨ and Tavutsi have mythological roles. In what is probably, in view of the racial memory upon which it is based, the most ancient Chemehuevi myth, the characters are Cottontail Rabbit, two orphans named Young Jackrabbit and Young Cottontail Rabbit, Immortal Water, Immortal Yucca Date, Sun, Moon, and the bushes of the desert.[36]

Kaatsi (plural kaatsiwɨ), rat.

Puʔ^wintcatsi (plural puʔ^wintcatsiwɨ), mouse.

Tavaʔatsi (plural tavaʔatsiwɨ), desert chipmunk, antelope groundsquirrel.

Sɨpiiya (plural sɨpiiyawɨ), whistling squirrel.[37]

Paatsatsi, bat. Bat has a prominent role in mythology and is also extremely important as a shaman's familiar, possessing and conferring power to cause extreme cold and therefore to heal burns.

Papawa (plural papawawɨ), bear. In pre-human times Bear was the aunt (paha, father's sister—and yet they had no father!) of Wolf and Coyote, and it was with the Bear People that they fought their last great war; there are also placenames which provide evidence of other myths involving a bear. As a shaman's familiar, the bear confers great strength. And Chemehuevis, encountering a bear while travelling, are privileged to address him as niwaani, my friend.

Huna (plural hunawɨ), badger.[38] In mythological times, the Badgers were allies and perhaps relatives of the Bears.

Yamasah (plural yamasaawɨ), raccoon.

Poniya (plural poniyawɨ), skunk. There was, it will be recalled, a Skunk Song, now extinct, which was either an
hereditary hunting group song or an hereditary shaman's song.

The generic name for all small, twittering, chirping birds is the
onomatopoetic word witciʔitsɨ (plural witciʔitsiwɨ). This name is
applied to birds of several differently named species, and perhaps
sometimes loosely to all land birds except the flesh-eaters, such as
buzzards, hawks, large owls, and eagles. It has been previously
remarked that the Salt Song (as George Laird knew it) chronicled
the travels of a large company of Birds and their selection of
various localities in the valley of the Colorado River.[39] Among the
many birds known by name to the Chemehuevis are:

ʔAnga (plural ʔangawɨ), bluejay. In the myths Bluejay was
a northern cousin of Southern Fox.

ʔAtapɨtsɨ (plural ʔatapɨtsiwɨ), crow; ʔatatuʔᵂatsɨ, young
crow. Like several other bird names, this terminates in
-pɨtsɨ, denoting respect or affection.

Kakara or kakarɨ (or possibly kakariʔ), quail. The plural
form does not occur in my original notes. George Laird
gave Kakarahuvᵂiyavɨ, Quail Song, but Kakarɨnarɨnapɨ,
Quail Used to Run (placename). In 1969 Gertrude
Hanks Leivas approved the plural form kakarawɨ (possibly because she was too polite to contradict me), but
her sister, Mary Hanks Molino, gave kakarɨmɨ. Wendell
Goodman, Sr. gave kakarɨmɨ but also used the phrase
kakariʸagantɨ, being quail, there are quail. The Chemehuevis have a great feeling for the quail, almost esteem-
ing it as a tribal symbol. It will be remembered that the
highly prized kaitcoxo, mountain hat, was trimmed with
rows of quail crests.

Hiʸovi (plural hiʸoviwɨ), dove, mourning dove. Doves figure
prominently in the mythology.

Maumáupɨtsɨ, nighthawk.[40]

Kwanantsitsɨ, red-tailed hawk. In one myth Kwanantsitsɨ is
a mighty hunter and shaman; in another his feathers,
attached to an arrow which Coyote shoots at the sky,
bring the false dawn.

Mɨngi, eagle. The eagle does not appear as a "person" in

the collection of myths included in this volume. It was a very sacred bird to the Chemehuevis. Its feathers were not used for "war bonnets" (which the Chemehuevis did not use) or ornaments, or even as part of a shaman's regalia. As described in Chapter II, whole skins of eagles, cured with the feathers, and also eagle feathers braided onto a sort of wand, were necessary adjuncts to a Cry or Mourning Ceremony.

Muhuumpɨtsi, owl species, the kind of owl which has what white people refer to as "horns" and the Chemehuevis call "ears."

Tavamuhuumpɨtsi, "day owl," owl species.

Paɨnʔnagwᵃitsi, burrowing owl. This is the owl that shares abandoned burrows with the rattlesnake, and the Chemehuevis therefore say the rattlesnake is its alter-ego. The sound that he makes is parangkwingkwiʔi, parangkwingkiʔi. It was due to this bird's persistence in holding up his small, three-toed foot that the seasons are three months long instead of four.

Povisatsi (plural povisatsiwɨ), a species of small bird resembling the kind known as "knee pounder."

Tangatcokotsi, knee pounder, small bird species.[41]

Wɨnʔnamakasaamaʔɨpɨtsi (also occurs in my notes as wɨnʔnamakasaamaʔapɨtsi), a bird, probably a small bird, identified in the myth "How Coyote Went to War Against Gila Monster" as the "grandmother" of Dove Boys. The etymology of the word (wɨnʔnapi, flint; makatcatsi, horned toad) suggests that this might also be the Bird who tied a wreath of flint around the head of Horned Toad when they paid a visit to the Giants.[42]

Yuʔuravatsi, a species of small bird identified in the myth "How Coyote Went to War Against Gila Monster" as the "other grandmother" of Dove Boys.

Wiwʔwiyatsi, a small brown bird, about the size of the bird called in Spanish la viejita.

Yampa, mockingbird.

Wiku or wikumpɨtsi, buzzard. George Laird used both forms, but I think the one in which -pɨtsi appears is preferred when occurring independently.

Pawanantsɨ, seagull—the bird whose feathers on Coyote's arrow brought the true dawn.[43]

Tcɨxa (plural tcɨgawɨ), duck.

Kwaroyaawɨ, chicken. Probably onomatopoetic, perhaps influenced somewhat by Spanish *gallo*.

Reptiles are classed as tɨɨravatcɨ, of the desert. They were therefore important to the Chemehuevis as food and also in other, more mystical ways. The following list is far from complete and is especially lacking in names for the various species of lizards. All reptiles named had prominent mythological roles.

ʔAya (plural ʔayawɨ), land turtle, tortoise. This reptile was desirable for food, but it also had a peculiar aura of sacredness. It was and is to this day symbolic of the spirit of the People. "A Chemehuevi's heart is tough, like the turtle's." This "tough-heartedness" is equated with the will and the ability to endure and to survive.

ʔɨtcivi (probable plural ʔɨtciviwɨ), Gila monster.[44]

Makatcatsɨ, horned toad.

Mugwiᵞa (probable plural mugwiyawɨ), lizard species called in Spanish *guico* (probably the gecko).

Tcagwara (plural tcagwarawɨ), chuckwalla,[45] a local variety of lizard. Its importance as a source of food is suggested by its mention in one myth as the companion of the mountain sheep and the deer.

Kwiyatsɨ (plural kwiyatsiwɨ), diamond-backed rattlesnake. George Laird indicated that there was a still larger species of rattlesnake, called in Mohave *haikwiira*, Chemehuevi name unknown.[46]

Tannakaitsɨ (plural tannakaitsiwɨ), sidewinder. He "sidewinds" when he travels on top of the ground, but when he "goes under the scum of the earth" his little "horns" can be seen going along in a straight line. He sleeps coiled up under the earth.

Nɨntɨnavi (plural nɨntɨnaviwɨ), red racer.

Along the banks of the watercourses were frogs, and various species of fish abounded in the Colorado River and its tributaries. The Chemehuevi word for frog is wagata, and for fish, pagɨɨtsɨ (pa-indicating the association with water). The Chemehuevis were strong swimmers;[47] in aboriginal times, as now, they bathed, played, and cooled themselves in the River. They must have been familiar with different kinds of fish, but George Laird supplied only the general term. Neither frog nor fish appears in their mythology,[48] at least not in the stories included in this volume.

On the other hand, all the insects had their names and were remembered as Immortal People in the Time When the Earth Was Young. It is charming to observe the mythological roles assigned to them, regardless of their size in this present era. Louse is the Chemehuevi Eve, consort of Coyote; Coyote with the greatest of ease turns himself into a water spider and back again; Sandbar Fly is nurse to Dove's infant son; and many Insects (in their anthropic phase) appear as fearsome warriors. The following is a partial list:

Muupitsi (plural muupitsiwɨ—the singular form occurs occasionally in my notes as mupitsi, which would indicate that the second syllable was sometimes accented), fly.

ʔAtarakamuupitsi (ʔotarakah, sandbar; but in this insect name the initial vowel is a and the last a is short), sandbar fly. This is a rather large fly with a tapering abdomen, seen hovering over sandbars in the River. Its peculiar shape is accounted for in the myth "How Dove's Son Escaped from Wind Woman."[49]

Pipita (plural pipitawɨ), horsefly.[50]

Muhuavi (plural muhuavimɨ), mosquito.

Hokosoʔʷavi, spider; perhaps this word was applied to several species.

Pahokosoʔʷavi, water spider. This insect carries its eggs in a sac, commemorating the manner in which Coyote brought Louse's eggs from the island to the mainland.[51]

Hukʷampi, black widow spider. I do not know whether the prominent mythological character Tavahukʷampi, Sun Spider,[52] is represented on earth today by a separate species or whether Tavahukʷampi is another rare mythological proper name. In his partially human form, Sun Spider is described as ʔangkasiʸakɨkɨpoʷakaiyu, having pink (light red) gaps between his teeth; when he let his grandson, Wildcat, down to earth, Wildcat looked up and saw himself descending from a red hole,[53] suggesting the red marking on the underside of the black widow. In another myth, "How Coyote Went to War Against

Gila Monster," Sun Spider is portrayed as the guardian
of the sky-hole.

Pooʔʷaviʔ, louse. In mythic times Louse was the woman
with the toothed vagina who became the mother of
mankind; in later times Pooʔʷavi also occurs as a man's
name.[54]

ʔAatakapitsi, grasshopper. In the myth "How Yucca Date
Worm Girls Went to Look for a Husband" Grasshopper
is sometimes an old man, sometimes a giant, sometimes
a swarm of small grasshoppers.

Tsasiyavi, large red ant. In what survives of my manuscript,
this occurs only in the phrase ʔavaʔatsasiyavi, many ants.

ʔAngavi (plural ʔangavimɨ), small red ant.[55]

Nanapaʔagaipuʔʷitsi, four-eyed insect, unidentified insect
species. The four-eyed insect is an actual insect. Since
its name was given by Wendell Goodman, Sr. as nanapuʔi, it is possible that Nanapaʔagaipuʔʷitsi is another of
those rare mythological proper names. Nanapaʔagaipuʔʷitsi was the anthropomorphic guard of one of the
watering places in the myth "How Coyote Went to War
Against Gila Monster," and it may be that the element
-paʔagai- refers to his function as guardian of the waters.

- ▦ - ▦ -

We have now looked briefly at the world with which the Chemehuevis were one, and we have looked, in part at least, through
the eyes of a Chemehuevi. The ancient words used to describe
things and phenomena, plants and animals, seem so peculiarly appropriate that we wonder how any other terms could be applied. I
think we may now realize that no matter how impoverished the
white man may consider this environment, to the People who
belonged there it was rich in resources and richer still in pleasures.

CHAPTER V

PLACES, TRAILS, AND TRIBES

S OME Chemehuevi placenames[1] were borrowed from foreign languages, predominantly from the Mohave in the area along the lower reaches of the Colorado River. Others commemorate events, mythological, legendary, or historical, but never the name of a person who actually lived. A few names are obscure in origin and meaning. However, the great majority of these names, even those which are quite poetic, are vividly and concisely descriptive. Obviously a descriptive placename had practical value: it enabled a man traversing a route he had learned about simply by word of mouth to know precisely where he was. This was of prime importance to persons going on foot across a country of great heat and great distances, where life itself depended upon knowing exactly how to get from one precious watering place to the next.

Mountains and mountain ranges loomed as large in the landscape as in Chemehuevi thought. These were the mountains each of which was traversed by its own version of the Mountain Sheep Song, delineating it as the hereditary hunting ground of a closely related group and thus making it part of that sacred tetralogy of man, song, mountain, and game animal. Here are the names by which some of them were known to the Chemehuevis:

Mug^{w}iyagaiv^{y}a, Guico Mountain. El Dorado Mountain.

ʔAagah (ʔAa- possibly for white clay, as in ʔAapanapɨ, White Clay Lightning Flash, and ʔaanovɨ, white clay fetus, echo), Spirit Mountains, especially the highest point thereof. This peak is known locally as Mt. Newberry, but the Government topographical map named it Dead Mountain and gave Mt. Newberry as a lesser eminence toward the River. ʔAagah is the sacred mountain of the Mohaves, who call it ʔAvikwamei.[2] The Chemehuevis attached no especial importance to it and were well aware, even in aboriginal times, that it is not, as the Mohaves are said to believe, the highest mountain in the world.

Yuvisaavitcɨ (yuvisavɨ, that which is dirty and greasy, like a black, greasy cooking pot; havitcɨ, lying), Greasy Substance Lying. Dead Mountains and the range west of Needles which appears to be a continuation of this chain. Tuuhʷavitcɨ, Black Lying, is another name for the same range. Both names were used, but (in George Laird's time at any rate) Yuvisaavitcɨ was thought to be the more correct term. Havitcɨ, from havigʸah, lies, is said of a long mountain range; karɨrɨ, from karɨgah, sits, applies to a mountain that is more rounded or "chunky."

ʔAmpanigʸaivʸa (ʔampagagah, talking), Talking Mountain. Paiute Mountains. A Tɨɨraʔayata, Desert Mohave, came upon a Tɨɨranɨwɨ, Desert Chemehuevi, and mistaking him for one of his own people, accosted him; whereupon the Chemehuevi began to shout for the rest of his band. The placename derives from this happening.[3]

Kɨtongʷa (kɨtongʷagah, pulls out three or more objects with the teeth; the use of the verb root without termination as a placename is quite rare), Pulled Out Several Objects with Teeth. A part of the Mohave Mountains. This range runs north and south, forming an angle with the range running east and west, identified on the map as the Chemehuevi Mountains. (The name of the latter range was unknown to George Laird; he spoke of it as the range which touches the River at the place called Sagwawayuʷapɨ.)

Wiyaatuʷa (apparently means towards Wiyaa-), Whipple Mountains. This was a very important range in Southern Chemehuevi mythology, notable as the home of Southern Fox and of the woman upon whom the Sun begot twin sons; also the Mountain Sheep Song which traversed it was the only version extant in 1919.[4]

Nantapɨagantɨ (nantapɨ, mescal plant), Mescal Being, Where There is Mescal. Turtle Mountains.

Si^yakarɨrɨ (si^yapɨ, schist), Schist Sitting. Riverside Mountains.

Wii^ʔwirah (no etymology). Maria Mountains, the southernmost mountain range claimed by the Chemehuevis.

ʔOk^wah (for ʔOk^wai-; no etymology). A mountain range lying a little northwest from Ivanpah.[5]

Kaiv^ya^ʔamantɨ, New York Mountains. Although this range figures prominently in the information given by George Laird, he was never able to remember what the Chemehuevis called it. The name was supplied in 1969 by Wendell Goodman, Sr. Mr. Goodman knew it well because he was born there.

Paasaruntug^wiv^yi (Paasa, Paiute Springs; tuntug^wiv^yi, lava, malpais, badlands), Paiute Springs Badlands. This name is applied to a black lava range which has Paiute Springs near its southern extremity.

Tɨmpisagwagatsitcɨ (the insertion of -tsi-, here probably locative, before the termination of sagwagarɨ places r between i and ɨ, where it becomes tc), Green Stone. Providence Mountains.[6]

Toyongkarɨrɨ, Boulder Sitting. Granite Mountains, commonly called Old Dad Mountains, according to George Laird; but the map assigns separate sites to the Granite and Old Dad ranges.

Kwaroyaawi Kotcovɨ (kwaroyaawi^ya, chicken's; kotcovɨ, comb, crest, as, for example, a quail's crest), Coxcomb. This is a range consisting of low peaks serrated like a rooster's comb; it is situated just north of Bill Williams Fork.

Kwiyarangkaiv^ya, Screw Mesquite Mountain. This is a range just across the River from Si^yakarɨrɨ, Riverside Mountains. The floodplain is about fifteen miles wide at that point.

Kuk^wnɨvagantɨ, Having Wood and Snow. San Bernardino Mountains. There were numerous places bearing Chemehuevi names located in this range, but they were unknown to George Laird. He had heard the name of San Gorgonio but could not recall it.

Yuvi^{y}avitcɨ (yuvimpɨ, pine species), Pinetree Lying. The Walapai Mountains.

Cɨnaˀagaiv^{y}*a*, Coyote Mountain. S. H. Mountain, located in Yuma County, Arizona, and called in Spanish *Sierra del Agua Nueva*.

Other mountains or mountain ranges which George Laird could not definitely locate were:

Nɨvagantɨ, Having Snow. George Laird said that this designated the highest point of the Panamint Mountains (all of which was holy ground), and also several times said he thought it might be Mt. Whitney. But at the present writing (1969) knowledgeable Chemehuevis positively identify it as Charleston Peak, in Nevada.[7] In pre-human times Nɨvagantɨ was the home of Wolf and his brother, Mythic Coyote. It was the very heart of Tɨwiin^{y}arɨvipɨ, the Storied Land. There seems to be a modern tendency to assign more definite locations to mythological placenames.

Hauwawangkɨgarɨ (wawangkɨgagah, tall points stand up serrated like the teeth of a comb; one may say with equal correctness Hauwawangkɨgatɨ, wawangkɨgatɨ deriving from the passive, wawangkɨgakaiy*u*, tall points have been stood up serrated), Bone-Gray Peaks. This mountain range was the home of all shamans' familiars except the bat.[8] George Laird spoke of this range as "somewhere northwest of the Colorado Desert."

Parɨˀasɨgaiv^{y}*a*, Ice Mountain. This was said to be a mountain of solid ice, the home of the bat familiar. It is probably an actual place, an unidentified mountain containing ice caves.

Mog^{w}ah (no etymology). A mountain or mountain range located somewhere in northern territory.[9]

Nog^{w}ah, another unexplained and unidentified northern range which George Laird had heard mentioned.

Beginning in the north, in Nevada, then following as best he could along the routes that he remembered, George Laird located the following places. It must be emphasized that these constitute but a fraction of those places named and known in aboriginal times:

ˀAvaˀapah (ˀavaˀa-, the free form of which is ˀavaˀan*a*, many; pah*a*, mortar), Many Mortars. This was originally the name of a place about two miles below the ferry at El Dorado, but came to be applied also to the site of the mill at the mouth of El Dorado Canyon.

Sawˀwiiv^y*a* (no etymology). Round Island.

Muuvi^y*a* (no etymology). Cottonwood Island.

Waas*a* (no etymology). This is the name of a large waterfall about two miles downstream from Cottonwood Island.

Hunaorap*ɨ* (horap*ɨ*, hole, from horagah, digging; in the compound h is omitted, thus forming a single accented syllable), Badger Hole. The site of the wing dam about six miles below Cottonwood Island.

Tɨmpiwɨˀananaˀats*i* (wɨˀap*i*, penis; nanaˀagah, grows or stands up of itself; here -ts*i* could be a verb termination, locative, or diminutive), Stone Penis Growing Up, Stone Penis Erected. Pyramid Rock. This rock formation resembles Tavaˀawɨˀananaˀats*i*, Chipmunk Penis Erected (Monument Peak), but is not so large.

Tɨmpipoˀok^wat*ɨ* (poˀok^wat*ɨ*, marked or written upon; also variegated, striped), Marked Rock. This is the name of a hill on the Arizona side of the River opposite the upper end of the valley called Hayak^*q*i. Here there are carvings on the rocks. Stones which bear these ancient markings are said to be tutuguuvoˀop*ɨ*, marked by tutuguuviw*ɨ*. It is thought that the spirit animals who act as shamans' helpers made these markings.

Hayak^*q*i (no etymology). A valley on the Nevada side of the River about twelve miles by road from Fort Mohave.

Wiyaanˀnik^y*aatɨ* (irregularly derived from wiyav*ɨ*, adobe, and yuwaanˀnik^y*aatɨ*, tears hanging on eyelashes), Adobe Hanging Like Tears. The name has reference to the peculiar structure of the adobe hills at that place. It is about four miles north of Fort Mohave. Quite a large band of Chemehuevis lived there under a lesser chief. They were, of course, designated as Wiyaanˀnik^y*aa*-tɨtsiw*ɨ*. This was the southernmost settlement on the Colorado River in Tantɨitsiw*ɨ* (Northerners) territory.

ˀAyatapagah, Mohave River. Fort Mohave. This was, as the

name implies, a Mohave settlement. No Chemehuevis ever lived there, but it was considered to be the dividing line between the Northern and Southern Chemehuevis.

Nagw^{a}ipap$i$ayay$a$ or Nagw^{a}ipat$i$gah (na-, reflexive or reciprocal; kwipagah, strikes with club; the suffixes -p$i$ayay$a$ and -t$i$gah are interchangeable, both indicating that the event referred to took place a long time ago), They Clubbed Each Other Long Ago. This is a small valley about ten miles north of Needles. No Chemehuevis lived there. The incident which gave rise to the placename has long been forgotten.

Haakw^{a}irox^{wa}i (from the Mohave $?Aha$ $Kwelox$). The little valley where Needles is situated. It used to be much larger but has been reduced by erosion.

Haataruump$i$ (from the Mohave $?Aha$ $Taloomp$). No location given.

Koh^{w}ain^yi (no etymology). A small valley about three miles north of Topok, at the upper end of which there was an apparently nameless Chemehuevi settlement. The site of the settlement is now marked by ironwoods that have grown up from seed brought there by the Chemehuevis.

T$i$mpi$^{?y}$angkagatsitc$i$ (compare T$i$mpisagwagatsitc$i$), Red Rock. This has reference to a natural rock formation located at Topok.

Sagwawayu^{w}ap$i$ (wayu^{w}agah, hangs, hangs down), Green Hanging. The name is applied to the mouth of a box canyon which is located about two miles downstream from T$i$mpi$^{?y}$angkagatsitc$i$.

W$i$$?i$in^{y}uah (w$i$$?i$ig^{y}ah, shoots; -nuwah, locative), Shooting Place. This is a high rock on the Arizona side of the River which used to serve as a target for archers. Here the trail passed over high, rocky cliffs.

Tukumumuuntsit$i$nah (-t$i$nah, at the base of; compare t$i$nav$i$, root), At the Base of the Mountain Lion. Here there are springs at the foot of a high cliff. This was the watering place which Tugumpayaa$?$o^{w}asi^{y}akar$i$mi, Yellow Sky, was trying to reach when he died of thirst in the desert.[10]

Hamatcuup$a$ (from the Mohave $?Aha$ $Matcuup$). Mohave Rock.

Tookovaronumpɨtsɨ, Material for Blackening the Face. A small deposit of black paint about two miles east of Hamatcuupa.

Papaway Paɨwaru^wapɨ (papawaya, bear's; paɨwaru^wapɨ, blood, that which has bled out, from paɨwaru^wagah, bleeds), Bear's Blood. A chain of black and red hills running from the foot of the large mountain across the River from Siwaʔavaatsɨ, Chemehuevi Valley, almost to Needles Peaks. It is said that Kwiyatsɨ, Rattlesnake, bit Papawa, Bear, at the hill called Muhungk^wanivɨ. Bear started to bleed where these black and red hills begin and died at their upper end, his blood forming the hills. This placename and its explanation were all that George Laird was able to recall of what must have been an important myth.

Tug^waruʔ^wintɨpah (tug^waruʔ^wintɨ, night), Night Water. Here the River flows between high sand banks.

Siwaʔavaatsɨ (siwaʔavɨ, hardpan; paha, mortar; -tsi, locative. Since this placename ends in -tsɨ, another -tsɨ cannot be added to signify "person of"; Siwaʔavaatsiwɨ means people of siwaʔavaatsɨ, but in the singular one must use nɨwɨ, person: Siwaʔavaatsin^yɨwɨ, a person of Siwaʔavaatsɨ), Hardpan Mortars. Chemehuevi Valley.[11] The name, George Laird stated, was originally applied to a place in a draw where a large wash comes in about half a mile from the valley proper, but has been extended to the whole valley on the California side of the River. He commented that all the washes thereabouts had once had Chemehuevi names which had already, in his time, been forgotten.

Kwayantu^watɨ. A place on the Arizona side directly across the River from Chemehuevi Valley. George Laird translated Kwayantu^watɨtsiwɨ as Across the River People.[12]

ʔAvaʔapah, Many Mortars.[13] A bend in the River on the Arizona side where there are large boulders containing many mortar holes.

Harimyiivɨ (probably from the Mohave; my does not occur in native Chemehuevi words). A notably frost-free strip of land, formerly of considerable size but now (1919, the last year George Laird saw it) much reduced by erosion. This was the home of a rather important Chemehuevi band (in speaking of them, George Laird used the word *ranchería* as the equivalent of nɨwɨavɨ). Here about 1880 or earlier lived the three very old men through whom much of the information contained in these notes was handed down. One of them was Tuuwɨnɨrɨ, Black Standing. George Laird could not recall the names of the other two, but it was one of these who went along as observer on the last Mohave expedition against the Halchidhoma.[14]

Muhungkʷanivɨ (muhuumpɨtsɨ, large owl species), Owl House. A rocky hill with a cave in it. People used to camp by this hill and take shelter in the cave when it rained.

Tcakwᵃivuʔʷivunavɨ (tcakwᵃivuʔi, testicles; punavɨ, bag), Testicle Bag. This is the name of a high hill down-river from Muhungkʷanivɨ.

ʔAvinʸootsɨ (nootsɨ, one who carried [something] on his back, from noogʷah, carries on back), One Who Carried White Clay on His Back. This is an overhanging bluff with a small layer of white clay near its apex, situated about four hundred yards from the River and a mile and a half from Steamboat Rock (the Chemehuevi name of which was not recalled). It is said that in very ancient times a man travelling with a load of white clay on his back died there, and his body became the bluff. The old, hard-beaten Indian trail goes by this spot.

Pagɨɨmuvɨ (muvɨ, nose), Fish Nose. Rincon. The name refers specifically to a group of upright rocks two or three hundred yards from the River which resemble fishes' "noses" sticking up into the air. This place is on the California side of the River, opposite ʔAvinʸootsɨ.

ʔOtavaʔantɨ (ʔotavɨ, fine sand; paʔantɨ, high), High Sand. A large sand dune on the Arizona side of the River about four miles below Pagɨɨmuvɨ and opposite the upper end of the valley known as Kakarɨnarɨnapɨ. This dune is not as high as those in ʔAyatanaugutɨvipɨ, Mohave Spirit Land, which is located across the River from Siwaʔavaatsɨ, Chemehuevi Valley.

Kakarɨnarɨnapɨ (kakarɨ, quail; narɨnapɨ from narɨnagah, three or more run), Quail Used to Run. This is a valley some six miles long, its head lying about four miles below Pagɨɨmuvɨ.

Miᵞaupitcaw ˀwagantɨ, Small (Place Where) There is Tc*awa*, Having Small Tc*awa*. This is a smaller wash than the one listed below as Tcaw ˀwagantɨ, but in both places one's footsteps in the sand make a whispering, crunching sound: tc*awa*, tc*awa*, tc*awa*. No exact location was given.

Panavatcawipɨ (navatcawigᵞah, flow together, meet), Water Confluence. This term is applied to any confluence of waters, but when used as a placename indicates the point where Bill Williams Fork empties into the Colorado River.

Pahuwipɨ (huwipɨ, stream, from huwigᵞah, flows), Water Stream. Bill Williams Fork. This watercourse is also known as Haakwitcapɨ, from the Mohave ˀ*Aha Kwi-tceipa*. Because of the similarity in sound, *kwitceipa* (no translation given) is replaced in the Chemehuevi version by kwitcapɨ, excrement.

Haikuuyɨwitcɨ (haiku, white man; yɨwigᵞah, three or more sit down), White Men Sitting Down. This was the name of the small, white hills about two miles north of the rocks called Nayɨɨpiyanagumatsɨ.

Nayɨɨpiyanagumatsɨ (nayɨɨpiyawɨ, brother and sister; nagu-mawɨ, husband and wife; -tsɨ, locative), Brother and Sister Married Pair.[15] Two rocky peaks standing side by side about eight miles from the mouth of the Bill Williams and four miles below Planet, Arizona. The Augdale Ranch is in a valley just west of this place.

Marahóxᵂᵃɨ (from the Mohave *Marahox*). The large whirlpool about four miles below the mouth of Bill Williams Fork.

Tcaw ˀwagantɨ, There is Tc*awa*. This is the larger of the two washes where one's footsteps sound like tc*awa*, tc*awa*, tc*awa*. It is the box canyon into which Copper Basin narrows and lies towards the River from Tavaˀa-wɨˀananaˀatsɨ (Monument Peak).

Muvaay*a* (no etymology). A spring at Billy Mack's place, north of Parker, Arizona.

Kᵻsagaivʸ*a*, Hawk Mountain. Black Mountain, the mountain which marks the northeast corner of the Colorado River Indian Reservation.

Kwiyarasapᵻ (sapᵻ, belly), Screw Mesquite Belly. The small valley on the California side of the River opposite the Agency at Parker.

ʔᵻnᵻpimahahuwitᵻah (-tᵻah, place, as in nᵻkatᵻah, dance ring, place where the Scalp Dance or any round dance is danced), Demon Bush Wash, Smoketree Wash. Location not described.

Tᵻhiyaʔᵻgatᵻah, Deer Entrance, Deer Entering Place. The large wash which runs from about eight miles below Parker up to Bouse. This was in Deer Song territory.

Kusir*a* (no etymology). A small, isolated mountain close to the River.

ʔAaparikʸiʔawaʔanuntᵻ (ʔawaʔanuntᵻ, wide), Wide Ironwood. A large wash with much ironwood growing in it, six or seven miles downstream from Kusir*a*.

Yamasaaganivʸ*a* (-v*a*, locative), Raccoon House. Location not described.

Tantᵻvaiyᵻpatsi Tangaronʔnᵻgipᵻ (Tantᵻvaiyᵻpatsiʸ*a*, Southern Fox's; tang*a*, knee; tonʔnᵻgigʸah, thrusts in), Southern Fox's Knee-Thrust, Where Southern Fox Thrust in His Knee. This placename and the following commemorate the adventures of the mythical hero, Southern Fox. Tantᵻvaiyᵻpatsi Tangaronʔnᵻgipᵻ is the place where Southern Fox, being at that time southbound, encountered his enemy and braced himself to shoot at him. The imprint of his knee may still be seen on the trail between Yamasaaganivʸ*a* and Hapuʷis*i*.

Tuhuʔungʷ*a* (tuhuv*i* is a very rare word for enemy; -ʔungʷ*a*, third person singular possessive, animate, invisible. The normal word for enemy is tuhugʷantᵻ, and this enemy has been dead a long time, so the normal usage would be Tuhugʷantᵻgaipᵻʔᵻngʷ*a*, but this is not the form of the placename), His Enemy. This is a place near Tantᵻvaiyᵻpatsi Tangaronʔnᵻgipᵻ, therefore near but probably not directly on the trail. Here the body of Southern Fox's enemy remains in the form of a large "blowout" on top of a hill.

Hapu^{w}is$i$ (from the Mohave *?Aha Puis*). The location of the Old Blythe Intake.

Si$^?$apiv^{y}aats$i$, Sage Water. A spring, not precisely located.

Muhunangkavik^{y}avo$^?o$ (muhuump$i$ts$i$, owl; nangk$a$, ear; pi-k^{y}avo$^?o$, natural tank in rocks), Owl Ear Tank. A natural water tank northwest of Wiyaan$^?$nik^{y}aat$i$. Nearby there is a cliff in the shape of an owl's head with the two little horns which the Chemehuevis call "ears." The water is located at the base of one horn.

Soovimp$i$ts$i$ (soovimp$i$, cottonwood; here -ts$i$ might be a characteristic of the Northern dialect rather than locative), Cottonwood. A spring at the north end of the mountain range called Yuvisaavitc$i$.

Paho^{w}aavo^{w}ak^ai (ho^{w}aavo^{w}ak^ai, humped-back; or Paho^{w}aa-vo^{w}ak^{a}its$i$), Humped-Backed Water. A round spring on top of a dome-like hill of clay or adobe which resembles an extinct mud geyser. A solitary mesquite and some arrowweeds grow there.

Hahaiv^{y}a (no etymology). Kleinfelter. This place is also connected with the adventures of Southern Fox. It is the second watering place that he made by pulling his arrows out of the ground as he journeyed northward to visit his cousin, Blue Jay.[16]

Nanangko$^{?wa}$ip$i$ayay$a$ or Nanangko$^{?wa}$it$i$gah (nana-, reflexive or reciprocal prefix meaning three or more; ko$^{?wa}$i-g^{y}ah, kills three or more animals, but preceded by nana- means three or more fight; as noted above, -p$i$ayay$a$ and -t$i$gah mean a long time ago), Where They Fought. This is the name of a draw or cut separating Yuvisaavitc$i$ from Kak$i$mp$i$. Long ago two bands (wahavant$i$niw$i$av$i$) of Chemehuevis were camped there at the same time. They fell to quarreling over the relative merits of the dogs belonging to each band, and a battle ensued.

Kak$i$mp$i$, Mesquite Seed. As previously stated, kak$i$mp$i$ is applied both to mesquite seed and to the hard, flattish seed of a species of *palo verde*; one might distinguish them by saying ?opik^{y}ak$i$mp$i$, mesquite seed, or ?atsita-k^{a}ik^{y}amp$i$, *palo verde* seed, but here the meaning is understood to be mesquite seed. An isolated mountain just south of the range called Yuvisaavitcɨ and cut off from it by Nanangkoʔᵂᵃipɨayaya.

ʔOpinʸawɨtɨmʔma or ʔOpinʸawɨtɨmʔmatsɨ (ʔopimpɨ, mesquite; na-, reflexive; wɨtɨmʔmagah, closes), Closed Itself with Mesquite. This is a small tank up a wash which is a tributary to the sandy wash on the road from Needles to Parker. It is so named because a mesquite grows in the mouth of the wash, and the water is hidden behind it. Tugumpayaaʔoᵂasiʸakarɨmɨ, Yellow Sky, was camped here when his horse got away from him; he struck out on foot across the desert and died of thirst before he could reach Tukumumuuntsitɨnah.[17]

ʔOᵂasopiʸamantɨ, Salty Tasting. The next water on the trail after ʔOpinʸawɨtɨmʔma. There is another spring some six or seven miles down the trail from ʔOᵂasopiʸamantɨ, but George Laird could not recall its name.

Hawayawɨ (no etymology). West Wells. This was the first spring or group of springs made by Southern Fox as he travelled towards the north.

Pagoosovɨtsɨ (pagoosovɨ, shrub called in Spanish *guatamote*), Guatamote. This is a spring situated just where the trail starts up the north side of Wiyaatuᵂa, Whipple Mountain.

Sohorah (horah, post, but sohorah, post with a U-shaped notch at its top such as is used in constructing the takaganɨ, shade house), Notched Post. This is the name of a U-shaped gap in the mountains where there is a spring.

Tookovaronumpɨ, Material for Blackening the Face. Compare Tookovaronumpɨtsɨ; but here -tsɨ is never used "because this deposit is larger than the other."

ʔOmpihorapɨ (ʔompɨ, red paint; horapɨ, hole, that which is dug), Red Paint Diggings. Both black and red paint were used as war paint. These two adjoining paint caves, Tookovaronumpɨ and ʔOmpihorapɨ, were worked in ancient times by Indians and during World War I as a manganese mine. George Laird worked there shortly before we met in 1919. These deposits bear only their purely descriptive names. If it becomes necessary in conversation to distinguish them from other paint caves, this may be done by referring to their proximity to Mamauʔuntɨngkanʔnɨ.

Mamauʔuntɨngkanʔnɨ, Woman Rock-Cave. This cave, situated under an overhanging bluff in the Whipple Mountain range, is said to have been the home of the woman who became the mother of the twin sons of the Sun.

Tavaʔawɨʔananaʔatsɨ (tavaʔatsɨ, chipmunk or antelope groundsquirrel; wɨʔananaʔatsɨ as in Tɨmpiwɨʔananaʔatsɨ), Chipmunk Penis Erected. Monument Peak. This marks the northwest corner of the Colorado River Indian Reservation.

Pasagwagarɨ, Green Water. A spring or seepage located back of Siʸakarɨrɨ, Riverside Mountain, where all the surrounding rocks are colored green.

ʔAyatapikʸavoʔo, Mohave Tank. This is probably the last watering place with a Chemehuevi name on the trail from Muuviʸa, Cottonwood Island, to Yuma.

ʔAvimpah or ʔAavimpah, White Clay Water. A spring on the mountain range called ʔOkʷah, possibly identified as Wheaton Springs. The town of Ivanpah derives its name from this Chemehuevi placename.

ʔAipavah (ʔaipatsɨ, preadolescent boy), Boy Water. Kessler Springs.

Tooyagah (George Laird stated that in this word too- might be interpreted as center or might equally well stand for toyompɨ, boulder), Center of the Pass or Boulder Pass. Rock Springs. Both suggested etymologies are appropriate, for this water is situated about the center of a pass, and there are many granite boulders scattered thereabouts.

Monompaagantɨ (monompɨ, bunchgrass, *zacaton*), Having Bunchgrass and Water. Vontrigger Springs.

Paasa (no etymology; the name does not derive from pasa, field). Paiute Springs. This was the third watering place that Southern Fox made on his northward journey.

Wikumpikʸavoʔo, Buzzard Tank. A watering place mentioned as located between Paasa and Siwayumitsɨ.

Siwayumitsɨ (siwampɨ, coarse sand; yumigʸah, caves in), Coarse Sand Caved In. Mohawk Springs.

Maupah or Mau'upah, Woman Water. Mopah Springs.

Saavahah (no etymology). Niggerhead Mountain. White people pronounce the Chemehuevi placename as Saavahu, and many young Chemehuevis have carelessly adopted this pronunciation.

Parimpa (timpa, mouth), Water Mouth. Pahrump, Nevada.

Pagangkwitcun'ni (pagampi, carrizo; kwitcupik^{y}aiyu, has been bunched up, has been gathered together in a bunch), Bunched Up Carrizo. Arrowweed Springs. The suggested origin of the English placename is as follows: in attempting to translate pagampi, the Chemehuevis stated that it was a plant used in arrow making, and the white men jumped to the conclusion that it was arrowweed. The English name is inappropriate, since no arrowweeds grow in this vicinity.

Tcupanihopak^{a}i or Tcupanihopak^{a}itsi (tcupani, *yerba del manso*; hopak^{a}i, hollow, dell), Yerba del Manso Hollow. Probably Willow Springs.

Cina'avah (cina'avi, coyote), Coyote Water. Chuckawalla Springs.

Other placenames not mentioned in any particular order were:

Yagah (yagah is a geographical term indicating a pass between two parallel mountain ranges whose ends overlap, but is used here as a true placename—just as pagah, river, means the Colorado River), Pass. This is located near the California-Nevada state line in the vicinity of Pahrump, Nevada.

Tivatsi Mo'opi, Cinawavi Mo'opi (Tivatsi^{y}a, Wolf's; Cinawavi^{y}a, Mythic Coyote's; mo'opi, mark made with hand, from mo'og^{w}ah, marks with hand), Wolf's Handmark, Mythic Coyote's Handmark. This is the name of the rock on which the imprints of Wolf's and Coyote's hands may be seen side by side. Although it commemorates one of the final episodes in the Wolf and Coyote saga,[18] it is, like Tantivaiyipatsi Tangaron'nigipi, an actual place. George Laird did not know its location, only that it is in northern territory.

Tutu'ugaiv^{y}a, Mountain of the Familiars.[19] A sacred cave, also in northern territory, "somewhere in Nevada, far up in the mountains," where the gift of any song or of any familiar may be obtained and where footprints, as of the feet of small children, are to be seen. George Laird knew a great deal about this cave but could never recall its name.

Kunayɨwaavɨ (kunɑ, fire), Fire Valley. Death Valley. Kunayɨwaavɨ was the name given to Death Valley by Southern Fox when he travelled across it, singing, while his body was consumed by its fire until only his head remained.[20]

Kwiyavaah (kwiyatsɨ, rattlesnake; frequently in compounds the final element representing paah is short, as in ʔAavimpah, ʔAipavah, Cɨnaʔavah, but here it is distinctly long, and this gives the effect of almost even accents on the second and third syllables), Rattlesnake Water. A spring situated about two days journey from Barstow in a direction slightly northwest. This was on the old Immigrant Trail.[21]

Kwinʸaváh (said to derive from the Apache). A sacred cave on the north side of the Sandy near where it flows together with the Santa Maria to form Bill Williams Fork. Here the Salt Song (George Laird's version) starts and finishes.[22]

Tɨhiyahivitɨah (hivigʸah, drinks), Deer Drinking Place. This is the name of a spring about two miles west of Signal, in Mohave County, Arizona.

ʔAngkapah, Red Water. A spring about forty miles upstream from Tɨhiyahivitɨah.

ʔAngkaturumpɨ, Red Adobe. The large valley running north and south which lies to the east of Kingman, Arizona.

Cɨnaʔahuwipɨ, Coyote Stream. The Gila River.

Hasiʸampɑ (said to derive from the Apache). The Hassayampa River.

Kamayaʔotavɨ (George Laird translated Kamayah both as Diegueño and Kamia, considering the three words to be equivalent in meaning), Diegueño or Kamia Sand. The sand dunes by Yuma.

Terms incorporating tɨvipɨ which means earth or soil, or by extension, land or territory (and in the creation myths especially the whole habitable world as distinct from ocean and sky) are applied to large areas; for example:

Tuhug^wantɨtɨvipɨ or Tuhug^wantɨrɨvipɨ (tuhug^wantɨ, enemy, from tuhug^waiyu, has been made or has become an enemy), Enemy Territory. This could, of course, be applied to any land occupied by enemies, but as a placename it designated specifically the lowlands on both sides of the Colorado River from Fort Mohave to the Palo Verde Valley. In this sense it came into general use during the wars which resulted in the expulsion of the Halchidhomas. At that time the area became a dangerous no man's land, and to avoid travelling over it the Chemehuevis had recourse to foothill trails where watering places were few and far between. George Laird said that ʔAhwei Nyamat was the Mohave equivalent of Tuhug^wantɨtɨvipɨ.

ʔAyatanaugurɨvipɨ or ʔAyatanaugutɨvipɨ (nauxu or nauguvi, spirit of the departed, ghost), Mohave Spirit Land. Mohave ghosts seem to like to stay as close to home as possible. ʔAyatanaugurɨvipɨ includes the large sand dunes across the River from Chemehuevi Valley and extends to Bill Williams Fork and far up that stream. As more and more Mohaves die, its boundaries are being constantly extended. Throughout the whole region which they occupy, the spirits of dead Mohaves may be heard singing and calling.

Naugurɨvipɨ or Naugutɨvipɨ, Spirit Land. The spirits of dead Chemehuevis are not home-keeping. The land to which they journey lies far to the north, even much farther north than Narɨwiin^yatɨvipɨ, the Storied Land of the Panamints. Quite possibly Naugurɨvipɨ once designated a specific area with more or less well-defined boundaries. But sometime in the course of a long, slow, southward migration its location became more and more vague, more and more invested with qualities not of the everyday world, more and more apt to have attached to it whatever greatly impressed the collective psyche of the People. As we have seen in Chapter I, the Chemehuevis were desultory agriculturists, by no means ready to surrender their nomadic habits. But it may have been that their first dramatic contact with a planting people, or a returned traveller's wonderful account of such a contact, left an imprint strong enough to change the image of Naugurivipɨ from a hunters' and gatherers' paradise to a land of equable and pleasant climate, "where the crops are always good," and where clan membership is no longer defined by the possession of a distinctive hunting song but by the exclusive claim to corn of a certain color; for so it was described to George Laird in the closing decades of the nineteenth century.

The following are among the placenames derived from a non-Indian source:

Piigisɨ (from Spanish *Vegas*). Las Vegas.

Kaampuʔu (from Spanish *Campo*). San Bernardino.

Rarantsɨ or Lalantsɨ[23] (from Spanish *la lancha*; the Mexicans had a large barge at that location which they called *la lancha*). Ehrenberg.

Puutsiyumah (from Fort Yuma). Yuma.

Trails

Trails made or travelled by the Chemehuevis spread their network over a great extent of territory. But even a hundred years ago this area had become much restricted, and many of the old routes and old placenames had passed into oblivion. Still in George Laird's youth, in the closing years of the nineteenth century, many trails were in use. Some of them may actually be seen to this day, worn down beneath the level of the desert floor, hard-beaten by the impact of generations of moccasined feet.

The word for trail or road is pooh. Trails along the River led from settlement to settlement. But during the long series of wars between the Yuman tribes, when these lowlands became Enemy Territory, the Chemehuevis came to rely whenever possible on routes traversing arid territory, well back from the River. These trails were infinitely more important than those in the lowlands leading from watering place to watering place. Sometimes a choice of routes was available, one offering more frequent water than the other at the expense of greater length. This would be the trail chosen by weaker persons or family groups. A strong, swift man travelling alone would take the more perilous way or, if he knew the country well, might even do a certain amount of short-cutting;

but for the most part established trails were followed—except, of course, by hunters in pursuit of game.

The trail from Cottonwood Island to Yuma, that is, to a point opposite the mouth of the Gila, approximately the site of Fort Yuma, was one frequently mentioned by George Laird; in his youth, he must have travelled over it many times.[24] Leaving Muu-vi^{y}a, Cottonwood Island, it crossed ʔAagah, passing a few springs or waterholes the names and exact locations of which were not remembered. The first water mentioned by name on this route is Muhunangkavik^{y}avoʔo, and the next is Soovimpɨtsi. Here the trail forks; one fork goes around Yuvisaavitcɨ, and the other passes to the west of Hahaiv^{y}a. Whichever way is chosen, the traveller must cross two long, waterless wastes before he reaches the point where the forks reunite at ʔOpin^{y}awɨtɨmʔma. Leaving ʔOpin^{y}awɨtɨmʔma, the next water is ʔO^{w}asopi^{y}amantɨ, after that a spring the name of which was not recalled, then Hawayawi. Here the trail divides again, one route going over Wiyaatu^{w}a and the other passing around it to the west. The old high trail from Hawayawi over Wiyaatu^{w}a is one which time has not obliterated. Where the ascent begins, there is the watering place called Pagoosovɨtsi. Further on the pitch approaches the perpendicular, and near the summit stones have been piled to form crude steps. There are springs at intervals along the top of the range, but the next named and located water is Sohorah. Thence the trail goes to Pasagwagarɨ, then on to ʔAyatapik^{y}avoʔo. After passing back of Wiiʔwirah, it turns down into the Palo Verde Valley and follows the River to its destination, Fort Yuma. From there on down the west side of the River belonged to the Kwitcaaniwɨ (Yumas), who were "friends and brothers" of the Chemehuevis.

The more modern horse trail does not pass over the waterless stretches crossed by the old foot trail. Going to Hawayawi, it leaves the River at Haataruumpi, then proceeds either to ʔOpin^{y}awɨtɨmʔma or goes straight on to ʔO^{w}asopi^{y}amantɨ.

From Hahaiv^{y}a to ʔAyatapik^{y}avoʔo there was an alternate route used by the Runners and occasionally by other men who were in a great hurry. Like the route previously described, it was well out of Enemy Territory, and it had the advantage of being much shorter, but it was virtually waterless. Between Hahaiv^{y}a and ʔAyatapik^{y}a-voʔo the only watering places were Wikumpik^{y}avoʔo and Maupah.

A trail that led from the Colorado River to the Mohave Desert and on to the San Bernardino Mountains left the River at Wiyaan?nik^yaatɨ and proceeded thence to Muhunangkavik^yavo?o, then on by way of Paas*a*, Tooyagah, and ?Aipavah. This trail went by Soda Lakes. George Laird commented that Soda Lakes and the sink of the Mohave River were in Chemehuevi Country, but being himself a Southerner he was not able to furnish placenames for that region.

Another trail left the River at Siwa?avaats*i* and went to Hawayaw*i*, thence to Siwayumits*i*, thence to a spring on Maa?ɨpɨgaiv^y*a*. There are many springs and tanks in the vicinity of that mountain the names and definite locations of which George Laird could not recall. Tɨmpisagwagatsitc*ɨ*, near which there are also many watering places, came next on this trail. A person travelling this route might or might not pass by Pagangkwitcun?n*i*; if he chose to do so, he would have to cross sand dunes between that water and ?Aipavah, at which point the trail united with the one from Wiyaan?nik^yaatɨ.

Yet another trail left the River at Nagw^aipapɨayay*a* and proceeded to Tɨmpisagwagatsitc*ɨ*. Placenames along this route were not given.

Tribes

All tribes, according to Chemehuevi mythology, sprang from the union of Coyote and Louse. As eggs, all were brought back by Coyote in a large storage basket from an island in the sea. During the journey they hatched out in human form, and upon reaching land Coyote allowed them to escape from the basket and gave them names.[25] Thus the Chemehuevis recognized a kinship between all native American peoples, no matter how remote their habitats or strange their customs; but where linguistic affinities were recognized a closer relationship was acknowledged. As far-ranging travellers, persistent visitors even where visiting was dangerous, curious and incurable gossips, the Chemehuevis knew or knew of many different tribes. Fifty years ago much of this knowledge had already been lost, blurred, or confused.

Collective terms, usually with a geographical basis, included various tribes or groups of tribes; and as will be seen below there were collectives within collectives. There were terms embracing several or more tribes based upon the words for north and west, but none deriving from south or east. In listing tribal classifications and tribenames I have used plural forms, which were those usually volunteered by George Laird; but it is always the singular form which appears in compounds and probably would be frequently employed in conversation, whereas the English tendency would be to use the plural.

Terms applied to tribal groupings are as follows:

Tantɨitsiwɨ, Northerners. As previously noted, this means (1) the northern branch of the Chemehuevis and (2) all northern tribes recognized as linguistically related to the Chemehuevis. Included within the Tantɨitsiwɨ were the Kohʷaitsiwɨ, for which no etymology was given. Kohʷaitsiwɨ also has a dual meaning: (1) a rather vaguely identified California tribe, possibly the Koso, and (2) a group of northern Shoshonean speaking peoples described by George Laird as "all Shoshoni tribes." Another name for the Kohʷaitsiwɨ was Nɨwɨrɨkawagamɨ, Person Eaters, Cannibals. "They hunted people," the Chemehuevis said, "as we hunted deer and mountain sheep." One of the band of Chemehuevis living at Victorville had a Kohʷaitsi wife.

Tantɨinʸɨwɨwɨ, Northern People. This designation included all tribes living north of the Chemehuevi range and speaking languages not recognized as related to Chemehuevi.

ʔɨgatuʷantɨmɨ, Those Towards the Entrance (towards the place where the sun and the heavenly bodies enter in), Westerners. All tribes west of the Chemehuevi habitat are Westerners. The term ʔɨgatuʷantɨmɨ includes Hutsipagɨwaatsiwɨ, Ocean Edge Dwellers, the Coastal Tribes.

A partial list follows of the tribal names and designations employed by the Chemehuevis. Alternative names or nicknames were usually derogatory or teasing, illustrating Chemehuevi humor.

Tuumontcokowɨ, probably Black Bearded Ones (although George Laird never analyzed the word), or more frequently, Nɨwɨwɨ, People. The Chemehuevis. They recognized three tribal divisions based on habitat: Tantɨitsiwɨ, Northerners; Tantɨvaitsiwɨ, Southerners; and Tɨɨranɨwɨwɨ, Desert People. The Tantɨitsiwɨ also called the Tantɨvaitsiwɨ ʔAngkanampawɨ, Red Feet.[26]

Kɨmanɨwɨwɨ (kɨma-, different, other, not one's own), Different People, that is, a different sort of Chemehuevi. The Cahuilla.

Kwitaanamuniwɨ (no etymology). George Laird at first gave this tribename as simply another name for the Kɨmanɨwɨwɨ; but after pondering for a time he thought it might be the name for the Kwitanemuk Serrano located on the Tejon Ranch.

Maarɨngʔngiyatsiwɨ (no etymology). The Serrano.

Pitantɨmɨ or Pitantɨmɨwɨ[27] (no etymology). Vanyume Serrano. The Mohave song, *Vanyumé Toman*, is called by the Chemehuevis Pitantacɨnaʔahuvʷiyavɨ, Vanyume Coyote Song.

Paanumiitsiwɨ (no etymology given). A tribe of Tantɨitsiwɨ (linguistically related Northerners) living in the vicinity of the Panamint Mountains.

Panamaitsɨwɨ. An unidentified northern tribe.

Paranʔnɨgiwɨ (tanʔnɨgigʸah, steps), Water Steppers. They are Tantɨitsiwɨ living along the Virgin River in Nevada.

Sivitsiwɨ (no etymology). A tribe of Tantɨitsiwɨ.

Yuwitawɨ (no etymology). Identified only as Tantɨitsiwɨ. The name, especially in the singular, Yuwit*a*, sounds very like Ute. Certain Tantɨvaitsiwɨ, Southern Chemehuevis, used to visit the Yuwitawɨ and brought back the report that they spoke a dialect somewhat more like the Southern dialect than that spoken by the Chemehuevis of Cottonwood Island who, like other Northerners, tended to speak too rapidly and made inordinate use of the particle -tsi-. The Yuwitawɨ did not have these peculiarities, but there were minor differences in their speech. Thus the Yuwit*a* word for grave is nɨntcumʔmap*i*; the Southern Chemehuevis say tcumʔmakat*ɨ*, covered with earth, but they do not use this term of a grave or a buried corpse, saying instead nɨngkuup*i* or nɨw kuukʷat*ɨ*. In times past the Chemehuevis ranged freely over the Tehachapi Mountains, and memory persisted of a tribe in that region who had many words similar to theirs (for example, por*o*, shaman's rod) and other words which were quite different. George Laird did not connect these people with the Yuwitawɨ. He knew no name for the Kawaiisu.[28]

Kohʷaitsiwɨ. A California tribe that was related to the Chemehuevis.[29]

Kaivʸahumpiwatsiwɨ (-humpiwa, across, over, on the farther slope of, is used only with the word for mountain), Dwellers on the Farther Slope of the Mountain(s). This tribe was not clearly identified; George Laird thought they might be the Luiseño.

Saimpivɨtsiwɨ (saimpivɨ, tule), Tule Dwellers. The Yokuts. They are Tantɨinʸɨwɨwɨ, Northern People, that is, a tribe living in the north and not linguistically related to the Chemehuevis. The Chemehuevis had considerable knowledge of these people. They said that the Saimpivɨtsiwɨ had houses, beds, and everything made of tule; also that it was their custom to gather duck and mudhen eggs and break a large quantity of them into a heated pit, thus making a sort of egg cake or baked omelet.

Muukʷiwɨ. The Hopi.

Hatpaawɨ (Chemehuevi plural adaptation of Mohave *Hatpa*). The Pima.

Kamayaawɨ (no etymology given). The Diegueño; the Kamia. George Laird used the designations Diegueño and Kamia interchangeably.

ʔAyatawɨ (no etymology). The Mohaves. They were said by the Chemehuevis to be descended from a mythical race of giants called Tutusiwɨ,[30] a name not now applied to any living tribe. The Chemehuevis also called the Mohaves Kwɨɨviwɨ. Peeled Ones (kwɨɨvɨ means a place where a person's outer skin has peeled off; it is used of people only, never of animals, fruit, or trees). This was a somewhat derogatory secret name, used in the presence of Mohaves or persons from other tribes when the speakers did not wish to reveal what people they were discussing. The Mohaves were the Chemehuevis' closest neighbors, co-inhabitors of much of the lower Colorado River Valley. The relationship between the two tribes was close, almost symbiotic. Each was to the other the essential enemy. To the Chemehuevis, tuhugʷantɨ, enemy, was virtually synonymous with Mohave, and the pole in the center of the dance ring was put there for "the Mohave's scalp." Mohaves ambushed Chemehuevis and vice-versa. Also they derived great satisfaction from their mutual contempt. Chemehuevis were revolted by the place that fish held in the Mohave diet, and Mohaves were equally disgusted by "lizard eaters." None of this prevented their visiting back and forth, intermarrying, and learning each other's language and songs—that is, many Chemehuevis spoke Mohave fluently, and the Chemehuevi passion for strange songs has already been commented upon; Mohaves seem to have been less proficient linguists. Single members of one tribe would sometimes live for long periods with the other. They traded artifacts, and no doubt to a certain extent each tribe assimilated the skills of the other,[31] the Mohave women being skilled potters and the Chemehuevi women weavers of elegant baskets. On occasion Chemehuevis and Mohaves fought side by side in the same war party, or Chemehuevi men accompanied a party of Mohaves into battle as observers.[32] Their enmity was almost (until recent years) without hatred, at least without deep, bitter, and enduring hatred; it was as though they united in playing out a stylistic (though deadly) game of war.

There is a tradition that "a long time ago" there used to be a large band or division of the Mohaves who were nomadic like the Chemehuevis, travelling about the desert from watering place to watering place. Like the Chemehuevis, they dressed in buckskin and had sinew-backed hunting bows. They were known as Tɨɨraʔayatawɨ, Desert Mohaves. Eventually the Chemehuevis exterminated them. The trouble started as ʔAmpanig^yaiv^ya, Talking Mountain (Paiute Mountains). A Desert Mohave came upon a Chemehuevi sitting down and, thinking he was one of his own kind, went up to him and thrust a bloody arrow in front of his face as proof that he had killed a mountain sheep. The Chemehuevi made no response whatsoever. Looking more closely, the Tɨɨraʔayata saw his mistake and took to his heels. Then the Chemehuevi began to shout for the rest of his band (and from the shouting back and forth which followed, the mountain took its name). The battle ended disastrously for the Mohaves, as did another later battle at Maupah, Woman Water (Mopah Springs), over possession of the water. All this happened long before the white men came. The surviving remnant of the Desert Mohaves joined their kinsmen who lived along the Colorado River and later tried to dissuade them from making war on the Chemehuevis. "We had good weapons like theirs," they argued, "and yet we were defeated. What can you do with your war-clubs and unbacked bows?" The (River) Mohaves persisted in their warlike intentions. At first they were defeated and suffered great loss. But there were so many of them. Finally, after the arrival of the white men, the Mohaves won a sort of victory over the Chemehuevis through sheer weight of numbers.

Haatcaruumiwɨ (from the Mohave tribename). The Halchidhomas. A fraternal bond existed between this Yuman tribe and the Chemehuevis. When a Chemehuevi and a Halchidhoma met, they addressed one another by the Yuman term *mát-havíky*, brother, which the Chemehuevi pronounced as though it was a Chemehuevi word, mataavik^{y}i. This form of address was retained even after the Halchidhomas became tuhug^{w}antɨmɨ, enemies. Ten Chemehuevis started out on the last expedition against the Halchidhomas, after the latter had taken refuge in Salt River Valley. The Mohaves who were in the war party taunted the Chemehuevis, telling them they were not needed, whereupon all turned back but two who continued on, as was their custom, to serve as eye witnesses and thereby furnish a check to Mohave boasting. When they approached the Halchidhoma village, one man came out alone to parley with the invaders. He asked how many tribes were represented. For sometime no one replied. At length one of the Chemehuevis stepped forward and said, "Mataavik^{y}i, here are Mohaves, Yumans, Apaches—and only two of us." "That is good, *mát-havíky*," replied the Halchidhoma, "that there are only two of you." The battle began, and the Halchidhomas were driven out of their first village. But while the aggressors were feasting on the melons and other food that they found there, the Halchidhomas came back with reenforcements and virtually annihilated them. The two Chemehuevis escaped. While the one who had parleyed with the Halchidhoma warrior was making his way home alone, he met a large party of Mohave women who had followed the war party carrying melons, large pots of beans, and much other food, and were expecting to meet their men and celebrate the victory. The Chemehuevi told them that most of their men were dead. Thereupon the women went home crying, leaving the food behind, where it was found and consumed several days later by a Chemehuevi hunting party. The Chemehuevi who parleyed with the Halchidhoma warrior and later gave the bad news to the Mohave women lived on to a high old age; he became one of the three wise old men of Harimyiivɨ, so frequently mentioned by George Laird.

Hatpaanyaawɨ (from the Mohave *Hatpa ʔanya*). The Maricopa.

Kwitcaaniwɨ (from the Mohave *Kwitcaana*). The Yuma; the Quechan. George Laird always spoke of a member of this tribe as a Yuma, but they now prefer their own name, transliterated as Quechan. The Kwitcaaniwɨ stood in a somewhat more intimate relationship to the Chemehuevis than the Halchidhomas. In old times when a Chemehuevi and a Yuma met, the Chemehuevi said, Tcak^ai-n^yi, my younger brother, and the other responded, *Mat haviky*, brother, not using the Yuman term for elder brother; and to this day, George Laird said, when old men of these tribes meet they greet each other with the Spanish word *hermano*, brother. These "brotherly" relations between tribes of entirely different linguistic stocks tell us of ancient alliances.

Paasawagarɨtsiwɨ (note -sawagarɨ- for sagwagarɨ, blue or green), Blue Water Dwellers. The Havasupai.

Waaripayatsiwɨ (from the Mohave *Huwalipaya*). The Walapais. The Chemehuevis also called the Walapais Hohora-payu^witsiw𝑖 (hohov𝑖, bone; tapayu^wig^yah, splits three or more objects), Bone Splitters. This was a secret name, used in the same way that Kw𝑖𝑖viw𝑖 was employed when speaking of the Mohaves.

Kwik^yapaaw𝑖 (derived from some Yuman source; to Chemehuevi ears the singular, Kwik^yapah, sounds like a Mohave trying to pronounce kuk^wapah, wood-water). The Cocopah. These people were always enemies of the Chemehuevis.

Yavipayaw𝑖 (from the Mohave *Yavipaya*). The Apaches.

Yavipayaagwatsiw𝑖 (derived somewhat loosely from the Mohave *Yavipaya ʔAwei*; *ʔawei* is usually translated into Chemehuevi as tuhug^want𝑖, enemy, but not in this tribename). The San Carlos Apaches.

The following terms designated non-Indian peoples:

Haikuuw𝑖 (from the Mohave *Haiku*), White Men, White Americans. Haikuuw𝑖 would be the proper plural form of the Mohave word in the old Southern Chemehuevi speech. Today it would not be so meticulously pronounced; in fact I doubt if any differentiation is made between singular and plural—except that when speaking in English the word is used with an English plural, Haikus. The white people (or perhaps Americans in general, as distinct from Mexicans) were also called Maarikaaniw𝑖, the Chemehuevi pronunciation of American with a Chemehuevi plural ending added. Huk^wantsiw𝑖 (possibly from huk^wamp𝑖, black widow spider) was another word for White Men; in George Laird's youth, Huk^wantsi and Haiku were interchangeable.[33]

Haʔ𝑖t𝑖haikuuw𝑖 (haʔ𝑖t𝑖-, real, genuine; the Chemehuevi term is a partial translation of the Mohave *Haiku Tahana*), Real White Men. The Mexicans. Since these were the first white settlers to arrive, they were considered to be the real white men.

Haikuurupagar𝑖m𝑖w𝑖 (singular Haikuurupagar𝑖m𝑖), Black Haikus, Black Americans. Negroes.

ʔAmpagapurig^yatsiw𝑖 (ʔampagagah, talks; purig^yagah, bubbles forth rapidly), Bubbling Talkers. The Jews. This conveys a similar concept to the Mohave word for Jews, *Tcakwaraturatura*, which is said to mean that their words come out like little round balls.

"One generation passeth away, and another generation cometh: but the earth abideth forever." One culture passes and another comes, but the earth endures—if not forever, at least longer than the transient life styles and systems of sentiments evolved by the successive races of men who dwell upon it. The desert in particular passes slowly. Slashed by freeways, torn by bulldozers and dune buggies, bearing upon its surface manmade oases and strangely incongruous resort developments, it remains for the most part a vast and empty country. Clouds cast their mysterious purple shadows upon it, thunder storms menace it, violent rainstorms drench it suddenly and briefly. These pass, and the desert lies pale and still and empty beneath the hot, empty, merciless sky.

From a helicopter, Chemehuevi country, I am told, resembles a great relief map, with many of the old landmarks still recognizable. The River and its environs have suffered the most drastic changes. Havasu Lake, backed up behind Parker Dam, has submerged Siwa?avaats*i*, with its brush huts, arable lands, and the graves of the fathers—and that spot where the three remaining chiefs conversed together in the twilight of their era. On the Arizona side of the lake, the noises of Lake Havasu City drown out the lamentations of Mohave ghosts in what was once Mohave Spirit Land.

Big game animals have all but vanished from desert and desert mountains. No more hunting parties go out, nor bands of warriors, nor solitary adventurers bent upon visiting strange tribes. No more moccasined feet tread silently on hard-packed trails or whisper tc*a*wa, tc*a*wa, tc*a*wa, tc*a*wa in sandy washes.

The most fatal difference is that a whole mode of perception is lost, forgotten, never to be regained. Even if the remaining native peoples increased and prospered, their thought has so departed from the old ways that there would be no eyes to see desert, mountains, and River as they once were seen.

CHAPTER VI

MYTHOLOGY:
THE ANCIENT TELLING

A MYTH is tɨwiinᵞapɨ, deriving from tɨwiinᵞagah, tells a myth, narrates an ancient tale. George Laird could give no etymology for tɨwiinᵞa-, but in attempting to convey the flavor of the word he suggested "ancient telling." This root and its derivatives may be used only of events or beings belonging to pre-human times, When the Animals Were People. Tɨwiinᵞagah[1] is not applied to the narration of exploits or adventures taking place in the world as it is at present, no matter how remote in time or drenched with magic these events may be. Tɨwiinᵞarɨvipɨ (or Tɨwiinᵞatɨvipɨ—whichever form strikes the speaker as the more euphonious) is the Sacred Land, the Mythic Country, "the place where the stories start and end," and where the Chemehuevis and kindred tribes are said to have been made by the power of Wolf. This Storied Land includes Nɨvagantɨ, Having Snow,[2] the great snow-covered mountain where Wolf and his brother, Mythic Coyote, lived together in a cave, and it includes all the vicinity of the Panamint Range. It is "open-ended" in space and time, extending up into the Never-Never Land of the mysterious North, and back beyond mankind to the time "before the World was." The myths range south to the low deserts and west to the sea, and although the immortal actors have long departed, many placenames and natural formations commemorate mythic events; so that in a sense the whole earth is or at one time was Tɨwiinᵞarɨvipɨ. The characters in the myths are Narɨwiinᵞapɨwɨ, Immortal Ones, Everlasting Ones, literally, Self-Mythologizing Ones.[3]

147

Myths must be told only in the wintertime, when the snakes are dormant. Should this taboo be violated, someone would be bitten by a rattlesnake.[4] When the snakes go to sleep, the Ancient Tales awake, and when the snakes come out of hibernation, the voice of antiquity must be silent. One result of this custom was to enhance enormously the aura of mystery and sanctity surrounding the ancient stories. A myth was bound to be more effective when its hearers were huddled together about a fire, sheltering themselves from the cold, menacing dark of an endless winter night—a night that became all too short when filled with high adventure, drama, and outrageous fun. For these myths, let us never forget, were not only the sacred scriptures but the comic theater of the People, who saw no incompatibility between the numinous and the humorous.[5] The narrator was in a sense both author and actor. While the framework of the myth remained fixed, the person who told it could embroider or even add episodes, adjusting its length to the long hours of darkness, just as, in the summertime, the leader of a song would shorten it to fit the brevity of a summer night. The narrator spoke with great style, with many dramatic pauses, with in-drawings of the breath through clenched teeth and frequent ejaculations of "Ha!" He also played all the parts, from weeping women to lisping children to stern warriors to clowning Coyote, changing his voice and rhythm of speech as he imitated the various speakers (whether or not these individuals had speech peculiarities which identified them).

This collection represents the merest fraction of the immense body of Chemehuevi oral literature. It is too much to claim that any of the myths included in it are complete, but some are obviously more complete than others. However, I have included all significant fragments in my possession.

How Ocean Woman Made the Earth

At first there was only water. This water is hutsip*a*, ocean; and in the ancient tales it is also spoken of as Nar*i*wiin*y*apah, Immortal Water, Everlasting Water.

In the very beginning of the time When the Animals Were People, four Immortals floated in a basket boat[6] on the Everlasting Water. They were Hutsipamamau?*u*, Ocean Woman; Tukumu-muunts*i*, Mountain Lion; T*i*vats*i*, Wolf; and C*i*nawav*i*, Coyote.[7]

Ocean Woman rubbed dead skin from the creases of her body. First she rolled it up into a little ball, then she crumpled it and sprinkled it on the surface of the Immortal Water. It floated and became land. She repeated these actions, slowly and patiently, many, many times. Each time there was a little more land.

Finally the earth became large enough for Ocean Woman to climb out on it. She lay down flat on her back with her head toward the west, her right arm extending towards the south, her left arm towards the north, and her legs towards the east. Then she began to stretch out the earth. She pushed hard with her hands, again and again. She pushed hard with her feet, again and again. There are three words that describe the way she was pushing with her hands: maviagah, mamaviagah, and mavɨn⁷nɨyagah; and there are three for the way she pushed with her feet: tapɨagah, tatapɨagah, and tapɨn⁷nɨyagah.

When the earth became so large that Ocean Woman could not see the edges of it, she sent out Wolf and Coyote[8] to see if it was large enough. Wolf ran very swiftly north and south, up and down the coast. Coyote ran over all the region to the east. Many, many times Wolf came back and chanted in his dignified way, "Katcusu, not yet." Coyote returned many, many times, and each time he said in his excitable way, "Haikʸa, haikʸa! Katcus-aikʸa, katcus-aikʸa, not yet-aikʸa, not yet-aikʸa." But finally Coyote announced, "Togʷaingutsa⁷aukʷ-aikʸa, it fits-aikʸa!"

Then Ocean Woman knew that the earth was finished.

How People Were Made

Wolf and Coyote were living together in their cave on Nɨvagantɨ. One day when Coyote was hunting in a valley near his home he saw a woman's tracks, going from east to west. He trailed her and soon overtook her. She was Poo⁷ʷavɨ, Louse. She wore only an apron made of a single jackrabbit skin which, as she walked or ran, flapped up and down to the rhythm of her motion, and she went along singing:

Ka′ mɨna′ wipɨ′ ɨptsi′	My little jackrabbit apron
wɨ′pukʷagai	flaps up and down
wɨ′pukʷagai	flaps up and down

The woman's great beauty and the way she moved and the movements of her little apron and the song she sang all combined to drive Coyote mad with desire.

Coyote told Louse what he wanted of her.

She consented. "But," she said, "you must run ahead and build a house for me. Because it is not fitting that the things you describe should be done out in the open."

Coyote rushed on ahead with his tongue hanging out. He hurriedly built a samarók^{wa}i, a brush house rounded at the top.[9] Then he went inside and lay down. When Louse came in sight of the house, she thought to herself, "Mangasuyaganu ?ipɨikwaigupɨ (or mangas ?ipɨikwaigupɨyaganuh), may that one fall asleep." Coyote fell at once into a deep sleep. The woman ran on past the hut, without looking inside or even slackening her pace. When she had left it far behind, she thought, "May that one wake up!" Instantly Coyote started up, crying, "Haik^{y}a, haik^{y}a! I must have fallen asleep-aik^{y}a!" He went outside, saw the woman's tracks going past, and took up the chase.

This happened three more times in exactly the same way. Coyote followed the woman's tracks west till he overtook her, ran on ahead and built a house, was made to fall asleep, and awakened only after Louse was long out of sight.

Now when he overtook her for the fifth time, they had reached the seacoast, and there was no brush growing there with which to build a house. Louse then pretended to be sorry for him and agreed to ferry him across the water to her island home. She allowed Coyote to climb on her back and swam strongly out to sea. But in mid-passage she dived and stayed on the bottom till she no longer felt his weight. Then she surfaced and swam on.

But Coyote had simply let go, risen to the surface, and turned himself into a pahokoso?^{w}av$i$, water-spider. Then he skittered along on top of the waves and reached the shore of the island while Louse was still far out at sea. Running out on the sand, he turned himself back into his natural form and set out to explore. He saw a samarók^{wa}i and went up to it. An old woman sat outside in the shelter of the windbreak. She was beginning to weave a large storage basket. Without speaking a word to her, Coyote went into the house and lay down.

Sometime later Louse arrived. "I saw Coyote," she said to her mother. "I drowned him. He is dead."

"Hush! Be quiet!" the old woman whispered, pointing with her lips and chin towards the house. "He's in there!"

The young woman went inside and lay down beside Coyote. Then he attempted to make love to her. But because she had a toothed vagina, his troubles were a long way from over. Eventually he succeeded in his purpose, but not without suffering some injury when he broke off the teeth. (That is the reason why, to this day, some Chemehuevi men have smaller and shorter [but not less effective] penises than the men of certain other tribes.)

By the time Coyote was ready to go home, the old woman had finished the storage basket. She sewed the top together tightly[10] and gave it to Coyote, telling him to take it to his brother, Wolf. She gave him strict orders not to open it till he reached his home on Nïvagantï. Coyote took the basket down to the shore, turned himself again into a water-spider, and ran off across the water, carrying it as a water-spider carries her egg-sac.

Coyote reached the mainland and resumed his own shape. The basket had already grown heavy, and he could sense movement within it. Soon he could no longer restrain his curiosity. He opened the basket, and immediately people began pouring out and scattering in all directions, over the whole face of the earth. The basket had contained Louse's eggs, which had hatched out during the journey into the first human beings.

Coyote was so excited and so busy exclaiming "Haik^{y}a, haik^{y}a!" and giving names to the various tribes, that he did not think to close the mouth of the basket until nothing remained within except a few weaklings and cripples, and the excrement. With this sorry load, he went dragging his tail back to Nïvagantï.

Wolf rebuked his brother sternly for having disobeyed the old woman. Then taking what was left in the basket, by his great power he made of it the best of all people: the Chemehuevis and their kindred.[11]

Wolf and Coyote had previously argued about how the people who were to come should propagate themselves. Wolf suggested that the embryo should form and grow in the little hollow at the back of a woman's wrist. In the fullness of time, the woman would toss her hand up over her shoulder in a back-handed gesture; then she would turn and see a young man, fully grown. "My son," she would say in greeting; and he would respond, "My mother."

Coyote had no use for that suggestion. "That is no good-aik^{y}a! That is no good at all-aik^{y}a! That is too magical-aik^{y}a, too easy-aik^{y}a, it would not be any fun-aik^{y}a!" Then he set forth his own ideas about the relationship between the sexes and the conception of children.

To this day the old people say, "And we followed Coyote."

How Cottontail Rabbit Conquered the Sun

In ancient times Tavapɨtsɨ, the Sun, was much larger than he now is and threw out much more heat. Then almost all the earth was so hot that people could scarcely live on it. Tavutsɨ, Cottontail Rabbit, set out to do something about this condition. He journeyed towards the east, to find the place where the Sun emerges.

As he came near to that place, crossing the hot desert, he came upon two small children, sound asleep. They were Tavo^{w}aatsɨ, Young Cottontail Rabbit, and Kamu^{w}aantsɨ, Young Jackrabbit. Now this was a desolate, waterless region, but the children did not look starved—they even had little potbellies. Cottontail Rabbit became very curious. He looked about till he found a very slender, sharply-pointed stick, then he twirled it upon the little round belly of one of the sleeping children. When he had made a tiny hole, he drew the stick out carefully and examined it. He saw that the child had eaten a few small seeds and yucca dates, and had drunk a little water. Then he woke the children up and questioned them.

"Where are your parents?" he asked.

"We are orphans," they answered.

"Then how do you get your water and food?"

The children were so young that they could not speak plainly, but they managed to explain that to obtain water they would approach the shore of Narɨwiin^{y}apah, Everlasting Water,[12] and sing to it:

Nara´ wampaa	Narɨwiin^{y}apah [sung in baby-talk]
Nara´ wampaa	Narɨwiin^{y}apah [sung in baby-talk]
mahaig^{y}in^{y}i	Pursue me with intent to injure!
mahaig^{y}in^{y}i	Pursue me with intent to injure!

Now since mahai- means with intent to injure and ki- to come towards or after, and nɨmaiwig^{y}ah is said of a person who goes to war, this was a challenge issued by two feeble babies to the great

Immortal Water, which would promptly and violently pursue them. The children would run away beyond the Water's reach, then when it had retreated they would come out and quench their thirst at the pools it had left behind.

Cottontail Rabbit told the orphans to sing their challenge just as usual while he hid nearby armed with a large rock. When Immortal Water came raging out of its banks, he flung his stone and caused it to splash all over the earth, forming all the streams, lakes, springs, tanks, and watering places of every sort from which people now drink.

At that time Narɨwiinᵞatcɨmpɨ, Immortal Yucca Date, floated in the air, out of reach of human hands. When they needed food, the children said, they would stand at a certain place and sing:

Nara' watcɨ' ɨmpɨ	Narɨwiinᵞatcɨmpɨ [sung in baby-talk]
Nara' watcɨ' ɨmpɨ	Narɨwiinᵞatcɨmpɨ [sung in baby-talk]
mahaiginᵞi	Pursue me with intent to injure!
mahaiginᵞi	Pursue me with intent to injure!

When the enraged Immortal Yucca Date came down to chase them, they would throw stones at it and break off small pieces to gather up and eat after it had returned to its place.

Again with the children's help, Cottontail Rabbit set an ambush. The large stone which he threw smashed the Immortal Yucca Date and scattered it far and wide. This was the origin of all species of yucca and of all yucca-like plants which bear the fruit called tcɨmpɨ.

Then the children told Cottontail Rabbit, "Before our mother died, she stored seeds in a crack in a rock."

Cottontail Rabbit went with them to see the place. The crack had all but closed up, and the orphans were able to extract only a few seeds at a time by thrusting in a slender, moistened stick. Cottontail Rabbit pried open the crack with his poro and gave to all the world a plentiful supply of plants bearing edible seeds.

Cottontail Rabbit took the children with him and wandered about over the desert asking every bush if it burned. Many bushes answered, "Yes, I burn." But at length one said, "My leaves burn, but my roots and branches do not burn." Cottontail Rabbit made a hole by the root of that shrub where he and the orphan children could take shelter from the fire to come.

Now Cottontail Rabbit set himself for his great task of ambushing the Sun. He selected a large stone that fitted well in his hand. Then he hid himself near the place where the Sun emerges. Innumerable crows appeared, flying about and crying, kak*a*, kak*a*. Thinking the Sun was about to come out, he gripped his stone tightly and prepared to throw. But it was Mi^{y}arogopits*i*, the Moon, who emerged, and the crows settled themselves upon his head. Cottontail Rabbit let him go by unharmed.

Next the Sun came out of the hole, throwing out intolerable brightness and heat. Cottontail Rabbit took careful aim and threw the stone. He struck his target, and at once great fiery chunks broke off of the Sun, and the whole desert took fire. But Cottontail Rabbit and the children ran to the place he had prepared beneath the bush that does not burn.

When the fire had burnt itself out, it became evident that the heat of the Sun had been so reduced that mankind could now endure it.

How Wildcat Brothers Recovered Their Hunting Song

Tukunanavaviw*i* (three or more) Wildcat Brothers, lived with their aged mother. They owned a song for killing kam*i*w*i*, jackrabbits, and tavutsiw*i*, cottontail rabbits. They would go along singing:

hii´ kwasii´	tail (kwas*i*)
hii´ kwasii´	tail (kwas*i*)
hii´ kwasii´	tail (kwas*i*)
hii´ kwasii´	tail (kwas*i*)

until they sighted a rabbit. Then one of the brothers would quickly point his finger[13] at it and exclaim: Tosatavitaakwa^{ʔ}a (tavi-, to tumble), White tumbling over! The animal would immediately fall over dead, exposing its white underside. Then a brother would gather it up, and the group would wander on singing until they sighted another rabbit.

Coyote[14] came to visit. He went out after rabbits with Wildcat Brothers and decided they had a pretty good way to hunt. He watched carefully and listened to their song. Then he went home and taught the song to his wife, son, and four daughters. The next day Wildcat Brothers went out to hunt, but they could not remember their song; Coyote had stolen it. Now they had to hunt in the ordinary, non-magical way with bows and arrows. They had bad luck and went hungry.

At long last the oldest brother[15] wounded a jackrabbit, who ran off with the arrow sticking in him. Wildcat followed him. The jackrabbit ran for a very long time, up a long, gradual slope. When Wildcat finally overtook him, killed him, and recovered the arrow, he looked about and saw that he was in unfamiliar territory. He was on top of the sky.

Wildcat saw smoke rising and went towards it. He found his maternal grandfather (tox$o$) making charcoal so that he would have a little something to bet in the peon game that night. The old man was Tavahuk^{w}amp$i$, Sun Spider.[16] Every night he gambled with the Rabbits of that country. At the time of his grandson's arrival he had already lost all his property and his wife and children; he had nothing left to bet except a little charcoal and his own life. To change the old man's luck, Wildcat gave him the jackrabbit to eat. Then he told his grandfather to make peon sticks out of the jackrabbit's leg bones and during the course of the game to substitute them for the sticks which his opponents would hand him. To make success certain, Wildcat made himself small and hid inside his grandfather's wrist protector.

That night Sun Spider won back his wife and family and all his property. Then he kept on winning. The Rabbits became suspicious. They muttered among themselves, "His grandson (togots$i$) must have arrived." But they continued playing and losing. Towards morning Sun Spider pretended to have diarrhea. Every time he left the gaming-place (ostensibly to relieve himself) he cast his net (spun his web) a little farther, until he had the area completely surrounded.

The Sky Rabbits lost everything. Finally they bet their lives and lost them too. Then the game broke up, and they tried to run away. But Wildcat leaped full-sized from his grandfather's wrist protector and killed them all. Because of the net that had been cast, not one escaped.

After that Wildcat asked his grandfather to help him to return to the land below the sky.

Sun Spider said, "First you must let me swallow you. And when you feel yourself descending, you must on no account look up."

Wildcat agreed and allowed himself to be swallowed. But as he was going down, curiosity overcame him, and he looked up. He saw that he was suspended by a thread that came out of a red hole in the sky, far above him. Immediately Sun Spider drew him up, disgorged him, and chided him severely for disobedience. Wildcat said he was sorry and promised not to repeat his offense. Then his grandfather swallowed him a second time and let him down to earth without further trouble.

When Wildcat returned to his home, he and his brothers turned themselves into tavaʔatsiwɨ, desert chipmunks. They watched Coyote's house till they saw him go out to hunt with the stolen song,[17] taking his family with him. Then they crept into his house and gnawed all his warm rabbitskin blankets into shreds. By the magic power which they now had, they caused extreme cold and heavy snow. Coyote and his whole family froze to death.

In this way Wildcat Brothers recovered their hunting song.

How the Pleiades Came to Be[18]

Coyote was living with his wife, son, and three daughters.[19]

One of the daughters became sick and was about to die. A shaman was summoned to cure her. After he had worked for awhile, he said that it had been revealed to him that in order for the girl to recover her health her father must fetch a jug of water from Narɨwiinʸapah, the Ocean. But this was only a pretext to get Coyote out of the way for awhile. After he had trotted off towards the seacoast, the shaman declared publicly that it was Coyote's incestuous relations with his daughter which had caused her illness.[20]

The young woman's body then expelled the cause of its sickness. But so deeply was everyone disgusted with Coyote and his behavior that the whole group, the shaman and Coyote's wife and children, betook themselves to the sky. Before they left, Coyote's wife tidied up the camp. She thrust the afterbirth into the hot ashes of the campfire.

Coyote came back with his jug of sea water and found no one at home. He smelled meat roasting, sniffed around, dug up what his wife had buried in the ashes, and began to eat it.

His wife looked down and saw what he was doing. "May that one look up!" she said.

Coyote looked up and saw the medicine man and his family among the stars. "Haik^{y}a!" he exclaimed. "You will become Soniyaw-aik^{y}a!"[21]

"You," his wife answered, "will become cɨna$^?$avi, coyote. You will poke your long nose into the filth of abandoned campsites and become a scavenger!"

How the Length of the Seasons was Determined

In the time When the Animals Were People, it devolved upon those Immortals to set the earth in order. They established four seasons, called tamana, spring; tatca, summer; yɨvana, autumn; and tomo, winter.[22]

Then the question arose as to how many months should be included in each season. The First People held a great Gathering to decide the matter. But of all those present there were only two who had fixed opinions on the subject. They were Coyote and Paɨn$^?$nagw^{a}itsi, Burrowing Owl.[23]

Coyote liked for everything to be arranged in groups of four. He stood up in the meeting and said loudly, "Haik^{y}a, haik^{y}a! The seasons shall be four months long-aik^{y}a!"

Burrowing Owl said not a word. He just held up his little three-toed foot.[24]

Coyote was noisier than ever. "Haik^{y}a, haik^{y}a! I say that four months is the proper length-aik^{y}a!"

Burrowing Owl silently continued to hold up his three-toed foot.

"No-aik^{y}a, no-aik^{y}a!" said Coyote, refusing to yield.

Still without saying a single word, Burrowing Owl left the Gathering and went into a nearby thicket. There, hidden from everyone, he began to utter his own peculiar cry: "Parangkwingkwi$^?$i, parangkwingkwi$^?$i, parangkwingkwi$^?$i."

Coyote pricked up his ears. He rushed into the thicket to investigate the strange noise. Burrowing Owl assumed his alternate form of Rattlesnake and promptly bit him.

"Haik^{y}a, haik^{y}a, haik^{y}a!" Coyote yelped, "I give up-aik^{y}a! I give up-aik^{y}a! The seasons-aik^{y}a shall consist of three months each-aik^{y}a!"

Then Coyote was left alone in the thicket. He looked around and saw that the squawberries were showing a little color. It was already the beginning of the first spring. Now he was not angry any more. He was glad that he had lost the argument. He realized that if winter was to be only three months long, spring and the time of ripening fruit would come that much quicker. Coyote loved to gorge himself on berries.

How Dove's Son Escaped from Wind Woman[25]

Nɨarɨmamauʔu, Wind Woman, was lustful and always on the prowl.

At that time Hiʸovi, Dove, was living with her infant son. She had a nurse to care for him while she went out daily to gather seeds. The nurse's name was ʔAtarakamuupitsi, Sandbar Fly. Whenever Dove returned from her seed gathering, she would identify herself by uttering the cry of the mourning dove, afterwards calling out, "Fetch my child!" Then Sandbar Fly would carry the baby out to his mother. Wind Woman, prowling in the thickets around Dove's house, listened and observed carefully. One day when Dove was far from home, Wind Woman hid in the brush and called, "Hiʸo, hiʸo, fetch my child!" Sandbar Fly came with the infant, and Wind Woman stole him from his nurse's arms. Later Dove came and called for her son. Sandbar Fly had to tell her what had happened. In her rage and grief, Dove squeezed the nurse so hard that to this day sandbar flies have a tapered shape.

Years passed. Dove's son grew up to be a young man in the house of Wind Woman. His whole desire was to escape from her, but he could not think how to manage it. Her incessant sexual demands had caused him to develop a very large and heavy penis which hampered him when he tried to run.

One day when Dove's son was out hunting he met four girls who were his cousins. They took pity on him and reduced his penis to its normal size. Also they gave him good advice. "When next you kill game," they told him, "tie it in the top of a tall tree. Then when Wind Woman goes to fetch it, you can get a headstart."

Dove's son followed their advice. He killed a deer very far from home and tied its carcass securely near the top of a tall tree. When he returned to Wind Woman's house, he lay down and told her where she would find the meat. As soon as she was out of sight, he began to run.

Wind Woman returned with her load and saw that her victim had escaped. She pursued him with the swiftness of the wind.

When he was about to be overtaken, the young man came upon a group of men playing a game of archery. They were shooting arrows at a single arrow which they had previously shot into the trunk of a tree to serve as a target. One of the archers removed the head of his arrow, made Dove's son very small, hid him in the shaft, and replaced the flint. Just as Wind Woman came in sight, he shot the arrow as far as he possibly could. As it struck the earth, Dove's son came out, resumed his normal size, and ran on.

Next the fugitive came to a cave where a man sat making arrows. He asked the man's help. Again he was made very small and hidden, this time in a bundle of arrow-making material. When Wind Woman came to the mouth of the cave, the man was receptive to her advances. He had no difficulty in getting her to enter the cave. Then watching his chance, he threw out all his possessions, including the bundle where Dove's son was hiding, leaped out after them, and tightly sealed the mouth of the cave.

Enclosed forever in the cave, Wind Woman became ʔAanoʔoví, Echo.[26]

The Journeys of Southern Fox[27]

Tantɨvaiyɨpatsí, Southern Fox, resembled present-day Chemehuevis in that he liked to go on long journeys to visit friends and relatives.

When Southern Fox left his home in Wiyaatuʷa, the Whipple Range, to visit his northern cousin, ʔAngá, Blue Jay, he travelled in the following manner: stringing his bow from end to end with arrows, he discharged them all at once,[28] outran them in their flight, and being like Coyote, manaikʸatɨ, a good dodger, he dodged them as they fell to earth around him. Then he collected the arrows. Whenever he pulled out one that had pierced the earth, water sprang forth. The first water that he made on this trip was Hawayawí, now known as West Wells. Again he shot all his arrows at once, and this time he made Hahaivʸa, Kleinfelter. Then he went on to make Paasa, Paiute Springs. Thus he made many springs all along his route.

Southern Fox had arrowheads made of black flint. On another journey, this time travelling south, he met his Tuhugʷantɨ, his Enemy. The Enemy taunted him because of the color of his arrowheads, saying that he could not kill anything with charcoal. Southern Fox and his Enemy then agreed to settle their quarrel by a duel. Retiring to a considerable distance from one another, each loaded his bow with arrows and discharged them all at once. Of the two, Southern Fox was the better dodger. He dodged all his Enemy's arrows. But the Enemy was killed, and the remains of his body may be seen to this day. Also the imprint of Southern Fox's knee, where he braced himself to shoot, may still be seen. It is called Tantɨvaiyɨpatsi Tangaronʔnɨgipɨ, Southern Fox's Knee-Thrust.[29]

On still another one of his trips, Southern Fox crossed Death Valley, which he named Kunayɨwaavɨ, Fire Valley. As he travelled over the floor of that Valley, he sang:

Kunayɨwaavaa	At Fire Valley
kuminʸak^{a}i	burnt off by fire
kuminʸak^{a}i	burnt off by fire

and as he sang, he burnt off to his ankles; still going on and still singing, he burnt off to his knees; then to his hips, to his waist, and to his chest. Finally only his head was left, rolling or bouncing along over the burning surface of the desert and still singing. But when he came out on the other side, Southern Fox had his complete body.[30]

How Horned Toad Visited the Giants

Makatcatsɨ, Horned Toad, lived all by himself in the desert. One day a cousin, Witciʔitsɨ,[31] Small Bird, stopped by to visit him.

"Where are you bound for?" Horned Toad asked.

"I am on my way to visit the Tutusiwɨ,[32] the Giants," Small Bird said.

"Oh, let me go too," Horned Toad begged. "I like to travel, I would like very much to visit the Giants."

"I am afraid to take you with me," Small Bird said. "These giants are cannibals and swallow anyone who laughs at them. That is their excuse for eating people alive. But they are also very comical fellows and will do every sort of stunt to try to make their visitors laugh. You are a person who laughs at everything. You are too easily amused. It would be the end of you if ever you walked into their camp."

"No, I won't laugh," Horned Toad promised, grinning broadly all the while. "I will not laugh at anything."

"Well, since you want to go so badly, you may come along," his cousin said. "But I don't trust you. I will have to fix you up with some sort of protection."

Small Bird looked around to see what he could devise. He gathered up some flint arrowheads and bound them into a wreath, which he tied tightly around Horned Toad's head. Then the two travellers went on their way.

As they approached the camp of the Giants, Small Bird again warned Horned Toad. "After supper they will test you," he said, "they will do everything they can to make you laugh."

"I won't even crack a smile," Horned Toad assured him, still wearing his broad grin.

The cousins arrived late in the afternoon. They sat down in the camp, and the Giants shared their food with them. These giants were very big, much bigger than Horned Toad had expected them to be, and they were stark naked. But he was sure he could keep from laughing at them.

Darkness fell, and the Giants began to dance and to cut capers around the fire. They openly practiced sodomy and indulged in all sorts of wild and outrageously funny sex play. They leaped and capered in the firelight, and their great, fantastic shadows leaped and capered with them.

Small Bird watched solemnly. Horned Toad watched grinning from ear to ear. There was a big rock sticking up in the midst of the fire. Suddenly a Giant went up to this redhot rock and thrust his huge penis against it. Everybody could hear it sizzling.

This was too much for Horned Toad. He burst out laughing, and the Giant promptly picked him up and swallowed him. But the wreath of flints tickled the Giant's throat so that he was forced to cough the little fellow up again.[33]

Then the cousins left that camp of the Giants and continued on their travels.

To this day the horned toads of this present world wear wreaths of flint and broad grins.

Twin Sons of the Sun[34]

A woman was living alone in a cave[35] on Wiyaatu^wa, Whipple Mountain. Each morning it was her custom to go outside her cave and lie down with her legs spread wide apart, opening herself towards the rising Sun. On one of these mornings, Tavap<del>i</del>ts<del>i</del>, Sun, by a sudden concentration of his rays, caused her to conceive. She gave birth to twin sons.

The woman never saw her husband in his human (or partly human) form. But every day, while she was out seed-gathering, he would visit and care for his sons. He also left them presents of warm clothing and red flannel.[36]

How Yucca Date Worm Girls Went to Look for a Husband

The two Yucca Date Worm Girls[37] were plump, cream-colored (?o^wakar<del>i</del>m<del>i</del>), and very desirable. They were old enough to be married, and they needed a man to hunt for them.

As they wandered about over the desert in search of a husband, they came to a house with much sinew hanging up outside.

"Look! Here is much sinew hanging up to dry," said the younger girl. "The man who lives here must be a good hunter. That is the kind of man we are looking for. He won't let us go hungry."

The sisters sat down side by side to await the owner of the house. Presently a man came in sight over the brow of a hill, packing a large load of sinew on his back. As he approached, the girls were nudging each other and smiling. "Look who is coming," they said, "just look at his big load!"

When Tu?upa?av<del>i</del>, Indian Asparagus Worm, arrived at his house, he cooked a big mess of sinew and gave it to the girls to eat. He was glad to get them for wives, because he had been living all alone.

In the morning the new husband arose very early. He told his wives, "I am going out to hunt big game." Late in the afternoon he returned, heavily laden with sinew. This procedure was repeated for four days. Each morning Indian Asparagus Worm announced that he was going out to hunt big game, and each evening he returned with a load of sinew and nothing else.

After he had left on the fourth morning, the older girl asked, "What kind of animal is it that our husband always kills? What kind of animal can it be that has no bones, no skin, no flesh? I don't believe it is real meat that he is bringing us. Tomorrow let us trail him and see what he really does."

On the fifth morning, as soon as their husband was out of sight, the girls began to follow his tracks. He came to a large bed of Indian asparagus and started to dig. There the two Yucca Date

Worm Girls overtook him and hid themselves to watch what he was doing. They saw him dig the toughest stalks and put them in his carrying net. This was the kind of sinew that he had bringing home every night!

"Look!" the girls exclaimed. "Just look what he has been feeding us! Let us go away." Immediately they set off across the desert.

After travelling for some distance they came to a house with much blood sausage hanging up outside.

"Look at that delicious blood sausage!" said the younger sister. "This must surely be the home of a good hunter. Let us stay here with him."

Again they sat down to wait for the owner of the house. When Nintinavi, Red Racer, came he brought with him a large quantity of blood for making blood pudding and blood sausage. The girls were happy to see this, for they had become very tired of sinew. Red Racer cooked blood pudding and gave it to his new wives.

Early in the morning he said, "I am going out to hunt big game"; and late in the afternoon he returned loaded down with blood.

On the fourth day, after Red Racer had left saying that he was going to hunt big game, the older girl said, "I am getting tired of eating nothing but blood pudding and blood sausage. What kind of an animal can it be that is without skin or bones or flesh? I wonder if it is real blood that he keeps bringing us? Let us follow him tomorrow and find out."

The next morning Red Racer left to hunt big game, with the two sisters hard on his trail but keeping out of sight. They watched when he came to a large thorn bush. First he tied the four corners of his buckskin so that it formed a bag and hung it under the bush. Then he dived through the thorns, crying "Paḧ'gurugurguru," and hung himself like a bow over the bush, letting his blood run down into the buckskin. Four times he dived through the thornbush and drained his own blood.

"Look! See what he has been giving us to eat! His own blood!" the Yucca Date Worm Girls cried in great disgust. And again they said, "Let us go away."

Off they went over the desert, still looking for a proper husband.

After they had walked for quite a long time, they came to another house. All around it much fat was hanging, nothing but fat.

"Here is where a good hunter lives," the younger sister said. "Look at all the fat he has hanging here! It will taste good after the stuff we have been eating."

The girls sat down to wait.

In a short time Paatsats*i*, Bat, came home, carrying a large load of fat on his back. He put it down and told the girls, "They say this is ice-fat; they say it should be eaten without letting it touch fire." That evening Bat did not make a fire nor cook anything. He fed the Yucca Date Worm Girls on raw fat.

The next morning he told his wives, "You stay here at the house. I am going out to hunt big game."

Late in the afternoon Bat returned with another load of fat, and again the girls had to eat it raw. The next day and the next and the next he came back with nothing but fat.

On the fourth day the elder girl said, "Why does not our husband want us to cook this fat? I am getting tired of eating it raw. Why does he not bring home the flesh and bones of the animals that he has killed? He must kill an animal that has nothing but fat. Tomorrow we shall follow him and find out."

In the morning Bat went flapping away, flapping away, flapping away to a deep and narrow box canyon through which a stream ran. By his peculiar magic he caused the water to freeze into solid ice. Then he picked up a large stone, flew across the canyon, and dropped it onto the ice, thus breaking it up into chunks. He repeated this action till he had enough chunks of ice for a large load. Thereupon the ice turned into fat, and he placed it in his carrying-net; this was the "ice-fat" that Bat had been bringing home to his wives.

Although when he flew he left no tracks, the Yucca Date Worm Girls had managed to follow. From a hiding place nearby they had watched everything he did.

"Look what he does," they said, "he has been feeding us nothing but ice! Let us go away at once."

Again they wandered over the desert.

At last they came to a house where they saw much jerky hanging up, also many hides, both tanned and untanned. Also around that house the bones of various kinds of animals lay scattered upon the ground.

"Look!" the elder sister said, "here a real hunter lives. This is a hunter indeed, the kind of man we are looking for. Let us stay here and wait for him."

Presently the owner of the house appeared. He wore a fine buckskin suit, and on his head a kaitcoxo, mountain hat—a pointed cap made of buckskin and trimmed with many rows of quail crests. On his back the hunter packed a great load of meat, together with the hide of the deer that he had killed. Arriving at his home, he made a fire and cooked meat for himself and the girls. Then they all went to sleep.

The next morning Kwanantsitsi, Red-Tailed Hawk, did not go out hunting. There was no need; he had plenty of food in the house. He stayed home all day, talking with his wives, getting acquainted with them, and enjoying their company. He also made them dresses and moccasins. Altogether he stayed with his wives four days, and two of those days he spent sewing clothes for them, because until this time the young women had been completely naked, without even aprons.

The fifth morning Red-Tailed Hawk said, "We are going to move to another place where there is more game. You two girls pack up all our belongings and carry them with you. Go around yonder mountain to the other side, where you will find a spring with a cave by it. Camp there, but do not go into the cave. I am going to travel across the mountain, hunting mountain sheep as I go. Perhaps night will overtake me, and I may not arrive till morning. Even if I do not come to you tonight, even if it rains and storms, do not enter the cave. You must sleep outside, even in the rain!

"We will do as you say," the sisters said.

Red-Tailed Hawk left them, and the Yucca Date Worm Girls packed everything into two big bundles and started around the mountain. In the afternoon they arrived at the place their husband had described. The sky had clouded over, and it looked like rain.

The younger girl climbed up to see the cave. Then the rain began to fall. She called down to her sister, "This is a good cave, there is nothing the matter with it. Come on up! You will get wet, and all our things will get wet!"

"No," replied the older girl, "our husband told us not to go into the cave, not even if it rained."

"But it is a good cave," the younger sister said, "there is nothing here to hurt us. It will be all right for us to go inside."

"No," said the other, "we must obey our husband."

The two girls argued for some time, calling back and forth while the rain continued to fall. Finally the younger one went down and brought her bundle up to the cave. Then the other girl had to follow with her bundle. "Yes," she agreed at last, "it is a good cave. We will stay in it."

They gathered wood and built a fire inside the cave. After it was dark, after they had lain down by the fire, they heard a voice calling far off. The younger sister called out an answer.

"Keep quiet!" said the older Yucca Date Worm Girl.

"No, I am going to answer, it is our husband calling," the younger said.

The voice sounded again, this time a little nearer.

"Here we are, in the cave!" the younger girl called in answer.

Nearer and nearer came the voice, and every time it sounded the younger sister replied.

At last the one who had been calling came into the cave. He was an old man with a long walking stick (a pi̵ri̵, not a poro which shamans use). He sat down by the fire.

"You may lie on that side of the fire," the sisters said, "there is plenty of room over there."

"No, I never sleep that way," the old man said, using an expression which meant "I never sleep in that position or direction."

"Well then," the girls said, "sleep crosswise down at our feet."

"No, I never sleep that way."

"Well, sleep here between us."

"No, I never sleep that way."

"Then sleep crosswise up at our heads."

"Yes, that is the way I sleep!" the old man said. He lay down above the fire with his head towards the wall of the cave and his feet in a line with the girls' heads. The cave was not very wide, so he had to sleep with his knees drawn up.

In the morning the younger sister said, "What a nice old man! He never even stretched all night long!"

She had no sooner made this remark than ʔAatakapitsi̵, Grasshopper (for that was who the old man was), groaned. Then he began to stretch. Then he kicked out suddenly across the faces of both girls, gouging out their eyes with the serrated undersides of his powerful legs. After that, Grasshopper got up, put their bundles on his back, and went down into the valley, leaving the two blind Yucca Date Worm Girls to stagger about helplessly in the cave.

Red-Tailed Hawk was a great shaman as well as a great hunter. He already knew what had happened to his wives. Therefore when he arrived at the cave later in the morning, he brought with him the eyes of two female mountain sheep which he had killed on his way across the mountain. He put the mountain sheep's eyes into the empty eyesockets of the Yucca Date Worm Girls and restored their sight.

Then he scolded them soundly. "Why did you two women not obey me? I told you not to enter the cave, not even if it rained. You disobeyed me, and now you have lost your eyes. If you had done as I told you, if you had remained outside, all would have been well."

Hot with anger, Red-Tailed Hawk then went down towards the valley, looking for the old man who had blinded his wives and stolen his possessions. While he was still high up on the mountain side, he saw a giant in the valley beneath him, strutting about and shooting arrows up into the sky as he sang:

> My eagle-arrows
> my eagle-arrows
> melting (that is, disappearing) one after the other.[38]

Red-Tailed Hawk hurried down into the valley, very angry and eager for battle. But as he approached, the giant became smaller and smaller; and when he reached the floor of the valley, there was no one to be seen.

Red-Tailed Hawk started back up the mountain. Far up on its slope, he paused and looked back. There was the giant, large as ever, capering below him and shooting his arrows at the sky! Again Red-Tailed Hawk rushed down, and again no one was there. This time he searched the valley thoroughly, but found no living thing except swarms of small grasshoppers, hopping about vigorously.

Again he climbed far up the mountain, turned to look back, and saw the giant. And again when he descended there was no one in the valley to fight.

After he had come down the mountain for the fourth time, Red-Tailed Hawk was in a fury. He looked at all the grasshoppers jumping about and shouted, "Perhaps it is these little ones! At least I will get rid of them." He took a stick and beat about among the swarms of insects till he had killed them all. Then once again he started back up the mountain. But this time when he looked back he saw the giant lying dead on the floor of the valley!

Red-Tailed Hawk went down again, and the corpse of the giant Grasshopper did not disappear as he approached. It still lay there, and beside it lay the two bundles that had been stolen. Red-Tailed Hawk put them on his back and carried them back to the spot where his wives were waiting.

Afterwards the three of them lived there in the cave and had no further trouble.

How Coyote Went to War Against Gila Monster

ʔɨtciv*i*, Gila Monster,[39] and ʔAy*a*, Turtle,[40] were companions and partners. Both were chiefs. Gila Monster was the High Chief (tɨ-vitsitog^{wa}intɨm*i*, Real Chief), and Turtle was the lesser chief (miʔ^yau-pitog^{wa}intɨm*i*). Those two were the heads of a very large band.

Gila Monster and Turtle instructed their people well. When a good year came, the women gathered seeds and stored them in large baskets capped with potsherds and sealed with greasewood gum. They gathered fruit and berries, which they dried and stored. They boiled the heart of mescal plants and pounded them out into slabs two or three feet across. The hunters brought in much meat. Some of it was pounded into slabs and dried, like the mescal hearts, and some was made into jerky. Then the people dug a big hole and buried all the food they had prepared. They covered it well and made the surface of the ground look like it had not been disturbed. Afterwards the whole band went to roam around the country. Because it was such a good year, they could find food everywhere and could travel wherever they pleased.

There came a bad year. Coyote and his people were living near the place where Gila Monster and his people had stored their food, but because it was so well hidden they did not know about it. Coyote had not told his people to prepare food and store it, and the result was that they now had nothing at all to eat. Coyote wandered off alone to see if he could find anything. He saw one solitary bean on a screw mesquite tree. He shot it down with an arrow, and the bean dropped into a little hole in the ground. Coyote went over to dig it out, but the more he dug, the further the bean rolled down along a crack in the dry earth. The bean kept rolling, and Coyote kept digging, till at last he uncovered the food that the people of Gila Monster had buried.

"Haik^ya, haik^ya, I have good luck-aik^ya," he shouted, "I have found much food-aik^ya!"

Coyote made his home right there. He did not go back and tell his starving people about the food. He just stayed there, eating his way deeper and deeper into the hole.[41]

In the meantime, Gila Monster and Turtle had said to their people, "We are having a bad year. Let us return to our food cache." Then they had started home.

As they approached the place where the food had been stored, Coyote heard voices. He looked out of the hole and saw many people coming. They were already very near. By this time Coyote had eaten almost all the food in the cache.

Coyote was frightened. "Haik^ya, haik^ya, my penis-aik^ya, what shall I do-aik^ya?" he cried.

His penis advised him, "Make yourself dead. Make yourself into cɨna^ʔagaipɨ, a coyote carcass."

Coyote became an old, dead coyote, one that looked as if it had been lying there for several months.

The people of Gila Monster and Turtle said, "This is the place all right—but look! Just look what that coyote has done to our food! And there he lies dead! He smells bad—somebody take a stick and throw him out!"

Two men took a long stick, worked it under the carcass, and tossed the stinking thing out of the hole. Coyote hit the ground alive and running, and with a good headstart.

"Haik^ya, haik^ya!" he called back over his shoulder, taunting the people he had wronged, "how could you know that I was fooling you-aik^ya?"

The people were terribly angry. They followed Coyote in hot pursuit.

As he reached his own camp he called out, "Haik^ya, prepare for war-aik^ya! Prepare for war-aik^ya! Gila Monster is on the war-path-aik^ya! His people are coming after us-aik^ya!"

Gila Monster and Turtle with all their warriors were right on his heels. Coyote's people were unprepared and weak from hunger. Almost all of them were killed or taken captive. When Coyote saw that his side was losing, he ran away and hid himself, and some of his people went with him.

With the exception of those who ran away, there remained of Coyote's band after the battle only one old woman, who had been left for dead, and her infant grandson (hutsits*i*, woman's son's child), who had been left to die when his mother was carried away captive. The old woman revived. Looking around among the dead, she saw the living child, picked him up, and comforted him. After that she gathered seeds and berries every day, always singing as she worked, and in this way she raised him.

When the boy began to creep, his grandmother would warn him whenever she had to leave, saying, "Do not go outside the house. It is dangerous, there are many enemies about." After he learned to walk, she continued to caution him, "Do not go far away, this is enemy country." But she never explained anything to him. She never told him who the enemies were nor how he had been orphaned.

Every day the little boy grew more daring and wandered farther and farther from the house while his grandmother was out gathering food. One day he made himself a toy bow and arrow. Then when he had grown bigger, he made himself a larger bow and arrow and took them with him to a little waterhole where he had observed birds coming to drink. He hid himself behind a bush to ambush whatever might come for water. After awhile a small brown bird (yu?uravats*i*) came down to water. The boy shot it and broke its leg.

The little bird flew off under a tree and called, "Hutsitsin^y*i*, come make me a leg! My grandson, come make me a leg!"

The boy was puzzled. He wondered, "How can that Bird be my grandmother, hutsin^y*i*, when hutsin^y*i* is out gathering seeds?"

Yu?uravats*i* (who was, of course, an Immortal appearing in her bird form) just kept calling, "My grandson, come make me a leg! My grandson, come make me a leg!"

After a long time the little boy went over to her and tied up her leg with splints. Then she asked him, "Has your grandmother never told you your history? Has she never told you anything about your parents or how you lost them?"

"No," said the boy.

Then Yu?uravats*i* told him the whole story of how Gila Monster's people had fought with and conquered Coyote's people. "Do you see all these bones lying around here?" she asked. "They are the bones of your relatives who were killed in the battle. This pile of bones is all that remains of your father. He was killed, and your mother was taken captive.

"Now you must go back," she went on. "You must pick out a good hard piece of wood, and you must smooth it and shape it until you have made it into a sharp knife. Then you must have your grandmother drop it down on top of your head and split you in two. In that way you will become two boys."

On the way back to his home the boy kept thinking of all he had been told. His mind was full of how his father had been killed and his mother carried away captive. He found a hardwood stick and began to shape it into a knife. When the afternoon was well advanced, he hid it and went on home. As soon as he entered the house, he lay down without speaking to his grandmother, who was preparing supper. When the meal was ready, he refused to eat. Then his grandmother began to cry.

"It must be that you have met hutsi⁀imi, your (other) grand-mother,"[42] she said, "and she has told you all about what happened when you were a baby. That is why you are angry." Then the old woman repeated to the boy all that Yu⁀uravatsi had already told him.

The boy did not say a word.

In the morning he did not eat. After the old woman had gone out as usual to gather seeds, he got up and left the house. He went to the place where he had hidden the stick he was making into a knife and resumed work on it. All day long he went without food. When the day had ended, he had finished the knife. He hid it near his house, went in, and lay down. Again he just lay there without eating or speaking.

Very early in the morning, the boy got up. He went out and got his knife and brought it into the house. Then he awakened his grandmother.

"Grandmother," he said, "take this and split me in two with it!"

"No, no, my grandson," she protested, "I do not want to kill you!"

"You do not need to strike me with it," the boy explained, "you just have to lay the edge of the blade on the top of my head."

The old woman was afraid to do even that. The boy went on insisting that she must split him in two. At length, in great distress, she picked up the knife and laid the blade on the crown of his head. Instantly she fell over in a faint, releasing the knife, which dropped and of its own weight split the boy in two. There stood two Dove Boys (Hi^{y}ovin^{y}a$^?$aiv^{y}atsiw$i$), where only one had been before.[43]

"Get up, get up!" the boys shouted in unison to their grandmother, "Now there are two of us!"

After quite a long while the old woman revived. She looked up and saw that her grandson had become two. Then she began to talk war. She painted her face black and her bangs red. She told the boys, "You stay here. I will go tell Coyote and the other people to prepare to go on the warpath."

The old woman went to the camp where Coyote was living with a number of his people. When these people saw her approaching with her warpaint on, they exclaimed to each other, "It must be that the grandson of Win$^?$namakasaama$^?$ap$i$tsi[44] has become two!" They had all known that this was going to happen some day. It was the sign they had been waiting for. Now the time for vengeance had come.

Then Win$^?$namakasaama$^?$ap$i$tsi told them plainly, "My grandson has become two, and I want all you people to go on the warpath."

Coyote came out in a high state of excitement. "Haik^{y}a, haik^{y}a, that is what we have been waiting for you to say-aik^{y}a, now I will go around-aik^{y}a and tell the others-aik^{y}a to get ready to go on the warpath-aik^{y}a, to go on the warpath-aik^{y}a! I will go get Tsasiyav-aik^{y}a (Large Red Ant) and his people-aik^{y}a, $^?$Angaav-aik^{y}a (Small Red Ant) and his people-aik^{y}a, Muhuav-aik^{y}a (Mosquito) and his people-aik^{y}a, Pipit-aik^{y}a (Horsefly) and his people-aik^{y}a, Kwiyats-aik^{y}a (Rattlesnake) and his people-aik^{y}a, Tannakaits-aik^{y}a (Sidewinder) and his people-aik^{y}a, Hun-aik^{y}a (Badger) and his people-aik^{y}a!"

All these whom Coyote named were lesser chiefs subject to him but not living with him at that time. In the same camp with him were other lesser chiefs and their bands, namely: $^?$Atap$i$tsi, Crow, with his people; Lizard[45] with his people; Wikump$i$tsi, Buzzard, and his people; and Mugwi^{y}a, Guico, and his people.

When all had been notified, and when the chiefs and warriors of all the bands subject to Coyote were assembled, they set out on the warpath. Dove Boys and Wɨnʔnamakasaamaʔapɨts*i* went with them.

They made their first camp. When all were seated about the campfire, Coyote, still very excited, addressed his people, calling them ʔaiv^yayawɨn*i*, my nephews, not because they were his real nephews but because that is the proper way for a Chief to speak to his warriors.

"Haik^y*a*, haik^y*a*," he said, "it is customary-aik^y*a*, it is the proper thing-aik^y*a*, when people are going on the warpath-aik^y*a*, when they camp-aik^y*a*, for all of them to sing their war songs-aik^y*a*! You sing first, my Lizard-nephew-aik^y*a*!"

Lizard sang:

Si'wampɨru'k^waiy	From under coarse sand
kwɨ' tɨkiyɨkwɨtɨkiy	(I) get up, get up
siwampɨru'k^waiy	from under coarse sand
kwi' tɨkiyɨkwɨtɨkiy	(I) get up, get up

"Haik^y*a*, haik^y*a*," Coyote said, "It is not good-aik^y*a*, it is not a war song-aik^y*a*, you are just singing about what you do-aik^y*a*!" He made fun of the song. "It is no good-aik^y*a*, it is no good-aik^y*a*!"

"Very well, hand me down my moccasins," said Lizard, rising from his seat by the campfire, "I will return home."

"Haik^y*a*, haik^y*a*," Coyote protested, "you must stay with us-aik^y*a*, I was just fooling-aik^y*a*, your song will go nicely-aik^y*a* when we all sing it together-aik^y*a*!"

Lizard took his seat, and all the warriors sang his song.

Then Coyote said, "Haik^y*a*, haik^y*a*, my Guico-nephew-aik^y*a*, you will sing next-aik^y*a*!"

Guico sang:

Su' kumungkwa' yungkway	(I am) shaped to a point
su' kumungkwa' yungkway	(I am) shaped to a point

"Haik^y*a*, haik^y*a*, it is no good-aik^y*a*!" Coyote exclaimed, making fun of him, "you are just singing about your own shape-aik^y*a*!"

"Well, hand me my moccasins, and I will go home," Guico replied.

"No-aik^y*a*, no-aik^y*a*," Coyote said quickly, "it will sound well when we all sing it together-aik^y*a*!"

Then they all sang Guico's war song.

When they had finished, Coyote said, "Haik^ya, my Crow-nephew-aik^ya, you sing next-aik^ya!"

Crow sang:

ˀUvanguntsi	Going yonder out of sight
ˀuvanguntsi	going yonder out of sight
tatsikwaakwaˀ	(I) come in sight now and then
ˀuvanguntsi	going yonder out of sight
ˀuvanguntsi	going yonder out of sight
tatsikwaakwaˀ	(I) come in sight now and then

Coyote despised that song too. "Haik^ya, it is no good-aik^ya, you are just singing the way you travel-aik^ya, that is not a war song-aik^ya!"

"Give me my moccasins," Crow said, "I am about to return home."

"No-aik^ya," Coyote said, "it will be all right-aik^ya, it will sound well enough when we sing it together-aik^ya!"

Then Crow led the whole war party in singing his song.

Next Coyote said, "Now you must sing your war song-aik^ya, my Buzzard-nephew-aik^ya!"

Now Buzzard was the most fearful to look at of all the warriors. He wore a live turtle for his nose ring, and it scrabbled continually at his breast. Therefore he sang:

ˀAyaʹmuviʹnˀn^yaʹkaʹniʹ	My turtle nose ring
hitsutawanayɨn	scratches me,
ˀayaʹmuviʹnˀn^yaʹkaʹniʹ	my turtle nose ring
hitsutawanayɨn	scratches me

But Coyote had no use for this song either. He said, "Haik^ya, he just sings what he has-aik^ya!"

The terrible Buzzard took offense. "Hand me my moccasins," he said, "so that I may depart for my home."

Coyote knew it would not do to lose such a warrior. "No-aik^ya, no-aik^ya," he said, "don't leave us-aik^ya, your song will sound all right-aik^ya when we sing it together-aik^ya!"

Buzzard sat down very slowly, and the company sang his song.

Coyote said, "Haik^ya, my Mosquito-nephew-aik^ya, you are the next one to sing-aik^ya!"

"Very well," Mosquito replied, "I will sing my war song. But I know it will be the same as with all the others. You will say it is no good."

Then he sang:

Nɨwɨ́ vaɨ́ pitan	People's blood I
hivi′gᵞah, hivi′gᵞah	am drinking, am drinking,
hi′ tokwaava	(I) will rise up
hi′ tokwaava	(I) will rise up

"Haikᵞa, haikᵞa, splendid-aikᵞa, splendid-aikᵞa!" Coyote was carried away with enthusiasm. "Who would think-aikᵞa of drinking live people's blood-aikᵞa? That is a real war song-aikᵞa! That is good-aikᵞa! Now let us all sing it together-aikᵞa!"

When they had finished singing Mosquito's war song, Coyote said, "Haikᵞa, my Horsefly-nephew-aikᵞa, let us hear your war song-aikᵞa!"

Horsefly sang:

Nɨwɨ́ vaɨ́ pita′ ni′	My people's blood
hi′vigᵞani′	I am drinking,
hi′vigᵞani′	I am drinking,
pihᵞɨ′wavi	(my) heart
tɨ′ n ʔnɨgani	I am palpitating,
tɨ′ n ʔnɨgani	I am palpitating

Coyote liked that song too. He said, "That is a fine song-aikᵞa! That is a good song-aikᵞa! Now let us all-aikᵞa sing together the war song of my Horsefly-nephew-aikᵞa!"

They all sang.

Then Coyote asked the other members of the party to sing, one after another, till each had had his turn and the whole war party had sung each song. But the only two songs that he approved of, the only two that he said were real war songs, were those of Mosquito and Horsefly.

When everyone else had sung, the people said to Coyote, "Now it is your turn. Now you must sing your war song."

"Haikᵞa, all right-aikᵞa!" Coyote was pleased that they had asked him. He sang:

Nagasagwᵃiy	Mountain sheep entrails
wɨtompoyaimi-haikᵞ	(I) bundle up,
ha′yɨnɨnɨha′yɨnɨnɨ-aikᵞ	[not translated]

nagasagw^aiy	mountain sheep entrails
wɨtompoyaimi-haik^y	(I) bundle up
ha'yɨnɨnɨha'yɨnɨnɨ-aik^y	[not translated]

"No good! No good!" the people shouted, getting even with him. "He is just singing what he always does." They said this because whenever they butchered a mountain sheep Coyote always bundled up the entrails and took them home with him.

Coyote's feelings were badly hurt. "Hand me down my moccasins-aik^ya," he said, "I will go home-aik^ya, there is no use in my going along-aik^ya!"

"No, no, Coyote," all the people said, "you must go with us, we need you! We were just fooling. Your song will go well when all of us sing it together."

The war party sang Coyote's song. Then they all went to bed.

In the morning all of them, including Dove Boys and their grandmother, Wɨn²namakasaama²apɨtsɨ, started on their way again. Soon they had to cross a wide stretch of desert. It was very hot and dry. The warriors used up all the water they had brought with them, and all began to suffer from thirst.

Coyote said, "Haik^ya, haik^ya, we shall send Dove Boys-aik^ya to find water-aik^ya!"

Then he told the boys how they should do. "You must fly high-aik^ya, and you must not stop at the first place where you see water-aik^ya. You must fly past it-aik^ya, and you must also-aik^ya fly past the second water-aik^ya and the third and the fourth waters-aik^ya! When you come to the fifth water-aik^ya you must sit on a sky-perch-aik^ya and look down below you-aik^ya! You will see many women-aik^ya gathering seeds-aik^ya, and one woman-aik^ya will be off by herself-aik^ya and every once in a while-aik^ya she will stop working-aik^ya, she will look all around-aik^ya and cry-aik^ya! That is your mother-aik^ya! That is the woman who was captured-aik^ya! You must go to her-aik^ya! She will show you the water-aik^ya, and she will explain to you-aik^ya about the waters between us and that place-aik^ya!"

Assuming the form of doves, Dove Boys took flight. They flew very, very high, as Coyote had ordered them to do. They flew over the first four watering places and went on to the fifth. There they stopped and sat on a sky-perch. Far beneath them they saw a crowd of women busily gathering seeds. One woman worked apart from the others; she stopped gathering frequently, looking around and weeping.

"That is our mother," said Dove Boys, "let us go down to her." They flew down and lit on her shoulders, one on each shoulder. "Our mother!" they said.

"My sons!" she answered.

Then the woman asked, "How did you happen to come?"

Dove Boys told her the whole story of the war party and of the events that had led up to it. They also told her that now the warriors were perishing of thirst and that they had been sent to her to find out how they might get water. Then the woman sat down and told them about the various watering places.

"The first water that you came to," she said, "is the watering place of kakarawɨ, the quail. Only quail drink there. It is guarded. The next water belongs to the wiwʔwiyatsiwɨ,[46] and it also is guarded. The third water is the antelopes'[47] watering place. It is guarded. The fourth water is in the center of a barren plain, where there is no brush nor any kind of cover. That whole plain is guarded by Nanapaʔagᵃipuʔᵂitsɨ, Four-Eyed Insect, who stands first on one side of the plain and then on the other.

"Now I will take you home with me so that you can get water. Gila Monster will try you," she warned, "to see if you are real doves. No matter what test he puts you to, you must not cry out, you must keep perfectly quiet and not even blink your eyes. When you have passed his tests, you may go to the water."

The captive woman started back to camp with her sons, who had now become very small young doves. On their way to find her, they had shot a jackrabbit, and this she carried with her along with the baby birds.

As was fitting for a great High Chief, Gila Monster chanted when he spoke, somewhat in the manner of Wolf and other of the great Immortals. As soon as the woman came near, he began to accuse her: "Those are – my enemies – that you are bringing, – they are not – real doves. Where did you get – that jackrabbit? You cannot – kill rabbits."

"I killed *this* jackrabbit," the woman said. "He was in the brush near where I was gathering, and I killed him with my crooked stick. As for these doves, I found a nest of young doves and brought these two home for the children to play with."

"I will test them," Gila Monster chanted, "I will try them – to see if they are – real doves."

He took a redhot coal from the fire and held it to their little beaks, burning them white (which is the reason why the doves of this present time have white beaks). Dove Boys remained perfectly quiet. Then Gila Monster gave them back to the woman. "It must be – that they are real doves," he acknowledged, "they did not even – blink their eyes."

The woman gave the doves to the children, saying, "Take them to the water. They must be very thirsty."

The children took the little doves down to the spring, where they drank and drank until it seemed that they would never stop. When they could drink no more, they fluttered up into a bush, perched there awhile, then suddenly took flight. They flew high and fast back to the camp of Coyote and his warriors. There they resumed the forms of young men, and each youth had a large jar of water on his back. (That is why to this day the male dove feeds his mate when she is sitting on the nest by swallowing and re-gurgitating food and water, and both parents feed their young in this manner.)

When the children realized that their pets were gone, they burst into tears. They went home crying, "We have lost our little doves!"

Then Gila Monster took up his chant: "I knew that they – were not real doves. I rightly suspected – that they were – my enemies."

He turned his attention to the woman, who was now grinding the seed that she had gathered. "Why are you – grinding all that seed? You never ground – so much at one time – before, you always grind just – what you are going – to cook. Now you – are grinding it all. You are preparing it – for the enemy."

"Oh no," the woman said, "I am just grinding it now so that I will not have to grind tomorrow when I come in tired from gather-ing. I want to have something ready to cook."

But Gila Monster said, "You are preparing – for the enemy."

When it became dark the woman was still grinding. For a long time Gila Monster continued to chant about his enemies, but he finally fell asleep. The woman ground on. Towards morning, when she thought it might be almost time for the war party to arrive, she took the sleeping man's stone shirt and hid it. Then she went back to her grinding.

Back in the warriors' camp, Dove Boys found everyone dead for want of water. They went about raising up certain ones by touching them with the *poro* and giving them water; then those resurrected ones set about reviving the others. The next to the last one to be brought back to life was Rattlesnake. As he recovered consciousness he rolled over against a water jug, upsetting it and spilling the water, which flowed out endlessly to form a creek. Now Coyote was still lying dead, directly in the path of the new stream, and the waters floated his body away like an old piece of driftwood. Some of the warriors ran after him and revived him.

"Haik^{y}a, haik^{y}a!" Coyote exclaimed as he regained consciousness, "I must have over-slept-aik^{y}a!"

Then Coyote called all his company together to hear what Dove Boys had to tell them. "Tell us-aik^{y}a," he said, "all about where you have been-aik^{y}a and how you fared there-aik^{y}a! Tell us about the watering places-aik^{y}a!"

When the young men had finished their account, he gave the order to proceed. "All right-aik^{y}a! Let us go-aik^{y}a!"

They travelled on across the desert till they came near to the first watering place. Then Coyote called for a volunteer. "Haik^{y}a, haik^{y}a, who will be the man-aik^{y}a to kill the guard-aik^{y}a?"

"Kwaagwaw*i*, I will," said Rattlesnake.[48]

"All right-aik^{y}a," Coyote said, "I will turn myself into a quail-aik^{y}a and take you along as my belt-aik^{y}a!"

Thereupon Coyote turned himself into a very large quail and turned Rattlesnake into a tu^{2}ur*u*, a buckskin strap suitable for belt or headband, which he tied about his middle. Then he proceeded to fly over the watering place.

As Coyote was flying around among a flock of quail, the guard[49] noticed him and said, "I think I see a spy. There is no real quail as big as that one over there. And he does not act like a quail, he keeps flying around to see what he can see."

The guard shot an arrow at Coyote, who at once dropped his belt and flew away.

"Aha! Just as I thought!" the guard exclaimed. "I missed him, but now I will go get his belt and take it home with me to prove that I really saw a spy."

He went over and picked up the buckskin strap, which at once became a rattlesnake and bit him so that he died.

Then the war party came up to the water, drank their fill, replenished their containers, and went on toward the next watering place.

When they were close by they halted, and Coyote again asked, "Haik^ya, haik^ya, who will volunteer-aik^ya to go with me-aik^ya to kill the guard-aik^ya?"

"Kwaagwawɨ, I will," Rattlesnake again said.

"All right-aik^ya," Coyote agreed, "I will take you along as my belt-aik^ya!"

Coyote turned himself into a wiw^ʔwiyatsɨ (a species of small bird), and Rattlesnake again became his buckskin belt. Then Coyote flew around among the real wiw^ʔwiyatsiwɨ that had come to their watering place.

"I think I see a spy," the guard said to himself, "that wiw^ʔwiyatsɨ is larger than the others and is acting suspiciously." He loosed an arrow at Coyote, who dropped his belt and flew away.

"I missed him," said the guard, "but I will pick up the belt that he dropped to prove that I have seen a spy." The belt became a rattlesnake in his hand, bit him, and he died.

Coyote and his people then came up to the water, drank and filled their water bags, and went on till they approached the antelope watering place. Hidden in the brush, they paused, and Coyote issued his call for a volunteer.

"Kwaagwawɨ, I will go with you to kill the guard," Rattlesnake said the third time.

They employed the same strategy as before. Coyote became an antelope, tied the buckskin strap which was Rattlesnake around his belly, and mingled with the herd of antelope drinking at that water. Because he was larger than the others, and because he appeared to be jumpy and frightened of everything, the guard noticed him and thought, "That must be a spy!" He shot and missed. Coyote ran away very fast, leaving his belt behind him. The guard picked it up, was bitten, and died.

The war party satisfied their thirst and travelled on toward the last watering place that lay between them and the camp of Gila Monster. This was the water that was situated in the center of a barren plain and guarded by Four-Eyed Insect.

They stopped to reconnoiter under cover of the brush that grew at some distance from the plain.

"Haik^ya, haik^ya, who will go over to kill that one-aik^ya?" Coyote asked.

"I will," said Tannakaitsi, Sidewinder, "watch me as I go!" He began to wind and wriggle over the ground, singing as he went:

Kotsimayo	[not translated]
Kotsimayo	[not translated]
tïvin^yasivïva ʔaagainguntsi	I have gone hidden under the top scum of the earth

As he went along singing his body penetrated beneath the surface of the plain till nothing could be seen by the watchers except his two little horns plowing along on top of the sand. Now and then he raised his head for an instant to locate the position of Four-Eyed Insect. He took note of one of the observation points at the edge of the plain where the guard always stopped to look around and headed straight for that place, timing himself to arrive when his victim would be on the opposite side of the stretch of barren land. There, under the earth,[50] Sidewinder coiled himself to strike.

When Four-Eyed Insect came and stood in his usual place, Sidewinder bit him. He ran only a little way before he died.

At this watering place in the midst of the plain, Coyote and his party assembled for a final council of war.

"Haik^ya, haik^ya, now we are rid of these fellows-aik^ya," Coyote said. "Now let us fall upon the enemy-aik^ya!

"You, Small Red Ants-aik^ya," he directed, "go to the swampy land-aik^ya! You, Large Red Ants-aik^ya, go to the adobe land-aik^ya! You, Mosquitoes-aik^ya, go to the water-aik^ya and the brush-aik^ya! Sun Spider-aik^ya, you close up his sky-hole-aik^ya with your web-aik^ya so that our enemy cannot go up that way-aik^ya! The rest of you-aik^ya will fight in the battle-aik^ya, get your arrows ready-aik^ya, we will strike the enemy before day-aik^ya, we shall surprise him while he is still asleep-aik^ya!"

Those to whom Coyote had assigned special places took up their positions, and members of the main war party paced themselves to arrive at the camp of Gila Monster and Turtle very early in the morning. There everyone was asleep except the mother of Dove Boys. In the house of the High Chief Gila Monster slept, his children slept, and the captive woman ground her seeds. She was still grinding when the battle began.

Finally Gila Monster and Turtle were the only enemies of Coyote and his people who remained alive. Gila Monster tried to escape by way of the adobe ground, but hordes of large red ants stung him and forced him back; he ran to the swampy land, but it was full of small red ants that stung him and made him turn back; he tried to flee through the brush, but there swarms of mosquitoes stung him and drove him back; then he tried to go up into the sky, but Sun Spider had spun his web across the sky-hole, and Gila Monster had to come down to earth. Then Coyote's warriors killed him.

All this time, Turtle sat in his house with his back turned to the fighting, protected by his stone shirt which was solid on the back but had spaces between the stones in front. After the death of Gila Monster, the warriors taunted him, calling out, "Why are you cowardly? Your partner is killed already, why don't you turn and give us a chance at you?"

Turtle stood up and looked over his shoulder. He saw that Gila Monster was indeed lying there dead. Then slowly, slowly, and with great dignity he turned to face Coyote's ranks of warriors. They loosed their arrows all at once, and like rain driving before the wind, those arrows flew straight into the interstices between the stones and killed him.

Then the war party feasted. The mother of Dove Boys had been grinding all through the battle. She prepared much food for them.

That is all; that is the end of the ancient story.

How Bat Killed Rattlesnake

Coyote and his people were camped in a certain place. Every morning early the men went out to hunt small game, and the women went to gather seed.

One of the men was Paatsats$i$, Bat. He was Coyote's son-in-law. Coyote said to him, "Haik^{y}a, haik^{y}a, my son-in-law-aik^{y}a, tomorrow morning-aik^{y}a you must go to the mountains-aik^{y}a to see if there is any big game about-aik^{y}a!"

"I will go," Bat said.

The next morning he went flapping away, flapping away to the mountain range called Sivin^{y}angkuvayawa, and there he sat on top of a peak. His eyes were very small and weak, so that he could scarcely see. But he could hear noises down the canyons and ravines and on the mountain sides. He heard the sound of many hoofs striking against fallen logs and stones, he heard mountain sheep playing and running and fighting all around him. Then he went flapping away, flapping away, flapping away to another peak. There it was the same as before: he could not see at all, but he could hear the noise of much big game all about him. He went flapping away, flapping away to a third peak, and there also many big game animals were making noises all around. Bat shot one arrow down a canyon in the direction of these noises. When he went down to see what he had killed, he found that he had shot a mountain sheep. He packed it back to camp to prove that there was much big game thereabouts.

Coyote came to him and demanded, "Haik^{y}a, my son-in-law-aik^{y}a, tell me-aik^{y}a all about where you have been-aik^{y}a!"

While Bat made his report, he and Coyote were already feasting on the mountain sheep. He said: "First I went flapping away, flapping away to the top of Sivin^{y}angkuvayawa. There I sat on a peak rubbing my eyes and trying to see. I could not see anything because my eyes are so weak. I heard mountain sheep running and playing and fighting all around me. I heard the sound of their hoofs striking against the fallen timbers in the canyons and on the mountain sides. Then I went flapping away, flapping away to another peak, and there, too, I heard the noises of big game all about me. Then I flapped away, flapped away to still another peak. There I heard the same noises. I shot an arrow down into a canyon where I heard the sound of many animals, and I killed this mountain sheep that we are now eating. Then I returned to our camp."

When the rest of the people had come back to camp, Coyote said, "Tomorrow-aik^{y}a we will all patch our moccasins-aik^{y}a, we will make arrows-aik^{y}a, we will string our bows-aik^{y}a, we will prepare food-aik^{y}a, because on the day after tomorrow we are going to the mountains to hunt big game-aik^{y}a!"

The people did as Coyote said. They worked all the next day patching their moccasins, putting their bows and arrows and carrying nets in good condition, and preparing food for the hunters to take with them. Early in the morning of the following day, the men started off on the big hunt while the women went as usual to gather seeds.

Except for the children, Bat remained alone in the camp. First he ground seeds, then he made a fire, then he put a pot on the fire to boil water for gruel. While the water was boiling, he went around the camp hiding all the dishes. Then he came back and made the gruel. When it was nearly done, he said to the children who had all gathered around to watch hungrily, "Go get your dishes, and I will give you some." But the children could not find their dishes. Then Bat said, "Hold out your hands, and I will put some gruel in them."

The children stood around in a circle holding out their little cupped hands, and Bat poured boiling gruel into them.

"ʔArɨrɨh! ʔArɨrɨh!"[51] the children cried.

Bat by his magic power quickly froze water into ice. Then he laid the children's hands on the ice and cured their burns. He had played this trick for the purpose of testing his magic. Having proved that it was working properly, he started out on the trail of the hunters.

Meanwhile the hunters had been playing gambling games as they journeyed along, and the two Sky Brothers,[52] Bat's grand-sons (his togotsiwɨ, son's sons), had been beaten in every game. This is the way they played: first one of the party shot an arrow ahead to serve as a target, and all the hunters shot at it, and Sky Brothers proved to be the worst marksmen; next they ran races, and Sky Brothers lost; then they had jumping contests, and Sky Brothers were beaten, both at the running jump and the standing jump; then they had wrestling matches, and Sky Brothers lost these too. Finally Sky Brothers had gambled away all their arrows; they had only their bows left. They dropped behind the others and stood leaning upon their long hunting bows, looking very sad.

As Bat travelled along on the trail of the hunting party, he saw where they had shot at a target arrow, and he knew that his grandsons had been beaten.

"Oh, my grandsons were beaten at this game," he said, "if I had been here I would have won, this is the way I would have shot!" With this, he shot an arrow and then shot another so that it touched the first.

A little further on he came to the place where the hunters had raced. "Oh, my grandsons are very poor runners," he exclaimed, "if I had been here, I would have won the race! This is the way I would have run." So saying, he ran over the same course the others had used.

Then Bat came to the scene of the jumping contests and saw that Sky Brothers had lost. "Oh," he said, "my grandsons lost these jumping contests—if I had been here, I would have won. This is the way I would have jumped!" He made both a running jump and a standing jump, and both times he jumped far past the marks left by the contestants.

Bat went along till he came to the site of the wrestling matches. "Oh, my grandsons are poor wrestlers," he said, "if I had been here, I would have won, I would have wrestled this way!" He went through all the motions of wrestling and soon made believe that he had thrown his opponent.

At last he came upon Sky Brothers as they stood leaning upon their bows. Then he scolded them.

"Why did you two boys want to play gambling games when you know that you cannot excel at anything?" he asked. "You cannot shoot, you cannot run, you cannot jump, you cannot wrestle. You ought to have known better than to have tried any of those things.

"I see you have lost all your arrows," Bat went on. "Now I will give you one arrow apiece, and you may come with me."

The three travelled on together. They came upon the hunters who were making a drive, so they themselves started toward the other end of the range, that is, toward the part of the range where the game would run before the drivers.

Bat told his grandsons to stop at a large, dry wash. "You stay here," he told them, "and ambush the big game animals as they come past. This is the way that they generally get down into the valley. I am going further up to another place to make my ambush. If a mountain sheep or a deer comes by, shoot at him! Do not miss! But if you do miss, do not follow him. Even if the arrow just sticks into his skin so that he carries it away with him, or if it barely grazes him, you must not follow!"

"That is the way we will do," Sky Brothers promised.

Bat then went on his way.

After the two brothers had remained in ambush for a little while, a very large buck came running down the wash. Both brothers shot at him, but just as they loosed their arrows he crouched for a spring so that the arrows passed over him, just grazing his back. He continued to run down the wash.

"Well, we must let him go," said the elder brother.

"No," answered the younger, "he is too big to let go. Let us follow him!"

The older brother gave in. They retrieved their arrows and followed the buck down the wash. They kept out of sight, trying for a second shot, but the deer kept running away in unexpected directions, and thus they were led along until they came down into the valley. There at last they killed and butchered their quarry. Then they lay down to rest in the shade of a tree.

It was now getting late in the afternoon, and both boys were very thirsty. As they lay there, hot and weary, a bird flew overhead and spattered water upon them from his wings.

"Why, there must be water somewhere nearby," the younger brother exclaimed, "for that bird has just come from water! Let us go up on our sky-perch and see if we can spy out the water."

The brothers flew up and sat on their sky-perch. At once the elder brother perceived that there was water directly under them, but he said nothing. The younger brother kept looking all around. At last he caught sight of the water.

"Why, can't you see?" he said, "there is water right under us!"

"Yes, but that is dangerous water," the older brother said, "dangerous people live there."

"Let us go down anyway and get a drink and see those people," the younger brother suggested boldly.

Again the older and wiser brother gave in. They flew back to earth, took some of the meat they had recently cut up, and then flew over the water. It was a rather large lake, so after they drank, they bathed. Then they approached the house which they saw near the lake. It was the home of Rattlesnake.

"Kwaagwawɨ I will bite you," he threatened the moment he saw the boys, "kwaagwawɨ make yourselves known at once!"

"We are your grandsons," Sky Brothers replied, "we have brought you some meat."

"Kwaagwawɨ all right," said Rattlesnake, accepting the meat. "Kwaagwawɨ but you must go as soon as you get a drink kwaagwawɨ, and when you go kwaagwawɨ you must fly straight up from here. Kwaagwawɨ you must not walk around and leave any tracks. Kwaagwawɨ I have two wives who are very vicious, kwaagwawɨ they are likely to come at any moment kwaagwawɨ, and if they see you they will kill you kwaagwawɨ!"

Then old Rattlesnake (for he was indeed a very old man) gave the boys some yucca dates to eat and a charm to guard them.

"When you lie down to rest kwaagwawɨ," he told them, "you must hang this charm above you kwaagwawɨ. When it falls kwaagwawɨ you will know that danger is approaching kwaagwawɨ, and you must get out of the way quickly kwaagwawɨ."

Sky Brothers rose straight up from that spot and flew part of the way back to the place where they had left their meat. Then they came down to earth and walked the remainder of the way. They were very tired. So they lay down to rest under a tree and hung the charm on a branch above them.

All this while Rattlesnake's two wives, Yucca Date Worm Girls, had been at work gathering yucca dates.

The younger girl said (or rather, chanted, for she had become a person of such powerful magic that she always spoke in a chant), "I have a presentiment that the old man, our husband, has company."

Now the presentiment or "hunch" to which she referred was a twitching in the thigh or some other part of the body, which she interpreted intuitively, as people customarily do. Therefore the older sister said, "Oh, no, you have that feeling because you have become very warm working. I often have that sensation, and it means nothing at all."

"Whenever I feel this," the younger girl chanted, "it is a sure sign that he has a visitor. Let us hurry back and ambush whomever he has with him."

The sisters stopped their work and hastened toward home. As they approached the house, they noticed strips of venison hanging outside to dry.

"When did the old man ever have meat before?" asked the younger girl in her awesome chant. "That meat proves that someone has visited him."

One sister hid to the right of the door, the other circled around back of the house and approached from the left. Then both pounced in at once. No one was there but old Rattlesnake.

"Where are your visitors?" asked the younger girl.

"Kwaagwawɨ there have been no visitors."

"Someone must have been here to give you that meat, and you are trying to protect him," the girl said.

"Kwaagwawɨ no," said Rattlesnake, "in my youth I used to

kill deer kwaagwaw*ɨ*, but now I do not go out hunting any more kwaagwaw*ɨ*. But this deer came to water here kwaagwaw*ɨ*, and I managed to get him kwaagwaw*ɨ*."

"No, you never killed that deer," his younger wife insisted.

The girls then went down to the lake to bathe and refresh themselves after their labors in the sun. Rattlesnake had already blotted out Sky Brothers' tracks and had made marks simulating deer tracks along the edge of the water. But while bathing the sisters found a hair.

"This is not my hair," the older girl said, "it is longer and darker than mine."

The younger sister compared it carefully with her own. "It is not my hair either," she chanted.

The girls came out of the water and circled around the lake, looking for signs. Then they went out a little further and made a wider circle, and kept casting about in wider and wider circles till they came upon Sky Brothers' tracks. They followed the trail and found the two youths asleep under the tree. Just as they had unsheathed their knives[53] and were about to spring the charm dropped, Sky Brothers rose straight up into the air, and the girls pounced upon nothing but the goodluck piece.

"Look!" exclaimed the older sister in great anger, "look what the old man gave them! No wonder they escaped."

Sky Brothers sat on their sky-perch, viewing the earth. At last the younger brother caught sight of the girls—the older, of course, having been aware of them all along. "Look!" cried the young man. "There beneath us are two girls! Let us go down to see them."

"No," said the older brother, "they are dangerous. We would do better to leave them alone."

"They are only girls, how could they hurt us?" the younger brother asked.

The girls were now making enticing gestures, inviting the brothers to come down to them. This was highly exciting to the younger man, and he entreated his brother to go down.

The older Sky Brother finally consented. "All right, we will go down as you wish. You take the younger girl, and as you descend, hold your bow so as to be ready to strike her knife with it. Be careful not to miss. If you break her knife she will have no weapon, she will be harmless."

The younger brother said, "I will do as you say. But I do not want the younger girl, I want the older one." After some discussion, the older brother agreed to take the younger girl for himself and leave the older for his brother.

Sky Brothers descended swiftly, striking with their bows at the girls' knives as they came down. The older brother broke his girl's knife and carried her with him up to his sky-perch. But the younger brother missed and was killed by the older Yucca Date Worm Girl.

Having killed her prey, the girl wondered where her sister and the other young man had gone. She looked all around. At last she saw them above her, far up in the sky. She took up the dead Sky Brother's bow, pulled out one of her hairs to use as an arrow, and shot it at them. The hair fell short. She pulled out a longer hair and shot it, and it too fell short. And thus she kept on, using longer and longer hairs, till finally she pulled out her very longest hair and shot it. It did not fall short. It pierced both the older Sky Brother and the younger Yucca Date Worm Girl and brought them to earth, killing them both.

First the older girl brought her sister back to life, then she took gum from a greasewood bush and mended her sister's knife. "Try it," she said, "on that large pine stump." The girl struck the stump in many places and found that her knife was strong and well mended. (And it is said that to this day that pine stump may be seen, still standing, gashed all over by the younger Yucca Date Worm Girl's knife.)

After she had proved her knife, the younger sister was thoroughly revived and more vicious than ever. "Let us back-track these Sky Brothers," she chanted, "let us see where they came from. There must be other people whom we can kill in that place."

The Yucca Date Worm Girls followed Sky Brothers' tracks till they came to the point where Bat's trail branched off. There night overtook them, and they slept. In the morning they followed Bat's tracks towards the camp of Coyote and his people.

Early that same morning Bat began to cry.

"Haikʸa, haikʸa," said Coyote, "tell us-aikʸa, my son-in-law-aikʸa, what is the matter with you-aikʸa!"

"My grandsons have been killed," Bat said. "I have had a bad dream, and I know that they are dead."

At sunrise the people in the camp saw the two Yucca Date Worm Girls coming up the hill towards them.

"Haik^{y}a, haik^{y}a, there are two girls-aik^{y}a!" Coyote exclaimed. He was very happy and excited because two new women were coming to his camp. "I am going down to meet them-aik^{y}a," he said, "I am going to be the first one to give them meat-aik^{y}a!"

Coyote took some meat and went down to meet the girls. They killed him immediately and came on up towards the camp without even stopping. As soon as they arrived, they began to kill people. Bat, seeing what was happening, made himself into a very small bat and crept inside the rib cage of an eviscerated mountain sheep carcass which was lying there waiting to be cut up.

Without stopping, Yucca Date Worm Girls killed all the people in the camp. Then they looked around to see if they had overlooked anyone. Bat squeaked like a mouse to attract their attention.

"What is making that squeaking sound?" they wondered.

Bat squeaked again.

"It comes from that mountain sheep carcass!" the girls cried. They rushed to the carcass and stabbed it through and through many times, one stabbing from one side and one from the other. Then they left it.

Bat squeaked. The sisters went back and stabbed the carcass still more thoroughly. No sooner had they finished than Bat squeaked again, and again they stabbed the carcass viciously.

Yet again Bat squeaked. "What could still live inside that carcass?" the girls asked. They examined it thoroughly. Clinging to the inside of a rib they found the tiny little bat, grinning up at them in a friendly way.

"What tiny eyes he has!" the girls said. "Oh, isn't he a cunning little creature! Let us take him home with us for a pet so that the old man will have something to keep him from getting lonely."

Yucca Date Worm Girls picked up Bat. He was exceedingly friendly, crawling all over them in a caressing, ingratiating way. His playful ways delighted them. They started home with their new pet.

As they went along, Bat maneuvered himself between them. Very gradually he was increasing in size, and presently he began to lift the girls a very short distance above the ground, so that they found themselves floating instead of walking.

"Oh, what a nice pet," they exclaimed, "he is carrying us

towards home! He will be able to carry us this way anywhere we want to go. This is probably the reason the people in that camp kept him for a pet." The girls began to sing for joy.

Still quite gradually, Bat increased in size, and as he grew he lifted the sisters little by little higher above the ground. As he lifted them, he worked himself under them until he was carrying a woman on each wing. Then suddenly he was a monstrous creature, flapping away, flapping away at great speed far above the earth. The sisters no longer sang. They had stopped exchanging remarks about their pretty pet and his endearing ways. They became terribly afraid, but they were helpless because they had no magic strong enough to use against Bat. Now he was carrying them above the lake where their home was situated; and now, by his magic, he froze the water of that lake into solid ice. Then he dropped Yucca Date Worm Girls upon it from a great height, killing them instantly.

Bat descended and made himself wrist protectors from the bones of the dead women. Then, wearing these wrist protectors, he went up to the house where old Rattlesnake waited for his wives to return.

"Kwaagwawɨ I will bite you," Rattlesnake threatened, "kwaagwawɨ make yourself known!"

"Why, don't you remember me?" Bat asked, "don't you remember that when the world was new and everything was covered with fog there was a great war[54] and you had to be carried on someone's back. I went along on that war party—don't you remember that I was there?"

"Kwaagwawɨ no, I don't remember you kwaagwawɨ," said Rattlesnake, "kwaagwawɨ I am going to bite you."

They argued back and forth for some time, Bat insisting that he was an old comrade-in-arms and Rattlesnake insisting that he had never known him. Presently Bat went over to a bunch of yucca dates that was hanging inside the house, helped himself to a handful, and sat roasting them at the fire with his back turned. But all the time he was alert, watching Rattlesnake closely for any sign of aggression. Bat could do this because he had plucked out one of his eyes and set it in the back of his head. It was such a small eye that Rattlesnake did not notice it.

But there was something else that the old man did notice. While Bat was eating, Rattlesnake cried out, "Kwaagwawɨ those look like my wives' bones that you are wearing for wrist protectors kwaagwaw*i*!"

"Why, no," Bat said, "you should remember these wrist protectors. I had them that time you were carried into battle when the earth was new."

"No kwaagwaw*i*, those are my wives' bones kwaagwaw*i*."

Seeing that Rattlesnake was about to spring upon him from behind, Bat turned to face him. They continued to quarrel. Rattlesnake declared repeatedly that he was going to bite. While he was making these threats, Bat secretly took a sharp flint and made himself a toenail from it.

When it was in place, he thrust out his foot. "All right," he said, "go ahead and bite me on that toe!"

Rattlesnake struck at the extended toe, and Bat kicked out strongly and split him in two with his flint toenail.

Bat left old Rattlesnake lying dead in two pieces in his own house and set out to find his dead grandsons. First he restored them to life; then he scolded them severely for disobeying him by coming down into the valley, when he had expressly forbidden them to follow any animal that they might wound.

"It was my brother's fault," said the older Sky Brother, "he was the one who said that we should follow the deer."

Bat and his two grandsons returned to camp, and there Bat brought back to life all the people whom Yucca Date Worm Girls had killed. Last of all, he revived Coyote.

"Haik^{y}a, I have overslept-aik^{y}a!" Coyote said. "I was coming down here-aik^{y}a to meet two girls-aik^{y}a and give them some meat-aik^{y}a! I must have fallen asleep-aik^{y}a!"

That is all; thus ends the ancient tale.

How Wolf and Coyote Went Away
(T*i*vats C*i*nawaviwa? ?Uru^{w}akwa?ip*i*)

Wolf and his younger brother, Coyote, were living together in a cave on N*i*vagant*i*, Having Snow.[55]

Wolf always spoke in a chant. In this way he said to Coyote, "C*i*nawávip*ii*ts*í*,[56] Respécted Óld Coyó-oté, go get some grass seed from our aunt.[57]

"Haik^{y}a, haik^{y}a, I did not know we had an aunt-aik^{y}a!" Coyote said. "But I'll go anyway-aik^{y}a, I'll do as you say-aik^{y}a!"

Coyote went down the slopes of the mountain almost into the valley. There he found a little brush house. No one seemed to be at home. Coyote thought it would be well to build a fire, and he did so. Then he picked up one of a number of little poker sticks that were lying in a row and poked the fire with it.

"ʔArɨrɨrɨh,[58] that burns!" the little stick cried.

Coyote dropped that stick in a hurry and poked the fire with another, and it also said, "ʔArɨrɨrɨh!"

He dropped that one and tried the next, and it also cried out in pain.

While Coyote was going down the line, poking the fire with one little poker stick after another, his aunt came home. She was Papawa, Bear, and she had been out seed-gathering. She saw in one glance what the visitor was doing, made a lunge at him, caught him with her powerful claws, and stripped the flesh from his loin.

Coyote went home.

Wolf was out hunting. By his great power he was aware of everything that went on. When he perceived what Coyote had done and what had befallen him, he killed a mountain sheep, cut off the loin, and brought it, together with the blood, home with him.

He found Coyote lying by the fire, trying to conceal his hurt.

"Respécted Óld Coyó-oté," Wolf chanted, "do not lie there on your back; take this flesh and make yourself a loin . . . . Respécted Óld Coyó-oté, I did not tell you to make a fire at our aunt's house, I did not tell you to poke it with those little poker sticks. They are our aunt's children. Because she lives all alone, the Fire Poker is her only husband. Those poker sticks are our little cousins."

Coyote took the piece of meat. "Yes-aikʸa, yes-aikʸa, I'll make myself a loin-aikʸa!" he said. "I don't know how you see everything-aikʸa! I don't know how you know so much-aikʸa!"

Coyote made himself a loin out of the loin of the mountain sheep. (And that is the reason that even to this day the loin of a coyote tastes like the loin of a mountain sheep—or at least, so it is said.)

Then Wolf said: "Respécted Óld Coyó-oté, tomorrow you must go down towards the valley again. You must take this blood with you and these flint-chippings. When you have come to our aunt's house, you will make a fire and put this blood into a pot and cook it, stirring in the flint-chippings. Then you will feed some to the little poker sticks, and they will all die. Presently our aunt will come home, and you will offer her some. She will eat it, because all the Bear People are very fond of blood pudding. As she eats, you must watch her carefully. When her eyes begin to change, be ready to dodge! She will try to leap upon you and kill you. Then she will die.

"When she is dead, you must pack up her body and all her possessions and bring them back with you. Bring everything, Oh Respécted Óld Coyó-oté! Bring everything! Do not leave one little thing behind you, Respécted Óld Coyó-oté!"

"All right-aik^{y}a! I'll do as you say-aik^{y}a!" Coyote promised. "I'll bring everything back with me-aik^{y}a!"

The following day he went down to his aunt's house, taking with him the blood and the flint-chippings. He was careful to do everything just as Wolf had directed. He prepared the blood pudding poisoned with flint-chippings and fed it to the little poker sticks. When they were dead he laid them out neatly all in a row on top of a rock.

Then Bear came home.

"Haik^{y}a, haik^{y}a, haik^{y}a! My aunt-aik^{y}a," Coyote exclaimed very quickly, before she had time to attack him. "Look at the nice blood pudding-aik^{y}a I have cooked for you-aik^{y}a! Your children-aik^{y}a have already had theirs-aik^{y}a, and now they are asleep-aik^{y}a!"

The sight of her favorite food made Bear's mouth water. She sat down and began to eat. She ate and ate, while Coyote watched her closely, especially her eyes. Bye and bye they began to roll wildly and to glow with a red and angry light. Coyote rose up on tiptoe.

Bear lunged at him ferociously.

Coyote dodged. "Haik^y-aik^y-aik^{y}a!" he screamed, "you can't catch me-aik^{y}a!"

Bear came after him. Coyote kept out of her way, screaming and yelping with excitement. She pursued him in great awkward lunges, growling terribly, her eyes rolling wilder and wilder. She was already in her death struggle.

Suddenly she tumbled over dead.

Coyote skinned her, cut up her body, and put it in his carrying net. He set fire to her little brush house. He packed up all her baskets and cooking pots, and all the rest of her belongings, together with the little dead poker sticks. Then he started home.

When he had gone about halfway, he had a sudden thought, "I wonder if I got all those little poker sticks?"[59] He went back to check. There on the rock was one little poker stick that he had forgotten.

Coyote put out his hand to pick it up. The little poker stick slipped off the rock. He tried again to grasp it, and it eluded him. He ran after it, and away it went, tumbling end over end, bouncing and skipping down the valley like a feather in the wind. As it went, it called out in its tiny little voice, "I am going to tell-sikwikwikwiꞋ! I am going to tell-sikwikwikwiꞋ!"

Coyote gave up. "All right-aikʸa!" he called after the little poker stick, "go on and tell-sikwikwikwiꞋaikʸa! Tell every-thing-aikʸa!"

Coyote took up his pack and went home.

Wolf already knew what had happened. He rebuked Coyote, telling him how grieved and disappointed he was. Wolf had put up with Coyote's carelessness and disobedience ever since the earth was made, and now he was getting very weary of the way things were going.

Coyote hung his head in shame. He tried to excuse himself by telling how it had all come about. "The little poker stick went off down the valley-aikʸa," he said, "it went away saying 'I am going to tell everything-sikwikwikwiꞋaikʸa!' "

"Respécted Old Coyó-oté," Wolf sang. "Straighten arrows! Straighten arrows!"

Now the word that Wolf used for "straighten" was one which would more usually be taken to mean "rub." Coyote knew per-fectly well what his brother meant. Nonetheless he pretended to misunderstand and went about rubbing the reeds which were to be made into arrow shafts against various objects in the cave.

"I did not mean for you to do that," Wolf chanted, "I meant for you to straighten your arrows."

Coyote pretended great surprise. "Haikʸa, haikʸa! Is that-aikʸa what you meant-aikʸa? Why didn't you say so in the first place-aikʸa?"

Coyote then built a fire and threw his arrow-straightening stone into it. When the stone was hot, he took it out, sat down by the fire, and began to rub the reeds one at a time back and forth in the little groove, straightening each separate reed very carefully.

Wolf looked on for a long time in silence. Then he said, "That is not the way, Respécted Óld Coyó-oté! That is too slow. This is the way you should do." He grasped a bunch of reeds and pulled them through his closed fist, straightening them perfectly all at once.

"No-aik^{y}a, no-aik^{y}a!" Coyote protested. "This way is better-aik^{y}a! Your way is unnatural-aik^{y}a, magical-aik^{y}a! It is more seemly and proper that Man-aik^{y}a shall sit by his fire-aik^{y}a straightening arrows as I am doing now-aik^{y}a!"

When the shafts were all straightened, the brothers began to feather them. Wolf merely touched the feathers to the arrow, and they were instantly and perfectly affixed to it. But Coyote wrapped each one with sinew, taking infinite pains, holding up the arrow and squinting along it to see that every feather was on straight. "It is more natural-aik^{y}a that Man-aik^{y}a should feather his arrows thus-aik^{y}a!" he said. And it was the same with attaching the flints: what Wolf did without effort, Coyote did with much labor so that he might set a proper pattern for Man.

After all the arrows were finished, Wolf chanted, "Respécted Óld Coyó-oté, go dig in the mountain."

"All right-aik^{y}a, all right-aik^{y}a, I'll go dig-aik^{y}a," Coyote said.

He went higher up on the slope of the mountain and began to dig vigorously with his paw-like hands, but he did not accomplish anything. After he had been digging for a long time, he could still be seen on top of the ground. He was just raising a dust.

Wolf came to him and said, "Respécted Óld Coyó-oté, this is the way to do." He thrust his *poro* into the earth, gave it a single twist, and immediately a tunnel opened, slanting upwards through the mountain to the other side. (And if we had followed Wolf, we too could dig without effort; but we followed Coyote.)

Wolf then said, "Respécted Óld Coyó-oté, pack up our belongings and carry them into the tunnel."

"All right-aik^{y}a! I'll do as you say-aik^{y}a!" For once Coyote did exactly as he had been told.

Wolf's next command was, "Respécted Óld Coyó-oté, stand out in the sun! Stand out in the sun!"

"All right-aik^{y}a! I'll stand in the sun-aik^{y}a! It's very hot in the sun-aik^{y}a! I don't know why I should stand out here-aik^{y}a!" Coyote kept up a noisy protest, pretending he did not know that Wolf meant for him to stand guard at the mouth of the tunnel.

"Respécted Óld Coyó-oté," Wolf then said, "no matter how hot it is, stand in the sun and watch!"

"All right-aik^ya, all right-aik^ya! Whatever shall I be watching for-aik^ya out here in the sun-aik^ya? I don't know why you want me to stand in the sun-aik^ya! I think you want to cook me-aik^ya! Whatever should I be watching for-aik^ya out where it is so hot-aik^ya . . .

"Haik^ya, haik^ya, haik^ya!" he cried suddenly, "It is dark to the southwest-aik^ya! There something lies like a rainstorm-aik^ya! Like dark fog-aik^ya!"

"That is what I want you to watch," Wolf chanted. "Watch well, Respécted Óld Coyó-oté! Watch well what becomes of it."

"It is coming toward us-aik^ya! It is getting nearer-aik^ya!"

"Watch carefully, Respécted Óld Coyó-oté."

"Haik^ya, haik^ya! Under the dark cloud-aik^ya things are moving-aik^ya! They are people-aik^ya! I can see sparks flashing-aik^ya like lightning from their arrowheads-aik^ya! Haik^y-aik^y-aik^ya! They are our aunts-aik^ya!"

Coyote had recognized the Bear People. They were approaching like rain under a dark storm cloud, and the sparks that glinted from their flint arrowheads were the lightning.

"Watch them closely, Respécted Óld Coyó-oté! Do not abandon your post."

But as the approaching army became more clearly visible, Coyote was overcome by fear. "Haik^ya, haik^ya, haik^ya!" he yelped, turning tail and running back into the tunnel.

"Respécted Óld Coyó-oté," Wolf commanded, "put on these clothes and go out to fight!"

With that he gave Coyote a suit of beautiful pink armor. Coyote put it on, and at once he felt big and brave. He took a bow and four arrows and showed himself at the mouth of the tunnel.

The Bear warriors were massed below him on the mountain side.

"There is Wolf!" some of them shouted.

"No," cried others, "it is not Wolf! Do you not see his squinting, slanted eyes? It is that Coyote!"

Coyote shot three times and missed. With his fourth arrow he wounded one of the Bears. Then he broke his bow, dropped it, and ducked back into the tunnel.

Now Wolf gave him a red suit of war clothes, and Coyote felt grander than ever. Again he went out, armed with a bow and four arrows.

"Ah, that one is Wolf!" some of the enemy exclaimed. Coyote heard them. He was grinning all over his face because he was being taken for his brother.

But others were looking more closely. "Don't you see his pointed nose?" they asked. "It is that same Coyote!"

Coyote missed three times, wounded one warrior with his last arrow, broke his bow, and ran back into the tunnel.

Wolf gave him yellow armor, and he wore it very proudly as he went out with still another bow and four arrows.

Again he fooled some of the Bears. "Surely that is Wolf!" they cried. Coyote smiled as he fought, hearing what they said.

"But no," others said, "don't you see his stubby, dog-like paws? He has no proper hands. It is just that Coyote again!"

Coyote wounded one Bear with his last arrow, broke his bow, and dodged back into the tunnel.

His brother gave him green war clothes. He showed himself again and heard voices calling, "There! At last Wolf has come out!"

But others answered in disgust, "Just look at his bushy tail! It is that same miserable Coyote!"

As before, Coyote used up his arrows and retreated.

Then Wolf chanted: "Respécted Óld Coyó-oté, make a bundle of all my belongings, and pack it on your back. Go through the tunnel. When you come out, keep on going straight north. Under no circumstances must you look back."

"All right-aikʸa! I'll pack everything-aikʸa!"

Wolf waited till Coyote was well on his way. Then he took his own armor from the place where he had hidden it, put it on, and went out to do battle. His fighting clothes were of all colors at once, every color of the primary rainbow, including, but far out-shining, all the colors that Coyote had worn—which is why, to this day, we call the primary rainbow "Wolf's war clothes" and the secondary rainbow "Coyote's war clothes."

The brilliance of this armor of light dazzled the eyes of the Bear warriors. They gasped in amazement. A great sigh went up from all of them, and they cried out with one voice, "Ah, that is Wolf! See how glorious he is to look upon! How unmistakable! How different from that Coyote!"

Wolf strung the whole length of his bow with arrows and, discharging them all at once towards the right flank of the enemy, he mowed them down. Again releasing innumerable arrows at one time, he mowed down the entire left flank. And shooting thus the third time, he destroyed half of those who were left standing in the center. Had he ever discharged his fourth volley, the battle would have been over.

But while Wolf was winning gloriously, Coyote was toiling through the tunnel. He came out onto a high ridge beyond it and wondered to himself, "Why did my brother tell me not to look back?" Then he turned around and looked. He saw Wolf in his dazzling rainbow armor mowing down whole masses of the Bear People.

Coyote's heart was filled with bitterness and envy. "Oh, why did he withhold that suit from me?" he thought. "If he had given it to me, I too could have dazzled the enemy, I too could have wiped them out with many arrows discharged at once. I cannot endure to watch him." Then Coyote thought, "Mangasuyaganu (would that that one) might get shot in the calf of his leg!"[60]

Coyote intended only to humble his brother and tarnish his splendid image, but no sooner had he made his wish than an arrow pierced Wolf's heart. Immediately the Bears fell upon him and butchered him.

Coyote squatted down and howled: "Kayuyayuyayuu^{w}aik^{y}a! Kayuyayuyayuu^{w}aik^{y}a! Oh, what made me think that? Oh, why did I make that wish? Kayuyayuyayuu^{w}aik^{y}a!"

After he had kept this up for awhile, his curiosity began to get the better of his grief. "Well-aik^{y}a, my brother is dead-aik^{y}a," he said, "I might as well go through his things-aik^{y}a before I burn them-aik^{y}a! I might as well see what he had-aik^{y}a! He would never let me-aik^{y}a do this while he was alive-aik^{y}a!"

Talking to himself, Coyote began to rummage among Wolf's belongings. Soon he found a bundle well wrapped and securely tied. This seemed like something worth looking into. He untied the string and removed the buckskin wrapping, only to find an inner wrapping just as well secured as the outer one. He untied that and found another; and another, and another, and another. He got tired of untying knots and used his knife to cut the string. Still there were more wrappings to remove, and more, and more, till only a tiny little bundle was left. Coyote cut the last string, spread out the last little scrap of buckskin—and immediately it was dark, completely, impenetrably dark! It was the Night itself that Wolf had kept in that bundle.

This time Coyote's mourning was long and sincere, because he was crying for himself. "Kayuyayuyayuu^waik^ya! Kayuyayuya-yuu^waik^ya! Whatever made me-aik^ya go through my brother's things-aik^ya? Now how shall I live-aik^ya? How shall I see to get my food-aik^ya? Now I must surely die-aik^ya! Kayuyayuyayuu^waik^ya!"

Coyote howled a long time. But he could not keep this up forever. Finally he felt around, found some pieces of wood and made a little fire. Then he squatted down beside it and began to make arrows. He had hope, because he knew that among his brother's possessions was a bag containing the feathers of every sort of bird that flies upon the earth. Coyote thought to himself that he would use them all if necessary.

Coyote finished an arrow, feathered it with crow feathers, and shot it up into the sky.

"Haik^ya! It just got darker-aik^ya," he said, "that won't do-aik^ya!"

On the next arrow he put buzzard feathers. He shot it up and immediately exclaimed, "Haik^ya! I believe it has become still darker-aik^ya!"

Coyote kept on trying arrows feathered with the feathers from a very great number of different kinds of birds, and the darkness lifted not at all. Then he used feathers from the red-tailed hawk, and there came a faint light!

"Haik^ya! Haik^ya! Cɨnaʔarɨsɨant-aik^ya! Coyote-dawn-aik^ya!" Coyote was wild with delight because the false dawn had come—and that is why to this day coyotes howl early in the morning.

The darkness thickened again. Undismayed, Coyote made another arrow, feathered it with seagull feathers, and shot it into the sky. The light came back.

"Haik^ya! Haʔɨtɨtasɨant-aik^ya! True dawn-aik^ya!" Coyote cried. Then the sun came up.

Coyote carried all his belongings and all his brother's belongings back to the cave and hung them up in their accustomed places. Then he went down to the battlefield to see if he could find any pieces of his brother's body. He found one small sliver of bone, one little hair, one speck of dried blood, and one flake of flesh. These he gathered up carefully and put under a large basket.

Then he went back into the cave and once more sat himself down to make arrows. He made an enormous stack of them. Then he began to make bows, one bow for every four arrows. When he had all the bows and arrows that he could possibly carry, he started out on the enemies' trail.

After travelling a long, long way it seemed to him that he had come to the proper place to leave a cache. He hid a bow and four arrows in such a way that they were well concealed but accessible in a hurry. Then he ran as fast and as far as he possibly could, and when his breath completely gave out so that he could not take another step, he again hid a bow and four arrows. Again he ran as hard and as far as he could, and left another bow with four arrows, and so he continued till he had only one bow and four arrows left. By that time he was getting well into enemy country.

"Haik^{y}a, my penis-aik^{y}a! Oh, my penis-aik^{y}a! What shall I do-aik^{y}a?" Coyote asked. "How shall I manage this business-aik^{y}a?"

Coyote's penis advised him how to proceed.

As he came near to the camp of the Bear People he saw two old women coming out to gather wood. He sat down and hastily painted himself so that he would not be recognized, and he also disguised his manner of speaking.

Then he approached the old women. "How are you-siviyau-kwi$^?i$?" he asked politely. "Are you well-siviyaukwi$^?i$? I am a traveller-siviyaukwi$^?i$," he explained, "and have not seen anyone for a long time-siviyaukwi$^?i$, and I do not know what is going on in the world-siviyaukwi$^?i$."

"Ye-es," the old women answered slowly and with relish, "what shall we tell you? Well, there is nothing to tell except that they have been to kill our nephew Wolf—"

"Ye-es-siviyaukwi$^?i$?"

"—and now they are having the Scalp Dance, and we are gathering wood for their fire."

"Yes-siviyaukwi$^?i$. And how do you two do after you gather the wood-siviyaukwi$^?i$?"

"We go grunting under our loads, $^?$unh, $^?$unh, $^?$unh. And when we are come near to the dancing place we sing:

yawaiya′ yawaiyawai ha
yawaiya′ yawaiyawai
tuwamɨ′
tuwamɨ′
yawaiya′ yawaiyawai ha
yawaiya′ yawaiyawai ?[61]

Then people say, 'Our mothers are acting like Coyote—Coyote has got into our mothers!' And we answer, 'How could he? He is all alone now, he has no one to come with him.' Then after this kind of talking and joking, we put our wood down and go to our house to lie down. Then our granddaughters go to the dance. Towards morning they come home, and we get up and go to the dancing place again. As we draw near, we sing. Then we get inside the circle of dancers and dance and sing. The scalp is passed from person to person till at last it comes to us, and we have it on our heads for awhile. Then we stoop lower as we dance and sing louder and act more fiercely. And people say, 'Now surely Coyote has got into our mothers! Just see how they are acting!' And again we answer, 'No, how could he do so? He is all alone!' "

"Yes-aik^ya!" shouted Coyote in his own voice, as he fell upon the women and killed them.

He skinned the old Bear women and put himself into one skin and his penis into the other; then having become two, he picked up the loads of wood and went along grunting towards the dance circle. And as he approached that place, Coyote and his penis sang the women's song just as they were accustomed to sing it. The people made sport, saying, "Look! It seems that Coyote has got into our mothers! Perhaps he has killed them and has put himself into their skins!" Whereupon Coyote and his penis replied in the voices of the old women, "How could he do so when he is all alone and has no one to come with him?"

Coyote and his double put down their loads and went into the old women's brush house. It was already sundown. The granddaughters came in, and all ate supper together, and the young women noticed nothing peculiar about their grandmothers. Then the false grandmothers lay down to rest, and the girls went to the dance. Towards morning they returned. Coyote and his penis sprang on them and killed them.

Still in the form of two old women, Coyote went to the dance ring. Oh, now he was singing with all his might!

"Just look at our mothers!" the people said. "They were never so fierce before—surely Coyote has got into them!"

"Oh, no," two cracked old voices answered, "he couldn't do that, he has no one to help him."

Coyote and his penis entered the circle and began to dance vigorously. Slowly the scalp progressed toward them. It was put first upon the head of Coyote's penis, which then stooped lower and danced harder and sang louder. Meanwhile Coyote, apparently absorbed in the frenzy of the dance, was selecting a good place to break out of the circle. He timed himself so that Wolf's scalp would come to him just as he danced by the Badger People, who were much shorter than their allies, the Bears. When he felt it on his head, he got a firm grip on it, cried "Haik^{y}a" loudly, took a tremendous flying leap over the heads of the Badgers, and made off at a dead run. In that instant the second "grandmother" vanished, and his penis was joined to him in its proper form.

Now Coyote was running for his life with his enemies close on his heels. He finally made it to his last cache of a bow and four arrows, tied the long hair of the scalp around his waist, snatched up his weapons, and stood off the Bears while he caught his breath. He only wounded one of them with his last arrow. Then he ran again, as hard as he could.

It was a long, long run to the next weapon cache. Coyote barely made it. He used his arrows as slowly as possible, to give himself time to breathe. When he had wounded one warrior with his last arrow, he broke his bow and began to run again.

In this way Coyote travelled till he had used up all the bows and arrows that he had hidden. Then there was nothing left for him to do but to run and run and keep on running. He became so tired that he could hardly put one foot before the other. Wondering what in the world he could do to save himself, he darted down into a dry wash where the bank concealed him momentarily from the Bears, who were now gaining on him rapidly. His eye lit on an old coyote track, and he turned himself into it.

His enemies rushed into the wash. "Which way did Coyote go?" they asked, "he can't have got very far!"

They scattered to search for him, but there was no sign. At last someone noticed the track and exclaimed, "Look! There is an old coyote track."

"That must be Coyote himself!" another surmised. "Get a rock and smash him quickly!"

"Haik^{y}a! How do you see me when I have made myself vanish-aik^{y}a?" Coyote leaped up and went away from that place. He had had a good rest, and for awhile he left all his pursuers far behind.[62]

At last he began to lose his breath again, and little by little they gained on him. This time they were sure they had him. But down in a hollow he spied an old coyote rolling-place and turned himself into it.

The Bears swarmed all over looking for him. "Where did he go? He can't have got far because he was pretty nearly done for." After a time someone exclaimed, "Look here! Here is an old coyote rolling-place—get a rock, it may be he himself!"

"Haik^{y}a! It is I-aik^{y}a! It is I-aik^{y}a!" yelped Coyote, starting off on another long run.

And so he travelled, running all out, running till he could run no more, then using his power as an imitator to gain himself a little breathing space. All the time he was getting more and more tired. There came a time when he could barely stagger along, but he could see no shape to assume, no way to disguise himself.

He rounded the point of a little hill and was hidden for a moment. "Haik^{y}a, my penis-aik^{y}a," Coyote begged, "what shall I do-aik^{y}a?" His penis advised him.

Quick as thought he collapsed into a heap and became invisible, projecting his semblance to run far off on the slope of a distant mountain.

The Bear People came rushing around the point. "Where can that Coyote have got to? Not far surely, because he was just barely creeping along." They looked in every direction and finally caught sight of what seemed to be Coyote running like the wind, far, far ahead of them.

"Look how he has out-distanced us!" they said in disgust. "He must just have been pretending to be tired. We'll never catch him now."

"Oh, well," some of them suggested, "let us call up a snow-storm and freeze him to death." '

"Yes, that is what we shall do," they all agreed.

The Bears turned around and started home. Of course all the time the real Coyote had lain there right under their feet, listening to every word.

"Haikʸa! My penis-aikʸa, what shall I do-aikʸa?" he said. "It would be better for me to hunt myself a cave-aikʸa! It would be better to gather up a quantity of wood-aikʸa! They say it is going to turn cold-aikʸa!"

Coyote ran all around till he found a nice, dry cave. Then he gathered a great pile of wood. By this time it was late afternoon. Soon cold, gray clouds spread all over the sky. It began to rain, and then the rain turned to snow. The night was dark, snowy, and bitterly cold. But there lay Coyote, snug and warm in his cave, waking up from time to time just long enough to put another piece of wood on the fire.

When he opened his eyes in the morning the storm was over. The sun shone brightly on a cold, white world. As far as he could see in every direction, the earth was covered with snow. "If I try to travel through that snow-aikʸa I'll freeze to death-aikʸa!" Coyote said. He went back and lay down by the fire to try to figure out a way to get home. Looking up at the roof of the cave, he saw where a very small spider had spun a very small web. In it was caught a tiny puff-ball,[63] such as one sometimes sees blowing along for miles over the desert.

"Haikʸa! That looks like it might be useful-aikʸa!" Coyote said.

He took down the puff-ball, weighed it in his hand, and felt how light it was. Then he took his awl and punched a little hole in it and looked in. Yes, just as he had thought, it was hollow! He placed the puff-ball near the opening of the cave, where the wind could catch it and swirl it away. Next he turned himself into a tiny little creature, no larger than the smallest ant, and crawled inside the puff-ball through the hole that he had made. When he was all curled up securely, he began to call the North Wind:[64]

Kwiyamayamayuuyuuʷaikʸ
kwiyamayamayuuyuuʷaikʸ!

Coyote kept this up for a long, long time. At last he could hear the wind, but he could not feel it. He called harder than ever and heard it roaring above him, but still he could not feel even a tremor in the little puff-ball. Then Coyote crawled out of his place and made himself as tall as the sky, and with his *poro* he hooked the wind down so that it raced along just above the ground. (Before this time all winds had stayed high up in the sky; it was Coyote who brought them down to sweep the earth.)

Quickly Coyote made himself small again and crept back inside the puff-ball. Soon it began to bounce and quiver. Then the wind picked it up and swept it away, and it floated light as a feather over mountains and valleys and across deep canyons. "Haik^{y}a, haik^{y}a," Coyote said, "this is a fine way to travel-aik^{y}a!"

But then the movement stopped. Coyote was puzzled. "Haik^{y}a, what can be the matter with this thing-aik^{y}a?" he said. "I wonder if it can be caught in a crevice-aik^{y}a?"

He took his awl, punched a small hole, and peered outside. "Haik^{y}a! That looks like my bundle hanging on the wall of the cave-aik^{y}a! That other one looks like my brother's bundle-aik^{y}a!" Coyote got himself out in a hurry. The puff-ball had come to rest back in his home cave on Nɨvagantɨ. "Haik^{y}a! What a good way to travel-aik^{y}a! And quick too—I didn't even get tired-aik^{y}a!"

Coyote went back to his normal size. He lay down and rested for awhile, then he got himself some food. After that he went outside the cave and placed Wolf's scalp beside the other fragments of his body, and replaced the large basket on top of the remains. Then he returned to the cave, lay down, and slept.

At midnight he awoke and lay listening. There was silence till the time when the morning star emerges. Then he heard a faint call: "Huuuu!"

"Haik^{y}a! That is my brother-aik^{y}a!"

Coyote listened intently. He was happy, because this time he had done everything exactly right. Now that his brother had come back to life, they would go on living together in the cave, and everything would be as it had always been.

The sound came again: "Huuuu!"

"Haik^{y}a! That is from the wrong direction-aik^{y}a!" Coyote cried. "It sounds as if he was going north-aik^{y}a! Why doesn't he come to the cave-aik^{y}a?"

And then a third time the call sounded, very faint and far: "Huuuu!"

"Haik^{y}a! He's going away-aik^{y}a! I am going to follow him-aik^{y}a!" Coyote started running in the dark, guided only by those distant, mournful wolf howls.

The two brothers ran on and on and on, always towards the North, the Storied Land where the Ancient Telling starts and ends. Coyote ran far behind. We are not told if he ever caught up with Wolf or ever saw his brother's face again. But even after he could no longer hear the guiding voice, Coyote knew he was on his brother's trail because he came upon a rock beside a spring which retained the clear imprint of Wolf's hand. Perhaps Wolf stopped to drink and rested his palm upon the rock; or perhaps he left the sign to guide his errant brother. However that may be, there was the print of the well-formed hand Coyote knew so well. Always the imitator, he put his own doggy paw-mark on the rock beside it (where those handmarks may be seen to this day) and ran on, even though ever so far behind.

That is all. That is the end of the tale and of the ancient telling.

There is also a mere fragment, no more than the closing passage, of another end-of-cycle myth, this one involving three animals important for food: Tihiya, Deer; Naxa, Mountain Sheep; and Tcagwara, Chuckwalla.[65] The three were companions, travelling together from north to south. When they came to the plains and foothills, Deer said, "I shall remain here." The other two journeyed on together to the foot of the rocky desert mountains. There Chuckwalla said, "I am cold," whereupon Mountain Sheep cracked a rock with his horns and said, "This will be your house." Peering out from his crack, Chuckwalla asked, "What do you intend to do?" Mountain Sheep[66] said, "I am going to live in those mountains."

CHAPTER VII

MYTHOLOGY:
THE MASTER KEY

BEING primarily nomadic hunters and gatherers, and only incidentally planters, the Chemehuevis never evolved an organized
priesthood (although, as we have seen, the Chieftaincy entailed
certain priestly functions), elaborate rituals, or great symbolic sea-
sonal dances. Their principal culture carriers were songs and
myths, primarily the latter, although songs were also tremendously
important in this respect, and the dying out of a single song is an
irreparable loss.

Chemehuevi myths transmitted racial and tribal memories and
traditions, ideals of correct behavior, and, through symbols, a
highly developed psychology. There are certain passages which
present in-depth analyses of the human psyche as the Chemehuevis
understood it—notably the dual nature of woman and the dual
nature of man; others dramatize a male and female tension which
may in part reflect the transition from a presumably female-domi-
nated gathering culture to a later phase where the skillful hunter
was the ideal and predominant figure. Many episodes illustrate the
bad effects of self-will and disobedience, while others appear to
favor independent action.

It would not be correct to say that the Chemehuevis' history
was to be found only in their myths, for they had a system of
learning by rote and thus transmitting events and exploits worthy
of remembrance from generation to generation. However, since
these happenings were not dated, not fixed in time, they must

have passed easily into myth. For example, "How Coyote Went to War Against Gila Monster" appears to be based upon an ancient—or perhaps not very ancient—feud resulting from the violation of a food cache, combined with a bereaved mother's dream, fantasy, or psychic experience, along with vaguely remembered puberty or shaman's initiatory rites, and a highly fictionalized account of a war party on the move.

Although this collection of myths is woefully incomplete, it is probably representative. Indeed, it may be said that if this were the only material available, and if no living memory remained of the ancient ways, one might from these myths alone gain a considerable understanding of the way of life of the Chemehuevis in aboriginal times, of their relationship and reaction to their environment, of their values and code of behavior, and especially of their strong, deeply poetic, and persistently humorous mental attitudes. And looking beyond what these ancient tales provide in the way of information about a specific ethnic group, we see that they also reiterate universal themes and afford universal insights.

It is the tendency of a person of non-Indian background to attempt to visualize the mythic characters. Even in their metamorphoses, the characters of Greek mythology are not hard to picture. Not so with those who people the Chemehuevi tales. Their forms are not easily grasped by the waking mind, for the actors in these dramas emerge from that deep layer of the unconscious where mystical and prophetic dreams have their origin. These creatures shift and shimmer between anthropic, semi-anthropic, and animal form and sometimes appear in two or more forms at the same time.

Let us look at some of the mutations of Sky Brothers. They are clearly birds or winged creatures of some sort—being Bat's grandsons, they might even sometimes look like bats, but in the logic of the myth this by no means follows, since the most disparate creatures are frequently represented as closely related. At the beginning of the myth "How Bat Killed Rattlesnake," Sky Brothers are pictured as inexperienced and inept young men, setting out on a great hunt and losing at all the games of skill and contests of strength and agility that the hunters engage in along the way. They are still human in form when Bat finds them leaning disconsolately upon their bows, having gambled away all their arrows, and they apparently retain this form when they wound the buck, follow it down into the valley, and butcher it. But when a passing bird drops water on them as they rest under a tree, they immediately fly up to their sky-perch to spy out the land. They are again young men when they approach Rattlesnake with a gift of meat, and apparently it was in the form of men that they bathed in the lake, for there one of the Yucca Date Worm Girls later finds a human hair. Rattlesnake advises them to rise straight up from that place and leave no trail, then he erases the human tracks on the shore of the lake, simulating deer tracks instead. And in what form Sky Brothers swoop down from their sky-perch to attempt the rape of Yucca Date Worm Girls is simply beyond conception!

Coyote was especially noteworthy for his shifting shapes. Labeled Trickster by anthropologists, he was known to the Chemehuevis as Imitator.[1] He could "imitate" anything, but preferred to assume the appearance of something associated with the coyote, such as a coyote carcass, coyote track, or coyote rolling-place. Having the advantage of a detachable penis, he could also appear in duplicate, as when he and his penis masqueraded in the skins of the two old Bear women. In "How Yucca Date Worm Girls Went to Look for a Husband," Grasshopper appears first as a feeble old man, next as a man-sized grasshopper (or at least a being with a grasshopper's legs), then alternately as a giant and a swarm of small grasshoppers. Thus the dream figures shift and change, while each dream unfolds in accordance with its own peculiar logic.

Myths shared their dream-quality with songs. The great hereditary songs could be learned by dreaming as well as by rote (or, more accurately, by dreaming in combination with rote), and this was also true of the Talking Song, although even in a dream it would come only to a member of the immediate family of the High Chief. A shaman's song, by which he summoned his familiar, always originated in a dream but was frequently passed on by rote to his descendants. These shamans' songs were particularly bound up with the body of mythology, since, as we have seen, the spirit-animal familiars with which they were associated were all, excepting only the deer and the mountain sheep, animals who had been themselves shamans in the pre-human times When the Animals Were People. But while a shaman's song was sung whenever he had occasion to perform his healing office, and the hereditary songs were sung, either ritually or for pleasure, at any season of the year, myths, as has been noted, might be told only in the winter. There was no taboo on telling them in the daytime, but they were usually told during the long, dark, winter nights, a time peculiarly appropriate for narratives springing from that sleeping under-mind which knows all things, forgets nothing, yet is unfettered by the restrictions of man's lately evolved intellect and reason. The People, huddled together in caves or huts, were enthralled by these vivid tales of the youth of the world. Whether told by a skilled storyteller to a family or a larger assemblage or simply on a one-to-one basis, by a grandmother, perhaps, to a solitary grandchild, or by a sick old man to the youth who cared for him, the myths were presented with verve and style. These sacred and mysterious tales, released only when the cold had sent venomous snakes to their long winter sleep, were splendid theater. They contained high tragedy, exciting adventure, and marvelous comedy. Even the grimmest tale was laced with that humor which has always armored the Chemehuevis against the rigors of existence; and the frequent pornographic passages were both outrageous and outrageously funny.

Although these myths embody many of the ancient and universal themes, they were with few exceptions thoroughly adapted to the Chemehuevi culture and environment, and they were even brought up to date with changing times—as witness the large, red penis of the man who trapped Wind Woman in a cave[2] and the red flannel brought by the Sun as a gift to his sons. Just as a Renaissance picture of the Holy Family might reveal little about the culture of Palestine in the first century A.D. but much about fifteenth century Italy, so most Chemehuevi myths purporting to deal with times long past give a reliable picture of aboriginal life in the heyday of the big game hunters; and yet faint intimations of immense antiquity may sometimes be detected.

From the Chemehuevi story of creation we learn that this tribe of desert dwellers, possessing a Desert Culture which may have been thousands of years in developing, had as their Magna Mater not the earth mother, but Ocean Woman, the sea mother, who was both honored as the prime creator and addressed in invocations, some of which are still in use.[3] Ocean Woman, we are told, made the earth entirely out of her own substance. Patiently collecting particles of her own dried and sloughed-off skin, she rolled this stuff into minute balls, which she crumbled and sprinkled upon the surface of the Primeval Sea. The dust produced by this process floated and became the land. Like all woman's work, this was repetitive and all but interminable. At length there was enough land for her to climb out of her boat or raft and lie down upon it. Then Ocean Woman began her tremendous task of stretching out the earth. Thrusting out strongly, slowly, and patiently with hands and feet braced against the still somewhat flexible substance of the land, employing rhythmic, powerful impulses like those of a woman in labor, she spread out the earth until Wolf and Coyote, racing back and forth to survey its extent, were satisfied, and Coyote reported, "It fits," that is, it is sufficiently large for the purpose for which it is intended.

In the primal tetrad of Ocean Woman, Mountain Lion, Wolf, and Coyote, Ocean Woman definitely outranks her companions. She creates, while the others (in the stories recorded here, only Wolf and Coyote) play their parts in setting the earth in order, establishing its times and seasons, and determining a way of life for the people who were to come. Even in the time of the hunters women were (as to a great extent they still are) the prime movers in Chemehuevi society. In very primitive times, in the time of the gatherers, they were possibly dominant. Later, every woman needed a man to hunt big game for her; but conversely, every man needed a woman to gather and to grind for him. So while it came about that women yielded their husbands proper respect and (when convenient) obedience, they never occupied a position of inferiority. Women's voices were heard in the Gatherings, and fierce and implacable women incited their men to take the warpath. The Chief, so it is said, was always a man. But in the older, darker, and more awesome world of the shamans there were at least as many women as men.

In the second creation myth, which describes Coyote's wooing of Louse and the origin of the tribes, the Sea Goddess appears in dual aspects which are also the two aspects of the female principle. Usually Chemehuevi mythology presents the two who are essentially one as siblings, but in this story they are mother and daughter; this is appropriate to the transformation which takes place in a woman's nature as she progresses from seductive and untamed youth to wise and respected age. As the mother of Louse, the Goddess is all-wise, all-knowing (in this respect her masculine counterpart would be Wolf), and we see her patiently weaving the great basket that is the symbolic womb, the *vas hermeticum*, which will contain the human race in embryo. As Louse, she is voluptuous, wild, elusive, dangerous, potentially castrating–but capable of being tamed, of submitting to male dominance. In Chemehuevi mythology prominent roles are sometimes assigned to the most unlikely creatures. It seems strange, at any rate to non-Indian thought, that the "mother of all living" should be identified as Louse. But it is also strangely prophetic, for her offspring have assuredly crept like lice over the beautiful body of the earth.

In this account Coyote is the indispensable male partner in the act of creation. Yet we are told that when it came to human procreation, if Wolf had had his way, sex would have played no part, and the child would have budded from its mother's wrist.

Wind Woman, as portrayed in the story called "How Dove's Son Escaped from Wind Woman," embodies the undesirable feminine traits of lust and possessiveness. Perhaps there was a period in the remote prehistory of the ancestors of the Chemehuevis when men were poorly armed and unskillful and failed frequently even in their efforts to secure small game. Then women were the main suppliers of food as well as the mysterious bringers-forth of new life. Woman's magic was in every way superior, and men could be driven away or accepted at will. But with the perfection of man's skills in the manufacture and use of weaponry, and possibly with a better understanding of the procreative process, men escaped from the humiliation of female dominance. The tale of Wind Woman would seem to dramatize this escape. Her effect upon her victim has been psychologically though not physically castrating. He has, in his constant attempts to satisfy her, developed an abnormally large male organ which handicaps him as a hunter and a runner. His first helpers are four female cousins (a cousin, it will be remembered, is "the same as" a sister), who evidently admire strong and swift young men and relieve him of his impediment. But significantly, all others who help in his escape are archers.

"How Cottontail Rabbit Conquered the Sun" differs in many respects from the other myths in this collection. Although it deals with the preparation of earth for human habitation, its hero is Cottontail Rabbit, not Coyote or even that typical Southern Che-

mehuevi, Southern Fox. This suggests that the story is based at
least in part upon some tale acquired by diffusion, or by very
ancient direct contact with those eastern tribes whose Rabbit
"trickster" became the "Br'er Rabbit" of Afro-American folklore.
The setting is the familiar desert, probably the hottest place which
the early Chemehuevi adapters of the myth could imagine. The
Rabbit children have the traits of Chemehuevi children in that
they are resourceful and able to survive under hard conditions.
Cottontail Rabbit himself displays a Coyote-ish curiosity as to the
contents of the children's bellies and picks up a small, sharp-
pointed stick to drill a hole in one of them—had Coyote been the
hero, we would have been told that he used his awl. Cottontail
Rabbit is in no way an inferior person. He is foresighted, preparing
a place where he and the children may shelter from the fire, and
he is also brave and skillful in setting an ambush. But the cultural
background is that of the wild chimpanzees: fire is an enemy, not
a servant, food (in this story the familiar yucca dates and edible
seeds) undergoes no preparation, and the only tools or weapons
are sticks and stones. The tale seems to reach back blindly to
pre-human antiquity, to a time when hominids survived an encounter with volcanic activity or—just possibly—some dreadful
solar flare. In this story nature is pictured as withholding the nour-
ishment which the hero must, by guile and bravery, wrest from
her and make available to those who are to come.

This myth is also unique in that hidden within it we find the
concept of the Earth Mother. The mother of the orphan Rabbits
has died, but before her death she had hidden seed in the crack of
a rock. But the crack has now closed up, and only with a moistened twig can the children extract a few seeds at a time. Cottontail
Rabbit with his *poro* (a typical Chemehuevi touch) opens the
crack, and an abundance of seeds pours forth. This is also an
occurrence (very far from home) of the basic mythological theme
of the planting peoples, which associates sex, death, and fertility;
only here the order of the elements is transposed, and we have
first death, followed by sex, revival, and fertility (just as in Hebrew mythology, in Genesis, they appear in still another order:
first the fertility of the earth, then sex, human fertility, and its
inevitable consequence, death). In the Chemehuevi story the dead
mother of the orphans is the dead and barren earth; but when the

poro opens the crack in the rock (vagina of the Earth Goddess), life and fecundity are restored. And this is probably the most important clue in all Chemehuevi oral literature and tradition to the true nature of the poro. That regenerating rod of power, by which those Immortals who had been killed in various ways were revived and by which in later times the shaman performed his curative work, is primarily the generative organ, the phallus. Like the phallus, the poro had on occasion a life of its own, for we have seen how in dreams the poro itself undertook to instruct John Smith in the arts of shamanism.[4] Here is evidence, clearer even than that afforded by Coyote's partnership with his penis, of the existence of a phallic cult such as one would expect to find associated with the worship of the Goddess.

The emergence of the Moon and Sun presents images of great beauty. Notably, the Moon is surrounded by innumerable crows; these are not precisely the white doves of Aphrodite, but the comparison comes to mind. Cunningly hiding himself and attacking the Sun with his only available weapon, a stone that balances well in his hand, Cottontail Rabbit performs an act of great valor and of great value to Man, for whom the earth is being prepared— an act worthy of Coyote, for whom, in this story, he substitutes. For it must be remembered that Coyote embodies some of the desirable as well as the reprehensible human qualities.

"How Wildcat Brothers Recovered Their Hunting Song" apparently pictures a period in Chemehuevi history when the hunters relied principally upon small game. Wildcat Brothers had the bow and arrow but not much skill in the use of this weapon, for they went hungry after their magic song was stolen. In a later episode the Sky Rabbits are slaughtered after being driven into a net (the web spun by Sun Spider).

Wildcat comes back from the Land Above the Sky with greatly enhanced powers. His journey to that place and return therefrom may be read as an account of a shaman's initiation, and viewed in this light furnishes extremely important information. For we know that a shaman dreamed, wandered by himself, and had certain mystical experiences, but we have no direct account from any Chemehuevi shaman of the nature of these experiences. Wildcat's wandering to a place on top of the sky may be taken as representing the apprentice shaman's entrance into the world of dream, the psychic world. There Wildcat meets an ancestor, his maternal grandfather, Sun Spider. Wildcat performs various services for this ancestor, changing his luck at gambling and helping to annihilate his enemies, the Sky Rabbits. Thereupon the old man agrees to help him to return to earth. It is this return which contains the classic elements of initiation, as abundantly recorded in various studies of shamanism: death (and/or dismemberment, the latter not represented in this story) and rebirth. To allow himself to be swallowed by an ancestor would be equivalent to death, a return to the womb of time when he was nonexistent; and the descent by means of a thread (in place of the umbilical cord) emanating from a red hole is certainly rebirth. Actually Wildcat dies symbolically (is swallowed) twice. This being a Chemehuevi tale, there is the act of disobedience (looking up) which causes the grandfather to draw him up swiftly, disgorge him, and administer a stern rebuke. The second time Wildcat is obedient, and all goes well. (But if he had not looked up the first time there would have been no knowledge of the means by which he was returned to his own world!)

In two myths in this collection, "How Yucca Date Worm Girls Went to Look for a Husband" and "How Bat Killed Rattlesnake," the two Yucca Date Worm Girls figure prominently. It would seem logical to tell these tales consecutively, but George Laird always insisted that "How Coyote Went to War Against Gila Monster" should be placed between them. This, together with the fact that "How Wolf and Coyote Went Away" was "the last of the myths," implies that anciently there was a definite order in which the myths were told; it also suggests the existence of a whole saga of Yucca Date Worm Girl tales spaced out in pre-human, mythic time. The change in the sisters between our first glimpse of them and their last appearance is enormous. There must have been narratives which explained this and told just how it came about that the younger displaced the elder in power and prescience. Particular mention is made in the first story of the Yucca Date Worm Girls' coloration. They are described as cream or buff-colored (ʔoᵂaka-rɨmɨ, the word also used of a white person whose complexion is not florid), a term doubtless appropriate to their counterparts in the animal kingdom, the worms inhabiting yucca dates. In the second story they know that the hair they find while bathing in the lake must have belonged to an intruder because it is lighter than theirs. The mention of light complexion and light hair might just possibly be a clue to some ancient contact of the Chemehuevis or their ancestors with a lighter colored race.

When we first meet the two Yucca Date Worm Girls wandering over the desert in search of a husband to hunt game for them, they are naked, nubile, naïve, stupid, and harmless; and according to the usual sibling pattern, the elder is wiser (not much wiser) than the younger, but invariably allows the younger and more foolish sister to have her way. It is stated that upon their arrival at the houses of the first three prospective husbands, it was the younger girl who jumped to the conclusion that good hunters must live in those places, while on the fourth day it was the elder who suspected that the meat they were being fed (first sinew, then blood, then raw fat) was not "real meat" and that the claim of these husbands to hunt big game was fraudulent; it is the elder sister who first recognizes, from the evidence of meat, hide, and bones, that the house of Red-Tailed Hawk is the home of a genuine hunter.

This story is a morality tale from first to last. It teaches young girls to choose carefully and not to be taken in by false appearances or by a man's boastful claims. Next it teaches that having found a worthy husband, a wife should be obedient in all things, respecting his superior wisdom, and that if she does not obey even the commands which appear unreasonable, dire consequences may ensue. In the last episode, which deals with Red-Tailed Hawk's revenge upon the giant Grasshopper, there is a preachment for man: the most skillful hunter, the wisest shaman may find himself faced with an insoluble problem—in which case, if he takes care of his smaller, more pressing difficulties he may find that the big trouble no longer exists. Incidentally, Red-Tailed Hawk is consistently presented as the ideal Chemehuevi hunter and warrior, who also possesses considerable shamanistic powers. We first see him as well-armed and beautifully clothed in buckskin, wearing a mountain hat ornamented with quail crests and bearing on his back—since at that time he had no wife to carry for him—a huge load of meat. The next day, piercing the buckskin with his awl, he makes clothing for his wives, thus fulfilling a hunter's duty.

The narrative ends on a fairy-tale note. Red-Tailed Hawk has clothed his young wives, taught them, tamed them, healed them of the blindness resulting from their disobedience, and destroyed his enemy; and from that time forward, we are told, "the three of them lived there in the cave and had no further trouble."

In the second myth involving Yucca Date Worm Girls, "How Bat Killed Rattlesnake," the mountain cave has disappeared and Red-Tailed Hawk along with it. The sisters now live by a lake in the desert, and their husband is Rattlesnake, upon whom the weight of mythic time lies heavily so that he can no longer hunt, although he is still capable of uttering dire threats. The girls themselves have undergone a dreadful transformation. In appearance they are still youthful and enormously seductive. Since this story takes place in a time of great heat, it would not be expected that they should be wearing buckskin clothing; but apparently they do not even have aprons since their "knives" (not mentioned in the previous tale) are said to be in plain view and in fixed position when they encounter Sky Brothers. Obviously they are now the anthropomorphic counterparts of dagger-leafed plants rather than of soft and harmless worms, and the projecting knife-sharp clitoris presents an interesting variation on the familiar theme of the toothed vagina.[5] The sisters have now become imbued with a maniacal hatred of all pre-human "people," excepting only old Rattlesnake. Not only their characters but their roles have been reversed: the younger sister is now dominant, so awesomely endowed with mana that she chants when she speaks, after the manner of Wolf and Gila Monster.

The vicious women carry out their grim intentions. They track down, entice, and then kill Sky Brothers. Then reasoning that there must be more people where they came from, they follow the trail to Coyote's camp, killing first Coyote and then every man, woman, and child of his band with the exception of Bat. But Bat has seen the fate of his grandsons in a dream and has saved himself by becoming a very small bat and clinging to the inside of a rib of the eviscerated carcass of a mountain sheep. When he reveals himself to the sisters, they do not even suspect him of being a "person." There is something peculiarly chilling in the way in which he ingratiates himself by crawling lasciviously all over their bodies. And the listener to the tale, foreknowing its outcome, must have been tempted to feel pity as the vicious sisters revert temporarily to their more innocent phase and exchange naïve remarks about their cunning pet. When he gradually becomes larger (which is, of course, a perfectly natural phenomenon in the era of the mythic dream), inserts himself between them, and gently bears them along in the direction in which they wish to travel, they are delighted and sing his praises back and forth as they drift along. But this episode builds to a climax of horror. Bat, having become enormous and now flying very high and fast, is bearing the two sisters to their doom. Now they realize this, as each clings precariously to a leathery wing. They sing no more, for they have no magic strong enough to cope with the situation. And Bat's power to produce cold is no longer to be used to heal burns (or, as in the earlier story, to make "ice fat"). He freezes the lake by which Rattlesnake and his wives have made their home into solid ice and drops the dreadful sisters upon it from a great height. This is the final episode in the pre-human lives of Yucca Date Worm Girls, who now continue only as spear-leafed plants or as soft worms within the yucca fruit.

Yet a rich vein of humor runs through this dark story. The tale begins with a situation which is by its very nature hilarious, though related with deadpan seriousness. Bat, who has notoriously weak eyes, is Coyote's son-in-law. But Coyote is the Chief of a very large band, and no daughter of a prominent man would be allowed to marry someone who had not proved that his eyes could endure strong smoke without watering! Then when Coyote orders a man to go out to scout for game, he chooses Bat rather than any one of a number of keen-sighted hunters. Bat flaps away to various mountain peaks where he sits pathetically wiping his streaming eyes and straining them in an attempt to see; although he proves to be an excellent scout after all, since his phenomenal hearing makes him aware of the presence of much game and even enables him to bring down a mountain sheep without actually seeing it.

The next series of humorous situations involves Bat's tracking of his grandsons, and his reconstruction of their ill-fated efforts to take part in games of strength and skill. We cannot but note that these Sky Brothers are the male counterparts of Yucca Date Worm Girls as they were when we first met them. Sky Brothers are bumbling, naïve young men, excelling at nothing. Following the usual pattern, the elder is more perceptive, resourceful, obedient, and generally better balanced than the younger, but the self-will of the younger always prevails.

As the story works up to the revenge taken by Bat upon the sisters and their ancient husband (who had actually done his best to warn and protect Sky Brothers), there is very little to laugh at. Only Coyote is comical as he goes blithely to his death, hastening to present a gift of meat to the new girls who are entering camp; and there is a certain grim humor in Bat's long, quarrelsome dialogue with Rattlesnake. Bat asserts that he and Rattlesnake are old comrades-in-arms and that they were members of the same war party when the earth was new, and everything was covered with fog, and Rattlesnake had to be carried into battle.[6] Rattlesnake repeatedly disclaims any memory of such an expedition and intersperses his disclaimers with threats to bite his unwelcome guest. During most of this colloquy Bat sits with his back turned roasting yucca dates in the fire, but all the time watching Rattlesnake's every move through one tiny eye which he has plucked out and relocated in the back of his head—and which now seems to see very clearly! Rattlesnake finally discerns that Bat's wrist protectors are made out of the bones of his wives, although Bat denies this and declares that he has had these same wrist protectors since the earth was new. This episode contains, in different relationship, the same constellation of elements mentioned in "How Wildcat Brothers Recovered Their Hunting Song," namely, bones of a slain adversary, wrist protectors, and the completion of vengeance. It will be recalled that, in the Wildcat story, Wildcat wounded a jackrabbit, followed it up to the Land on Top of the Sky, killed it, and gave it to his grandfather to eat, afterwards making peon sticks of its bones; he then made himself small and hid in his grandfather's wrist protector, preparatory to leaping out and slaughtering the Sky Rabbits. In the Bat and Rattlesnake tale, Bat makes the bones of his enemies into wrist protectors, and it is implied that this enhances his power as well as providing an additional provocation to Rattlesnake. The long quarrel between these two culminates in another scene of horror as Bat splits Rattlesnake in two with his flint "toenail."

Then the atmosphere brightens as the story turns towards its happy ending. Bat finds and resuscitates his grandsons and administers the ritual scolding. Returning to camp, he proceeds to restore life to all those whom Yucca Date Worm Girls had killed, leaving Coyote till the last. And according to pattern Coyote, springing up at the touch of the *poro*, exclaims that he must have fallen asleep suddenly on his way down to give a gift of meat to two girls. This is the inevitable humorous touch, always anticipated and always laughed at by those who listen to the stories of Coyote as Chief.

Of the myths recorded here, "How Coyote Went to War Against Gila Monster" is the one most heavily weighted with doom and foreboding.

The violation of the food cache illustrates Coyote's selfishness, greed, and foolishness. A Chief who had proper care for his people, even though he had neglected to instruct them in the ways of prudence, would surely have led them to the cache; then the food might have been quickly transferred to their own encampment and their tracks covered. But Coyote "wants it all for himself"—a grave fault to the Chemehuevi way of thinking. He remains in the hole where the food was buried, eating and sleeping, until he finds himself trapped by the approach of the rightful owners. Then he consults his penis, turning, as always in a tight spot, to the instinctual and unconscious wisdom of the body rather than to reason or to the higher wisdom of the shaman controlling (or controlled by) powers beyond himself. Coyote's ruse of turning himself (following the advice of his penis) into a stinking coyote carcass which the outraged people themselves toss out of the hole furnishes a typical bit of Coyote-ish humor; but the story immediately turns grim as Gila Monster's and Turtle's angry warriors pursue him to his camp and slaughter his weak and unprepared people. On this occasion, Coyote is not killed; as the battle goes against him, he and a remnant of his followers run away.

Then follows a long, strange, dream-like interlude. The only survivors of the massacre are an old woman, left for dead, and her grandson, abandoned and left to die when his mother is taken captive. The grandmother regains consciousness and cares for the infant. She raises him in an atmosphere of secrecy and fear, and yet there is a hint of magic, for we are told that she always sings as she works at her daily task of seed gathering. From the first the boy is daring, creeping away from the house despite his grandmother's warnings and while still very small making himself a toy bow and arrow—the ability to construct such a weapon appears to be an innate masculine skill which does not have to be learned.

When he has grown bigger he makes himself a better weapon and with it wounds a little brown bird (Yu'uravats*i*), who turns out to be his "other grandmother." (And here again is the sibling motif, for the relationship term employed for both grandmothers indicates that they are sisters or cousins.) From this newly discovered "grandmother" comes the revelation of the tragic events which heretofore have been unmentioned and the instructions on how to make a knife and how he must require the grandmother who has raised him to use it to divide him into two boys. With great difficulty the old woman is persuaded to place the edge of the blade on top of the boy's head; she then faints, the knife falls of its own weight, and immediately there are two where only one had been before. And while the single youth has been simply referred to as "the boy," the two now have a name: Dove Boys.

With this the secret is out. We see clearly that what has previously been merely hinted at or implied must be accepted as a definite psychological statement, namely, that each of the unitary pairs who appear so frequently in Chemehuevi mythology represents dual aspects of a single entity. All has been spelled out in the division of one youth into Dove Boys. Only in this instance, because there is no "elder" or "younger," a differentiation in character does not occur; the two continue to speak with one voice and to act in obedience to one will, although with a great access of ability and maturity. It also becomes evident that the two grandmothers (sisters or cousins) constitute another duad representing two types of maternal instinct: one which would protect the charge, keep him in ignorance, and prolong his state of childish dependence; the other willing to teach, to impart information even on painful subjects, to strengthen and push the youth toward adulthood. Significantly, it is the protective grandmother who is required to wield the dividing knife.

It is now apparent that the feeling "my sibling is the same as myself" has been projected back into mythological times, there to become reinforced by its presumed origin in a pre-human era, and also that the Chemehuevis had a profound, even tragic sense of the cleavage in the individual human psyche and expressed this metaphorically in the myths.

Is the division of Dove Boys a mythologized account of some ancient puberty ceremony, or is it another reference to a shaman's initiation? Whichever rite of passage is implied, its effect is not restricted to the individual(s) directly concerned. At this time, the grandmother who raised the boy, heretofore called merely "the grandmother" or "the old woman," begins to be spoken of by name (Wɨnʔnamakasaamaʔapɨtsi, a word which, like Yuʔuravatsi, is the name of a species of small bird). It should be noted that, on occasion, the names of mythic beings are mentioned only after a certain change in, or more precise definition of, character has occurred—this is the very old and widespread custom that can still be seen in the Christian practice of bestowing a new name to emphasize the new nature presumably received at the time of baptism. In the case of Dove Boys' grandmother, her nature changes from quiet and timid to active and belligerent. She paints her face for war and goes to rouse Coyote and his people. All those in Coyote's camp at once become aware of the appearance of the long-awaited sign and emerge from their dream-like lethargy, while Coyote himself, highly excited, goes to notify those lesser chiefs subject to him but not at the moment living in the immediate vicinity. Thus the great war party gets under way, with Dove Boys and Wɨnʔnamakasaamaʔapɨtsi accompanying the warriors.

Now the war song sequence provides another comic interlude. Coyote makes fun of everybody's song with the exception of those of Mosquito and Horsefly, both of which appeal to him as warlike because they mention drinking the blood of living persons. Each warrior takes offense at Coyote's criticism and must be placated and persuaded not to leave the expedition. Last of all, the warriors ask Coyote to sing his song. Greatly flattered, he accedes to the request, only to be met by a storm of ridicule. Then in turn his feelings are hurt, and he threatens to go back home, whereupon all the people assure him that they need him and that they were "only fooling." Coyote obviously has the very human trait of being able to dish out more than he can take in return.

The following morning the war party travels on. In the midst of a burning, waterless desert Coyote sends Dove Boys to scout for water, instructing them to fly high over four "dangerous waters" and telling them by what signs they will recognize their mother, the woman who was taken captive, near the fifth water where Gila Monster and his band are camped.

Thus we are introduced to the tragic figure of the captive

woman, gathering seed like the other women in the band but working apart from them and stopping at intervals to weep and to look around. Spying on her from their sky-perch, Dove Boys descend in the form of doves and alight on her shoulders. She recognizes them at once and listens eagerly to what they have to tell her of the approaching war party. Then after explaining to them the nature of the danger at each of the intervening watering places and warning them to give no sign when Gila Monster puts them to the test, she takes them home with her, ostensibly as pets for the children. Gila Monster at once becomes suspicious. He states that the doves are "not real doves," that they are his enemies in the form of doves, and he accuses the woman in his ominous and doleful chant. He also questions the woman about the dead jack-rabbit she carries (actually a present from her sons). "You cannot kill jackrabbits," he declares. But the woman calmly replies that she has killed that rabbit with her "crooked stick."[7] There is a dreadful touch in the casual manner in which the captive woman parries Gila Monster's questions and accusations and in her iron composure while he tests the baby doves (for by this time they have become very small and young) by burning their beaks with hot coals. When they have endured their ordeal without the blink of an eye, the woman, still casual, hands the little doves to her children, suggesting that they be taken to the water. There they drink and drink, then flutter clumsily up into a small bush only to mount suddenly and swiftly and fly high and fast back to the waiting war party while the children return to their house crying for their lost pets and setting Gila Monster off on another round of suspicious chanting.

Back at the camp, Dove Boys find all the warriors dead of thirst and go about reviving them and giving them water to drink from the large jugs which they (now in the form of young men) carry on their shoulders.

(At this point the narrator remarks parenthetically that male and female doves feed each other during the nesting season, and feed their fledglings after they are hatched, by regurgitating food and drink because of the example set by Dove Boys; also that the doves have white-tipped beaks because the young doves were burned by Gila Monster. The tellers of stories also say that horned toads appear as they do because in mythic times Horned Toad laughed too easily and had a wreath of flints tied about his head to keep him from being swallowed by a Giant; and that the loin of a coyote tastes like the flesh of a mountain sheep because this is what Coyote used to "make himself a loin" after he had been lacerated by Bear. Thus the game goes on. Appearances, habits, and traits observed in animals, as well as human beliefs and customs, are projected back into mythic time and there assigned origins and causes.)

The resurrection scene in the camp of the war party ends with the revival of Coyote, always eagerly anticipated by the listeners. In this case there is an added touch of humor. Rattlesnake, next to the last to be revived, moves convulsively as he regains consciousness and overturns a jug of water, which immediately becomes a fountain in the wilderness, pouring forth its magical and inexhaustible contents. Coyote's carcass, helpless and inert as a piece of driftwood, floats swiftly down the newly formed stream, and his warriors must run after it and bring it back before they can resuscitate their leader. Whereupon he protests in his usual manner, oblivious or pretending to be oblivious of recent events, that he must have fallen asleep.

Once revived, Coyote is full of energy. No wonder the people said, "We need you, Coyote." He calls upon Dove Boys for a full report and at once acts upon it, planning step by step the conquest of the watering places. Giving himself successively the appearance of a quail, a wiwʔwiyatsi, and an antelope, he mingles with the flocks of birds flying over the waters and afterwards with the herd of antelopes, carrying Rattlesnake in the form of a buckskin strap tied around his waist. But he is not a very convincing quail, wiwʔwiyatsi, or antelope. It is part of his plan that the guard should suspect him and shoot at him, giving him an excuse to drop his fatal belt so that Rattlesnake may do the assassin's work for which he has volunteered. Then at the last water, when Four-Eyed Insect has been disposed of by Sidewinder, Coyote holds a council of war, deciding which warriors shall fight in the main engagement and which—Large Red Ants, Small Red Ants, and Mosquitoes in their insect forms—shall block off Gila Monster's various routes of escape. Also at this conference an ally not heretofore listed, Sun Spider (whom we first met as Wildcat's grandfather in the Land on Top of the Sky), is directed to spin his web over Gila Monster's sky-hole, cutting off his final exit. (And thus the myths are tied together, and even in the pitiful remnant that has been preserved we find hints and shadows of what must have been a glorious network of sagas.)

Back in the house of Gila Monster the captive woman is grinding seed. Still filled with foreboding, Gila Monster charges her with grinding for his enemies, but she parries his accusations by saying that she is merely grinding for the next day. Unconvinced, Gila Monster keeps up his grim chanting, again voicing his conviction that the doves were his enemies in disguise, charging the captive woman with treachery, and foretelling the approach of enemy warriors. All through this part of the tale there is a heavy sense of doom and fatality. Gila Monster has been presented as an able and foresighted Chief. Yet he now makes no effort to alert his people or to prepare them for war. Eventually he even falls asleep, and the captive woman ceases her grinding long enough to hide his stone shirt, leaving him defenseless. It is now toward morning, and she knows the war party is approaching. But she goes back to her grinding and continues to grind out vengeance all through the battle. Afterwards we are told that the victorious warriors feast on the quantities of food that she has prepared. The children whom she bore to Gila Monster are not mentioned after the episode with the baby doves. Presumably they perished in the general massacre while their mother ground on, not raising hand or voice to save them.

Turtle also expresses a sense of inevitable doom by remaining in his house with his armored back turned during the whole course of the battle. When it is over, seeing that all is lost and that the High Chief lies dead, he turns to face the warriors and dies with great dignity. Thus he expresses the Chemehuevi ideal: patience to endure, strength to survive, courage when all hope is lost.

The very first episode in the myth entitled "How Wolf and Coyote Went Away" contains material of enormous importance in the field of comparative mythology. After describing the "sending away" or sacrificing by the Ainus of a bear cub that has been captured and raised for this purpose, a ceremony which includes offerings made to the dead bear's head of dishes prepared from its own flesh, Joseph Campbell writes:

> When a wild bear is killed in the mountains it is carried into the hunter's house with honor, by way not of the door but of the so-called "god's window"; and such an entry is known as a "god's arrival." The old goddess of the fire, guarding the fire in the center of the house, is thought to have welcomed the guest invisibly from afar, and the god and goddess now talk together by the fireside all night . . . .
>
> In this goddess of fire, Fuji, the "ancestress and protectress" of the house, we have a counterpart, in some way, of the goddess-figurines found in the dwellings of the mammoth hunters; for they too, apparently, were the guardians of the hearth. In the Ainu household there is a place in the sacred northeast corner of the lodge, behind the family heirlooms, where a special prayer-stick is kept, with a little gash at the top to represent the mouth, which is known as *chisei koro inan*, "ancestral caretaker of the house"; and he is addressed as the husband of the fire.[8]

If we compare this account of observances connected with the circumpolar bear cult[9] with Coyote's encounter with his aunt, Bear, we see that they contain precisely the same elements, although these elements are rearranged or reversed. In the Chemehuevi story the Bear, not the fire, is feminine, and the special poker stick (since the Chemehuevis did not have prayer-sticks) is the husband of Bear, not of the fire. Although in certain North American Indian myths the Bear is the custodian of fire, this is not the case with the Chemehuevis; Coyote, prototype of man, knew how to make fire before his contact with his aunt, Bear. But in making a fire at his aunt's house he violates an implied taboo, that is, he does something which Wolf has not specifically told him to do. He also commits an indiscretion in poking the fire with the little living poker sticks (his "little cousins"). The story now goes on to imply (without ever so stating) that Wolf in his great wisdom sees the necessity for eliminating all trace of Bear and her progeny, so that no word of Coyote's offense may reach the Bear People and precipitate war. Therefore on his second trip to his aunt's house, Coyote, following Wolf's instructions, feeds Bear and her poker stick children blood pudding (of which she is supposed to be inordinately fond) mixed with flint chippings. This pudding is made of mountain sheep's blood, not bear's blood, and the intent is to destroy, not to honor; but the offering of food again parallels an element of the Ainu practice. The plan is foiled by the escape of one little poker stick who tumbles away down the valley threatening to "tell all"; and (we have been told) the Ainu term for prayer-sticks is *inao*, meaning message bearers.

Later in the same myth Coyote brings the dawn (after he has loosed the Night from the bundle in which his brother kept it) by shooting an arrow feathered with seagull feathers at the sky, which would seem to indicate that at one time the Chemehuevis or their ancestors looked eastward to the sea. Also, still later in the tale, the frustrated Bear warriors cause a tremendous blizzard, freezing everything and covering the whole earth with snow (a blizzard comparable to that produced by Wildcat Brothers when they caused Coyote and his family to freeze to death and thus recovered their stolen song.)

Summing up, we find in Chemehuevi mythology these tenuous but significant clues to a persistent racial memory of a northern origin coupled with a coastal habitat (at least at one time) and possibly a passage over water: (1) the evidence just noted of the presence of a bear cult; (2) the Land of the Dead was located in the north, and at the end of the mythic age Wolf and Coyote (and presumably all surviving pre-human beings) "went north"; (3) references to blizzards more severe than any which could have occurred in territory occupied by the Chemehuevis for some time prior to the coming of the white man; (4) the reference to a time "when the earth was new and everything covered with fog"; (5) these long-time desert dwellers, possessing a typical Desert Culture, held Ocean Woman, the sea goddess, as the primary creator and worshipped her after their casual fashion; (6) Louse's eggs, the seed of mankind, were fertilized by Coyote on an island in the sea, placed in a storage basket woven by Louse's mother,[10] and brought back to the mainland by Coyote in the guise of a water-spider carrying its egg-sac on its back; (7) the seagull's feathers were associated with the dawn. It is tempting to surmise that the whole story of Wolf's and Coyote's war with the Bears might be a metaphorical account of the struggle between the old circumpolar mythology where Bear was the dominant character and the desert mythology in which Coyote is typical. This conflict is clothed in poetic imagery; it is seen as typified in the natural world by the dramatic confrontation between the darkness of an advancing storm and the brightness of the double rainbow.

"How Wolf and Coyote Went Away" illumines Chemehuevi psychology by its presentation of the contrasting characters of the two brothers and the relationship between them. As we have seen, in these dream-stories siblings are always "the same as" one another, the one who became two, that is, the dual nature of a single entity. However, the other mythological pairs of siblings do not present completely divided personalities. The dialogue between older and younger sibling always goes somewhat as follows:

"Let us do so-and-so."

"No, to do so would be disobedient and/or dangerous."

"I am determined to do so anyway."

"Very well, that is what we will do."

Then comes the unwise action and penalty followed by rectification. In the case of Wolf and Coyote the cleavage is complete. They are shown either as opposites or as superior and inferior, with Coyote acting out a poor imitation of Wolf. Clearly they represent two aspects of the human psyche (potential and actual), and therefore two patterns between which mankind may choose. Wolf is described as perfect and Coyote as imperfect, and the old people say, "We followed Coyote," we chose the inferior model. But we as non-Indians must avoid the mistake of projecting upon this division of the self the categories of "good" and "evil," "light" and "darkness." The Chemehuevis had such terms, but they are not applicable here. It is said that Wolf when he appeared in human form was noble, perfect man; Coyote at all times (except in temporary disguise) was only incompletely anthropomorphic. But Wolf was not so much the perfect model for an ordinary human being as for a shaman. It is said that in other stories not recorded here he appeared as a Chief leading his warriors; but this activity and his prowess as a hunter are not inconsistent with shamanhood. Wolf and Coyote are both Immortals, Self-Mythologizing Ones, belonging to the age of myth. But about Wolf particularly there is a constant aura of the supernatural. He would accomplish

all things by magic, from the birth of a child to the digging of a
tunnel or the feathering of an arrow. Coyote argues that these
things should be done in such a way as to set a fitting pattern for
the race of mortals. In almost every way he typifies the human
element. Even his magic is of a different order than Wolf's. Wolf
has the divine attribute of foreknowledge. In every event he knows
"the end from the beginning." Therefore the implication is that he
foresees Coyote's errors, disobediences and failures, and also their
consequences. Then the whole procedure of solemnly imparting
detailed instructions which, through carelessness or incompetence
are not precisely carried out, the ritual scolding of Coyote, his
fawning, tongue-in-cheek repentance, and the ensuing chain of di-
sastrous events, becomes a sort of elaborate play deliberately de-
signed, a divine maya with a predestined end.

Wolf is the Elder Brother. There is no doubt of his superiority,
and in the pairs of siblings it is always the elder who is the
wiser—with the curious exception, noted above, of the second
appearance of the Yucca Date Worm Girls after the killer instinct has grown like a cancer and assumed control of the dual
organism, so that the younger sister becomes dominant. But whereas Coyote simply calls Wolf by name or addresses him by the
term which means "my elder brother," Wolf unfailingly adds the
honorific -pitsi to Coyote's name. This seems to be a tacit ac-
knowledgement of the physically instinctual as antedating the
spiritually intuitive.

It has been said that the Trickster figure separates out and
embodies all that is evil and undesirable in human nature. However
true this may or may not be of other American Indian mythic
characters (and on this I am not qualified to speak with authority), it is most emphatically not true of the Chemehuevi Mythic
Coyote. He embodies *all* the human traits: cowardice and incredible daring; laziness and patient industry or frantic exertion; foolishness and skillful planning; selfishness and concern for others. If
he were simply the dark shadow of Wolf, the People would not
say, "We followed Coyote." True, he is the incomplete and the
imperfect; but although his war clothes are the secondary rainbow,
they are nonetheless an arc of light. And Coyote has one very
important attribute which seems quite foreign to Wolf's extreme
and even pompous dignity—namely, a sense of humor. Coyote has

fun, and it is fun to hear about him and his exploits. What he lacks in dignity he makes up in sheer exuberance.

When Coyote tries to obey the instructions of Wolf (his higher self) he invariably bungles his mission; but when he turns to his penis, that organ which has an instinctual life of its own, independent of reason, will, or spiritual control, he receives appropriate guidance and succeeds superbly. To borrow Freudian terms—not completely applicable—Coyote does better when dominated by his id than by his superego. From his premature opening of the basket containing the newly hatched people (by which he disobeyed the mother of Louse, an aspect of Ocean Woman and feminine counterpart of Wolf, and for which he was duly scolded by Wolf), on through his offense to his aunt, Bear, his carelessness in permitting the escape of one little poker stick, and his fatally misdirected curse on Wolf, he piles up a long record of failure—although, as always, we feel that these very failures were predestined parts of an orderly and inescapable design; but on his own, throughout the wild series of adventures culminating in the return of his brother's scalp to their home on Nɨvagantɨ, he handles himself superbly.

The myths of the Two Brothers also dramatize the age-old confrontation between God and man, which is actually subjective, simply another way of looking at the conflict between man's "higher" and "lower" natures, though always pictured as taking place between divine and human entities. Many ancient scriptures aver that God (or the gods) became fed up with man. In Genesis we read, "And it repented the Lord that he had made man on the earth, and it grieved him at his heart." In the myth now under consideration it is plainly stated that Wolf has grown tired of Coyote's fecklessness and general unreliability, which no amount of teaching, preaching, or scolding was able to correct. But the reverse is also true. Man grows tired of God, or of those who claim to enforce His will, or of that part of himself which sets impossible standards and makes impossible demands and takes everything too seriously. Coyote is fully as weary of Wolf as Wolf is of him. He finds it very trying to live with someone who knows everything and from whom he cannot conceal any of his actions. He is tired of Wolf's always being in the right, and he has had enough of Wolf's humorless pomposity and intentional obscurity. When Wolf uses archaic or unusual words, or words in their less familiar sense,

Coyote asks petulantly, "Why don't you say what you mean?" Moreover, Coyote begins to feel that Wolf is deliberately withholding power from him or not giving him the equipment or regalia by which he could acquire power. As he toils with his bundles up the mountain while his brother remains for the final encounter with the Bears, he disobediently turns and looks back and sees Wolf shining in the glory of the primary rainbow and mowing down the ranks of the Bear warriors, and at that moment his envy and resentment culminate in the curse. This curse was intended to disable the Glorious One only slightly, to humble him a trifle, to make life with him somewhat more endurable; but it took form and force less from Coyote's consciously formulated words than from his smoldering hatred, and Wolf, struck through the heart (not through the calf of the leg as Coyote has desired), tumbles from his mountain like Lucifer falling from heaven and is immediately torn to shreds by the Bears.

Thus one more ancient tragedy finds its distant echo. Coyote has slain Wolf even as Cain rose up against Abel and slew him. But because our narrative has the quality of a dream rather than the pseudo-historicity of the Hebrew scriptures, the events which follow are quite different.

At first Coyote is like a child left to his own devices or a man who has succeeded in silencing his conscience. He gives only a few perfunctory howls of mourning before hastily beginning to look through the possessions which Wolf in his lifetime has not allowed anyone else to see. However, it so happens that the very first bundle Coyote opens contains the Night, and squatting there in the primeval darkness he mourns long and loud, not for his brother, but for his own probable fate in a world without light. But as the prototype of man, Coyote cannot yield forever to despair. By his own ingenuity (though only with the help of his brother's store of feathers) he brings the dawn, followed by full day. And by that time Coyote is fully bent on achieving Wolf's resurrection.

His first task is to seek for and find minute flecks of each of the four elements of his brother's body: bone, flesh, blood, and hair. Next he is faced with the all but impossible undertaking of retrieving Wolf's scalp from the Bear People. Preparing for this feat, Coyote adheres to his pattern of fours, making four arrows for each bow and leaving them in caches along the way as he journeys to the country of the Bears. Arriving there, he disguises himself (in speech as well as appearance, for he now speaks very deliberately and adds siviyaukwiⁿi instead of haikʸa to each sentence) and talks with two old Bear women who are gathering wood for the fire around which the Scalp Dance is danced. They tell him that Wolf has been slain and that now Coyote is all alone, with no one to help him; and from them he extracts the information that will enable him to enter the dance ring unsuspected. Then he leaps upon the old women, kills them, skins them, and stuffs himself into one skin and his ever-available penis into the other—thus regaining the semblance at least of being two, not one. In this double disguise, he boldly dances in the Scalp Dance until the scalp is placed upon his head,[11] whereupon he leaps out of the ring and makes off with the precious trophy. The Bears pursue him hotly, and Coyote has many narrow escapes. At last his enemies decide that the simplest way to dispose of him will be to produce a great blizzard and freeze him to death. They return home, and Coyote takes shelter in a cave. Waking to a world covered with snow as far as the eye can reach, Coyote makes himself small, inserts himself into a tiny puff-ball which he finds caught in a spiderweb, and calls for the North Wind to blow him home. But the wind, as was its wont in that era, roars in the sky high above him. So then Coyote makes himself sky-tall and with his *poro* hooks it down to sweep across the surface of the earth. This is the last act recounted in the myths by which an Immortal remakes conditions on earth into what they are today.

Back in the home cave, Coyote rests and refreshes himself, then places the scalp under a basket with the other fragments of Wolf's body, and awaits the moment of truth. In the eerie pre-dawn hours he lies awake and listens; and when the morning star emerges he hears the "Huuuu" that tells him his brother is restored to life. Now Coyote is highly excited, mad with joy. Now the murder has been undone, wiped out. He and his brother will live on in the cave as they have lived through endless time, and all will be as it has always been. But the next "Huuuu" sounds farther away and the next still farther. Wolf is not coming back to the cave, he is "going north!" Coyote scrambles to his feet and runs after him frantically, guided only by ever fainter wolf howls and once, much farther on, by the imprint of a well-known "perfect" hand upon a stone. Thus we last see Coyote as he runs on forever in pursuit of the lost Brother, mentor, guide.

Those ancient dreaming mythmakers, who were not afraid to journey deep into the cave of the collective unconscious, brought back with them many parables descriptive of the human psyche, and a prophecy perhaps more applicable to our time than to theirs. Modern man has destroyed or outgrown the beliefs which he once accepted as verities, only to find, like Coyote, that life is scarcely worth living without the mystery and the magic, the dignity and the authority of Something beyond himself. Now he runs on, blindly pursuing he knows not what, never reassured by the traditions and imprints (the symbolic wolf howl and handprint) of the past.

NOTES

NOTES

Introduction

1. There are Chemehuevis on the Colorado River Reservation now who say that this was her name. There was a younger woman called Cloud Flower, but they also connect the name with this woman, who is still remembered for her heroism.

2. This is the way Chemehuevis translate ʔAyarupagarimɨ. ʔAya is the desert tortoise; it is tɨɨravatcɨ, a product of the desert intimately associated with the Desert Culture.

3. I assumed for a time, because George Laird often spoke of "the trouble at the building of the Old Blythe Intake" and of "the killing of Calloway," that the construction job where his father was employed was the building of the intake, and that the man whom he saw killed was Calloway. I can find nothing in my notes to justify this assumption. George Laird correctly dated the "trouble" at Blythe as taking place in 1880, five years after the death of the Old Chief, yet he was positive that he was no more than seven years old when his father left him. Persons now living, who have heard of the episode, say that young George provoked the killing by teasing a man who was trying to light his pipe. But George himself recalled nothing of that. He only remembered singing and drumming his heels to keep warm in the chilly dawn while watching his father (who surely made the best flapjacks in the world!) split kindling to start a fire.

4. Words of Chemehuevi origin have no l, but the sound presents no difficulty to the Chemehuevi tongue; l or r is substituted indifferently for dh (th as in "those") of Yuman words.

Chapter I: Identity, Distribution, and Organization

1. Padre Francisco Garcés, on encountering a party of "Chemebets" in 1776, observed that they ran "with the speed of deer," and added "These Indians give me the impression of being the most swift-footed of any I have seen" (Elliott Coues, *On the Trail of a Spanish Pioneer: The Diary and Itinerary of Francisco Garcés* [New York: Francis P. Harper, 1900], I, p. 220). He also wrote: "They conducted themselves with me most beautifully; by no means were they thievish or troublesome, but rather quite considerate" (Coues, pp. 224-225). To this day the older Chemehuevis deplore loud talk and aggressive behavior as "bad manners."

2. Although George Laird spoke much of the sinew-backed hunting bow and described the manner in which men went additionally armed with the short, powerful war bow and quiver of war arrows, he did not describe the war bow in detail. In 1969, several Chemehuevi women denied that there were different bows and arrows for hunting and for war. However, Wendell Goodman, Sr. confirmed George Laird's information, agreeing that the war arrows were shorter than the hunting arrows and stating that "they flew like bullets." Mr. Goodman thought that the war bow was made of the antler of the mule deer. There was such a bow, but it was not the war bow. At Christmas, 1971, Mr. Goodman was visited by an elderly Chemehuevi friend, now living up north in Paiute country, who reminded him that the war bow was made of sinew-backed hickory and that it required great strength to draw it. Mr. Goodman said the war bow was called huntangatsi and that ?atsi meant gun—possibly ?atsi was originally the word for the hunting bow. Mr. Goodman and others gave niwihutsi as the word for the complete weapon, bow and arrow. Mr. Goodman and his friend agreed that awls and tools for chipping flint were made of deer antlers.

3. Padre Garcés described the dress of the "Chemebets" as follows: "The garb of these Indians is, Apáche moccasins (*zapato*), shirt of antelope skin (*vestido de gamuza*), white headdress like a cap (*gorra blanca á modo de solidéo*) with a bunch of those very curious feathers which certain birds of this country have in their crest" (Coues, p. 220).

4. George Laird mentioned only the cowrie shells. But women now living on the Colorado River Reservation say that the dew claws of mountain sheep were also so used. These had to come from animals that the man had killed himself; so that the pleasant susurrus accompanying the woman's movements bore witness to her husband's prowess. After contact with the whites small bells were used, and these were sewn on the elaborate full-skirted garments adopted as standard dress for the Indian woman and still used on ceremonial occasions.

5. See Note 3, this chapter. The "headdress" which Padre Garcés describes was without doubt the kaitcoxo, and it was apparently worn by all the

Chemehuevi men in the party of forty. The question arises, why "mountain hat" rather than simply "hat?" It was a highly valued article of clothing, and the temptation is strong to associate its name with the mystique linking man and mountain (see p. 12). But it was surely not worn in the mountains only and not exclusively by men who were Mountain Sheep (owners of some variant of the Mountain Sheep Song). Also the basketry hat worn by women was called "woven mountain hat." It would seem that the most logical explanation for the appearance of the element kai- (-gai-), mountain, in the names of these head coverings is that their shape was reminiscent of mountain peaks.

6. Beautiful specimens of Chemehuevi baskets are extant, and the not-altogether-forgotten art of basketry is being revived.

7. This area was also home to the Serrano and Wanakik Cahuilla people, another example of the close coexistence of Southern California Indians.

8. Tantiitsiwɨ was also applied to Shoshonean-speaking tribes recognized by the Chemehuevis as related. For example, the Paranʔnɨgiwɨ, Paiutes living along the Virgin River in Nevada, were Tantiitsiwɨ but not Tuumontcokowɨ. On the other hand, unrelated (non-Shoshonean) northern tribes were simply Tantiinʸiwɨwɨ, Northern People.

9. It is said that a small group of Chemehuevis always lived close to the Colorado River and "played with" although they did not eat fish, and that the word "Chemehuevi" derives from the Mohave name for this band. This information is possibly correct, although it was not mentioned by George Laird. But considering that the inhabitants of a place were called by the name of the locality they principally occupied, it does not indicate that these river dwellers constituted a major subdivision of the tribe.

10. Actually a man may have inherited songs from both sides of the family, since some men claimed two or more songs.

11. Nowadays when a song is sung it takes great leaps from one locality to another, because there is no one who remembers the route in its entirety.

12. Another greater story involving a Mountain Sheep has left traces in the names of certain stars and groups of stars (see pp. 91-92).

13. Spirit-animal helpers, tutuguuviwɨ, discussed in detail in Chapter II.

14. In 1969, I was told that there is one man who still "sings Mountain Sheep—but only when he is drunk." The old, proud culture is now buried under layers of powerful inhibitions.

15. George Laird said that he had known well the Chemehuevi name of New York Mountains, but it had slipped his mind, and he was never able to recall it. Wendell Goodman, Sr., who was born there, gave the name as Kai-vʸaʔamantɨ. Compare Nɨvagantɨmantɨ, given by Stella Smith as the equivalent of George Laird's Nɨvagantɨ.

16. The Cry, or Yagapɨ, is discussed in Chapter II.

17. When George Laird left the Reservation in 1919 he knew of no proficient Deer Singer; fifty years later it is forgotten except for the name.

18. ʔAtatuʔᵂatsi never learned the Deer Song but became a Ghost Dance singer instead, and ʔOpitcokotsi had done the same. Kiipisi, the second son, had no interest except in food and drink; ʔApati, the youngest, might have learned the Deer Song from his uncle had he not died before reaching maturity.

19. This song, or rather portions of it, is still remembered. It was a song with which George Laird felt closely identified and the only song whose route he could trace. Yet much of the information now attainable does not check with that which he gave. The statement that the song is divided into two branches is not contradictory, considering its length and importance. But while George Laird located the starting point far up Bill Williams Fork, Wendell Goodman, Sr. says it started "at the Salton Sea"–probably at that low point on the desert now occupied by the Salton Sea. Although George Laird mentioned its funerary or ritualistic use, he considered it primarily a song of fun and gaiety, eminently suited to entertain the People; but today it is reverentially regarded, held to be too sacred to be lightly used. On the other hand, the Bird Song (modern Chemehuevi Witsihuvᵂiyav or Witsihuvᵂiyap), which George Laird did not list as an hereditary song (although he stated that the Chemehuevis greatly admired the Cahuilla Bird Song) is for amusement– and yet the Mohave Bird Song was sung on the solemn occasion of Mike Tobin's funeral. Still they say, "Bird Dance [dance and song are used interchangeably in translation] is for fun." The Salt Song, according to George Laird, traces the travels of a great variety of birds, each searching for its proper home; but it seems unlikely (though it is possible) that the present Bird Song is actually identical with or a part of the Salt Song as he knew it. Recently, when a group was singing, one woman admonished another, "Don't sing Bird, sing Salt." To avoid confusion so far as possible, I have given in the text what George Laird told me, recording contradictions–or at least some of them–in this note.

20. All Mohave words recorded in connection with this song and elsewhere in the book are recorded as I heard them from George Laird. The pronunciation given is probably fairly accurate, since George Laird spoke Mohave fluently (though obviously with a Chemehuevi accent), but I can convey no idea of the structure. I have used th to indicate unvoiced th as in "this"; dh for the voiced th of "those"; and t-h to represent t plus a strong aspirant, as in "get hurt."

21. But Fort Mohave was reached by the song before midnight!

22. Tavamuhuumpɨtsi indicates a different species from muhuumpɨtsi. But compare Tavahukᵂampi, Sun Spider, in the myth "How Wildcat Brothers Recovered Their Hunting Song," in which Sun Spider is a purely mythological name.

23. If a man's eyes watered easily, it was believed that he had limited eyesight. Compare the pathetic picture of Bat, Coyote's son-in-law, wiping his weak eyes when Coyote sent him out to scout for game (in the myth "How Bat Killed Rattlesnake").

24. Also occurs, perhaps more frequently, as niwi?avi.

25. George Laird stated that irrigation had been introduced by the first Mexican settlers; but it seems possible that the Chemehuevis may first have learned this method of farming by contact with other tribes who irrigated their crops.

26. But tribal memories are sometimes extraordinarily short. We must remember that we are not dealing with a linear or historical time sense. If an event or circumstance or cultural condition became incorporated into myth it might be transmitted in that form for centuries or even millenia (as is probably the case with the incredibly primitive way of life pictured in "How Cottontail Rabbit Conquered the Sun"); but if there is no storied record, a few generations are apt to become "always." There are young people today, born on the Colorado River Reservation, who insist that the Chemehuevis have always been "Arizona Indians," none of whom ever lived in California; and on that reservation there are middle-aged persons, persons moreover vitally interested in Chemehuevi culture and history, who are, for example, ignorant of the fact that yucca dates were once an important item in the Chemehuevi diet.

27. George Laird translated Kwayantu^watɨtsiwɨ as "Across the River People." Since this is clearly not the etymology of the word, he must have given this meaning simply because Kwayantu^watɨ was on the Arizona side. At another time he said that ?Ayarupagarɨmɨ was chief of the "Across the River People," and once he located ?Ayarupagarɨmɨ's band in the vicinity of Bill Williams Fork. I would suggest that these contradictions arose from the fact that ?Ayarupagarɨmɨ was closely associated with the Deer Song, which began up Bill Williams Fork; that ?Ayarupagarɨmɨ may actually have been chief of the Kwayantu^watɨtsiwɨ, which would account for his frequent presence in Chemehuevi Valley; and that just possibly ?Otawinɨrɨ was chief of the more remote nɨwɨavi.

28. Ben Paddock's maternal grandfather, Indian name unknown. This refers of course to the Ben Paddock who was George Laird's contemporary, not to the white trapper and ex-soldier whose union with a Chemehuevi woman started the Paddock line.

29. Calloway. See Note 7, Chapter III.

30. Or ?Opin^yawɨtɨm?matsɨ. This is the name of a small tank (a natural catch basin in rock) concealed by a mesquite growing in the mouth of a wash.

31. No etymology was given for Nagarɨpɨ. It looks as though it might be derived from a form of karɨgah, sits, with the reflexive or reciprocal prefix

na- and therefore might mean something like "a sitting down together"–
but karɨgah is applied to one or two persons only; for three or more the verb
is yɨwigʸah.

Chapter II: Shamanism and the Supernatural

1. George Laird offered no etymology for puhʷagantɨ. The word appears
in my original notes more often as puʷagantɨ and sometimes as puʔʷagantɨ.
Recent informants pronounce the h clearly and strongly but elide it (as
George Laird did) in derivatives such as navuʷaganumpɨ, medicine, or naga-
vuʷagantɨ, mountain sheep shaman. (This normal elision of h between vowels
when compounding produces a shift of accent which might account for my
error of omitting it when the word occurred independently.) A modern informant, Mary Molino, connected puhʷagant (in her pronunciation) with puhavak (which she pronounced with h, not hʷ!), a curse of "witching." She
illustrated the word by the following sentences: huʔungatsa nɨɨni puhavak,
that person "witched" me; puhavakatsani, you put a curse on me.

2. The People had knowledge of healing herbs. Yatampɨ, greasewood
(creosote bush), was an almost universal panacea, and there were many others
used to alleviate various complaints. These medicinal herbs are classed as
navuʷagantɨ, medicine, that is, material used for self-curing or self-medica-
tion. The work of the shaman, for good or ill, was not on a material plane and
required no material accessories.

3. I am inclined to think that the expression "he carried the poro" may
have been used symbolically rather than literally. Since Padre Garcés noted,
on encountering a party of Chemehuevis in 1776, that "They all carried a
crook besides their weapons" (Coues, p. 225), it is obvious that a crooked
stick for pulling lizards, gophers, etc. from their hiding places was an ordinary
piece of equipment. Is it not possible that this implement, like the shepherd's
crook in other times and in another part of the world, became, in certain
hands, the rod of power?

George Laird did not say of what kind of wood the poro was made, but
he stated that it was shaped by heating and bending.

4. A daughter of ʔOomposɨ became the wife of Tom Murango and lived
with him in the vicinity of Banning, California. The pronunciation Murango
was George Laird's. It probably should be Morongo, the family name used in
Morongo Reservation, Banning.

5. Her husband was formerly known as van Winkle but changed his name
to Jim ("or something") Hawk.

6. George Laird said that at the moment this information was recorded,
he could not recall the Chemehuevi equivalent of *haikwiira*. He frequently
gave kwiyatsɨ as meaning diamond-backed rattlesnake, and I do not know if
he meant to imply that *haikwiira* denoted another species. But compare

references to "Hikwi:r (supernatural snake illness)" and "Hikwi:r hahnok (supernatural snake contamination)" in George Devereaux, *Mohave Ethnopsychiatry: The Psychic Disturbances of an Indian Tribe* (City of Washington: Smithsonian Institution Press, 1969), p. 586.

7. "Doctor" Billy Eddy died on the Colorado River Indian Reservation in the spring of 1969. He was two years older than George Laird would have been had he lived. "Doctor" Billy Eddy was the last of the shamans, well-known and highly respected. I am told that he was tivitsipuhʷaganti, a genuine healer, up until the time when age impaired his powers. He was one of those real Chemehuevis who refused to talk to white people; and in his high old age he became so withdrawn that he did not even talk to his own family. I am told that the bat was his familiar.

8. At one time George Laird, trying very hard to recall the name of this lame Tantivaitsi, tentatively identified him with Yaariʔivʸa; but Yaariʔivʸa, though a mountain sheep shaman, was a Deer by inheritance, not a Mountain Sheep as this man was said to have been, and there is no mention elsewhere of his having been lame. It will be recalled, however, that Yaariʔivʸa claimed power to protect "his" game, both deer and mountain sheep.

9. This shaman, like ʔOomposi, was remembered in 1969 and subsequently along the Colorado River.

10. Although these songs mapped the mountains and deserts of this present, daylight world and had secular and purely social uses as well as ritualistic, they were strong in numinous overtones. It will be remembered that they had their dreamed versions; and they were probably sung principally, if not exclusively, at night.

11. Possibly Lehman Cave, Wheeler Peak, Nevada.

12. Hi Stewart is still remembered. His mother, Helen, deeded ten acres in Las Vegas to the Indians in 1912, the section now known as Indian Village. Stella Smith Mike, who resides there, estimated that there were about sixty people, many of them children, living there in 1969. She knew of the great cave and gave its name as Tutuʔugaivʸa, Mountain of the Familiars.

13. As will be seen a little later, the root of the jimson weed could also bring visions of the dead, but in a culture such as that of the Chemehuevis, where the very mention of the dead was taboo, such a dream would seldom be requested.

14. As the old culture passed, only fragments of the Talking Song were remembered and sung. And after the relatives of the old High Chief had died off or had lost their vocation, only the deceased's own song was sung. Finally, the time came when, in certain cases, that too had been forgotten. Then anyone owning an hereditary song would sing what he remembered of it, whether or not he belonged to the dead person's group. Even so, George Laird felt that certain restrictions and proprieties should be observed; for

instance, he did not think that it would be appropriate to sing the Salt Song at the Cry for a Mountain Sheep.

15. In modern times the funeral and the Cry have been combined; the Cry lasts all night, and the funeral takes place the following morning. (Throwing light on this transition, Wendell Goodman, Sr. told me in 1971 that the last big "powwows" he had attended—he mentioned one in 1915—were "memorials" for the dead.) The Cry is held in an available public building, a "flat house" no longer being erected for the occasion. Mike Tobin, the last of George Laird's contemporaries, died in the autumn of 1969. Because his death marked the passing of a generation and of an era, representatives of six tribes gathered to mourn him. Georgia Laird Culp, my daughter, had the very great privilege of being present at these rites. In the early part of the evening Christian hymns sung to guitar accompaniment alternated with the songs of various tribes, but after midnight the old ways took over completely. No property was burned. The deceased's good hat, blankets, cigarettes—whatever he might need for his journey—were placed in the coffin, together with a hunting bow (made by a Mohave who remembered the old Chemehuevi way) and two willow wands with eagle feathers braided onto them. A young Paiute stood at the head of the coffin and declaimed powerfully what must have been a version of the Talking Song. Afterwards the mourners formed a circle and danced the Circle Dance. Only then was the white undertaker allowed to enter and remove the coffin, taking it first to church for services conducted by a minister, then to the cemetery.

16. In 1971, Wendell Goodman, Sr. did not think that young eagles were caught and raised, but he well remembered shooting eagles with a rifle so that their skins could be used at a "powwow."

17. Compare the passing of the scalp from head to head of those dancing and singing within the circle at the Scalp Dance, as described in "How Wolf and Coyote Went Away." Could it be that the eagle skin represented the dead friend even as the scalp represented the dead enemy? Wendell Goodman, Sr. knew nothing about the eagle skin with feathers being placed on anyone's head.

18. Single families sometimes built themselves houses of this type, but these were much smaller than the ones constructed for Cries.

19. Since this song ranged territory "not of this world," it is perhaps not too much to assume that it directed the soul of the dead on its perilous journey. George Laird always spoke as though the singer of the Talking Song sang alone, and this was the case at Mike Tobin's funeral (see Note 15, this chapter). But Wendell Goodman spoke of him as leading the singing.

20. A pan-Indian religious movement, started in 1886 by Wovoka, "the Paiute Messiah." Actually it was an attempt to translate Christian teachings into the Indian idiom.

21. See p. 139.

22. The role of Ocean Woman as sole creator of the earth, and the dual roles she played in the creation of mankind, will be fully dealt with in the chapters on mythology (Chapters VI and VII).

23. See "How Wolf and Coyote Went Away" (pp. 192-207) and comment on the first episode of this myth (pp. 227-229).

24. I do not know whether they were called by a plural form of nuk^wi, runner, or by a word related to kwaingkati, swift runner over mountains, or by their own distinctive name. The Chemehuevi term is not among my existing notes. In 1971, an informant said voluntarily, "I don't know what they called those Runners."

25. When George Laird "ran with the Runners" he was probably the youngest of the group. To the end of his life he moved with great swiftness and ease, but he insisted that he had been "wind-broke" as a youth by carrying a message for a white man fifty miles at top speed, and therefore, like a "wind-broke" horse, was no longer capable of sustained effort.

26. Usually George Laird spoke of Kaawiʔa and Pagiiwixi as cousins—his cousins, and cousins to each other—but just once, after giving the matter long thought, he announced: "Black Turtle was the father of those two."

27. Pagiiwixi lived on for a long time. He had a woman once, but she left him, and he never took another. The aged ʔAyarupagarimi, Black Turtle, had lived much with the Mohave and liked a warm shelter in winter; so each year Pagiiwixi made an earth house for him (tivikʸani), building it bit by bit as he could spare the time. Pagiiwixi was also notable as having been the last man to own a kaitcoxo, mountain hat. Once when he and other young men were playing the stick-and-pole game, he hung this precious pointed cap with quail crests, together with his bow and quiver, on a bush. A party of Mohaves attacked suddenly. Pagiiwixi leaped for his weapons and helped drive off the enemy, but never recovered his hat.

28. The Spaniards called their captive converts "neophytes"; the Indians, more realistically, said "slaves."

29. I remember George Laird's half-sister, Anna Gonzales, speaking with gentle amusement of her "*muy catolica*" mother-in-law and the respect she demanded for her numerous images of saints. It must be remembered that in recent times the Catholic church has developed a happy faculty for coexisting with those symbols of an earlier belief which it cannot assimilate—as in the Pueblos, where the same men attend ceremonies in both church and kiva.

Chapter III: Kinship and Personal Relationships

1. Even now (in 1969), there are those who carefully obliterate the image of a deceased person from group photographs.

2. Final a plus initial a of postfix becomes aa or simply a, according to the amount of stress that falls upon the syllable.

3. The term for "older sister" appears in my notes both as patc*i* and pats*i*. I am inclined to think the form with tc is correct, but it was not so recorded in the collectives. It will be recalled that c in Chemehuevi is much lighter than the English sh, tc lighter than English ch.

4. In the myths included in this collection, only the exploits of Mythic Coyote in the capacity of leader are dealt with, and only he uses this term; but George Laird said that ʔaiv^yayaw*i*n*i* was also employed by Wolf and Mountain Lion in stories that he had heard but remembered only very vaguely.

5. In Chemehuevi, as spoken by George Laird, only certain names of tribes and words terminating in strongly nasal vowels took -m*i* as the plural termination meaning two or more; in all other cases it indicated two only. But today plurals in -m*i* (reduced to m when not followed by another element) seem to be preferred, especially with many words ending in -ts*i*. Perhaps this is characteristic of the Northern or Desert dialects.

6. The form of the suffix is -gaip*i* after all relationship terms except mon*a*, son-in-law. One may say either monangkaip*i* or monagaip*i*, former son-in-law. Monam*i* is the plural form of mon*a*. See Note 5, this chapter.

7. During this disturbance, Calloway was later killed by a Chemehuevi. The Chemehuevis were then displaced from one of their hereditary sites, and the Colorado Irrigation Company was left in sole possession. The Indians (304 in number, according to a letter to the Commissioner of Indian Affairs from the Indian Agent, Johnathan Biggs) were removed to a new site downriver, where (again according to Agent Biggs) they suffered great destitution. According to letters from Biggs, the Chemehuevis originally occupied land on the Arizona side and were moved across to California; according to George Laird, his n*i*w*i*av*i* belonged on the California side, at the present site of the city of Blythe.

8. One of the few persons living in 1969 who had the blood of the "Old Chief" was Wendell Goodman, Sr. His Chemehuevi name was Sawatosar*i*m*i*, White Arrowweed (sawap*i*, arrowweed; tosagar*i*, white). Mr. Goodman was born at New York Mountain and considered himself T*ii*ran*i*w*i*, Desert Chemehuevi. I do not know whether the form of his name (Sawatosar*i*m*i* instead of Sawatosagar*i*m*i*) is due to dialectic difference (he said t*i*h*ii*, deer, not t*i*hiy*a*) or to the process of simplification and shortening that has taken place in modern times, e.g., Siwavats for Siwaʔavaats*i* as the name for Chemehuevi Valley.

9. Billy Calloway, Chemehuevi or part Chemehuevi, is not to be confused with the white man mentioned simply as Calloway, who killed an Indian, ʔAapanap*i*, at the time of the building of the old Blythe Intake and was in turn killed by the Chemehuevis. Could Billy Calloway have been this man's son by a daughter of Nagaramaup*a*?

Chapter IV: The Natural World

1. A few years later George Laird and his cousins, the Runners, were to propose the tracking of Kaawiʔa, Rat Penis, on one of his supranormal journeys. See pp. 48-49.

2. This is the only reference to pottery making to be found in my notes, although there are many times when the *use* of pottery is mentioned. The Chemehuevis were notable for their basketry, the Mohaves for their pottery.

3. In the myth "How Wildcat Brothers Recovered Their Hunting Song," Wildcat wandered into that realm by accident in pursuit of a jackrabbit that he had shot on earth but which was actually a sky-jackrabbit; and in "How Coyote Went to War Against Gila Monster" we hear that Gila Monster tried to escape through his sky-hole.

4. In one myth (surviving only as a brief fragment in notes recorded in Poway but complete in my notes in the Harrington Collection) it is told how the Sun begot twin sons upon a woman; in "How Cottontail Rabbit Conquered the Sun," Sun and Moon are both animate and probably both male.

5. In this loanword George Laird clearly voiced the d. In 1969 I heard at least one person say duʔu instead of tuʔu for Indian asparagus. It would appear that familiarity with English tends to pull unaspirated Chemehuevi t towards d.

6. After Coyote had loosed the Night he shot arrows feathered with the feathers of various birds into the air to bring back the light. When he saw the false dawn he howled with delight, and that is why coyotes howl at that time even now (see p. 200).

7. The myths tell of a land on top of the sky; the terms for the entrance and emergence of the sun, moon, and stars imply a region below the earth, but such a place is not mentioned in this collection of myths.

8. A rather lengthy, but still far from complete version of this myth is given in Chapter VI, pp. 192-207.

9. See p. 244.

10. See pp. 243-244.

11. "How Wolf and Coyote Went Away."

12. See p. 28.

13. See p. 40.

14. As recorded by John Peabody Harrington in *The Ethnogeography of the Tewa Indians*, extract from the 29th Annual Report of the Bureau of American Ethnology (Washington, D.C., 1916), p. 43. There are probably many other correspondences between Chemehuevi and the Tanoan languages.

15. Probably ʔangkagah, being red, because ʔangkakagah would be awkward to pronounce.

16. See p. 88.

17. In 1969 I heard Wendell Goodman, Sr., speaking in Chemehuevi to Mary Hill, describe the Gila monster as po^ʔok^watɨ.

18. The Spanish name of the small and extremely palatable seed of a small species of sage, also of the plant which bears it. I do not have the Chemehuevi name at present. *Chia* was a food prized by many California tribes. I tasted it many years ago at a small ranchería on the Tejon Ranch.

19. See pp. 42-43 and Note 2, Chapter II.

20. An amusing touch in the story of Coyote's wooing of Louse is the statement that the successive houses he built for her were samarók^{waↄ}ik^yanɨ, not the more easily erected tcuupik^yanɨ (see p. 150).

21. In modern times tɨvik^yanɨ means adobe house.

22. Pagɨɨwɨxɨ built one annually for ʔAyarupagarɨmɨ (see Note 27, Chapter II). The implication is that this form of house construction was borrowed from the Mohaves.

23. This and associated words were obtained from Stella Smith Mike in 1969. According to Mrs. Mike, the willow was shaped while green to form the body of the cradle. The havaganuh, shade, was also of willow and was hung with shells, beads, or bells, to entertain the child by their pleasant sound and movement; the cradle strings were called konoowɨkwapɨ, and the roll of cloth bound over the baby's breastbone was nɨarɨtakampɨ. But George Laird had stated that a piece of wood was placed over the breastbone, producing a permanent indentation. He himself had such an indentation and said that it, in addition to an upright carriage and the maintenance of one position while asleep, marked a person who had been a cradleboard baby. He remembered the comfort of the cradleboard and how, when he was already walking, he would, when sleepy, drag his board after him and beg his mother to tie him on it.

24. Wendell Goodman, Sr. said that to make arrows they would select a patch of arrowweed growing on the edge of a mesa, because that is stronger than the sort found in the valley. They would burn off the patch, then straighten the reeds in the hot sand. He said that war arrows were made of willow and were about twenty inches long.

25. Wendell Goodman, Sr. identified ʔuuvimpɨ as Spanish dagger. Another Chemehuevi told me in 1969 that the weapons with which the pre-human Yucca Date Worm Girls killed in their later murderous phase were connected with their sex, though George Laird had described these weapons simply as their knives. The sharp leaves of all three plants would suggest a weapon growing out from the body.

26. A modern Chemehuevi trying to recall the word for yucca date (tcɨmpɨ) came up with yuvimpɨ, which I have many times in my notes as pine tree. This illustrates how rapidly an unwritten language may be distorted when words are no longer in common use.

27. See pp. 182-192.

28. See pp. 39-40, 41.

29. According to Wendell Goodman, Sr. cholla is hintcungᵂaramp. Mr. Goodman also mentioned sagwakoᵂap, Indian tobacco (from George Laird I had only the root form, koʔᵂa-, in koʔᵂatcomigʸah, chews tobacco); of plants cultivated for food he named kamitu, cantaloupe and pavonokᵂatsi, watermelon.

30. See pp. 192-207.

31. Recently I have heard pungku; but George Laird always used the form ending in -tsi.

32. Clearly pronounced tihii by Wendell Goodman, Sr.—possibly a dialectic variation. Mr. Goodman stated that the Chemehuevis did not distinguish the two species of deer by name, and only one name was given to me by George Laird.

33. I believe the Chemehuevi word for antelope is wantsi, but I have not been able to verify this. Although antelope were plentiful in Chemehuevi territory and must surely have been one of the big game animals, there is no remembrance of an antelope song. The antelope does, however, appear in the myths (see pp. 177, 180).

34. See Note 2, Chapter I. Mr. Goodman also stated that the quiver was usually made of the hide of a mountain sheep.

35. The Mountain Sheep and Deer Songs have been discussed in detail in Chapter I, and the role of these animals as shamans' familiars in Chapter II.

36. "How Cottontail Rabbit Conquered the Sun" (see pp. 152-154).

37. This word was given in 1969 by Mary Hanks Molino, who approved the plural in -wi. Mrs. Molino described these animals with great gusto: "They sit up and make a whistling sound. They have big, sparkling eyes and tough little bodies." Mrs. Molino thought tavaʔatsi would be the kangaroo rat.

38. Pronounced in 1969 with fully voiced a.

39. Stella Smith Mike mentioned Witsihuvᵂiyav as one of the dances that would be danced at the Cry for Mike Tobin (see Note 15, Chapter II), but she probably referred to the Mohave Bird Song. Chemehuevis now pronounce the word for bird witsiʔits and translate huvᵂiyav as either "song" or "dance."

40. Supplied by Gertrude Hanks Leivas. No word obtained from George Laird had repeated diphthongs or accent on the second syllable if the first was long or a diphthong.

41. Since only the translation appears in my notes, I reconstructed this by analogy with ʔOpitcokotsi, Mesquite Bean Pounder (tanga, knee); this might be logical in some languages, but in Chemehuevi there is no reason why "knee pounder" should resemble "mesquite bean pounder" any more than kamitaroso, rabbit hole, resembles hunaorapi, badger hole.

42. See p. 161.

43. See p. 200.

44. This is a Chemehuevi name reconstructed from words given in 1969 by Gertrude Hanks Leivas and Mary Hill, Wendell Goodman, Sr. translating for Mrs. Hill. Mrs. Leivas thought ʔitsiv (pl. ʔitsiviw), the modern word for crocodile, might also mean Gila monster. Mrs. Hill gave ʔitciv, (pl. ʔitcivu). She distinctly gave the possessive as ʔitcivi: ʔitcivi kan, Gila monster's house. The word is recorded as ʔitsivi in notes in the Harrington Collection, which do not distinguish between ts and tc.

45. Commonly pronounced "chuckawalla." The English name clearly derives from tcagwara or some word in a closely related language.

46. Possibly belonging solely to Mohave mythology. See Note 6, Chapter II.

47. In his youth, before dams were built to hold back the waters of the Colorado, George Laird swam across the broad river many times—twice under very severe conditions, with his clothes and rifle tied on top of his head, in bitter cold, contending with a swift current that carried large chunks of ice.

48. The Mohaves, neighbors, intermittent companions, and perennial enemies of the Chemehuevis, have a legend in which the Frogs acted as their saviors; and fish have always been an important item in Mohave diet (see p. 141).

49. See pp. 158-159.

50. The words for horsefly and mosquito, missing from my original manuscript, were resupplied by Mary Hanks Molino. She pronounces muhuav without ᵂ between u and a and gives the plural in -mɨ, the form which she seems to prefer for words ending in the singular in i. These words are contained in the Harrington Collection.

51. See p. 151.

52. It is noteworthy that George Laird always translated Tavahukᵂampi as Sun Spider and just as consistently gave Day Owl for Tavamuhuumpɨtsi.

53. See p. 156.

54. According to Mary Hanks Molino, pooʔᵂavi also means flea.

55. See p. 18. In 1969, Mary Hanks Molino gave the word as tasiyavi (pl. tasiyavimɨ); she also resupplied the word for small red ant.

Chapter V: Places, Trails, and Tribes

1. Almost all of the placenames discussed in this chapter were painstakingly located by George Laird on tracings made from Government topographical maps. Regrettably these tracings have been lost. I shall list the names in the order in which they were recorded, hoping that some kind of pattern will emerge for those who are interested enough to study the terrain.

2. Modern Mohaves consider Monument Peak (called by the Chemehuevis Tavaʔawɨʔananaʔatsi) to be their sacred mountain.

3. George Laird always pronounced Mohave words with the strong initial glottalization characteristic of Chemehuevi. No Mohave words given by him have been checked with a Mohave informant.

4. See Note 14, Chapter I.

5. See Note 6, this chapter.

6. Under "tribes or local divisions that may fairly be included among the Chemehuevi," Kroeber gives "Hokwaits, in Ivanpah Valley," also "Tümpisa-gavatsits or Timpashauwagotsits, in the Providence Mountains (A. L. Kroeber, *Handbook of the Indians of California* [Berkeley: California Book Company, Ltd., 1970] , p. 595). ʔOkᵂaitsɨ (pl. ʔOkᵂaitsiwɨ) would mean a person living at ʔOkᵂah, and there would be a similar plural form at least for the people of Tɨmpisagwagatsitcɨ (-tsɨ, person of, would not be used in the singular when -tsɨ in its locative or diminutive sense was already present in the placename). As mentioned in Chapter I, every habitable valley was home or headquarters for a nɨwɨavɨ (band), and if the nɨwɨavɨ consisted of more than two or three families it would be under the leadership of a lesser chief; but such bands or groups of families scarcely constituted "tribes or local subdivisions." See pp. 22-23.

7. This agrees with Kroeber's "Nüvant, Charleston Peak in Nevada, the most famous place in the mythology of both the Chemehuevi and the western bands of the Southern Paiute" (Kroeber, p. 596). Stella Smith Mike, one of those who identified this mountain as Charleston Peak, gave the name as Nɨvagantɨmantɨ, probably a dialectic variant; compare Kaivʸaʔamantɨ, the name supplied by Wendell Goodman for New York Mountains.

8. Animal familiars are discussed in Chapter II.

9. On Kroeber's "Mokwats, at the Kingston Mountains" (Kroeber, p. 595). A person of Mogᵂah would be Mogᵂaatsɨ.

10. See p. 26.

11. In 1969, Gertrude Hanks Leivas gave the name of Chemehuevi Valley as Siwavaatsɨ, and derived it from siwampɨ, sand. Her sister, Mary Hanks Molino, concurred, and did not recognize paha as mortar; "Pah is water," she said, although agreeing that pahatsɨ (paha- plus diminutive) means handstone, pestle. This is an example of the changes and simplifications which have taken place in the Chemehuevi language within fifty years or less.

12. See Note 27, Chapter I.

13. The second place of this name along the River. See p. 123.

14. See pp. 23, 142-143.

15. According to Devereaux (pp. 360-361) the Mohave legend is that a mythological brother and sister contracted an incestuous marriage and were later turned into this rock formation; the Mohave name is given as *Hamasem Kutco:yva*.

16. See p. 159.

17. See p. 26.

18. See pp. 192-207.

19. See p. 39 and Note 13, Chapter II.

20. See pp. 159-160.

21. See p. 28.

22. See pp. 16-18, 38-39, and Note 19, Chapter I.

23. In native Chemehuevi words l does not occur, and r does not occur initially (see p. 281).

24. See p. 48.

25. See p. 151.

26. See pp. 3, 8.

27. Although from the plural one would suppose that the root form ends in -ɨ-, the singular in compounds ends in -a-; compare kakara and kakarɨ, quail. For plurals in -mɨ and triplurals in -mɨwɨ, compare plurals of sibling terms formed from personal pronouns, p. 60 and Note 5, Chapter III.

28. The term "Hiniima or Hinienima," given by Dr. Kroeber as the Chemehuevi name for the Kawaiisu (Kroeber, p. 595) is obviously hin^{y}i mah, "who then?" or "whom do you mean?" This expression would be used in bewilderment or irritation after repeated failure to understand a question.

29. See under Tantɨitsiwɨ, p. 138.

30. See p. 160.

31. The bow that accompanied Wagatamuh^{w}aratɨmɨ, Bitter Frog (Mike Tobin), on his last journey was made by a Mohave who happened to remember the way the Chemehuevis used to make them (see Note 15, Chapter II).

32. See p. 142.

33. Wendell Goodman, Sr. said that when the first white people crossed at Lalantsɨ (Ehrenberg), the Chemehuevis thought they were "ghosts." They exclaimed, ʔinɨpiw punik^{y}aiyu, tuhu^{w}agant, look at the devils, they are enemies!

Chapter VI: Mythology: The Ancient Telling

1. See p. 122 and Note 7, Chapter V.

2. In 1970, a Chemehuevi pronounced this word as tɨwinggah: "I'm not going to tɨwinggah this time of year [in summer]." This could be due to a dialectic difference.

3. I am quite sure that Wendell Goodman, Sr. referred to them as ʔɨitipiwɨ, Ancient Ones, literally, Early Ones, People of the Morning [of Time]. Compare ʔiitcuku, forenoon, morning.

4. Several years before I met George Laird I tried to get some of the people of the ranchería located on the Tejon Ranch to tell me their myths in the summertime. All steadfastly refused, but I had at least turned their thoughts in that direction, and when a small boy was bitten by a rattlesnake, I do not think that I was held entirely blameless.

5. Even the great hereditary hunting songs, which were (and are, when remembered) sung ritually at the funerals of their legitimate owners, were, it

will be recalled, also sung for entertainment; only the Talking Song was too sacred or too closely associated with death to be used in this way.

6. George Laird used the word boat and said he thought it was made by some process of weaving. Wendell Goodman, Sr. told me that the Chemehuevis used to make rafts which they bound together with arrowweeds to use in crossing the River.

7. Cinawav*i*, Mythic Coyote, as distinct from cina?av*i*, coyote. He is one of the few Immortals who has what might be called a proper name. The appearance of the Immortals will be described in the various narratives and more fully discussed in Chapter VII. But it is helpful to bear in mind that their forms fluctuated from animal to human. In this anthropomorphic phase Wolf was the very model of a perfect man, and it is said that this was also true of Mountain Lion; but Coyote, even when he looked like a man, usually had four distinguishing marks: his little, squinting, slanted eyes; his long, pointed nose, suitable for poking into various things; his hands, the fingers of which were folded under so that they were paw-like; and his bushy tail. This is the only story I had when writing this book in which Mountain Lion appears, and here he is simply mentioned, completing the primeval tetrad; but in the Harrington Collection there is a story in which Mountain Lion appears as a chief, equal in power and dignity to Wolf.

8. When George Laird was pressed to account for the origin of Wolf and Coyote, he sometimes said that Ocean Woman made them when she needed them to explore the earth. But this does not account for Mountain Lion. I believe the more authentic version is that which pictures the Primal Four together in the beginning, "without father, without mother, without descent."

9. See p. 105. This is not the type of brush house that is most easily and quickly built.

10. She sewed the top together instead of covering it with a potsherd sealed around with greasewood gum, as is the usual practice.

11. Shoshonean-speaking peoples.

12. Apparently in this context applied to the primeval freshwater lake, not to the ocean.

13. One never points with the finger except to do harm. To indicate a perticular melon or squash, for example, and avoid blighting it, one points with the knuckle; and a person is designated by pointing with the lips and chin.

14. In the myths Coyote is always Cinawav*i*, Mythic Coyote. This is true even when he does not live with his brother on Nivagant*i* but is represented as a Chief or merely as the head of a family.

15. The oldest of the Wildcat Brothers is spoken simply of as Tuk*u*, Wildcat.

16. Huk^{w}amp*i*, black widow spider. In his mythic, partially human form Sun Spider is described as ?angkasi^{y}akikipo^{w}akaiy*u*, having light red gaps between his teeth.

17. If Coyote had sung the song for entertainment only he would merely have "borrowed" it, and this would have been no crime (see p. 16). But by using it as if it were his own and teaching it to his family, thus making it his own hereditary song, he stole it and deprived the legitimate owners of its use.

18. The account given here is a brief summary of a very long, very outrageous, and very funny story. The complete version of this classic example of Chemehuevi pornography has been lost.

19. Here only three daughters are mentioned instead of four as in "How Wildcat Brothers Recovered Their Hunting Song." The Chemehuevis count six stars in the Pleiades.

20. Usually it was necessary for the culprit to confess his fault. Perhaps in this case it was not needed, since the daughter's illness was due to a violation of taboo and not to malicious mental practice.

21. See p. 92.

22. See pp. 93-94.

23. See p. 12.

24. This shows that patterns of three as well as four occur in nature.

25. This myth is still extant. The episode involving the four girl cousins and the final episode in the cave may be obtained in more detail than in the version given by George Laird. In the latter episode, as told to Georgia Laird Culp, it is said that the man in the cave had a "large red penis"—possibly a later touch influenced by the appearance of the white man's genitalia. While this man was having intercourse with Wind Woman, attempting to satisfy her, he was also busily throwing his bundles out of the cave and attempting to get in position to jump out himself, and all the while the entrance to the cave was growing smaller and smaller!

26. ʔAavi, white clay; noʔovi, fetus. The name implies that Wind Woman is shut like a fetus in the womb of earth.

27. Excerpts from three separate myths are included under this heading. There was a whole cycle of stories dealing with Southern Fox, but the fragments given here are all that George Laird could recall.

28. Wolf also discharged all his arrows at once in his final battle with the Bear People (see p. 199).

29. For the location of these places, see Chapter V.

30. This is an allusion to the heat mirage, which appears to make objects disappear.

31. I believe Witciʔitsi was the word George Laird used. This, as has been previously explained, is a general term for a bird of any small species or sometimes, more loosely, for any land bird except a buzzard or large predator. But see under winʔnamakasaamaʔapɨtsi, p. 115.

32. The Chemehuevis say that present-day Mohaves are remotely descended from this mythical race.

33. In an extant version of this tale Horned Toad was not coughed up but had to pass out with the Giant's excrement.

34. The fragment given here is all that remains of a very long myth which George Laird knew well; but even the fragment is important, for it places the Sun firmly among the immortal First People.

35. See p. 131.

36. This mention of red flannel illustrates how details of the myths changed with the changing culture of the People.

37. Tciimpaawaanaintsiwi (tcimpi, yucca date; pa?avim, worm; waha-, two; naintsiwi, girls), Yucca Date Worm Girls. From text in the Harrington Collection.

38. I do not have the Chemehuevi words for this song.

39. See Note 44, Chapter IV.

40. Land turtle, desert tortoise.

41. In the version of this tale which Anna Smith Gonzales (George Laird's half-sister) told to her granddaughter, Nina Murdoch, Coyote took a little food to his people then went back to eat the rest himself; also in this version his difficulty in escaping from the hole was because he had grown so fat.

42. Since both grandmothers were hutsi, Yu?uravatsi must have been the sister or female cousin of the old woman who raised the boy.

43. Up to this point the grandson has been simply "the boy"; from now on the two that were one are always referred to as "Dove Boys."

44. A small bird species; see under win?namakasaama?apitsi, p. 115. This is the first time the old woman has been mentioned by name. In the telling of the tale it gradually becomes apparent that both grandmothers and the grandson(s) were Birds.

45. This Lizard is probably Sigipitsi, but without access to the Chemehuevi texts I recorded in 1919-1920 (now in the Harrington Collection at the Smithsonian Institution) I cannot state this with absolute certainty; it is certainly not Mugwiᵞa, Guico (probably Gecko, though George Laird always used the Spanish term), nor is it Tcagwara, Chuckwalla, not listed in this myth as an ally of Coyote. The behavior described is characteristic of the genus *Uma*.

46. Wiw?wiyatsi, a small, brown bird; the English name was not given.

47. See Note 33, Chapter IV.

48. Kwaagwawi marked the speech of Rattlesnake, just as haikᵞa distinguished that of Coyote.

49. This guard was some sort of Person, man-like in form, as were the guards at the next two watering places. But the quail were real quail, birds and not Bird People—just as at the next water the wiw?wiyatsiwi were birds, and at the third the antelopes were merely antelopes.

50. To this day, sidewinders only "sidewind" when they travel on top of the ground; after they have worked themselves under the surface, they go

in a straight line. And they sleep coiled up under the earth where they cannot be seen.

51. ʔArɨh, ʔarɨrɨh, and ʔarɨrɨrɨh are exclamations of pain, used only of the pain caused by a burn.

52. Tugumpiinʸaaviwɨ (tugumpa, sky; pɨhɨvɨ, downfeather, also fuzz of cottonwood seed and soft fur of animal), Sky Brothers, literally, Sky Downfeather Brothers. From text in the Harrington Collection (see p. 59).

53. From mention of the girls' "knives" in the version given by George Laird, I had assumed that they were of hardwood, like the knife made by the boy who became Dove Boys (p. 171). I am now informed that "the way in which they killed people was connected with their sex" (see Note 25, Chapter IV). Perhaps a girl's knife was a dagger-like development of her clitoris, growing out from her body like the sharp leaf of a plant. The girls must have been entirely naked since the story indicates that the "knives" were in plain sight and held in a fixed position.

54. When asked about this war, George Laird said he thought the reference might be to the expedition on which Coyote went to kill Gila Monster—and that Bat was lying, because he was not included in the roster of warriors. But it seems unlikely that such a sun-drenched, heat-parched adventure should be described as taking place "when the world was new, and everything was covered with fog." Rattlesnake was not sluggish with cold when he went with Coyote to make war on Gila Monster.

55. See p. 122 and Note 7, Chapter V.

56. It is stated that Coyote is the *younger* brother, yet Wolf always addresses him with the honorific -pɨtsɨ, usually connoting age.

57. Paha, father's sister; yet if Wolf and Coyote had any antecedent at all, it was Ocean Woman. The seed he was to fetch was ʔantsɨ.

58. See Note 30, Chapter IV.

59. The narrator only says "haikʸa" when mimicking Coyote's spoken words, not when reporting his thoughts.

60. Any spoken or unspoken thought containing -suyaganu is imbued with power; -suyaganu implements the will and causes wicked or malicious wishes to come true. But it seems that Coyote could not do anything right, at least not anything connected with his brother. In this case his magic overacted—or perhaps secretly he really desired his brother's death.

61. George Laird was unable to translate this song. The third syllable in each line is heavily accented, high in pitch, and strongly nasal.

62. Coyote now has one hairbreadth escape after another. Two episodes in this series which were known to George Laird were omitted from the manuscript from which this narrative was taken. There were probably many others, added or deleted at the will of the storyteller.

63. This is the seedpod of the bladderweed.

64. Coyote must have travelled north to the Bear country, since he called for a wind from the north to blow him home; but the Bears had circled around and approached Nivaganti from the southwest.

65. The mythic association of these three animals raises the question, was there at one time a Chuckwalla Song Group? (For Deer and Mountain Sheep Song Groups, see Chapter I.)

66. Another myth involving Mountain Sheep survives solely in the names of certain stars and groups of stars (see p. 91); while of yet another we have (in what is left of the later material obtained from George Laird) only the statement that a son who had been magically born to a foster daughter of Coyote was turned into a Mountain Sheep by sleeping in an enchanted cave.

Chapter VII: Mythology: The Master Key

1. Probably in Old Chemehuevi Nitari, from nitagah, imitates or mocks, the word used of imitating a song which does not belong to one.

2. See Note 25, Chapter VI.

3. See p. 46.

4. See p. 47 and Note 6, this chapter.

5. See Note 53, Chapter VI. George Laird gave sovarampi as the name of a species of yucca; in 1969, I was told that soovarant means "mean, vicious" and might be applied to a vicious dog.

6. See Note 54, Chapter VI.

7. George Laird always translated poro as "crooked stick," but I do not know if poro was the word used here in the Chemehuevi text. When we are told that Coyote used his poro to hook the North Wind down from the sky, a practical usage is implied. I do not know whether the tool used for hooking lizards or small rodents out of their hiding places, killing rabbits caught in bushes, or even beating seeds from plants was also the most sacred symbol of shamanistic power; but there would have been nothing contradictory in this dual usage (see p. 47 and Note 3, Chapter II).

8. Joseph Campbell, *The Masks of God: Primitive Mythology* (New York: Viking Press, 1959), I, p. 338.

9. For further vestigial remains of the Bear Cult among the Chemehuevis, see p. 46.

10. See pp. 213-214.

11. See Note 20, Chapter II.

APPENDICES

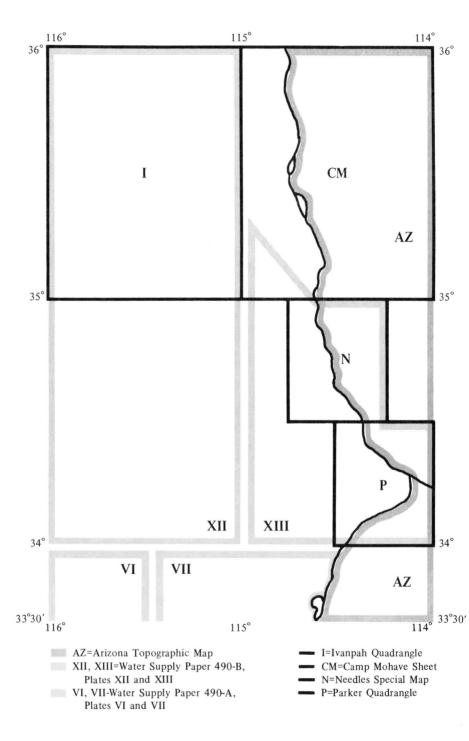

AZ=Arizona Topographic Map
XII, XIII=Water Supply Paper 490-B,
   Plates XII and XIII
VI, VII-Water Supply Paper 490-A,
   Plates VI and VII

I=Ivanpah Quadrangle
CM=Camp Mohave Sheet
N=Needles Special Map
P=Parker Quadrangle

A BRIEF NOTE ON
THE MAPS

Herta B. Caylor

IN the introduction, Carobeth Laird mentions that she and George Laird discussed Chemehuevi territory with the aid of maps on which he located many of the places and traced the trails mentioned in Chapter V. After her husband's death, these maps, to her infinite regret, were lost; otherwise they would have been included here.

This book, however, would not have been complete without some means of visualizing the many places she describes. Many readers will be unfamiliar with the Chemehuevi homeland on the Colorado River and the California desert, or need a guide to modern placenames. Moreover, the detailed discussion of the Chemehuevis' kinship with their land calls for some mapping of the original placenames, however incomplete.

The maps in this book had their beginnings in a glance at a perfectly ordinary automobile club map of San Bernardino County, which covered much of the territory under discussion. During the preparation of the index an astonishing number of trails and placenames had emerged, both English and Chemehuevi, often very descriptive and surprising. I could not resist trying to find at least some of them, and that is how I started: with a road map and the journey of Southern Fox.

Anyone familiar with the California desert is aware of the reaches and terrain of Southern Fox's northbound journey from the Whipple Mountains near the Colorado River to Death Valley.

Shooting arrows ahead of him which start springs flowing where they land, he covers the distance in five steps. This intrigued me.

Four of the places mentioned in the myth—Whipple Mountains, West Wells, Paiute Springs, and Death Valley—soon formed their pattern on the map. But Kleinfelter was not to be found. A look at Gudde's *California Placenames* solved that problem, and with Kleinfelter in place, the trajectory of Southern Fox—one curve from southeast to northwest—revealed itself clearly.

The convolutions of the wandering Salt Song invited the next attempt. It soon became clear that I would have to find maps showing the area as it was in George Laird's lifetime, especially from the period in which he and his wife worked on their maps. Not only has the river changed course since then, but many of the sites along its banks have been drowned by Davis, Parker, Palo Verde, Imperial, and Laguna Dams; in some cases the places and the names have shifted or disappeared.

A thorough search of the Bancroft and Doe Libraries of the University of California at Berkeley turned up some topographic maps of the proper vintage. Most of the remaining information needed to trace the placenames was obtained from maps in the *Water Supply Papers* at the library of the University of California at Riverside, to which James Rothenberger kindly granted me access, and from *Plans and Profile of the Colorado River*, generously given to me by James J. Parsons, Chairman of the Earth Sciences Department, University of California at Berkeley.

Finding the places required cross-referencing the information given throughout the text and checking it step by step against the available maps. I am not trained as a geographer and had serious doubts about the chances of tracking down the myriad placenames. But after seeing the striking patterns traced by the Salt Song and Southern Fox's journey, I had to try.

Carobeth Laird begins her chapter on places and trails by listing peaks and ranges associated with the Mountain Sheep Song. Among these is Pulled Out Several Objects with Teeth. This is described as part of the Mohave Mountains running north and south, forming an angle with a range running east and west which touches the Colorado River at a place called Green Hanging. Elsewhere, in a section on names along the River, Green Hanging is identified as the mouth of a box canyon west of the River, two miles south of Topock. This turns out to be Mo-have Wash.

Looking across the river from Mohave Wash, the part of the Mohave Mountains referred to turns out to be The Needles—a spectacular group of distinctly separate, very sharply pointed peaks east of the Colorado—and suddenly the Chemehuevi place-name comes alive. Pulled Out Several Objects with Teeth. What kind of creature came down, bit chunks out of the earth's crust, and left The Needles standing?

It was this discovery* that changed the mere paper search for names and places into something altogether different. The place-names and their patterns on the maps became the far-away but very clear echoes and traces of the Peoples' voices, speaking of their daily life, and of their past: of real fights, of real hunts; of green moss at a canyon mouth, making it a landmark in arid country; of far-off hills becoming signposts by clay or chalk out-croppings at their top; of flats with many grinding mortar holes at the River's edge, known to everybody because it must have been comfortable there; of all their landscape and what it was like for them to live in it.

The search for placenames also rewarded me with several quite unexpected corroborations of tentative mappings, as well as with other sometimes rather delightful surprises.

For instance, Adobe Hanging Like Tears was of great interest. Not only was it the home of George Laird's own tribal group, but the text places it precisely. On page 23, it is said to be four miles south of Hardyville. On page 123, it is placed four miles north of Fort Mohave. Gregory Smith, geographer at California State Uni-versity, Dominguez Hills, who visited the site, says that the place-name does indeed describe the scalloped clay formation of the area.

Another example was Shooting Place. It is described as a high rock on the Arizona side of the river (below Green Hanging) with a trail passing over it, which served as a target for archers. A look at Sheet E, *Plans and Profile of the Colorado River*, shows this as

---

* The question arises: why did George Laird not give the English name for so prominent a piece of topography? Mrs. Laird suggests that it must have been so obvious to him that he did not bother.

Pulpit Rock, with the trail clearly marked. The contour lines show how steep the promontory is—a natural target.

Another: a spring at Billy Mack's place north of Parker, Arizona is called Muvaaya by Mrs. Laird. On the AAA map called *Guide to the Colorado River* there is a Billy Mack's Mine in the proper place. At the foot of the hill in which it is located, the river forms a lake called Lake Moovalya Keyes. Moreover, Mrs. Laird lists the name of a box canyon as There is T*cawa* (an onomatopoetic description for the sound of footsteps echoing). It is below Copper Basin, east of Monument Peak. At the mouth of that canyon the AAA map now shows an "Echo Trailer Park"!

To list one final item: should any readers be as baffled by the entry "S. H. Mountain" on page 122 as I was, they may turn to page 385 in *Arizona Placenames*; it will be rewarding.

The final phase of the search dealt with the trails used by the Chemehuevis to travel along the river and through the desert. These trails are described in the text in great detail, primarily by the routes through the watering places which determined them. However, only a few of the springs could be located on the maps. All I was able to do was establish a pattern of the trails, a pattern which shows the endurance and resourcefulness of these people in their demanding and dangerous terrain.

When I had finished with the first draft of the many places on the maps for this book, I found myself filled with the greatest respect for this one man's knowledge of his land. His memory, his precision, and his gift for the pertinent description were such that decades after he looked at maps the modern reader can follow him. Carobeth Laird says that in his youth her husband ran with the Runners. He must have seen everything there was to be seen; and forgotten nothing.

Maps and Books

USGS Topographic Map. California-Nevada, Ivanpah Quadrangle. Edition of June 1912. 1:250,000. Bancroft Library, University of California at Berkeley.

USGS Topographic Map. Arizona-Nevada-California, Camp Mohave Sheet. Edition of March 1892, reprinted October 1898. 1:250,000. Bancroft Library.

USGS Topographic Map. Arizona-California, Needles Special Map.

Edition of November 1904, reprinted September 1911. 1:125,000. Doe Library, University of California at Berkeley.

USGS Topographic Map. Arizona-California, Parker Quadrangle. Edition of March 1911, reprinted 1921. 1:125,000. Doe Library.

USGS Topographic Map. Arizona-California, Blythe Quadrangle, Grid Zone "F." 1942. 1:250,000. Bancroft Library.

Arizona Bureau of Mines in cooperation with the USGS. Topographic map of the State of Arizona. 1923, reprinted 1925. 1:500,000. 100 m contours. Doe Library.

USGS Relief Map. State of Arizona. 1925. 1:500,000. Doe Library.

USGS Water Supply Paper 490-B. Relief Maps of Part of the Mohave Desert Region, California. Plates XII and XIII. 1921. 1:250,000.

USGS Water Supply Paper 490-A. Relief Maps of Part of the Mohave Desert Region, California. Plates VI and VII. 1917 and 1918. 1:250,000.

USGS Topographic Maps. Plans and Profile of the Colorado River from Black Canyon, Arizona-Nevada to Arizona-Sonora Boundary (19 plan sheets, 1 profile sheet). 1902-1903, reprinted 1927. 1:31,680.

USGS Topographic Maps. 2° Quadrangle. Kingman, Arizona; California. 1954, revised 1963. 1:250,000.

USGS Topographic Maps. 2° Quadrangle. Needles, California; Arizona. 1956, revised 1969. 1:250,000.

USGS Topographic Maps. 2° Quadrangle. Salton Sea, California; Arizona. 1959. 1:250,000.

USGS Topographic Maps. 2° Quadrangle. El Centro, California; Arizona. 1958. 1:250,000.

Automobile Club of Southern California. Map of San Bernardino County and Lake Mead (no date).

Automobile Club of Southern California. Guide to the Colorado River (Map). 1976.

California Placenames. Erwin G. Gudde, University of California, Berkeley and Los Angeles, California. Third edition. 1969.

Arizona Placenames. Will C. Barnes. Revised and enlarged by Byrd H. Granger, University of Arizona Press, Tucson, Arizona. 1960.

Index Map

The index map facing page 263 refers specifically to the Trails and Colorado River Region map. Its outlines indicate most of the older maps used in locating the places.

Chemehuevi Mythological and Hunting Song Territory Map

This map deals with some of the placenames associated with the Mountain Sheep Song, the Deer Song, the Salt Song, the Journeys of Southern Fox, and the Sacred Land. For the most part, the list below follows the order used in Chapter V. The names listed are those cited by Carobeth Laird; they are either the English names in use at the beginning of the twentieth century, or English transliterations of the Chemehuevi terms. Their possible modern equivalents or locations are in parentheses. Map references, i.e., the abbreviations used on the index map facing page 263 for the maps consulted (I = Ivanpah Quadrangle, CM = Camp Mohave Sheet, etc.), are given only for places not found as such on present-day maps.

Mountain Sheep Song (pages 120-122)

El Dorado Mountains
Spirit Mountains
Dead Mountains (and the range west of Needles) Sacramento
    Mountains
Paiute Mountains
(A part of the Mohave Mountains) The Needles
Whipple Mountains
Turtle Mountains
Riverside Mountains
Maria Mountains
(Mountain range west of Ivanpah) Ivanpah Mountains
New York Mountains
(Paiute Springs Badlands) Paiute Range
Providence Mountains
Old Dad and Granite Mountains
San Bernardino Mountains

The following ranges east of the Colorado River are listed as Mountain Sheep Song territory by George Laird:

(Coxcomb: unnamed range north of the Bill Williams River and
    east of the Mohave Mountains)
(Screw Mesquite Mountains: unnamed range across the river
    from Riverside Mountains and south of Parker)
Walapai Mountains
(S. H. Mountain) Kofa Mountains (see *Arizona Placenames*,
    page 385)

Deer Song

The Deer Song is described as "(roaming) about in rolling,
hilly country east of the Colorado River" (page 14). The Salt Song
is also said to have "traversed Deer territory as part of its course"
(page 16).
    (Deer Entrance) Bouse Wash (page 128) **AZ**

Salt Song

George Laird's version of the Salt Song starts and ends at "a
sacred cave on the north side of the Sandy where it flows together
with the Santa Maria to form Bill Williams Fork" (page 133).
    The Salt Song route is as follows (page 17):
Sacred cave
Bill Williams-Colorado River confluence
North to Fort Mohave **CM, AZ**
East to the vicinity of Mineral Park **CM, AZ**
South into Walapai Valley
North and across the Colorado River at an unspecified point
Southwest to Las Vegas
(Through the valley of dry lakes) Roach, Ivanpah, and Jean
    Dry Lakes
Past New York Mountains
Through the valley in which Danby is situated
Past a rock salt mine
Southeast into Palo Verde Wash below Blythe
North along the California side of the Colorado River
Across the Colorado River about three miles from (Old) Blythe
    Intake **VII**
Into Parker Valley
To within some three miles of Parker
Up Bouse Wash **AZ**

Northeast to the Bill Williams
Back to sacred cave

The Journeys of Southern Fox

The route of Southern Fox is as follows (page 159):
Whipple Mountains
West Wells
Kleinfelter **XIII**
Paiute Springs
Pahrump (see Laird, Carobeth. "Two Chemehuevi Teaching Myths." The Journal of California Anthropology. Vol. 2, No. 1. 1975. pp. 18-24)
Death Valley

Sacred Land

Having Snow, the heart of Storied Land (page 122) is variously located as follows:
Panamint Mountains
Mt. Whitney
Charleston Peak

Trails and Colorado River Region Map

This map shows some of the locations along the Colorado River and along the trails as described by George Laird. He follows a north-to-south pattern, beginning (page 122) with Many Mortars as the northernmost site in Nevada (page 123) and following the Colorado to the Old Blythe Intake (page 129) as the southernmost point in California. The next placename description—Owl Ear Tank (page 129)—again refers to the northernmost location listed in the section on the Trails (in the Spirit Mountains of Nevada, page 136); from then on he lists the placenames associated with the trails south through Mohave Tank (page 131) to Yuma, follows these with sites along the west-bound trails through the Mohave Desert (pages 131-132), and then adds locations east of the Colorado River in Arizona. The same pattern will be used below.

Locations Along the Colorado River (pages 123-124)

(Many Mortars) El Dorado Canyon **CM**
Round Island **CM**

Cottonwood Island **CM**

(Waterfall) **CM**

(Badger Hole) **CM**

Pyramid Rock (see *Plans and Profile of the Colorado River, Sheet B*)

(Marked Rock) Boundary Cone (I am indebted to Ike Eastvold for this location)

(Valley, twelve miles by road from Fort Mohave) old road to Paiute Springs **CM**

Hardyville **CM, AZ**

(Adobe Hanging Like Tears) four miles north from Fort Mohave and two miles south of Hardyville (pages 23-24) **CM**

Fort Mohave **CM, AZ**

(They Clubbed Each Other Long Ago) **N**

Valley in which Needles is situated **N**

Red Rock (*California Placenames*, page 342)

(Green Hanging) Mohave Wash **N**

(Shooting Place) Pulpit Rock (see *Plans and Profile of the Colorado River, Sheet E*)

Mohave Rock **N**

(Bear's Blood) Mohave Mountains and Grossman Peak **AZ**

(Hardpan Mortars) Chemehuevi Valley, California side of the river **N, P**

(Across the River) Chemehuevi Valley, Arizona side of the river **N, P**

(Free from Frost) Little Chemehuevi Valley **P**

(Owl House: not located on map. A hill with a cave in the Mohave Mountains: see pages 125 and 126)

(One Who Carried White Clay on His Back) near Steamboat Rock **P**

(Fish Nose) Rincon Flat (see *Plans and Profile of the Colorado River, Sheet E*)

(Quail Used to Run) **P**

Bill Williams Fork

(White Men Sitting Down: not located on map. About two miles north of Brother and Sister Married Pair)

(Brother and Sister Married Pair: not located on map. Carobeth Laird describes this formation as about eight miles from the mouth of the Bill Williams and four miles below Planet,

Arizona. George Devereaux [see Note 15, Chapter V] lo-
cates it thirty miles from Parker and a quarter of a mile
from the Bill Williams, and includes a photograph of it in
his book.)
Planet **AZ**
(Whirlpool) **P**
(There is T*cawa*) box canyon below Copper Basin (see AAA
Guide to the Colorado River)
(Spring at Billy Mack's place) Billy Mack's Mine (see AAA *Guide
to the Colorado River*)
Black Mountain
(Screw Mesquite Belly) Valley across the river from Agency
at Parker **P**
(Deer Entrance) Bouse Wash **AZ**
Old Blythe Intake **VII**
Ehrenberg (page 135)

*Locations Associated with the Trails from Cottonwood Island
South to Yuma* (pages 129-131, 132, 136)

Kleinfelter **XIII**
(Where They Fought) Monumental Canyon **N**
(Mesquite Seed) **N**
West Wells
(Guatamote) Whipple Well **XIII, P**
(Notched Post) Chambers Well **XIII, P**
(Material for Blackening the Face and Red Paint Diggings)
American Eagle Prospect and D & W Prospect **XIII, P**
Monument Peak
(Mopah Springs) in Mopah Range east of Turtle Mountains (see
AAA *Map of San Bernardino County*)
Mohave Tank **XIII**

Locations Associated with West-Bound Trails (pages 131, 137)

(White Clay Water) Wheaton Springs **XII**
Kessler Springs
Rock Springs
Vontrigger Springs
Paiute Springs
Mohawk Springs

Arrowweed Springs
Chuckawalla Springs
(They Clubbed Each Other Long Ago) N
Providence Mountains

The Trails

Some of the locations described by George Laird as being along certain trails, as well as portions of the trails themselves, can be found on the maps referred to above. Although tracing them in their entirety was not possible at this time, their routes are indicated on the Trails and Colorado River Region map. Their general pattern illustrates Carobeth Laird's description of Enemy Territory on page 134.

The first and second trails described on page 137, from the Colorado River west towards the Mohave Desert and the San Bernardino Mountains, follow this scheme:

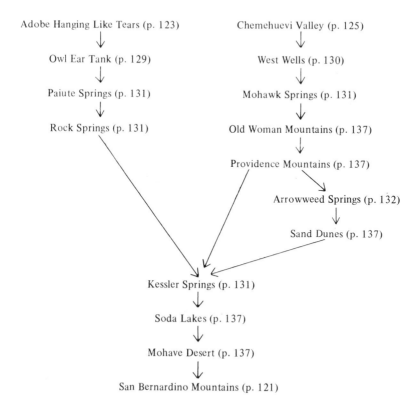

The first and third trail described on page 136, from Cottonwood Island in the north towards Yuma in the south have the following scheme:

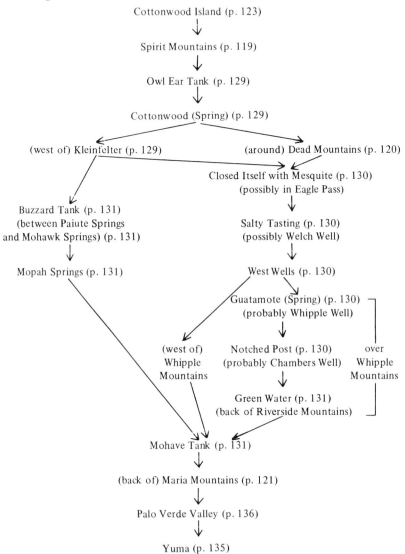

The final trail on page 137, from They Clubbed Each Other Long Ago to the Providence Mountains, has no intermediate points listed along its route.

List of Placenames

---

* Page numbers appearing in boldface type indicate the page(s) on which the Chemehuevi word for the placename may be found. Entries appearing in parentheses have no English names.

A BRIEF NOTE ON THE CHEMEHUEVI LANGUAGE

WE are fortunate to have some record of the Southern Cheme-huevi dialect as it was spoken by an expert teller of ancient tales or a member of a chief's household around the turn of the century. The full value given to each syllable, the coloration which strong vowels lent to following and sometimes to preceding vowels, and the presence of an unvoiced vowel or distinct aspiration at the end of every phrase or detached word combined to produce a sonorous, flowing, and dignified impression. This language appears to possess the felicitous quality of having been peculiarly suited to those who spoke it and to the environment in which they lived. Even those words which are not onomatopoetic seem to fit perfectly the object or action which they represent. "Dragonfly" is not a prosaic word, but wiw?wingngkuratsi is an incomparable way to designate the fragile insect that darted and hovered between the visible world of the shaman and the invisible realm of his familiar.

Chemehuevi as now spoken is still beautiful and expressive, though varying from speaker to speaker, as it always has done to a certain extent and as is probably natural in an unwritten language which is now an amalgam of at least three dialects, Northern, Desert, and Southern Chemehuevi. It has also obviously suffered from the conscious or unconscious attempts of literate present-day Chemehuevis to force it into the mold of English phonics and even to some extent of English syntax. Many words as now articulated by perhaps the majority of speakers are considerably shortened, and voiceless vowels are either completely lost (except when voiced in compounds) or fully voiced. For example: miᵞarogopitsɨ, moon, is generally pronounced miᵞaropits, although there are still some who say miᵞarogopits; Siwaʔavaatsɨ was given by George Laird as the name of Chemehuevi Valley and explained as meaning Hardpan Mortars (siwaavɨ or siwaʔaavɨ, hardpan, deriving in turn from siwampɨ, coarse sand, and ʔaavɨ, white clay; -vaa- for pahₐ,* mortar; -tsɨ, locative termination), but now everyone says Siwavatsɨ and derives the name simply from siwampɨ; hunₐ, badger, is now pronounced huna, with fully voiced a; but tɨmpₐ, mouth, and tɨmpɨ, stone, are both commonly given as tɨmp. In rapid, normal speech, George Laird omitted voiceless vowels between words, but pronounced them carefully at the end of sentences or phrases: tɨvip kosoʷagah, the earth is steaming (vapor is rising from the earth), but Tɨwiinᵞatɨvipɨ, Storied Land, Land of the Myths; katc tɨpiʔᵞatɨ, has no money, but always katcu, no, in answer to a question (nowadays many people say kats instead of katc, while others preserve a trace of the *u*).

Unless otherwise indicated, the words in this book are as they were spoken by George Laird. I have represented the sounds by the following letters and symbols:

Vowels

a as in father (aa, aʔa).

ɨ, an impure vowel somewhat resembling oo in book, but with slightly different position of lips and tongue; not to be confused with u in but (which does not occur in Chemehuevi), or oo in boot (ɨɨ, ɨʔɨ).

i as in machine but somewhat more open, sometimes approximating i in it, especially when there is a nasal quality (ii, iʔi).

o very open as in for; in loanwords close o is rendered as u: kamuutɨ for Spanish *camote*, sweet potato (oo, oʔo).

u like oo in boot (uu, uʔu).

Long vowels are accurately represented as doubled, since they

---

* This was the only word in the material obtained from him which George Laird did not normally pronounce with final voiceless *a*; he sometimes demonstrated to me that the word was indeed pahₐ, but normally he said pah.

are twice as long as single vowels, are treated as diphthongs in regard to accent, and have the last half unvoiced (becoming h) at the end of words; but in words of one syllable the vowel tends to remain long and to be followed by the aspirant—I find I have written paah, water as often as pah, and huuh, arrow, more frequently than huh. Since vowels may be treated differently in different situations, long and broken vowels have not been assigned separate places in the alphabetical order.

In compounds, a and o tend to influence adjacent vowels; for example, a followed by ki or $^{\gamma}$i usually produces k^ai (g^ai) or $^{\gamma a}$i, while o would produce k^{wa}i (g^{wa}i) or $^{\gamma wa}$i, and o sometimes turns the preceding u into o. To a degree, u and o are interchangeable, that is, a particle may appear with u in one compound and o in another (tu-, tuu-, to-, and too- all appear in different words meaning "black"), and to a lesser extent this applies to a and o. The influence of i, o, and u on certain consonants is noted below.

The Chemehuevi language must once have had a complete category of nasal vowels which have now lost their nasal quality except in certain rare instances: pahomp*a*, hail, has a strong and unmistakably nasal o, the second i in wiw$^{\gamma}$wingngkurats*i* is nasal, and there are a few other instances recorded in this material. In songs and chants, nasalization is more frequently preserved. For example, lines ending in fully voiced ya$^{\gamma a}$i, died (which would be ya$^{\gamma}a$ in normal speech), present the broken diphthong as strongly nasal. For the most part in ordinary speech, vowels do not sound nasal, even when they have a nasalizing effect on the following consonants, turning k, p, and t into ngk, mp, and nt.

Except in songs and formal chanting, all vowels have the quality of voicelessness in terminal positions. When George Laird was asked, for example, the word for "house," he always said kan*i*, carefully and unmistakably, and for "my house" he said kanin^y*i*. Nowadays these words would be pronounced most often as kan and kanin, the latter form (noun plus possessive pronominal postfix) showing that the final vowel is still a part of the word.*

---

* In modern Chemehuevi niw*i*, person, and its plural niwiw*i* are sometimes pronounced nu and nuwu respectively (perhaps at least partially as a result of writing both i and u as u); but in compounds such as niwi$^{\gamma}$ampagar*i*, Chemehuevi speaker, one who speaks Chemehuevi, the original form of the word appears.

Diphthongs and Triphthongs

aɨ, ai (ah in final position), ao, au. In ai, ao, and au, a is stressed; in aɨ the stress falls on ɨ. It seems that ao occurs only as the result of elision of an intervening consonant: hunaorapɨ, badger hole (hunα, badger, plus horapɨ, hole).

ɨa, ɨi (ɨh in final position). In both these diphthongs, the stress falls on ɨ; ɨo and ɨu do not occur, but when a word ending in -ɨwɨ is so placed as to cause the final ɨ to be omitted, the resulting ɨw is virtually ɨu (see preceding footnote).

iʸa, iʸo. In this material, i does not occur before ɨ or u.

oʷa. This is apparently the only diphthong beginning with o.

uʷa, uʷi. u does not occur before ɨ or o.

Diphthongs beginning with a and ɨ are true diphthongs and are treated essentially as long or doubled vowels; those beginning with i, o, or u are pronounced in most positions virtually as two syllables. A light ʸ is almost always audible after i, and a light ʷ after o or u; but in pahoavitcɨ, hail lying on ground, no w is audible. Perhaps this is because the o of pahompɨ is so strongly nasal, or it may be because the diphthong results from the elision of h (havitcɨ, lying). In some positions -tuʷa-, towards, is distinctly -tua-.

Since both aa and ai at the end of a word become ah, they may be distinguished only by adding another particle.

Triphthongs sometimes occur as the result of elision of an intervening consonant: paɨɨigʸamagah, has a fishy flavor, derives from pagɨɨtsɨ, fish, and kamagah, has or having a taste or flavor.

Consonants

h like h in English. As noted above, this light aspirant is frequently elided in compounds; h usually becomes hʷ after u, as in muhʷintɨ, leader, and muhʷaratɨ, bitter.

k (variants not occurring initially: ngk, g, x). This sound and its variant, g, are harsher than English k and g, being pronounced with the back of the tongue; x is like Spanish j. After nasalizing vowels, k becomes ngk, in certain other positions, g; and when g is followed by a voiceless vowel, it in turn becomes x: naxα, mountain sheep (singular), nagawɨ (plural); k and g are palatalized after i (kʷ, gʷ), labialized after o or u (kʸ, gʸ).

kw (variant, gw) is a true consonant, occurring after any vowel and (as kw) initially.

l does not occur in words of Chemehuevi origin, although offering no difficulty to the Chemehuevi tongue. In words taken from the Mohave, it substitutes for heavily voiced dh (th as in "those"), and when such words are thoroughly Chemehuevi-ized, is replaced by r. For example, there is the personal name ʔIluh or ʔIruh, derived from Mohave *idho*, willow. Either l or r may be used in loanwords from the Spanish beginning with l: Lalants*i* or Rarants*i* for Spanish *La Lancha* (The Barge), which was the early name for Ehrenberg. In true Chemehuevi words, as opposed to loanwords, r is a variant of t and does not occur initially.

m (mm, mʔm). Occasionally labialized (m^w), but my occurs only in loanwords of Yuman origin, and then not necessarily following i.

n (nn, nʔn). Palatalized (n^y) after i. Only in loanwords may ny occur after any vowel.

ng (ngng, ngʔng), ng as in "sing," but not, as pronounced by some persons, with hard and distinct g; ng does not occur initially but is frequently found within words (e.g., ʔangaav*i*, small red ant species). It may be palatalized or labialized: ʔing^y*a*, this animate; ʔung^w*a*, that invisible animate.

p (non-initial variants: mp, v) is never aspirated, and this leads some modern speakers who have not a very good ear and are familiar with English to pronounce it sometimes as b; but b is not a Chemehuevi consonant. The variant form, v, may be labialized after u or o, palatalized after i. In loanwords, it seems to be a general rule that p replaces initial v, as in Piigis*i*, (Las) Vegas; but v occurs initially in Vin^y*a*, for Ben.

s is never voiced—there is no z-sound in Chemehuevi. Between i and ɨ it is palatalized: ʔAngkasɨʔ*i*, Red Flower (woman's personal name), but Timpicɨʔ*i*, Stone Flower.

c represents a lightly palatalized s, less heavy than English sh, more like c in "optician" or "racial."

t (nt, r, tc) like p, is never aspirated, and is now sometimes pronounced as d by persons much influenced by English pronunciation; r replaces t as g replaces k and v replaces p. Where t is present or dominant in the first part of a compound word or phrase, either r or t may be used in the latter part, which, as an independent word, would begin with t. One may say, for example, either tuhugᵂantɨ-tɨvipɨ or tuhugᵂantɨrɨvipɨ, enemy country (tuhugᵂantɨ, enemy; tɨvi-pɨ, earth, land); r becomes tc between i and ɨ or between i and u; thus sagwagarɨ, green, but in the placename when the particle -tsi- is inserted, Tɨmpisagwagatsitcɨ, Green Stone.

ts is a true consonant, occasionally occurring initially.

tc is like ch in "change," but somewhat more lightly palatal-ized. It frequently occurs initially and may be used before any vowel. In modern times, there is a tendency to substitute ts for tc, though never initially: witsiʔits for witciʔitsɨ, bird, and sometimes kats for katcu, no.

w (wʔw).

y (yy, yʔy).

ʔ represents the glottal clusive. It is labialized or palatalized according to position. Usually it is treated as a consonant, some-times simply as a break or catch dividing doubled vowels, diph-thongs, and doubled consonants. I find that I have sometimes written a word both with and without ʔ (as nɨwɨʔavɨ or nɨwɨavɨ, band); yet its presence may make a difference in meaning: ʔuruᵂa-gah, goes, but ʔuruʔᵂagah, wants. In certain compounds, a nasal or nasalizing vowel plus ʔ results in unbroken nn: pahonnɨwarɨ, fall-ing hail (ʔɨwarɨ, rain); tatcannɨwarɨ, summer rain (tatca, summer). In wiwʔwingngkuratsɨ, a strongly nasal second i results in a length-ening of the first element of ngk.

Structure and Accent

Chemehuevi words and compound phrases are built up of par-ticles consisting of consonant (or glottal clusive) plus vowel or diphthong. The prime accent falls always on the second syllable in words or compounds of more than two syllables, unless the first vowel is doubled or a diphthong.* For example, tɨvi′pɨ, earth; tɨɨ′ra-vi, desert; mamau′ʔu, woman; but maa′ʔɨpɨtsɨ, old woman, and Mau′pah, Woman Water (Mopah Springs). Words of two syllables only, standing alone, sound almost like words of one syllable,

---

* For principally stressed vowel of diphthong, see under Diphthongs, p. 280. In doubled vowels, there is no rising stress toward the end. In the material recorded from George Laird, reduplicated syllables containing diphthongs did not occur; but in 1969 I was given maumaupɨtsɨ, with accent falling on the a of the *second* diphthong. It occurs to me that this might be a corruption of mamaupɨtsɨ.

since the terminal vowel is voiceless; and when a word so stands it is difficult to determine if the first vowel is long or short, since there is a tendency to prolong it. For instance, I am not sure whether the word for shaman's crook is poro or pooro; it is written both ways in my notes, and I either did not record or have lost an example of it in such a position that the length of the first vowel could be clearly determined (George Laird always articulated it very deliberately, but that does not prove anything). On the other hand, kani, house (for example), presents no such difficulty, since the addition of -ni, my, produces kani'n^yi, with the first vowel definitely short and accent shifting to the second syllable. Words of a single syllable always contain either a long vowel or a diphthong, and when standing alone tend, as noted above, to be pronounced with the vowel very long, followed by aspiration; but at the end of compounds, the diphthong is reduced to vowel plus aspiration (e.g., Maupah, Woman Water). As the first element of compounds, paa- (pah, paah) is frequently shortened: pagah', river, with accent on the second syllable. When words of three or more syllables are combined, the lengthy components retain the original stresses: tɨvi'tsi, real; tog^{wa}i'ntɨmɨ, chief; tɨvi'tsitog^{wa}i'ntɨmɨ, real chief, the term by which a High Chief was designated.

However, in chants or songs the accent tends to fall on the first syllable and thereafter on alternate syllables, although this sometimes involves the stressing of single vowels at the beginning, the artificial lengthening of others, and either the full voicing or the omission of final vowels. In the myths, Wolf, chanting in his great dignity, always addresses his brother as Cɨ'nawa'vipɨ'ɨtsi' (Cɨnawavi, Mythic Coyote; -pɨtsi, honorific postfix); and Louse's song begins: ka'mɨna'wipɨ'ɨtsi', (my) jackrabbit apron (kamɨ, jackrabbit, in which a is normally short and unaccented, as shown by the plural, kamɨ'wɨ; nawi, apron).

In view of the fact that diphthongs beginning in i, o, or u tend to sound like two syllables, it is sometimes difficult to determine how a word should be written. Sometimes the structure of the language gives a clue. Muwani, my father, is clearly made up of mu- plus -wa- (as in hiwani, my relative; piwani, my wife), so I have written muwa, father, and piya, mother. Also, doubtfully, I have written kwiyatsi, rattlesnake; but hi^yovi, mourning dove, because the i and o seem to blend as in the cry of that bird and because -yo- as a separate syllable is rare or nonexistent.

Sometimes it is possible to break down long compounds into single elements of one syllable each, every one of which is distinct in meaning and indispensable to the whole; in other compounds, one or more components remain obscure. As an example of word building, consider the first element in timpi, stone. Obviously the i is a nasalizing vowel, otherwise the ending would be -pi or -vi. Frequently the whole word is used in compounds, as Timpisagwa-tsitci and Timpici⁷i, cited above; but the root ti- occurs in tingka-n⁷ni, cave in rock (kan⁷ni might be an archaic diminutive of kani, house; compare nami⁷i, younger sister, little sister). Then one is led to wonder about the ti- in tivipi, earth; could it be that tivipi is simply timpi- softened and with the -pi added? (-pi or -vi is a common ending, found frequently in mineralogical or botanical terms but sometimes in words applying to intelligent beings—as in Nariwiinʸapi, Immortal, Self-Mythologizing One.) Again we have tiiravi, desert. Here tii- is possibly identical with the ti- of rock and earth, for a particle may have a long vowel in one context and a short one in another. Since r substitutes for t, tiiravi breaks down into tii- plus tavi; tavapitsi, sun, is made up of tava- with the honorific postfix -pitsi, but in compounds, sun is also represented by ta- and tavi-. Therefore, tiiravi might possibly derive from earth plus sun.

Many particles have two or even more meanings. Thus -tsi is a diminutive, as illustrated by many kinship terms (for example, togoni, my mother's father, said by a person of either sex, has as its reciprocal togotsinʸi, my daughter's child, said by a male). As a diminutive, -tsi- may also be used with verbs: ⁷ipiingu⁷u, sleep! but ⁷ipiitsingu⁷u, sleep! said to a small child. Frequently -tsi is a locative, appearing in many placenames, as in Siwa⁷avaatsi, (place of) Hardpan Mortars, or Tookovaronumpitsi, (place where there is) Material for Blackening the Face (too- for tuu-, black; kova, face; -ro- for -tu-, causative; numpi, postfix indicating instrument or material). In the placename previously cited, Timpisagwatsitci, -tsi- might be construed as either locative or diminutive, indicating possibly that the deposit of green stone is smaller in that place than in another. Also -tsi may mean "person of": thus Wiyaan⁷ni-kʸatsi, plural Wiyaan⁷nikʸatsiwi, person(s) of Wiyaan⁷nikʸati,

Adobe Hanging Like Tears (wiyavi, adobe; yuwaan[?]nik^yati, tears hanging from the eyelashes); however, if the termination -tsi is already present in a placename, it is not doubled—to indicate a single person of Siwa[?]avaatsi one would have to say Siwa[?]avaatsin^yiwi (niwi, person), although the animate plural termination added to the placename, Siwa[?]avaatsiwi, would indicate people of Hardpan Mortars. Many animal names terminate in -tsi, as yipatsi, fox, apparently without diminutive significance; and the excessive use of -tsi is claimed by Southerners to be characteristic of the Northern dialect. In addition to all this, -tsi forms an immediate tense of verbs, indicating a single action, which might also be translated in many instances by a noun; tonagah, thrusting, stabbing, is stabbing repeatedly or continuously; but tonatsi, thrust or stabbed, said of a single thrust. This is illustrated by the phrases [?]iwar panatonagah, rain is light-thrusting, used when sharp flashes of lightning are recurring, but [?]iwar panatonatsi, rain light-thrust, if there is a single flash. (Incidentally, pana-, light, appears as panapi, lightning flash, in the personal name [?]Aapanapi, White Clay Lightning Flash, and together with -numpi in pananumpi, lamp, instrument for making light.)

Animate nouns, those referring to human beings or animals, take plural endings, by far the most common of which (as given by George Laird) is -wi. For these nouns, there are also terminations signifying two only, -mi, and three or more, -miwi. George Laird also gave -mi as the plural (two or more) for some words ending in strongly nasal vowels. Verbal derivatives ending in -ganti have -gami in the plural (e.g., tuku^watikawaganti, flesh-eater, carnivore, plural tuku^watikawagami), but sometimes, as in tuhug^wanti, enemy, the plural is tuhug^wantimi. Apparently the old dual and triplural forms are now in less common use, while -mi is quite frequently given as the simple plural where George Laird would have used -wi—or this variation may be, at least in part, due to dialectic difference.

Words designating objects or concepts which are neither animal, human, nor personified have no plural terminations. Plurality may be indicated by prefixing [?]ava[?]a-, many, or sometimes by the reduplication of a syllable. For convenience, I have classified these nouns as inanimate, including plant names in this category.

Nouns have case endings, or rather, one case ending with triple significance: -a, -a- (or -ya after words ending in a) indicates objective or possessive case. Occurring (as it usually does) in sentences, the voiceless vowel is omitted, but has the effect of fully voicing the terminal vowel of the substantive to which it is appended. Of course the y of -ya is retained, and this turns final a of the preceding word into -ay. Thus we have tugumpay ʔiv^yaʔana, on top of the sky; kani ʔiv^yaʔana, on top of this house; Tɨvatsi^ya, Wolf's, but Tɨvatsi moʔopɨ, Wolf's handprint; nɨɨni^ya, mine, but nɨɨni kanɨ or emphatically, nɨɨni kanin^yɨ), my house. Again -a- is added irregularly (sometimes as -aa-, never as -ya, but sometimes as -wa after final -a-) to certain nouns to indicate their intimate connection with the person or thing by whom or by which they are possessed, or to which they are attached. Thus pɨhɨvɨ means "body hair," or "hair," or "fur" of an animal, but one says pungkutsi pɨhɨʔah, (the) dog's hair; tcopivɨ, hair of human head, but tcopivɨʔaanɨ, my hair; wɨnʔnapɨ, flint, but huu wɨnʔnawa, the arrow's flint; and, most interesting of all, kaiv^ya, mountain, but kai^yanɨ, my mountain, said by a man of the mountain over which his hereditary song ranges.

Pronouns, whether free or postfixed, never distinguish between male and female. But third person pronouns always differentiate between animate and inanimate, and also indicate whether the person or thing referred to is close at hand, more remote but visible, or remote and invisible. The second person pronominal postfix -ʔɨmɨ, tends to assimilate the initial ɨ with the last vowel of the word to which it is attached. This is also true of the third person pronominal postfixes -ʔung^wa, that animate invisible, and -ʔuk^wa, that inanimate invisible, if the terminal vowel is ɨ or i, but when this assimilation takes place, both retain the ^w; -ʔuk^wa also doubles as a copulative, and when used thus may be appended to animate substantives: ʔinɨpiʔik^wa, it is a demon; nɨʔɨk^w nɨwɨ (or nɨʔɨk nɨwɨ), I am a Chemehuevi, I am a person.

One might say that Chemehuevi is primarily a verbal language, a language of doing. Many nouns are verbal derivatives. Even the color names (except when the root only is used in compounds) are primarily verbs: tosa-, white; but independently, tosagarɨ, white, deriving from tosagah, is white, being white, having the quality of whiteness. Panatonatsɨ, light (or lightning) flashed, could also be translated as "a flash of lightning."

Active verbs, whether transitive or intransitive, take the present or continuative present -gah (probably for -gai- rather than

-gaa-), and I have chosen to list verbs in this form, since it brings out clearly the final vowel of the root. It is the form usually given by George Laird and by informants that I have talked with recently. When asked, "How do you say 'to eat'?" the answer would be tɨkagah, which would be translated back as "eats," "is eating," or most frequently, simply "eating," although it is in no way equivalent to the English participial. But when the verb indicates the presence of a state, condition, or quality that results from something having been done (to a person or an object), the passive ending -gaiyu is employed. Thus poʔogʷah, marking, writing upon, and poʔokʷaiyu, being marked, written upon, streaked, striped, or smeared. The descriptive word deriving from verbs in -kaiyu ends in -tɨ, not -rɨ. Both the rainbow and the gila monster are described as poʔokʷatɨ. Certain nouns ending in -ntɨ and -pɨ (though by no means all of the latter) are clearly verbal derivatives.

There are still persons who speak Chemehuevi, and now, after long neglect, there are competent linguists working in that field. I have no doubt that a satisfactory record of the language, including a grammar, will be produced, and for this I am grateful. But I believe that many grammatical and phonetic complexities are no more. It will probably be impossible to reconstruct the Chemehuevi language as it was spoken in the days when every winter the great mythic cycles were recited by skilled tellers of tales, when High Chiefs or their specially selected spokesmen harangued the People and instructed them in the way of life.

GLOSSARY

GLOSSARY

Alphabetical order: a (aa, aˀa), e (in loanwords only), ɨ (ɨɨ, ɨˀɨ), h, i (ii, iˀi), k (ngk, g, x), kw (gw), l (in loanwords only, where r may be substituted), m (mm, mˀm), n (nn, nˀn), ng (ngng, ngˀng—ng never occurs initially), o (oo, oˀo), p (mp, v), s (c between i and ɨ), c, t (nt, r, tc when r occurs between i and ɨ), ts (nts), tc, u (uu, uˀu), w (ww, wˀw), y (yˀy).*

-a, -a- (*-ya*, -ya- after words ending in a), objective and possessive case ending. Since usually followed by another word, in which case voiceless vowel** is elided, it has the effect of fully voicing final vowel of the substantive to which it is added, or of turning final *a* into -ay.

-a, -a-, -ah, -aa-, *-wa*, -wa-, case ending indicating that the object designated is intimately possessed; always preceded by noun in the possessive case, or used with free standing or postfixed possessive pronoun.

ˀaipavah, Boy Water. Kessler Springs.

ˀaipatsɨ, preadolescent boy.

---

* The glottal clusive (ˀ) precedes all initial vowels (even Mohave loanwords were so pronounced by George Laird); it is sometimes treated as a consonant, sometimes merely as a break between doubled vowels, doubled consonants, or diphthongs. Broken doubled vowels are treated as one in the alphabetical order, except when this doubling results from the combination of two words (as in **tɨɨraˀayat*a*, Desert Mohave). When h appears as a mere aspiration substituting for final element of doubled vowel or diphthong, it has been ignored in the alphabetical listing.

** Voiceless vowels in Chemehuevi words are rendered in italics.

ʔaivʸatsi, adolescent boy; youth.

ʔaivʸaya, man's sister's son; man's female cousin's son: ʔaivʸaya-
wini, my nephews, is the term used by mythic chiefs when
addressing their hunters or warriors.

ʔaka, plant called in Spanish *palmita*; ʔakaʔiwari, *palmita* rain, a
very fine, mist-like rain.

ʔaagah (no etymology). Spirit Mountain.

ʔangkagah, is red, being red; ʔangkari, ʔangka-, red.

ʔangkanampawi, sing. ʔangkanampa, Red Feet. Nickname applied
to Southern Chemehuevi by Northern Chemehuevi.

ʔangkapah, Red Water. Placename.

-akaavi, postfix meaning "someone's" (e.g., kaniʸakaavi, someone's
house; muwaakaavi, someone's father).

ʔakasiʔi, Palmita Flower. Woman's personal name.

ʔangkasiʔi, Red Flower. Woman's personal name.

ʔangkasiʸakagah, being pink, literally, being pale red; ʔangkasiʸa-
kari, ʔangkasiʸa-, pink; ʔangkasiʸakikipoʷakaiyu, having light
red (pink) gaps between the teeth.

-aganti (-waganti), there being, place where there is (kaniʸaganti,
where there is a house or houses; or, "there are houses there").

ʔangkaturumpi, Red Adobe. Placename.

ʔanaʹsiʹpakaiyooʹkaiyooʹ, a corruption of Mohave *ʔanya itcpak ki-*
yuk. From Salt Song. Translated: "the sun is rising, look!"

ʔaanoʔovi, "white clay fetus," echo.

ʔanuh or ʔanunih, it hurts! it pains! Said of backache, e.g.

ʔanga, bluejay.

ʔangngavi, arm; ʔangngaviang ʔiaruʔʷatsi, wound in the arm of that
one visible; wound in his arm.

ʔangaavi, small red ant species.

ʔampa, voice (root word rarely occurring except in Talking Song).

ʔampagagah, talking; ʔampagapi, speech, oration, language (tivitsi-
ʔampagapi, "real speech," the language of chiefs); ʔampagari,
speaker, one who speaks; ʔampagavaigʸah, shouting.

ʔampagahuvʷiyavi, Talking Song (also known as Crying Song).

ʔampagangkiavi, spokesman (for the High Chief or for a group of
people).

ʔampagapurigʸatsiwi, sing. ʔampagapurigʸatsi, "Bubbling Talkers,"
Jews. The Mohaves have a similar expression, *Tcakwaratura-*
tura, meaning their words "come out like little balls."

ʔavaʔan*a*, ʔavaʔa-, many; ʔavaʔatsasutav*i*, many ants (phrase from Salt Song); equivalent of Mohave *tcamdhulya ʔapaʔya*.

ʔaapanap*i*, White Clay Lightning Flash. Man's personal name.

ʔampanig^yaiv^ya, Talking Mountain. Paiute Mountains.

ʔavaʔapah, Many Mortars. Placename applied to two separate locations.

ʔampaarɨʔamayʔ, ʔampaarɨʔamayuʔ, phrases from Talking Song, translated: "on top of the voice."

ʔapat*i* (probably from the Apache). Man's personal name.

ʔaaparik^y*i*, ironwood species.

ʔaaparik^yiʔawaʔanunt*i*, Wide Ironwood. Placename.

ʔav*i* or ʔaav*i*, white clay.

ʔavin^yoots*i*, (One Who) Carried White Clay on His Back. Placename.

ʔavimpah, ʔaavimpah, White Clay Water. Possibly Wheaton Springs. The town of Ivanpah derives its name from this Chemehuevi word.

ʔasi, corruption of Mohave *ʔathʔi*, salt; used only in Salt Song.

ʔasihuv^wiyav*i*, Salt Song.

ʔasomp*i*, ʔasomp*i*, salt.

ʔaasukit (no etymology). Name of the chief of a marauding band which contained Apaches and some Chemehuevis.

ʔaatakapits*i*, grasshopper.

ʔantamuw*a*, brother-in-law, male cousin by marriage; ʔantamuwav*i*, a brother-in-law, etc.

ʔatapits*i*, pl. ʔatapɨtsiw*i*, crow; ʔatatuʔ^wats*i*, young of the species, also, Young Crow, man's personal name.

ʔatarakamuupits*i*, sandbar fly.

-ʔat*i*, not having, negative of -gant*i*: katc tɨmpiʔ^yat*i*, has no money.

ʔarɨh, ʔarɨrɨh, or ʔarɨrɨrɨh, it burns! ouch! Said only of pain caused by heat.

ʔants*i*, an edible seed, described also as grass seed.

ʔats*i*, gun; possibly the original term for the hunting bow (o).

ʔatsit*a*, wheat.

ʔatsitak^a*i*, *palo verde* species; ʔatsitak^aik^yakɨmp*i*, *palo verde* seed.

ʔawaʔanunt*i*, wide.

ʔawats*a*, several.

ʔay*a*, land turtle, desert tortoise.

ʔaya´muvinʔn^ya´ka´niʔ, from Buzzard's war song (mythology); translated: "my turtle nose ring."

ʔayatawɨ, sing. ʔayata, the Mohave.

ʔayatanaugutɨvipɨ or ʔayatanaugurɨvipɨ, Mohave Spirit Land.

ʔayatapagah, Mohave River. Fort Mohave.

ʔayatapikʸavoʔo, Mohave Tank. Placename.

ʔayarupagarɨmɨ, Black Turtle. Man's personal name.

ʔayatsɨ, Turtle (diminutive form but not so translated). Woman's personal name (o).*

ʔayɨh, ouch, it's cold! Said only of pain caused by cold.

ʔɨaruʔʷatsɨ, wound.

ʔɨitipɨwɨ, ancient ones, literally, "early ones," people of the morning of the world (o). Equivalent to George Laird's narɨwiinʸapɨwɨ.

ʔɨitɨtɨniʸagah, telling a myth, telling an ancient (early) tale; equivalent to tɨwiinʸagah.

ʔɨitcuku, morning, forenoon.

ʔɨgagah, entering, going in or into, as an animal goes into its den; ʔɨgapɨ, having entered, refers to the sun having set or being in the process of setting. ʔɨgapɨ designates sunset or late afternoon, the same time of day as wisɨpapɨ.

ʔɨgatuʷa, towards the entrance, towards the place of entering. West. ʔɨgatu ʔuruʷakwaʔinguʔu, go west!

ʔɨgatuʷantɨmɨ, people towards the entrance, Westerners. Applied to all tribes living west of the Chemehuevis.

ʔɨmɨ, you (sing.); mɨmɨ, you (pl.).

ʔɨmɨʸa, your (sing., free form); -ʔɨmɨ, your (postfix), assimilates first vowel to last vowel of noun or becomes simply -mɨ; thus for "your father" one may say ʔɨmi muʷa, ʔɨmi muwaʔamɨ, ʔɨmi muwamɨ, muwaʔamɨ, or muwamɨ.

ʔɨmiwantɨ, thy sibling; mɨmiwantɨ, your sibling, sibling of you (pl.).

ʔɨnɨpɨ, pl. ʔɨnɨpiwɨ, demon, devil, spirit-being (but not ghost); ʔɨnɨpɨʔikʷa, it is a devil (e.g., that animates the whirlwind).

ʔɨnɨpimahahuwitɨah, demon bush flowing-place, Smoketree Wash. Placename.

ʔɨnɨpimahavɨ, demon bush, smoketree.

ʔɨpɨigʸah, sleeping; ʔɨpɨinguʔu, go to sleep! ʔɨpɨitsinguʔu, diminutive imperative, said to an infant or young child; ʔɨpɨikwagupɨ, fell asleep, one who has fallen asleep.

---

* Words not in my original notes and which I do not remember hearing from George Laird are designated as (o) for "other."

ʔipinitsi (no etymology). Man's personal name (o).

ʔisaaviwa, father's brother or mother's brother; includes all relationships embraced in the English word "uncle" except aunt's husband, who is not recognized as a relative; ʔisaaviwavi, an uncle.

ʔirinapiwinih (no etymology). Man's personal name (o).

ʔitcivi, also given as ʔitcivi by other informants. Gila monster (o).

ʔiwagah, raining; ʔiwari, rain; ʔiwar panatonagah, rain light-thrusting, rain thrusts (with a lance of) light, and ʔiwar tonagah, rain thrusting, rain stabbing, are expressions that mean lightning is flashing continuously; ʔiwar panatonatsi or ʔiwar tonatsi, lightning flashed, a flash of lightning; ʔiwar panatonapagᵃigʸah or ʔiwar tonapagᵃigʸah, rain going along light-thrusting or rain going along thrusting. This is said of a thunder storm which is seen to be progressing, travelling along in a certain direction—probably toward the speaker; ʔiwar yagagah, rain weeping, rain crying, rain crying out (as if in pain); said of sharp, crashing thunder.

ʔiwapuʔᵂikʸaiyu, being cloudy (said of a cloudy day); ʔiwapuʔᵂaatsi, clouded over, became overcast.

ʔiwaringkova, Rain Face. Man's personal name.

haʔiti-, real, genuine; this prefix is frequently used to narrow or define ambiguous relationship terms, e.g., haʔitikinuni, my real kinu, that is, my grandfather or great-uncle, excluding male cousins of grandfather; haʔitiniwaantsi, "real cousin," first cousin of either sex; haʔitinaniwaantsiwi, two first cousins; haʔitinananiwaantsiwi, three or more first cousins.

haʔitihaiku, "real white man," Mexican.

haʔititogʷᵃintimi, "real chief," High Chief; equivalent to tivitsitogʷᵃintimi, though the latter term seems to be preferred.

hahaivʸa (no etymology). Kleinfelter. Placename.

hai (loanword—final i fully voiced), father's younger brother or father's younger male cousin (said by man or woman); step-father.

haikʸa, -aikʸa, Mythic Coyote's speech peculiarity.

haiku (from the Mohave—frequently given by George Laird with final aspiration and, in the plural, as haikuuwi). White man. haiku katc muguʔᵂatimi, the white man has no sense, literally, no semen.

haikurɨmpa, White Man Mouth. Man's personal name.

haikuurupagarɨmɨwɨ (sing. **haikuurupagarɨmɨ**), "black white men," Negroes.

haikuuyɨwitcɨ, White Men Sitting Down. Placename.

haikwiira (Mohave), a large variety of rattlesnake.

haitsɨ, man's older brother's or older male cousin's child; step-child.

hagani?ᵞamɨ, "how to you?" How is that person related to you?

haagaru?ᵂapɨ, man's clothing; **haagaru?ᵂagaipɨ**, old, worn-out, or discarded clothing. **Tɨvatsi haagaru?ᵂagaipɨ**, Wolf's former clothes, and **cɨnawavi haagaru?ᵂagaipɨ**, Mythic Coyote's former clothes, are terms for the primary and secondary rainbows, respectively.

haakwᵃiroxᵂᵃɨ (from the Mohave *?aha kwelox*). Placename. The valley where Needles is now situated.

haakwitcapɨ (from the Mohave *?aha kwitceipa*). Bill Williams Fork.

hamatcuupa (from the Mohave *?aha matcuup*). Mohave Rock.

hanih, what? **hani mah**, what did you say?

hanopaitɨmɨ, how big? **hanopaitɨm ?aipatsɨ**, how big a boy? how big is the boy?

havaganɨ, shade house; flat-topped shed also called **takaganɨ**.

havavɨ shade; **hava?ɨgangumpaanɨ**, I am about to enter the shade, I am going into the shade.

havigᵞah, lying down; **havitcɨ**, lying, that which lies—said, e.g., of an elongated mountain or mountain chain, a fallen tree, hail lying on the ground, etc.

hapuᵂisɨ (from the Mohave *?aha puis*). Placename, site of old Blythe intake.

hasiᵞampa (from an Apache word). Hassayampa River.

haataruumpɨ (from the Mohave *?aha taloomp*). Placename.

harimyiivɨ (from the Mohave or some other Yuman source). Placename.

hatpaawɨ (Chemehuevi plural of Mohave *hatpa*). The Pima.

hatpaanyaawɨ (from Mohave *hatpa ?anya*). The Maricopa.

haatcaruumiwɨ (from the Mohave tribename). The Halchidhoma.

haungkagah, being gray in color, like an old bone that has bleached gray rather than white; **haungkagarɨ**, **hau-**, bone-gray.

hauwawangkɨgarɨ or **hauwawangkɨgatɨ**, Bone-Gray Peaks. Home of the spirit-animal familiars.

hawayawɨ (no etymology). West Wells.

hawivɨ, corn.

hayak^ai (no etymology). Name of a valley in Nevada.

ha′yɨninɨha′yɨnini-aik^y. From Coyote's war song. Untranslated.

hɨvɨngkagah, being bright yellow, like the yolk of an egg; hɨvɨngka-
    rɨ, hɨvɨ-, bright yellow.

hiĭ′kwasi′ (kwasɨ, tail). Wildcat Brother's hunting song (mythology).

hin^yih, who? hin^yi or hin^yi^yaukwaik^ya, whom did you say?

hɨ^yo′, hɨ^yo′. Cry of mourning dove; also, in mythology, the call by
    which Dove Woman signaled her return home.

hɨ^yovɨ, mourning dove.

hɨ^yovin^ya^ʔaiv^yatsiwɨ, Dove Boys. Mythological characters.

hivig^yah, drinking; in Mosquito's war song, translated: "(I) am drink-
    ing"; hi′vig^yani′, from Horsefly's war song, translated: "I drink"
    or "I am drinking."

hi′tokwaava, from Lizard's war song. Translated: "(I) will rise up."

hitsutawanayɨn. From Buzzard's war song. Translated: "scratches
    me."

hiwa, (1) parent, (2) relative; hiwavɨ, a parent, a relative; hiwanɨ,
    my relative (unspecific term); hiwawɨnɨ, my parents; hiwagaipɨ,
    deceased relative, euphemism for "deceased parent," used
    however only in the absence of bereaved son or daughter.

ho^waavo^wak^ai, humped-back, hunchback.

hohoguma, "bone-husband," husband who was formerly the hus-
    band of a deceased sister or deceased female cousin; hohogu-
    mavɨ, a "bone-husband;" hohonagumawɨ, husband and wife,
    one of whom was formerly spouse of deceased sibling or cousin.

hohovɨ, bone.

hohoviwa, "bone-wife," wife who was formerly the wife of a de-
    ceased brother or deceased male cousin; hohoviwavɨ, a "bone-
    wife."

hohorapayu^witsɨ, Bone-Splitter. Secret or derogatory name for a
    Walapai, used when one of that tribe is present.

hokoso^{ʔw}avɨ, spider species.

hokontɨ-, large.

hopak^ai, hollow, dell.

horah, post.

horagah, digging; horapɨ, hole; that which has been dug.

howarɨ, scout (e.g., the scout that travels back and forth between a
    shaman and his familiar to report on the latter's progress).

huuh, huh, huu-, hu-, arrow, bullet.

huk^wamp*i*, black widow spider.

huk^wants*i*, pl. huk^wantsiw*i*, White American, haiku; maarikaan*i*.

huk^wi-, charcoal (termination not recorded).

huk^wivu?*i*, Charcoal Eye. Man's personal name.

hukun*i*agah, dust wind blowing; hukun*i*ar*i*, dust wind.

hukump*a*, dust.

hun*a*, badger.

hunaorap*i*, Badger Hole. Placename.

hu?un*i*vav*i*, frost; hu?un*i*vaavitc*i*, frost lying on ground.

hu?up*i*, squawberries.

-humpiw*a*, over, across or on the farther slope of (the mountain).

huv^wiyagah, singing; huv^wiyav*i*, song; huv^wiyanitagah, imitating a song (which one does not "own"); huv^wiyati?agah, borrowing a song.

huv^wigaiy*u*, owning a song, having hereditary right to a song; huv^wiyagant*i*, pl. huv^wiyagam*i*, one who owns a song.

huv^wu^wagant*i*, "wound doctor," literally, arrow (or bullet) shaman, shaman who can cure wounds.

huts*i* (also recorded as hutsi?*i*), father's mother; father's mother's sister or female cousin; father's father's sister or female cousin; hutsin^y*i*, my paternal grandmother, etc.

hutsip*a*, ocean; hutsipag*i*wah, "ocean-edge," the seacoast.

hutsipag*i*waatsiw*i*, Ocean Edge Dwellers (includes all coastal tribes).

hutsipamamau?*u*, Ocean Woman; invoked as hutsipamaa?ip*i*ts*i*, Old Ocean Woman.

hutsimpiy*a*, daughter-in-law (of man or woman); also husband's sister; woman's older or younger brother's wife; hutsimpiyav*i*, a daughter-in-law, etc.

hutsits*i*, woman's son's child; woman's sister's son's child; woman's brother's son's child.

huu w*i*n?naw*a*, Arrow's Flint. The cluster of stars forming Orion's head.

huu wisi?^yah, Arrow's Feathers. The three stars in Orion's sword.

huwig^yah, flowing; huwip*i* (sometimes huwip*i*), stream, wash, arroyo (this is applied to any tributary of the Colorado, no matter how much water it carries).

?ierateiva, Chemehuevi pronunciation of the name of the Mohave chief referred to in documents as *Irataba*.

ʔiluh (from the Mohave *ʔidho*, willow); also ʔiruh. Man's personal name.

ʔilyaalyiʔiv^ya (from the Mohave); also pronounced **yaariʔiv^ya**. Man's personal name.

ʔing^ya, this animate; ʔimɨ, these (two or more) animate.

ʔing^yawantɨ, sibling of this one; ʔimɨwantɨ, sibling of these two or more.

ʔiv^yaʔana, on top of this visible.

ʔisagawɨ (no etymology). Unidentified constellation.

ʔitcikaava (Chemehuevi pronunciation of a Mohave term for "cousin.") Used "only when we talk to the Mohaves."

ʔitcuk^wa, under this visible inanimate object.

ʔiyaavɨ, wild grape; ʔiyaavimpɨ, wild grapevine.

kaiv^ya (kai-), mountain; kai^ya-, mountain when intimately possessed, e.g., kai^yanɨ, my mountain (mountain over which my song travels and where I have the right to hunt); kaiv^yaya, obj. or poss. case, e.g., kav^yay ʔug^waavaʔanguntsɨ, having gone over the mountain; kaiv^yahumpiwa, on the farther slope of the mountain; kaiv^yagwaɨngkatɨ, one who runs swiftly in mountainous country, Span. *ligero*; kaipipovɨ, "mountain canteen," rumen of mountain sheep used as water container; kaitcoxo, "mountain hat," man's buckskin cap ornamented with quail crests; kaakaiv^ya, three or more mountain ranges.

kaiv^yahumpiwatsiwɨ, Dwellers on the Farther Slope of the Mountain(s). Tribename. Possibly the Luiseño.

kaiv^yaʔamantɨ, New York Mountains. Placename.

-gaipɨ (-ngkaipɨ after strongly nasal vowel), dead or former when postfixed to animate noun; added to inanimate, old, worn-out, former, discarded.

ka´ipipoo´vɨɨ´tsini´ (kaipipooviitsin). From Mountain Sheep Song. Translated: "my mountain canteen."

kaiwaɨkatɨ (derived from kaiv^yagwaɨngkatɨ), Swift Mountain Runner. Man's personal name.

-gaiyu, has, owns; -gantɨ, having, owner; e.g., nɨvagantɨ, (a mountain) having snow; huv^wiyagantɨ, owner of an hereditary song.

kakara (kakarɨ, possibly sometimes kakarɨ), quail; kakarahuv^wiyavɨ, Quail Song.

kakarɨ, sat down (in phrase mi^yarogopits kakarɨ, "moon sat down"). See under karɨgah.

kakaɨnarɨnapɨ, Quail Used to Run. Placename.

kakɨmpɨ, (1) mesquite seed; (2) seed of a species of *palo verde* which bears seed resembling that of mesquite; (3) placename.

kaxu, mother's mother; mother's mother's sister or female cousin; mother's father's sister or female cousin; **kagunɨ**, my mother's mother, etc.; **kagugʷaipɨʔɨmɨ**, your dead mother's mother, etc. (said only in insult to an enemy).

kagutsɨ, woman's daughter's child; woman's sister's or female cousin's daughter's child; woman's brother's or male cousin's daughter's child.

kama- (-gamagah), to taste (intrans.), having taste or flavor (occurs initially only in reference to a salty taste); **kamaiyɨraʔauk ʷa**, is it salty enough? Literally, "has it taste?"; **kamasɨʔigʸah**, being very salty, having a very salty taste. Said, e.g., of over-salted beans or of sea water.

kammagah, parching, e.g., grain.

kamayaʔotavɨ, Diegueño (or Kamia) Sand. The sand dunes near Yuma.

kamayaawɨ (from a Yuman source). The Diegueño; the Kamia.

kamɨ, jackrabbit, hare; **kamuʷaantsɨ**, young jackrabbit; **kamɨmugʷɨ-gʸarɨtɨah**, "jackrabbit sitting place," (1) a place which each jackrabbit has where he sits under a certain bush; (2) the name of an unidentified group of three dim stars; **kamɨtaroso**, jackrabbit hole; the hole into which the jackrabbit goes to shelter himself from the summer heat.

ka′mɨna′wipɨ′ɨptsi′. From Louse's song (mythology). Translated: "My little jackrabbit apron."

kamɨnukʷitavipagaipɨ, "Where the Jackrabbit Went Along Run-Throwing," Where the Jackrabbit Made Tracks as He Leaped. Three or four pairs of dim stars leading away from the three stars called "Jackrabbit Sitting Place." These two names of star-groups refer to events in the myth "How Wildcat Brothers Recovered Their Hunting Song." See Chapter VI.

kamitu, cantaloupe (o).

kamuutɨ (Span. *camote*, sweet potato). Reciprocal nickname between two of the Runners. See Chapter II.

kanavɨ, small willow species; Span. *saucillo*.

kanahiʸutsɨ (no etymology, possibly foreign origin). Man's personal name.

kan*i*, house; also, nest of bird; obj. and poss., kani^y*a*; kani ʔiv^yan*a*, on top of this visible house; kani mavaʔan*a*, on top of that visible house; kani ʔuv^wan*a*, on top of that invisible house.

kaamp*i*, hill; a chain of hills; kaangkarir*i*, "hill sitting," an isolated hill.

kaampuʔ*u* (Span. *campo*). San Bernardino.

kas*a*, wing.

kar*i*gah, sitting, sitting down; karir*i*, sitter, sitting, one who sits; mi^yarogopits kakar*i*, "moon sat down," the moon has taken its place in the sky.

kaats*i*, rat.

katc*u*, no.

katcus*u*, not yet; katcus mawʔwisiwaʔ*a*, it (a watched-for star) has not yet emerged.

kaawiʔ*a*, Rat Penis. Man's personal name.

kaayuvimp*i*, yucca species.

kayuyayuyayuu^waik^y*a*. Coyote's mourning cry.

k*i*ma-, pertaining to another, not one's self; different.

k*i*mamoʔ*o*, Different Hand. Man's personal name.

k*i*man*i*wiw*i*, "Different People," i.e., Different Chemehuevis. The Cahuilla.

k*i*n*u*, father's father; father's father's brother or male cousin; father's mother's brother or male cousin; k*i*nun*i*, my paternal grandfather, etc.; k*i*nug^waip*i*ʔim*i*, your dead paternal grandfather, taboo except in insult; haʔ*i*t*i*k*i*nun*i*, my real paternal grandfather or great-uncle, excluding cousins of grandparents.

k*i*nuts*i*, man's son's child; man's brother's son's child; man's sister's son's child.

k*i*sagaiv^y*a*, Hawk Mountain. Black Mountain, at northwest corner of the Colorado River Reservation.

k*i*savi, hawk species.

k*i*tong^w*a*, Pulled Out Several Objects with Teeth. Placename.

k*i*tong^wagah, pulling out three or more objects with teeth.

k*i*wah, edge; as in hutsipag*i*wah, seashore.

-ki-, particle added to verbs to signify motion towards speaker.

kiipis*i* (no etymology). Man's personal name.

koʔ^wa-, tobacco (ending not recorded from George Laird); koʔ^wa-tcomig^yah, is chewing tobacco.

koh^wain^y*i* (no etymology). Placename.

koh^waitsiwɨ, sing. koh^waitsɨ (no etymology). (1) a California tribe, possibly the Koso; (2) all Shoshone-speaking people.

ko^{ʔwa}ig^yah, killing three or more animals.

kok^{wa}i, mother's older brother or mother's older male cousin; ko-k^{wa}in^yi, my mother's older brother, etc.

konoh, cradleboard (o).

konoowɨkwapɨ, cradle strings (o).

kova, face.

koso^wagah, steaming; koso^wavɨ, steam or vapor; tɨvip koso^wagah, "the earth is steaming," vapor is rising from the earth.

kotsimayo. From Sidewinder's song as he went to kill the Four-Eyed Insect (mythology). Untranslated.

kotcovɨ, crest (of bird).

-ku-, particle occurring with certain numerals.

kuk^wanɨvagantɨ, Having Wood and Snow (i.e., timbered and snowy). San Bernardino Mountains.

kuk^wapɨ, wood, timber; kuk^wagantɨ, place or person having wood or timber.

kuuk^watɨ, buried; said only of a person, as in nɨw kuuk^watɨ, a buried person.

kuma, husband; kumavɨ, a husband.

kumin^yak^ai. From Southern Fox's song as he crossed Death Valley (mythology). Translated: "burnt off with fire." See under kuna.

kuna, fire; ku-, with or by means of fire, or with heat caused by fire; kukwɨɨngutsɨ, got scalded so that his (a person's) skin peeled off; cp. kwɨɨvɨ; kumin^{ʔny}ak^ai, burnt off; kutuutsig^yah, being hot, becoming hot (from fire, not sun); kutuutsitcɨ, anything which has become heated by fire; kutusik^yamagah, having a burnt taste; kutsik^yig^yah, burning (trans.), said, e.g., of a person burning trash.

kunayɨwaavɨ, Fire Valley, Death Valley.

kusira (no etymology). Placename.

kuu^ʔutsɨ, man's younger brother's or younger male cousin's child.

kuyuutɨ (possibly from Eng. "coyote"). Man's personal name.

-kwa^ʔi-, particle signifying motion away from speaker; opposite of -ki-.

kwaagwawɨ, Rattlesnake's speech peculiarity (mythology).

kwanantsitsɨ, red-tailed hawk; also the name of a mythological personage.

kwas*i*, tail.

kwas*u*, woman's clothes; dress.

kwaroyaaw*i* (probably from Mohave), chicken.

kwaroyaawi kotcov*i*, "Chicken's Crest," Coxcomb. Placename.

kwayantu^w**at***i* (no etymology). Name of a place in Arizona opposite Chemehuevi Valley where a band of Chemehuevis lived; **kwayantu**^w**atitsiw***i*, people of **kwayantu**^w**at***i*.

kwiiv*i*, peeled one, person whose skin is peeled off in patches. This is employed as a derogatory nickname or secret name for a Mohave.

kwi´tikiyikwitikiy. From Lizard's war song (mythology). Translated: "rise up, rise up."

kwik^y**apaaw***i*, sing. **kwik**^y**apah**. The Cocopah.

kwin^y**aváh** (no etymology, possibly an Apache word). Name of a sacred cave; **kwin**^y**avaantu**^w**avan***i*, I am going to **kwin**^y**aváh**.

kwipagah, clubbing; beating (to death) with a stick or club; **kwikwipakagah**, they three or more clubbing (person, animal, or demon).

kwitaanamuniw*i* (no etymology). Tribename—another name for **kimaniwiw***i*, the Cahuilla, or possibly the Kwitanemuk Serrano.

kwitump*i*, anus.

kwitutcapiats*i*, Spread Anus or Anus Spreader. Man's personal name.

kwitcaaniw*i* (from Mohave *Kwitcaana*), the Yuma; the Quechan.

kwitcap*i*, excrement.

kwitcuvakat*i* or **kwitcuvar***i*, a single mountain peak.

kwitcupik^y**aiy***u*, being bunched up; having been gathered together into a bunch.

kwituyaw*i* (suggested etymology: anus carries), half-sibling with a common father.

kwiyaik^y**amagah**, having a burnt taste; the same as **kutusik**^y**amagah** (see under **kun***a*).

kwiyamayamayuuyuu^w**aik**^y***a*. Coyote's call for the north wind (mythology).

kwiyavaah, Rattlesnake Water. Placename.

kwiyar*a*, screw mesquite bean; **kwiyaramp***i*, screw mesquite tree.

kwiyarangkaiv^y***a*, Screw Mesquite Mountain. Placename.

kwiyarasap*i*, Screw Mesquite Belly. Placename.

kwiyats*i*, (diamond-backed) rattlesnake; **kwiyavu**^w**agant***i* or **kwiya-**

vu⁊ᵂagant𝑖, "snake doctor"; (1) shaman who has rattlesnake familiar; (2) shaman who can cure snakebite; (3) shaman who can take away the pain of toothache because he has been bitten by a rattlesnake on the hand or foot and has recovered.

kwiyavu⁊i, Snake Eye. Man's personal name.

lalants𝑖 or rarants𝑖 (from Span. *la lancha*). Ehrenberg. Placename.

ma-, with the hand.

maa⁊ipɨgaivʸa, Old Woman Mountain. Old Woman Mountains.

maa⁊ipɨts𝑖, old woman.

mahᵃi-, sometimes mai-, with intent to harm; mahaiginʸi, pursue me with intent to harm! (Challenge of Rabbit Children to Immortal Water and Immortal Yucca Date—mythology).

mahav𝑖, bush; brush.

makatcats𝑖, horned toad.

mamau⁊u, woman; mamau⁊uhiwagaipi⁊ɨngᵂa, that (invisible) one's deceased female parent (polite circumlocution for "dead mother"); mamau⁊uhutsitsiwiwa⁊a, woman and son's children.

mamau⁊untɨngkan⁊n𝑖, Woman Rock-Cave. Placename in the Whipple Mountains.

manaikʸat𝑖, skillful dodger (of arrows or missiles).

manav𝑖, (1) thorn; (2) new branch budding out on a cholla cactus.

manaviso⁊ots𝑖, Thorn Baby. Man's personal name.

mang𝑎, that one visible animate; mam𝑖, those (two or more); manga-suyaganu ⁊ipɨikwaigup𝑖 or mangas ⁊ipɨikwaigupɨyaganuh, may that one fall asleep—illustrating use of the -suyaganuh formula (q.v.) with mang𝑎.

mangawant𝑖, sibling of that one visible; mamɨwant𝑖, sibling of those visible.

mava⁊an𝑎, on top of that visible.

maviagah, stretching out the arm and pushing with the hand; ma-maviagah, performing this action repeatedly.

mavin⁊niyagah, equivalent of maviagah or possibly of mamaviagah.

máskwaw𝑖 (from Mohave *maskwaw*). Plant name.

masuupaaru⁊ᵂagah, gathering up anything (clothes, leaves, trash) with the hand; masuupaaru⁊ᵂavaan𝑖, I shall gather up (e.g., the clothes).

marahóxᵂᵃi (from Mohave *marahox*), name of a large whirlpool in the Colorado River.

matav𝑖, tick; also said to mean flea (o).

mataviyum*i*, Having Ticks. Man's personal name or nickname (o).

mataavik^y*i* (corruption of Yuman *mat-haviky*, brother). Reciprocal form of address between a Chemehuevi and a Maricopa.

maari̇̀ng^ʔngiyatsiwi̇̀ (no etymology). The Serrano.

maarikaniwi̇̀, Americans.

maruk^w*a*, there visible under; preceded by noun in obj. case, that visible under.

maumáupi̇̀ts*i*, nighthawk (o).

maupah or mau^ʔupah, Woman Water. Mopah Springs. Placename.

mawi̇̀^ʔi̇̀, mother's older sister or mother's older female cousin.

mawisiyi̇̀ or maw^ʔwisiyi̇̀, emerges; comes out (said of sun, star, etc., emerging as an animal from its den); maw^ʔwisitca^ʔak*a*, it has emerged; katcus maw^ʔwisiwa^ʔ*a*, it has not yet emerged.

mayaangakutca^ʔak*a*, they have emerged (said of a constellation or group of stars); katcus mayaangawa^ʔ*a*, they have not yet emerged.

-m*i*, dual ending; (1) plural ending, formerly after nasalizing stems, now in common use, frequently becoming simply -m; (2) termination added to color name to signify "person of" that color—e.g., ^ʔo^wakari̇̀m*i*, cream-colored (not florid) white person. -mi̇̀wi̇̀, triplural ending, now virtually unused.

mi̇̀ants*i* (unrecognized as a loanword, but almost surely from Eng. month), month. Usually supplants mi^yarogopits*i*, moon.

mi̇̀m*i*, you (two or more).

mi̇̀ng*i*, eagle; mi̇̀ng tcaku^{ʔw}in^yakat*i*, eagle skin with feathers used in Mourning Ceremony.

mi̇̀ntcats*i*, lamb; young mountain sheep.

mi^yarogopig^yaiv^y*a*, Moon Mountain. Placename.

mi^yarogopits*i*, moon; mi^yarogopits kakari̇̀, moon sitting, moon sat down, is said of the new moon, indicating that the moon has taken its place in the sky; mi^yarogopits nanawa^{ʔa}ig^yah, moon going to grow itself, moon going to its growth, said of the waxing moon; mi^yarogopits putcawa^{ʔa}ig^yah, moon going to fill, moon going to its fullness, equivalent to the above and an expression in common use, but it is a Chemehuevi translation of the English idiom; mi^yarogopits tog^{wa}inti̇̀rawaagantu^w*a*, moon at half-center, describes the full moon, "half-center" here implies the very center, Span. *el mero medio*; mi^yarogopits ya^ʔ*a*, moon died, said both of the dark of the moon and of an eclipse; **mi^yarogopits ya^{ʔa}iwa^{ʔa}ig^yah**, moon going to die, moon going towards death; the moon is waning.

mi^{ʔy}aup<i>i</i>, small, little; **mi^{ʔy}aupitog^{wa}intim<i>i</i>**, a lesser chief.

mi^{ʔy}aupitcawaw^ʔwagant<i>i</i>, Small Place Where There is T*cawa*. Place-name describing a smaller wash than **tcaw^ʔwagant<i>i</i>**, q.v.

moh^wagamagah, being bitter, having a bitter taste. (But **muh^warat<i>i</i>**, bitter.)

moh^wav<i>i</i> or **muh^wav<i>i</i>**, bitter substance (e.g., quinine).

mo^ʔog^wah, marking with the hand. Cp. **po^ʔog^wah**, marking.

mog^wah (no etymology). Placename.

momomp<i>i</i>, jimsonweed.

mon*a*, son-in-law, pl. **monam<i>i</i>** or **monaw<i>i</i>**; **monangkaip<i>i</i>** or **mona-gaip<i>i</i>**, (1) former son-in-law, one who is no longer a son-in-law because of death of or separation from wife; (2) dead son-in-law—in latter sense an offensive or taboo expression.

monomp<i>i</i>, bunchgrass; Span. *zacaton*.

monompaagant<i>i</i>, Having Bunch Grass and Water. Vontrigger Springs. Placename.

mo^ʔop<i>i</i>, hand (but **ma-**, with the hand).

montc*o*, beard.

muh^warat<i>i</i>, bitter.

muh^wint<i>i</i>, Leader. Aldebaran.

muhuav<i>i</i>, mosquito (o).

muhu^wat<i>i</i>, crazy, insane (o); a modern word, possibly deriving from **mugu^{ʔw}atim<i>i</i>**. See under **mugu-**.

muhungk^waniv<i>i</i>, Owl House. Placename.

muhunangkavik^yavo^ʔo, Owl Ear Tank. Placename.

muhuumpits<i>i</i>, owl species.

muuk^wiw<i>i</i>, sing. **muuk^w<i>i</i>**, the Hopi.

mug^wi-, generic term including both jackrabbits and cottontails; **mug^wig^yarigah**, sitting as a rabbit sits (not as a person); **mug^wi-g^yaritiah**, rabbit sitting place; **mug^wiv<i>i</i>**, same as **mug^wig^yaritiah**.

mugu-, semen (termination not recorded); **mugu^{ʔw}atim<i>i</i>**, not having semen; **katc mugu^{ʔw}atim<i>i</i>**, he has no semen, i.e., no sense, no understanding or sensibility.

mugwi^y*a*, gecko, Span. *guico*.

mug^wiyagaiv^y*a*, Guico Mountain. El Dorado Mountains.

muumu^ʔitu^{ʔw}in^yump<i>i</i>, bull-roarer (-**nump<i>i</i>**, instrument).

munuukw*a*, Round. Woman's personal name.

mun⁷nukwivitsɨ, Round. Woman's personal name.

mun⁷nukwitcɨ, anything round like a ball.

muvɨ, nose; muvin⁷nʸangkа, nose pendant, nose ring.

muuviʸa (no etymology). Cottonwood Island.

muupitsɨ, fly.

musimpiya, woman's sister-in-law or woman's female cousin-in-law; musimpiyavi, a woman's sister-in-law, etc.

musitsɨ, woman's brother's child or woman's male cousin's child.

murih, beans; kakaramurih, black-eyed peas.

murunavɨ, sage species.

muwa, father; muwanɨ, my father; muwavɨ, a father; muwagaipɨ, dead father, a taboo expression except as deadly insult—e.g., muwagaipɨ⁷imɨ, your dead father.

na-, reflexive or dual reciprocal; nana-, triplural reciprocal; also indicates a multiple of two, as in nanapa⁷agaipu⁷ʷitsɨ, "four-eyed insect"; or continuing self-action, as in tava⁷awɨ⁷anana⁷atsɨ, "chipmunk penis erecting itself," a rock formation.

na⁷antamuwawɨ, two brothers-in-law or two male cousins-in-law; nana⁷antamuwawɨ, three or more brothers-in-law, etc.*

na⁷isaaviwɨ, uncle (father's or mother's brother) and nephew or niece; na⁷isaaviwawɨ or nana⁷isaaviwawɨ, uncle and two or more nephews and/or nieces.

nahaitsiwɨ or nahaiwɨ, (1) man and older brother's child; man and older male cousin's child; (2) step-father and step-child; nanahaitsiwɨ or nanahaiwɨ, man and two or more children of older brother or older male cousin; man and two or more step-children.

nahagani⁷ʸaawɨ, how are they to each other? How do they relate to each other? Asked to secure a more accurate definition of relationship when a vague or indefinite term has been used.

nahiwawɨ, two relatives; nanahiwawɨ, three or more relatives.

nahontsiwɨ, (1) two co-spouses or two consecutive spouses; (2) husbands or two sisters or female cousins, or wives of two brothers or male cousins; nanahontsiwɨ, three or more co-spouses or consecutive spouses, or spouses of three or more siblings or cousins. -hontsi- occurs only in collective terms.

---

* In the alphabetical order employed here I have found it expedient in most cases to disregard broken vowels, listing a⁷a simply as a; but here a⁷a is the last a of na- followed by the first of ⁷antamuwa.

nahutsimpiyaw*i*, parent-in-law and daughter-in-law; nanahutsimpi-
yaw*i*, parent-in-law and two or more daughters-in-law.

nahutsiw*i*, paternal grandmother and grandchild (collective embracing all relationships described by huts*i* and hutsits*i*, q.v.).

naig^yah, getting revenge.

naingkum*a*, "vengeance husband," woman's brother-in-law or male
cousin-in-law; naingkumav*i*, a "vengeance husband"; nanaingku-
maw*i*, man and sister-in-law or man and female cousin-in-law.

na²aiv^yayaw*i*, man and son of sister or of female cousin; nana²ai-
v^yayaw*i*, man and two or more sons of sister, etc.

naimpiw*a*, "vengeance wife," man's sister-in-law or female cousin;
naimpiwav*i*, a "vengeance wife."

naints*i*, adolescent girl; young woman.

naintsi^y*a*, man's sister's daughter or man's female cousin's daughter.

na²ªitcikaavaw*i*, two cousins (of either sex). See ²itcikaav*a*.

nax*a* (naga-), mountain sheep; nagay tamaup*a*, left the mountain
sheep behind. The plural, nagaw*i*, Mountain Sheep, is the name
of Orion's Belt, Span. *Las Tres Reyes.*

nangk*a*, (1) ear; (2) earring or pendant (cp. muvin²n^yangk*a*, nose
ring).

nagahuv^wiyav*i*, Mountain Sheep Song, one of the major hereditary
songs.

nagavu^wagant*i*, medicine, i.e., material used for self-curing.

nagaguw*i*, maternal grandmother and grandchild (embracing all relationships expressed by kax*u* and kaguts*i*).

nagasagw^aiy. From Coyote's war song (mythology). Translated:
"mountain sheep entrails."

nagaramaup*a*, Left the Mountain Sheep Behind. Man's personal
name.

nagarip*i*, Gathering (of people); same as suupaaru²^wap*i*.

nagumaw*i*, husband and wife; nanagumaw*i*, two or more married
couples.

nagw^aipapiayay*a* or nagw^aipatigah, They Clubbed Each Other Long
Ago. Placename. Also nanag^waipapiayay*a* and nanag^waipatigah.

nagw^aitunayawiw*i*, two half-siblings with a common father.

nam*a*, two adjoining; two close together; nam kani^yagant*i*, two
houses being close together, two adjoining houses; namangku-
tcats*i*, twin; namangkutcatsiw*i*, twins; namant*i*m*i*, two siblings;
nanamant*i*m*i* or nanamant*i*m*i*w*i*, three or more siblings.

namiʔi, younger sister or younger female cousin; direct or collateral ancestress more remote than grandmother.

namonamɨ or namonawɨ, parent-in-law and son-in-law.

namusimpiyawɨ, woman and sister-in-law, woman and female cousin by marriage (same as naʔunyiiwɨ); nanamusimpiyawɨ, woman and two or more sisters-in-law, etc.

nanaʔagah, growing up; erecting itself.

nanangkoʔʷᵃigʸah, three or more fighting (among themselves or with others); cp. koʔʷᵃigʸah, killing three or more animals.

nanangkoʔʷᵃipɨayayᵃ or nanangkoʔʷᵃitɨgah, Where They Fought. Placename.

nanapaʔagaipuʔʷitsɨ, four-eyed insect; insect species and mythological character. Given by another informant in 1970 as nanapuʔi.

nanawaʔᵃigʸah, going to grow (see under miʸarogopitsɨ, moon).

nanɨmpiyawɨ, woman and child of older sister or of older female cousin; nananɨmpiyawɨ, woman and two or more children of older sister, etc.

naniwaantsiwɨ, two cousins of either sex, or one male and one female; nananiwaantsiwɨ, three or more cousins.

naʔontokʷaavɨwɨ, two male cousins, or a male and a female cousin (but never two female cousins); nanaʔontokʷaavɨwɨ, three or more cousins, predominantly male.

nampₐ, foot (but ta-, with the foot).

navaviwɨ or naaviwɨ, two brothers, two male cousins; nanavaviwɨ, three or more brothers or male cousins; a name may be prefixed, e.g., tukunanavaviwɨ, Wildcat Brothers (mythology).

navatsiwɨ, two sisters or two female cousins; nanavatsiwɨ, three or more sisters or female cousins.

navatcawigʸah, coming together, meeting; (water) flowing to a confluence; navatcawipɨ, confluence (of waters).

navaawɨ, woman and brother's or male cousin's child; nanavahawɨ, woman and two or more children of brother or of male cousin.

napɨw, old man (o).

naviyawɨ, mother and child; nanaviyawɨ, mother and children; name of husband may be prefixed, e.g., tavahukʷananaviyawɨ, Sun Spider and family (mythology).

navuʷaganumpɨ, medicine, that with which one cures one's self. Cp. puhʷagantɨ, "doctor," shaman.

navuniwatuʔʷatsɨ, became self-seen, acquired visibility. First light, or the time when day is just beginning to break and objects are becoming visible.

nan*ta*, mescal; nantap*i*, mescal plant; nantapik^{y}ov*i*, heart of mescal; nantawip*i*ap*i*, large, flat, flexible cake or slab made of dried heart of mescal.

nantap*i*agan*ti*, There Being Mescal, Place Where There is Mescal, Turtle Mountains. Placename.

nara´wampaa, nar*i*wiin^{y}apah, Immortal Water, as sung in baby-talk by the Rabbit Children (mythology).

nara´watc*i*´impi, nar*i*wiin^{y}atc*i*mp*i*, Immortal Yucca Date, as sung in baby-talk by the Rabbit Children (mythology).

nar*i*nagah, three or more running; nar*i*nap*i*, used to run.

nar*i*wiin^{y}apah, Self-Mythologizing Water, Immortal Water; poetic or mythological name for the ocean (hutsip*a*), also for the primal freshwater lake mentioned in the myth "How Cottontail Rabbit Conquered the Sun," whence all rivers, streams, lakes, springs, and tanks are supposed to have come. Cp. t*i*wiin^{y}agah, telling myths.

nar*i*wiin^{y}ap*i*w*i*, Immortal People, the people who lived in mythological, pre-human times.

nar*i*wiin^{y}at*i*vip*i*, the Storied Land, or Land of Myths.

nar*i*wiin^{y}atc*i*mp*i*, Immortal Yucca Date (mythology).

naro?o, shirt; also protective armor, whether material or magical.

na?unyiiw*i* (from Mohave *unyi*), woman and sister-in-law or woman and female cousin by marriage; nana?unyiiw*i*, woman and two or more sisters-in-law, etc. Same as namusimpiyaw*i*.

naux*u* (naugu-) or nauguv*i*, spirit of the dead, soul, ghost.

naugupoh, Spirit Road, Ghost Trail. The Milky Way.

naugut*i*vip*i* or naugur*i*vip*i*, Spirit Land; Land of the Dead.

naawaw*i*, father and child; nanaawaw*i*, father and two or more children.

naw*i*, apron.

nayaig^{y}ap*i*tsiw*i*, parent-in-law and child-in-law; nanayah^{a}ig^{y}ap*i*tsiw*i*, father-in-law and two or more children-in-law.

nayaakaing*u*, is brought, has been brought.

nay*ii*piyanagumats*i*, Brother and Sister Married Pair (translation of Mohave Incest Rock). Placename.

nay*ii*piyaw*i*, brother and sister; nanay*ii*piyaw*i*, two or more couples each consisting of one brother and one sister.

ni⁷i̵, I; tami̵, we two (you and I); ni̵mi̵, we two or more.

ni̵agah, wind blowing; ni̵ari̵, wind.

ni̵ari̵mamau⁷u, Wind Woman. Mythological character.

ni̵kapi̵, Scalp Dance, Ghost Dance, Circle Dance danced at Cry; any dance that is danced in a circle.

ni̵kati̵ah, dancing place; ring around sun or moon.

ni̵maiwigʸah, going on the warpath, setting out for war (literally, "to harm people").

ni̵mi̵, we two or more; ni̵mi̵ʸa (ni̵mi), obj. and poss., free form.

ni̵miwanti̵, our sibling, sibling of us two or more; ni̵miwantimi̵, our two siblings; ni̵miwantimi̵wi̵, our three or more siblings.

ni̵i̵ni̵ʸa, me, my, mine (poss. and obj. free form of ni̵⁷i̵); ni̵i̵ni muwa or ni̵i̵ni muwani̵, my father.

ni̵ngkuupi̵, grave, buried person; same as ni̵w kuukʷati̵.

ni̵va⁷i̵wagah, "snow-raining," snow is falling; ni̵va⁷i̵wari̵, "snow-rain," said of falling snow.

ni̵vaganti̵, Having Snow. Placename actual and mythological, not definitely placed by George Laird; also said of any place which is snowy.

ni̵vaganti̵ or ni̵vavi̵ʸaganti̵, there being snow, place where there is snow.

ni̵vagantimanti̵, alternate form of placename, ni̵vaganti̵, identified as Charleston Peak in Nevada (o).

ni̵vasi̵⁷i̵, Snow Flower. Woman's personal name.

ni̵vavi̵, snow; ni̵vaavitci̵ (ni̵va- plus havitci̵), snow lying on ground. See ni̵va⁷i̵wagah.

ni̵mpiya, mother's younger sister or mother's younger female cousin; ni̵mpiyavi̵, a younger sister of a mother, etc.

ni̵nti̵navi̵, red racer, snake species.

ni̵ntcum⁷mapi̵, grave, place where a person is buried, in the language of the **yuwitawi̵** (see section on Tribes, Chapter V).

ni̵wanti̵, my sibling; ni̵wantimi̵, my two siblings; ni̵wantimi̵wi̵, my three or more siblings.

ni̵wi̵, person; a Chemehuevi; ni̵wi̵wi̵, people, Chemehuevis; the Chemehuevi (these words are now frequently pronounced nu and nuwu respectively, but the original form appears in compounds). **Ni̵wi̵wi̵**, like **tuumontcokowi̵**, embraces all three divisions of the Chemehuevi. A desert Chemehuevi is **ti̵i̵rani̵wi̵**, but **tanti̵i̵tsi̵** is a Northerner, and **tanti̵vaitsi̵**, a Southerner (**tanti̵i̵-**

nʸiwɨ would be a northern person of an unrelated tribe). The Mohave called the Southern and Desert Chemehuevis *tcamuweiva*, said to mean "mixed with all"; but the Northern Chemehuevi were distinguished as *tcamuweiv tahaana*.

nɨwɨʔampagarɨ, "person speaker," one who speaks Chemehuevi.

nɨwɨavɨ or nɨwɨʔavɨ, band of people (Chemehuevis) living under a lesser chief.

nɨwɨʹvaɨʹpitan hiviʹgʸaniʹ. From Horsefly's war song (mythology). Translated: "I drink people's blood."

nɨwɨrɨkagantɨ, "person eater," cannibal; pl. nɨwɨrɨkagamɨ. The plural form was given as another name for kohʷaitsiwɨ (see section on Tribes, Chapter V).

-nɨ, pronominal suffix, I, me, my.

nitagah, imitating (any sound, but specifically a song which does not belong to one).

niwah (niwaa-), friend; niwaanɨ, my friend.

niwaantsɨ, cousin of either sex or any degree of relationship; haʔɨtiniwaantsɨ, real or genuine cousin, i.e., first cousin.

noogʷah, carrying on back, as one carries a load.

nogʷah (no etymology). Placename which George Laird had heard of but could not locate.

nookʷaiyu, being carried or borne (load on back, dew on grass, etc.); -kaiyu, intransitive postfix.

noʔovi, fetus; ʔaanoʔovi, "white clay fetus," echo (into which Wind Woman was transformed when she was sealed into a cave—mythology).

nukʷi, runner (as last element in masculine names); nukʷigʸah, running.

-numpɨ, instrument or material with which or by which something is made or done.

-nuwah, locative postfix.

-ngu, -ngu-, particle signifying immediate action; -nguʔu, imperative.

ʔoʷakagah, being cream or buff colored; ʔoʷakarɨ (ʔoʷa-), cream or buff.

ʔoʷakarimɨ, (white) person of a fair (creamy) but not florid complexion.

ʔoʷavi, rock salt.

ʔoʷasiʸakagah, being pale yellow (literally, "pale buff," but used to indicate a yellowish tinge); ʔoʷasiʸakarɨ, pale yellow.

ʔoʷasiʸapɨ, stone which furnishes red color in pottery; it is a buff-colored stone which turns red when fired.

ʔoʷasopiʸagamagah, having a salty taste, tasting salty.

ʔoʷasopiʸagamantɨ, Salty Tasting, Having a Salty Taste. Name of a place where there is a brackish spring.

ʔokʷah (ʔokʷai-) (no etymology). Name of an unidentified mountain range.

ʔonosɨatugʷanu (also recorded as ʔonosɨantugʷanu), the first half of the night; period between sunset and midnight.

ʔompɨ, "red paint" (red clay or earth which was used for painting the face).

ʔompihorapɨ, Red Paint Diggings. Placename.

ʔopikʸakɨmpɨ, mesquite seed.

ʔopimpɨ, mesquite.

ʔopinʸawɨtɨmʔma or ʔopinʸawɨtɨmʔmatsɨ, Closed Itself with Mesquite. Placename.

ʔopitcokotsɨ, Mesquite Bean Pounder. Man's personal name.

ʔoomposɨ (no etymology). Personal name of a famous shaman.

ʔotavaʔantɨ, High Sand. Placename.

ʔotavɨ, fine sand.

ʔotarakah, sandbar (but ʔataɽakamuupitsɨ, sandbar fly).

ʔotawɨnɨɽɨ, Sand Standing. Man's personal name.

ʔontokʷaavɨ or ʔontokʷavɨ, male cousin; reciprocal form of address used between male cousins; ʔontokʷavɨakaavɨ, someone's male cousin, but ʔontokʷavɨ, a male cousin.

ʔontokʷarɨmɨ (referring to brownish color of hair). Woman's personal name (o).

ʔootca (no etymology). Woman's personal name.

pah or paah (paa-, sometimes pa- in compounds), water.

-vah (-va-, -vaa-), postfix indicating (1) at; (2) future tense.

paɨɨigʸamagah, having a fishy taste (but pagɨɨtsɨ, fish).

paɨɨ'guruguruguru. Red Racer's cry as he dived through a "thorn bush" to make himself bleed (mythology).

paɨnagah, light breeze blowing; paɨnarɨ, gentle breeze.

paɨnʔnagwᵃitsɨ, burrowing owl.

paɨpitα, blood; nɨwɨpaɨpitα, human blood.

paɨwaruʷagah, bleeding; paɨwaruʷapɨ, blood.

pahα (paha-), (1) mortar; (2) father's sister or father's female cousin; pahanɨ, my mortar; my paternal aunt, etc.

pahats*i*, handstone.

pah^aik*u*, three.

paho^waavo^wak^a*i* or paho^waavo^wak^aits*i*, Humped-Back Water. Placename.

pahokoso?^wav*i*, water-spider.

pahomp*a*, hail; pahoavitc*i* or pahompahavitc*i*, hail lying (on ground after a storm); pahonni̵wagah, "hail-raining," it is hailing; pahonni̵war*i*, "hail-rain," said of hail while it is falling.

pahoompari̵gats*i*, Hail Gatherer. Woman's personal name.

pahuwip*i*, Water Stream. Bill Williams Fork.

pagah, river; specifically, the Colorado River.

pa?agah, being high, having height; pa?ap*i*, high (as in tavava?ap*i*, q.v.); pa?ant*i*, high (free adjective).

pagangkwitcun?n*i*, Bunched-Up Carrizo. Arrowweed Springs.

pagamp*i*, Span. *carrizo*.

pagaip*i*, went along.

pagaarayuningk*i*, Kicker Against the River Bank to Make it Cave In. Personal name of a woman shaman.

pagari̵r*i*, "water sitting," lake.

pagi̵imuv*i*, Fish Nose(s)—descriptive of rock formation. Rincon.

pagi̵inamp*a*, Fish Foot. Man's personal name.

pagin?nava, cloud.

pagin?nasi̵?*i*, Cloud Flower. Woman's personal name.

pagi̵isagw^aiv*i*, Fish Intestines. Man's personal name.

pagi̵its*i*, fish.

pagi̵iwi̵x*i*, Fish Vagina. Man's personal name.

pagoosov*i*, *guatamote* plant.

pagoosovi̵ts*i*, Guatamote Place. Placename.

pana-, light; with light; panakaiy*u*, has been lit up or illuminated.

panangkwangu?*u*, come down! (e.g., from sky, tree, stairs, hill, the north).

panamaitsiw*i*, unidentified northern tribe.

pananump*i*, lamp, torch (instrument for making light).

panap*i*, lightning flash; light.

panavatcawip*i*, Water Confluence. Placename.

panatonagah, "light-thrusting," lightning flashing; panatonats*i*, lightning flashed, a flash of lightning.

panatci̵mpi̵?ig^yah, lightning flashing. This denotes a quicker, more vigorous movement than panayi̵mpi̵?ig^yah.

panayimpi⁷ig^yah, "light-vibrating"; said of the type of lightning known as heat lightning, when the whole sky is lit up but no lightning flash is seen.

panook^waiyu, water is being carried (i.e., borne on grass or shrubs); said of dew.

paanumiitsiwi, sing. paanumiitsi. Tribe linguistically related to the Chemehuevi, living in the vicinity of the Panamint Mountains.

papawa, bear; obj. or poss., papawaya; papaway tutugu^wanti, one having the bear as his spirit-animal familiar. Same as papawa-pu^waganti, bear shaman.

papaway paiwaru^wapi, Bear's Blood. Placename.

pavi, man's or woman's older brother or older male cousin; direct or collateral male descendant more remote than grandson.

pa⁷avi, worm.

pavonakwatsi, watermelon (o).

pasa, field.

paasa (no etymology). Paiute Springs.

pasagwagari, Green Water. Placename.

paasaruntug^wiv^yi (tuntug^wiv^yi, lava, malpais). Paiute Springs Badlands (applied to a black lava mountain range).

paasatsi (no etymology). Woman's personal name.

paasawagaritsiwi, sing. paasawagaritsi, Blue Water Dwellers. The Havasupai (George Laird called them "Supais").

paran⁷nigiwi, sing. paran⁷nixi, Water-Steppers. The Paiute of Virgin River, Nevada.

parangkwingkwi⁷i. Burrowing Owl's characteristic call (mythology).

pari⁷asikaiv^ya, Ice Mountain. Mythological and probably actual placename.

pari⁷asipi, "frozen water"; ice.

parimpa, Water Mouth. Pahrump, Nevada.

paati (no etymology). Man's personal name (o).

paroog^waagari, water purple; said (1) of the collective colors of the rainbow, and (2) of the darkness of an approaching storm.

paroog^watsiwi⁷ik^yaiyu, "water purple is streaked," "water purple being streaked." Descriptive of the rainbow "streaked" across the sky.

paroog^waawiniri, water purple standing; rainbow.

pantu^wakaiyu, is hung, is suspended vertically (as a waterbag hangs from the hunter's belt).

pantungkwagaig^yah, bouncing up and down.

pantu´ngkwaa´gaiv^ya´ (same as pantuk^ʔkwagaiv^yah). From Mountain Sheep Song. Translated: "will go along bouncing up and down."

parunuk^witcɨ, "water circle"; island.

paatsatsɨ, bat.

paatcaa´witsi´ya (paatcaa´witsi´). From Deer Song. Translated: "where water seeps."

patcɨ, man's daughter; patcɨnɨ, my daughter.

patcɨ, older sister or older female cousin; direct or collateral female descendant more remote than granddaughter.

pawanantsɨ, seagull.

-vɨh, past tense.

-pɨayay*a*, suffix added to placenames to indicate that the event commemorated took place a long time ago; same as -tɨgah.

pɨhɨvɨ, fur, hair of animal, body hair; but pɨhɨʔah when used with possessive of animal or person to whom it is attached; pungku-tsi pɨhɨʔah, the dog's hair.

pɨɨrɨ, crooked stick.

-pɨtsɨ, honorific postfix: old, little old, revered, respected.

-vɨ, noun termination; postfix which may be added to certain relationship terms with the force of an indefinite article: muwavɨ, a father.

pih^yagamagah, being sweet, having a sweet taste; pih^yagamayɨ-raʔᵃuk^w*a*, does it taste sweet enough?

pih^yavɨ, sweet substance, e.g., sugar or syrup.

pih^yɨwavɨ, heart (of person).

pih^yɨ´wavi tɨ´nʔnɨgani. From Horsefly's war song (mythology). Translated: "my heart palpitates."

pik^yavoʔo, natural tank in rock (Span. *tinaja*).

piigisɨ (from Span. *Vegas*). Las Vegas, Nevada.

pik^yovɨ, heart (of plant); as in nantapik^yovɨ, heart of mescal plant.

vin^y*a* (Eng. Ben). Ben Paddock. This is the only loanword in my notes where p does not substitute for initial v (o).

piviis*a* (no etymology). Man's personal name.

pipisoʔ^w*a*, woman's child of either sex; pipisoʔ^wanɨ, my child; pipi-soʔ^wagantɨ, woman who has a child.

pipisoʔotsɨ, child from about four months to six years of age.

pipit*a*, horsefly (o).

pipovɨ, "round gut" (rumen) of mountain sheep or other ruminant.

piisop*i* (bishop). Nickname sometimes applied to John Smith, George Laird's half-brother (o).

piso?orimp*a*, Baby Mouth. Man's personal name.

piso?ots*i*, baby; infant under four months.

pitantacɨna?ahuv^wiyav*ɨ*, Vanyume Coyote Song.

pitantɨm*ɨ* or pitantɨmɨw*ɨ*, sing. apparently pitant*a* (no etymology). The Vanyume Serrano.

pitantiw*ɨ*, sing. pitant*i*. Possibly the Indians who lived in the Tejon region.

piw*a*, wife; piwav*i*, a wife.

piy*a*, mother; piyav*i*, a mother; piyan*ɨ*, my mother; piyagaip*ɨ*, dead mother, taboo expression except as insult.

poh or pooh, trail, road.

poo?^wav*i*, louse. Occurs as a man's personal name and also as the name of a mythological female character.

po?og^wah, marking (transitive).

po?ok^waiy*u*, being variegated, marked, or written upon; po?ok^wat*ɨ*, variegated, piebald, striped, marked, smeared, written upon (po?o- does not occur as an adjectival prefix).

poniy*a*, skunk.

poniyahuv^wiyav*ɨ*, Skunk Song.

povisats*i*, small bird species; personal name of a woman.

por*o* or poor*o*, shaman's rod, usually translated by George Laird "crooked stick."

puh^wagant*ɨ* (in notes from George Laird, often pu?^wagant*ɨ*; first syllable frequently pu^wa- in compounds), shaman, "doctor."

pu?^wi- (termination not recorded), eye; -vu?*i* as last element in masculine names.

pu?^wintcats*i*, mouse.

pungkuts*i*, dog, pet; never given by George Laird without the diminutive, but from present-day sources I have pungk*u* or pungku.

puk^wig^yah, blowing (with mouth or bellows—not said of wind).

pukwitu?^win^yump*ɨ*, bellows.

punav*ɨ*, bag.

punik^yaing*u*, hortatory, as in "see, the sun rises!"; but the imperative is punik^yaingu?*u*; puni-, to see.

puus*i* (Eng. pussy), domestic cat; now preferred to tukupukuts*i*.

purig^yagah, bubbling out rapidly.

puutsiv*i*, star; puutsiv*i*agah, being stars; ?ava?an puutsiv*i*agah, there
are many stars; puutsiv ?*i*gatuʷar*i*, star(s) going west (said of
movement across the sky); puutsiv w*i*?igʸah, star drops, or star
shoots (said of a shooting star); hokont*i*puutsiv*i*, large star,
said of any star or planet conspicuous by its size; tas*i*ant*i*-
puutsiv*i*, "dawn star," the morning star.

puutsiyumah (from Fort Yuma). Yuma, Arizona.

putcakaiy*u*, being full, having been filled (said of a vessel).

putcawa?ᵃigʸah, going to fill, going to its fullness (said of moon—
an adaptation of the English idiom).

saimpiv*i*, tule.

saimpivitsiw*i*, sing. saimpiv*i*ts*i* (literal translation of Span. *Los Tu-*
lareños). The Yokuts.

sagah, willow species; sagaavas*i*?ap*i*, willow sapling used in house
construction.

sagwakoʷap, Indian tobacco (o).

sagwagagah, being blue or green; sagwagar*i* (sagwa-), blue or green.

sagwamuvin?nʸangkav*i*, "green nose pendant material"; turquoise.

sagwawayuʷap*i*, Green Hanging. Placename.

sagwᵃiv*i*, intestines.

samarókʷᵃ*i* (loanword) or samarókʷᵃikʸan*i* (samaro kʷᵃ*i*-, house),
rounded brush house.

samikwituts*i* (no etymology). Man's personal name.

saavaha (no etymology). Niggerhead Mountain. Young Indians
have adopted the non-Indian corruption, saavahu.

sap*i*, belly.

saandip*i* (from Eng. Sunday—only word from George Laird in which
voiced d occurs), week; pahᵃikusaandip*i*, three weeks; cuuku-
saandin w*ii*kav*i*h, I worked three weeks.

sawap*i*, arrowweed.

saw?wiivʸ*a* (no etymology). Round Island.

si?anup*i*, species of shrub.

si?ap*i*, sage species.

si?apivʸaats*i*, Sage Water. Placename.

s*i*h*i*v*i*, anything woven; s*i*h*i*gaitcox*o*, "woven mountain hat"; woman's basketry hat.

si?ip*i* or si?itc*i*, flower (from the latter form one might deduce
si?igʸah, blooming, being in flower); -si?*i* as final element in
feminine names.

sɨna, mother's younger brother or mother's younger male cousin.

sɨpanguntsɨ, cooled off (said of anything—e.g., food or weather—which was warm or hot and has now cooled off).

sɨpiiya, "whistling squirrel (o).

siˠakarɨrɨ, Schist Sitting. Riverside Mountains.

siˠapɨ, schist.

sikwikwikwiˀ. Speech peculiarity of the little poker stick, the offspring of Bear and her husband, the Fire Poker (mythology).

sivinˠangkuvayawa, mountain where Bat went to scout for game (mythology).

sivitsiwɨ, sing. sivitsɨ. Related tribe of Northerners.

siwaˀavaatsɨ, Place of Hardpan Mortars. Chemehuevi Valley.

siwaˀavaatsiwɨ, people of Chemehuevi Valley; since the placename ends in -tsɨ, the singular would be siwaˀavaatsinɨwɨ, person of Chemehuevi Valley.

siwavaatsɨ (sand). Modern name for Chemehuevi Valley (o).

siwampɨ, coarse sand.

siwampɨruˊkʷaiy. From Lizard's war song (mythology). Translated: "from under coarse sand."

siwaavɨ or siwaˀaavɨ, hardpan.

siwayumitsɨ, Coarse Sand Caved In. Mohawk Springs.

siiwɨntɨˀipɨ (no etymology). Man's personal name (o).

siyawˀwa, captive.

sohorah, post with natural U-shaped fork; also Notched Post, a placename.

sonitcugʷah, making a soft, fur-lined nest or den (like a rabbit's); soniyavɨ, such a nest (as distinct from a bird's nest, which is kanɨ, house).

soniyawɨ (soniya- with animate plural ending), Nests. The Pleiades (mythology).

sovarampɨ, yucca species.

soovarantɨ, "mean," vicious (o).

soovimpɨ, cottonwood.

soovimpɨtsɨ, Cottonwood. Placename.

sotanavagayˀyagah, changing the voice at adolescence; sotanavagayˀyapɨmɨ, an adolescent (said in answer to the question, hanopaitɨm ˀaipatsɨ, how big a boy? how big is the boy?).

suʷapɨ, breath.

suʷatavoʷaatsɨ, "breath-health recovered," came to life, revived.

sukumungkway*u*, is shaped to a point.

su´kumungkwa´yungkway. From Guico's war song. Translated: "(I) am shaped to a point" (mythology).

supaaru?ʷagah, going to the gathering; suupaaru?ʷap*i*, gathering of people.

-suyaganuh. Formula for willing a person to do something, or for willing bad luck upon a person.

cina?ahuwip*i*, Coyote Stream. Gila River.

cina?ahuvʷiyav*i*, Coyote Song (Chemehuevi translation of the name for a Mohave song).

cina?agaivᵞ*a*, Coyote Mountain. S. H. Mountain (Span. *La Sierra del Agua Nueva*).

cina?avah, Coyote Water. Chuckawalla Springs.

cina?avi, coyote; cina?agaip*i*, coyote carcass; cina?arasiap*i*, "coyote dawn," false dawn (the time when the coyotes howl).

cinawavi, Mythic Coyote, the pre-human, immortal personage; cinawavi haagaru?ʷagaip*i*, Coyote's former or discarded clothes, the secondary rainbow; cinawavi naro?ogʷaip*i*, Coyote's former shirt, another name for the secondary rainbow.

citu?ʷigᵞah, it is cold (literally, cold making). Said of weather.

cuuk*u* (cuuku-, cuu-), one. Cuuku- is the prefix before words for night, month, year, etc.; apparently the shorter form may be used only before -tava-, sun, day; thus one may say cuutavan wiikavih or cuukutavan wiikavih, I worked one day, I worked the whole day.

ta-, (1) sun, or by the sun; (2) with the foot; (3) (nasalizing) directional prefix.

takagan*i*, flat-topped house, shed; a large house of this type was built for the Cry.

tagutuutsitc*i*, anything heated by the sun (not by fire).

tamun*a* (tama-), spring; tama?iwar*i*, spring rain; tamamiants*i*, spring month; tamawi?ats*i*, beginning of spring.

tamaupats*i*, left behind (e.g., said of outrunning an animal).

tam*i*, we two; you and I only.

tamiwant*i*, sibling of us two; tamiwantim*i*, dual; tamiwantimiw*i*, three or more.

tannakaits*i*, sidewinder, snake species.

tan?nigigᵞah, stepping.

tang*a*, knee.

tangatcokots*i*, small bird species (hypothesized from George Laird's English translation, "knee-pounder").

tava-, -tav*a*, prefix or postfix meaning day, sun; **tavava'ap***i*, "high sun," time of day when the sun is two or three hours high; **cuutav***a* or **cuukutav***a*, one day; **tavamawisiy***i*, the sun emerges (rises).

tavahuk*w*amp*i*, Sun Spider. Mythological character.

tavamuhuumpits*i*, day owl; owl species.

tavamuhuuhuv*w*iyav*i*, Day Owl Song.

tavaap*i*, species of shrub.

tavapits*i*, sun (animate form, but sun is not always personified); **tavapits kutsik***y*ig*y*ah, the sun is burning something, e.g., burning trash or making a bonfire; said of the reddish glow that is sometimes seen around the sun at its rising or setting; **tavapitsi maruk***w*atu*w*a*, "toward (the region) there visible under the sun"; the east; **tavapits montco**, "sun's beard," or **tavapitsi montco'***a*u-k*w*a*, literally, "sun its beard," or "it is the sun's beard." Said of the phenomenon colloquially known as "the sun drawing water," also of the rays of light that are sometimes seen extending across the sky at sunrise or sunset; **tavapits ya'***a*, sun died, eclipse of the sun; **tavapits ya'ak***a*its*i*, the sun disappeared; same as **taviyi'ak***a*its*i*.

tava'ats*i*, chipmunk (desert chipmunk or antelope groundsquirrel).

tava'awi'anana'ats*i*, Chipmunk Penis Growing Up (continuously erecting itself). Placename. Monument Peak.

tavay*u* (adverbial form not used with numerals), day, in the day, by day; **tavay 'uru***w*agah, travelling in the day, travelling by day.

tapayu*w*ig*y*ah, splitting.

tapiagah or **tapin'niyagah**, stretching out the leg and pushing with the foot; **tatapiagah**, performing this action repeatedly.

tavig*y*ah, throwing (transitive), said (but not exclusively) of the sun throwing out light and heat; **tavip***i*, sunlight, that which is thrown (by the sun); whence **tavi-**, sun; **tavi'igangunts***i*, went in out of the sun (does not refer to the sun "going in" or setting); **tavi'igangumpaan***i*, I am about to go in out of the sun; sounds as if it meant "I am about to enter the sunlight," but is the same as **hava'igangumpaan***i*, I am about to enter the shade; **tavimaw'wis***i*, the sun emerged (as an animal from its hole); **tavimawisits***i*, sun emerged, sunrise; **taviyi'ak***a*its*i*, the sun disappeared; indicates sunset or the time immediately thereafter.

tapitcapɨ, knotted string (string tied with knots to indicate the number of days that will elapse before an event takes place); **tapitcap nayaakᵃinguɨ**, the knotted string is brought (messenger has arrived with knotted string).

tapitcapɨyawitcɨ, bearer of the knotted string.

tavoʷaatsɨ, (1) young cottontail rabbit; (2) got well, recovered health.

tavutsɨ, cottontail rabbit.

tasɨagah, dawning, day is dawning; **tasɨanguɨ**, it became morning, day broke; **tasɨapɨ**, early morning before sunrise; dawn.

tasɨantɨ, dawn; **tasɨantɨ marukʷatuʷa**, "towards (the region) under the there-visible dawn," the east (see under **tavapɨtsɨ**); **tasɨantɨ marukʷatu ʔuruʷakwaʔinguʔu**, go east! **tasɨatugʷanu**, dawn-night, the period of darkness between false and true dawn.

tasɨpanguntsaʔᵃukʷa, it (the weather) has cooled off. Said of any time of day when it becomes cooler.

taasi, familiar name or nickname of the woman shaman called **pagaarayuningkɨ**.

tasuupaaruʔʷagah, gathering up clothes, leaves, trash, etc., with the foot.

tantɨh (tantɨɨ-), north; **tantɨɨnguʔu**, go north! **tantɨɨtuʷa**, towards the north.

tantɨinʸɨwɨwɨ, sing. **tantɨinʸɨwɨ**, Northern People, persons of northern tribes unrelated to the Chemehuevis.

tantɨɨtsiwɨ, sing. **tantɨɨtsɨ**, (1) Northern Chemehuevi; (2) persons of any related tribe living to the north.

tantɨvah (tantɨvai-), south; **tantɨvainguʔu**, go south! **tantɨvaituʷa**, towards the south.

tantɨvaitsiwɨ, sing. **tantɨvaitsɨ**, the Southern Chemehuevi.

tantɨvaiyɨpatsɨ, Southern Fox. Mythological character.

tantɨvaiyɨpatsi tangaronʔnɨgipɨ, "(Where) Southern Fox Thrust in His Knee." Placename commemorating a mythological event.

taruʔʷigʸah, it is hot (literally, heat making), said of hot weather.

tatsikwaakwaʔa. From Buzzard's war song. Translated: "comes in sight now and then" (flying too high to be seen, he becomes visible occasionally). Mythology.

tatca, summer; **togʷaitatca**, "half-summer," midsummer; **tatca-**

miants*i*, summer month; tatcanni*wari*, summer rain; tatca-wi*ʔ*ats*i*, the beginning of summer.

taw*a*, we three or more.

tawawant*i*, sibling of us three or more.

taw*ʔ*wats*i* (taw*ʔ*wa-), man; taw*ʔ*wahiwagaipi*ʔ*ing*ʷa*, his or her (invisible) deceased male parent, euphemism for "his dead father"; and even this is not used when bereaved son or daughter is present; taw*ʔ*wats kinutsiwa*ʔa*, man and son's child; taw*ʔ*wats kinutsiwiwa*ʔa*, man and son's children.

-t*i*, -nt*i*, -r*i*, -tc*i*, verbal postfix sometimes translated as roughly equivalent to English present participial.

ti*ʔ*agah, borrowing.

ti*ʔ*amay*u*, top; on top of.

ti*ʔ*asigah, freezing; ti*ʔ*asip*i*, frozen, anything frozen.

tihiy*a*, deer; dialectic variant: tihii (o).

tihiya*ʔ*igatiah, Deer Entering Place. The long sandy wash that runs from Bouse to Parker.

tihiyahivitiah. Deer Drinking Place. Placename.

tihiyavhuv*ʷ*iyav*i*, Deer Song.

tiho*ʷ*agantim*i*, Ambushers. Probably Betelgeuse and Rigel.

tih (tii-), up (loosely also north, but to be specific as to direction one must say tantih); tiingu*ʔu*, go up! (e.g., hill or stream), go north!

-tigah, suffix indicating time long past; same as piayay*a*.

tikagah, eating; tikakagah, three or more eating; tikangkiav*i*, boarder.

tingkan*ʔni*, rock cave; cave in rock, lava, or *malpais*.

timimi*ʔ*agah, thundering (with a deep, prolonged, rumbling sound).

-tinah, at the base of.

tinav*i*, root, i.e., unpronged root or single prong; tirinav*i*, branching root, root with prongs; tasianti maruk*ʷ*atu tirinav*i*, "east root," root prong that points towards the east.

tinangkwangu*ʔu*, come up! Opposite of panangkwangu*ʔu*.

tin*ʔ*nigah, palpitating.

tivah, pinenut, piñon (o); from George Laird I have only tivatikawagant*i*, piñon eater, pl. tivatikawagantim*i* or tivatikawantimiw*i* (he knew of no such tribename).

timp*a*, mouth.

tivah (tivai-), down, or loosely south (tantivah is specifically directional); tivaingu*ʔu*, go down!

tivats*i*, wolf; also the Wolf of mythology, elder brother of Mythic Coyote; tivatsi haagaru?ʷap*i*, Wolf's former clothes; the primary rainbow; tivatsi mo?op*i*, c*i*nawavi mo?op*i*, Wolf's Handprint; Coyote's Handprint. Name of a place where these prints may be seen on a rock (mythological event); tivatsi naro?o-gʷaip*i*, Wolf's former shirt. All these phrases derive from the myth "How Wolf and Coyote Went Away," which ends the great cycle of Wolf and Coyote myths.

timp*i*, (1) stone; (2) money.

timpi?ʸangkagatsitc*i*, Red Rock. Placename.

timpimo?o, Stone Hand or Money Hand. Man's personal name.

tivinʸasiviva?aagaingunts*i*. From Sidewinder's song as he went to kill the Four-Eyed Insect. Translated: "I went under the top scum of the earth" or "I having gone under the top scum of the earth." Mythology.

tivip*i*, earth, land, territory; tivip*i* ?itcukʷa, under this-visible earth; underground; tivikʸan*i*, earth house; tivinʸawingk*i*av*i*, workman; tivinʸawingk*i*avinʸ*i*, my workman, the man who is working for me. Cp. t*i*kangk*i*av*i*, boarder (see under t*i*kagah); tivip kosoʷagah, earth is steaming. Said of vapor rising from the earth.

timpipo?okʷat*i*, Marked Rock. Placename in Arizona.

timpisagwagatsitc*i*, Green Stone. Providence Mountains.

timpic*i*?*i*, Stone Flower. Woman's personal name.

tivitsi-, real, genuine (with possible connotation of grand or large); tivitsi?ampagap*i*, "real speech," the dialect which chiefs were privileged to use; tivitsitogʷaintim*i*, "Real Chief," the High Chief.

timpiwi*i*?anana?ats*i*, Stone Penis Growing Up, Stone Penis Erected. Pyramid Rock.

t*ii*ra?ayataw*i*, sing. t*ii*ra?ayata, Desert Mohaves (band of Mohaves who formerly lived in the desert and dressed and had weapons like Chemehuevis).

t*ii*raniwiw*i*, sing. t*ii*raniw*i*, Desert People, Desert Chemehuevi.

t*ii*rav*i*, (1) desert; (2) "Indian mile," the desert lying between one mountain range and the next; cuukut*ii*rav*i*, space between top of one range and top of the next, one "mile." Later t*ii*rav*i* was also used to indicate the white man's mile; t*ii*ragant*i*, bare, literally, having desert; t*ii*ravatc*i*, that which is of the desert; said of meat, seed, or anything that originates in the desert.

tɨrapuk^wipɨ, Desert Blower. Man's personal name.

tɨrɨnapɨgantɨ, Follower. Sirius.

tɨwiin^yagah, telling myths, narrating a myth; tɨwiin^yapɨ, myth, story of pre-human times.

tɨwiin^yatɨvipɨ or tɨwiin^yarɨvipɨ, Mythic Country, Storied Land.

too-, (1) center; (2) granite; (3) black (for tuu-).

toog^wagah, being purple (cp. ʔangkagah, being red); toog^waarɨ, purple.

tog^{wa}i-, half, middle, midway, center; tog^{wa}itavayu, "half-day," midday, noon; tog^{wa}itatca, "half-summer," midsummer; tog^{wa}intɨrawaagantu^wa, at half-center or mid-center (equivalent to Span. *el mero medio*), used in the expression mi^yarogopits tog^{wa}intɨrawaagantu^wa, full moon; tog^{wa}itomo, "half-winter," midwinter; tog^{wa}itug^wanu, "half-night," midnight; tog^{wa}itug^wanu ʔug^waavaʔangutsɨ, having gone over midnight, the time immediately past midnight.

tog^{wa}ingutsaʔauk^wa, "it fits." Said to Ocean Woman by Coyote when she had stretched the earth to sufficient size.

tog^{wa}intɨmɨ, lesser chief.

tok^wavin^yakaiyu, having been broken or shot off; tok^wavin^yakatɨ, anything broken or shot off, as in kasatok^wavin^yakatɨ, broken-winged.

toxo, man's or woman's mother's father; mother's father's brother or male cousin; mother's mother's brother or male cousin; togonɨ, my maternal grandfather, etc.

togotsɨ, man's daughter's child; man's brother's daughter's child; man's sister's daughter's child.

tookovaronumpɨ, "face blackening material," black paint. Also the name of a place where black paint is dug (manganese deposit).

tookovaronumpɨtsɨ, name of a place where there is a small deposit of black paint.

tomo or toovɨ (too-), winter; tomomɨantsɨ, winter month; toowɨʔatsɨ, the beginning of winter.

tonagah, thrusting, stabbing; tonapag^aig^yah, going along (or coming along?) thrusting or stabbing.

tonʔnɨgig^yah, inserting, thrusting in.

toovɨ, year, winter; ʔawats too^wagantɨ, several years being.

toopoxɨ (suggested etymology: tuupog^{wa}ig^yah, having black lumps). Woman's personal name.

tosagagah, being white; **tosagarɨ** (tosa-), white.

tosaˊmɨntcaˊtcungʷaˊ. From Mountain Sheep Song. Translated: "that unseen white lamb."

tosatavitaakwaˀa. Magic formula by which Wildcat Brothers killed rabbits. Translated: "white tumbling over." **tavi-** here said to mean "to tumble," but cp. **tavigʸah**, throwing.

torosakagah, being gray (literally, black-white); **torosakarɨ** (torosa-), gray.

totsaarɨmɨ (no etymology). Man's personal name, alternate name or nickname of **tugumpayaaˀoʷasiʸakarɨmɨ**.

totsɨ, head.

tooyagah, Center of the Pass or Boulder Pass (see **too-**). Placename.

toyongkarɨrɨ, Boulder Sitting. Granite Mountains or Old Dad Mountains.

toyompɨ (too-), boulder.

-tu- (-ru-, -ro-, -tcu- after i), causative particle.

tu-, tuu- (to-, too-, -ru-, -ro-, etc.), black, dark.

tuˀu, Indian asparagus.

-tuʷa, towards; **-tuʷavanɨ**, I shall go to or towards (place named in prefixed word).

-tuˀʷatsɨ, young of animal.

tuuˀʷatsɨ, woman's sister's or female cousin's child of either sex.

tuuhʷavitcɨ, Black Lying. Placename.

tuhugʷaiyu, being an enemy, having been made into an enemy; **tuhugʷantɨ**, pl. **tuhugʷantɨmɨ**, enemy (the plural form was used to designate any tribe in a state of enmity with the Chemehuevi); **tuhugʷantɨgaipɨˀɨngʷa**, his (that invisible one's) dead or former enemy.

tuhugʷantɨsagwagarɨmɨ, Green Enemy. Man's personal name.

tuhugʷantɨtivipɨ or **tuhugʷantɨrɨvipɨ**, Enemy Country; specifically, the lowlands on both sides of the Colorado River from Fort Mohave to Palo Verde Valley. The Mohave equivalent was *ˀahwei myamat*).

tuhuˀungʷa, His Enemy. Placename.

tuhuvɨ, enemy (an unusual or archaic word from which the above placename derives; **tuhugʷantɨ** is generally used, even in compounds).

tugʷanu (obj. **tugʷanuʷa**), **tugʷavi** or **tugʷaruˀʷintɨ**, night.

tugʷavayu, at night, by night.

tug^waru?^wintɨpah, Night Water. Placename.

tuku, wildcat.

tukunanavaviwɨ, Wildcat Brothers (three or more).

tuku^wavɨ, meat; tuku^wawɨpɨapɨ, large, flat, slab of meat pounded and dried in preparation for storing.

tuku^warɨkawagantɨ, pl. tuku^warɨkawagamɨ, flesh-eater; any of the ferae; also applied to flesh-eating birds but not to snakes.

tukumumuuntsɨ, mountain lion.

tukumumuuntsitɨnah, At the Base of the Mountain Lion. Placename.

tugumpa, sky (obj. tugumpaya); tugumpay ?iv^ya?ana, "on this-visible sky," on top of the sky.

tugumpayaa?o^wasi^yakarɨmɨ (also recorded as tugumpa?o^wasi^yakarɨmɨ), Yellow Sky (literally, "light yellow sky"). Man's personal name.

tugumpiin^yaaviwɨ (tugumpa, sky; pɨhɨvɨ, downfeather, also fuzz of cottonwood seed and soft fur of animal), Sky Brothers, literally, Sky Downfeather Brothers. Mythological characters.

tukupɨra (no etymology). Personal name of a respected High Chief of the Desert Chemehuevis.

tukupukutsɨ (tuku- plus pungkutsɨ, pet, but here ngk becomes k), domestic cat. Now generally called puusɨ.

tukwaiyu, from under.

tuukwarɨ, anything stretched, e.g., elastic.

tuukwatsɨ, Stretched. Woman's personal name.

tumiingu (Span. *Domingo*). Man's personal name.

tuumontcokowɨ, sing. tuumontcoko (George Laird gave no etymology, yet the word obviously contains the elements tuu-, black, and montco-, beard). The Chemehuevis, including all three branches.

tunuk^witcɨ, that which is circular (e.g., like a plate).

tupagagah, being black; tupagarɨ (tupa-, tu-, tuu-; frequently to- or too- if followed by syllable containing o or a), black.

tu?upa?avɨ, Indian Asparagus Worm. Mythological character.

tupasi^yakagah, being brown, literally, pale black; tupasi^yakarɨ (tupa-si^ya-), brown.

tumpig^yamagah, having a puckery taste, being puckery; tumpitcɨ, that which is puckery, Span. *agaroso*.

tuupog^{wa}ig^yah, being black lumps.

tupunu^want*i*, dark (as the night is dark).

tu^ʔur*u*, buckskin strap two or three inches wide, suitable for belt or carrying strap.

tutu^ʔugaiv^y*a*, Animal Familiar Mountain (o). Placename, given as name of a sacred cave (possibly Lehman Cave in Nevada).

tutuk*i*waay^ʔyun*i* (no etymology). Woman's personal name.

tuntug^wiv^y*i*, lava, *malpais*.

tutuguuv*i*, pl. tutuguuviw*i*, spirit-animal familiar; shaman's helper; tutuguuvo^ʔop*i*, "animal familiar marked," i.e., marked by animal familiars; said of all rocks which bear paintings or carvings.

turunni^{ʔy}agah, whirlwind blowing; turunni^{ʔy}ar*i*, whirlwind (of it they say, ^ʔ*i*n*i*pi^ʔik^w*a*, it is a devil; turunni^{ʔy}ari kwikwipakagah, three or more (children) clubbing a whirlwind; turunni^{ʔy}ari may*i*wa^{ʔa}ingk*i*ts*i*, they (three or more) killed the whirlwind; turunni^{ʔy}ar su^watavo^waats*i*, the whirlwind came to life.

turump*i*, adobe.

tutup*i*, (1) the white opaque glass that is formed by lightning striking and fusing sand; (2) small species of shrub.

tutusiw*i*, mythological race of giants, said to be the ancestors of the Mohave.

tuw*a*, man's son (dual, tuwam*i*; triplural, tuwam*i*w*i*); tuwan*i*, my son.

tuwam*i* nturutsig^yam (ha!). From Old Bear Women's song, sung as they carried wood to the place of the Scalp Dance—probably Scalp Dance song). Untranslated (mythology).

tuuwin*iri*, Black Standing. Man's personal name.

tsasiyav*i*, large red ant; modern form, tasi^yav (o).

-tsi-, -ts*i*, (1) diminutive; (2) locative; (3) person of; (4) verb postfix indicating past or completed action; (5) noun ending with no particular meaning (especially in northern dialect).

tsiw*i*^ʔik^yaiy*u*, being streaked, having been streaked; tsi^ʔw*i*^ʔi^yats*i*, streaked (said of the streak of light left across the sky by a falling star).

tcak^ai^ʔ*i*, younger brother; younger male cousin; direct or collateral ancestor more remote than grandfather; tcak^ai^ʔin^y*i*, my younger brother etc. But tcak^ain^y*i*, my younger brother, was the customary form by which a Chemehuevi addressed a Quechan.

tcaku^{ʔw}in^yakat*i*, (eagle) skin which has been removed and cured with feathers intact.

tcagwara, chuckwalla.

tcakwᵃivu⁷ʷi, testicles.

tcakwavu⁷ʷivunavi, Testicle Bag. Placename.

tcaw⁷waganti, Having (or There Being) Tcawa. Name of a box canyon where one's footsteps sound: tcawa, tcawa, tcawa (a rough, whispering sound).

tcawiih (no etymology). Man's personal name.

tcawitsi-, to seep; rare word referring to the seepage of water.

tcixa (tciga-), duck.

tcikavi, anything tangled (e.g., a tangled vine); tcikamasuupaaru⁷ʷa-vani, I am going to gather up a tangle of things.

tciga⁷uruʷanti (sometimes recorded as tciga⁷uru⁷ʷanti), Duck Walker, Walks Like a Duck. Man's personal name.

tcig kasarokʷavinʸakati, Broken-Winged Duck. An unidentified constellation.

tcimpi⁷igʸah, quivering, vibrating with a quicker or more vigorous movement than that expressed by yimpi⁷igʸah (said of lightning).

tcimpi, yucca date; fruit of all three species of yucca.

tciimpaawaanaintsiwi (tcimpi, yucca date; pa⁷avim, worm; waha-, two; naintsiwi, girls), Yucca Date Worm Girls. Mythological characters.

tcomaruripanga'i. From Salt Song. Translated: "many ants." A corruption of Mohave tcamadhulya ⁷apalya, the equivalent of Chemehuevi ⁷ava⁷atsasiyavi.

tcomigʸah, chewing.

tcopivi, hair of human head; but tcopivi⁷aani or niini tcopivi⁷ah, my hair.

tcungkʷapi, granite.

tcum⁷makati, anything covered with earth; but not said of a buried corpse.

tcupani, yerba del manso.

tcupanihopakᵃi, Yerba Del Manso Hollow. Placename, probably Willow Springs.

tcupi, anything gathered to a point, e.g., a bunch of grass tied together at one end; tcuupikʸani, pointed, wigwam-shaped brush house.

-⁷ukʷa (1) inanimate possessive pronominal postfix; its; (2) copulative: am, is, etc. In both usages u tends to assimilate with preceding verb but continues to influence k as k^w—e.g., ni?ik^w niwɨ, I am a Chemehuevi.

?ug^waava?anguntsɨ, went over something (e.g., over a mountain, or the night "went over midnight").

?ung^wa, that invisible animate; pl. ?umɨ.

-?ung^wa, pronominal postfix, his or her invisible; u assimilates to preceding vowel but ng remains ng^w—e.g., hiwagaipi?ing^wa, his or her dead parent.

?ung^wawantɨ, sibling of that one invisible; ?umɨwantɨ, sibling of those invisible.

?unyih (from the Mohave), woman's sister-in-law or woman's female cousin by marriage; unlike the loanword hai, this word has ii in compounds, e.g., ?unyiinɨ, my sister-in-law, etc., and na?unyiiwɨ, two sisters-in-law. Exact equivalent of native Chemehuevi musimpiya, which it tends to supplant.

?uv^wana, on top of that invisible.

?uvanguntsɨ. From Crow's war song. Translated: "going yonder out of sight."

?uuvimpɨ, yucca species.

?uru^wagah, travelling, going, walking; ?uru^wantɨ, walking, walker (last element in masculine names, as tcɨga?uru^wantɨ, Walks Like a Duck, but never used in feminine names); ?uru^wakwa?ingu?u, go!

?uru?^wagah, wants.

?uruk^wa, under that invisible.

wahavantɨnɨwɨavɨ, two bands (of Chemehuevis).

-wa?ᵃi-, particle used with verbs to signify motion away from speaker (opposite of -ki-).

-wa?i-, -wa?a, and.

waiyo?ongo haniyanga´. From Salt Song. Untranslated.

wagata, frog.

wagatamuh^waratɨmɨ, Bitter Frog. Man's personal name.

wangkasɨ or wangkasih (Span. vaca), cow.

wangkasiigwasɨ, Cow Tail. Man's personal name.

waasa (no etymology). Name of a large waterfall below Cottonwood Island.

waaripayatsiwɨ, sing. waaripayatsɨ (from Mohave huwalipaya). The Walapai. But if a Walapai is present when a Chemehuevi is speaking, he says hohorapayuwitsɨ).

watsamamau⁷*u*, Bee Woman, or watsamaa⁷ipits*i*, Bee Old Woman
(o). Chemehuevi name sometimes given to Georgia Laird Culp.

watsav*i*, bee.

wawangkɨgagah, standing up serrated like teeth of a saw, but tall,
like mountain peaks; wawangkɨgar*i*, serrated peaks (but a single
peak is kwitcuvar*i*).

wayu^wagah, hangs, hangs down.

wayukwagaig^yah, swinging back and forth.

wayukwagaiv^yah (wayuk´, wa´yuk^waa´). From Mountain Sheep Song.
Translated: "will go along swinging back and forth"; said of
"mountain canteen" tied to hunter's belt.

wayukwakaiy*u*, "hangs" (*sic*) crosswise, being projected in a hori-
zontal direction.

-wɨ, plural termination.

wɨ⁷ap*i* (-wɨ⁷*a* as termination of masculine names), penis.

-wɨ⁷ats*i*, the beginning of; as in tamawɨ⁷ats*i*, the beginning of
spring.

wɨ⁷iig^yah, shooting (arrows); but tuguwɨ⁷ig^yah, shooting arrows at
the sky.

wɨ⁷iin^yuah, Shooting Place, Target. Placename.

wɨ⁷ik*u*, dropped, fell.

wɨɨkagah (Eng. work), working; cuutavan wɨɨkavɨh, I worked one
day.

wɨgimp*i*, vagina.

wɨgintirav*i*, Bare Vagina. Man's personal name (o).

wɨn⁷namakasaama⁷apits*i* (possible etymology: wɨn⁷na-, flint; ma-
katcats*i*, horned toad; maa⁷ipits*i*, old woman). Species of small
bird; also the name of a mythological female character (see
Chapter VI, stories of "How Horned Toad Visited the Giants"
and "How Coyote Went to War Against Gila Monster").

wɨn⁷nap*i*, flint; but when attached to arrow, huu wɨn⁷naw*a*, arrow's flint.

wɨnɨgah, stands, is standing; wɨnɨr*i*, standing, stander, he who or
that which stands; as in ⁷otawɨnɨr*i*, Sand Standing, personal
name.

-wɨpiap*i*, large, flexible slab of dried foodstuff, e.g., meat or mescal; cp. mapɨagah, stretching out with the hand, and tapɨagah,
stretching out with the foot.

wɨpuk^wagah, jumping up and down; flapping.

wɨ´pukʷagai. From Louse's song. Translated: "is flapping up and down" (mythology).

wɨsɨpagah, being cool; wɨsɨpapɨ, cool of the day, late afternoon (all forms of wɨsɨpagah refer only to the coolness of late afternoon).

wɨtɨmˀmagah, closing (transitive); nawɨtɨmˀmagah, closing itself.

wɨtompoyaimi-haikʸa. From Coyote's war song. Translated: "(I) bundle up." Mythology.

wikʸamagah, having an oily or greasy taste.

wikʸigʸamagah, having a jelly-like "taste" (texture or feel in the mouth); said, e.g., of chia, tapioca, okra, or manavɨ, the tender young branch of the cholla cactus.

wikʸivɨ, jellied substance, e.g., meat broth when jelled.

wikontotsɨ, Buzzard Head. Chemehuevi name of George Laird.

wikɨ, also wikumpɨtsɨ, buzzard.

wikuntɨpa (but tɨmpa, mouth), Buzzard Mouth. Man's personal name.

wikumpikʸavoˀo, Buzzard Tank. Placename.

wipusiyavɨ, lard. Also name sometimes given to George Laird because the Chemehuevis pronounced Laird as "lard."

wisiʸavɨ, feather; but witciˀitsi wisiˀʸah, bird's feather, huu wisiˀʸah, arrow's feather (if attached to bird or arrow).

witca-, calf of leg or thigh*; witcaˀaitɨɨgupɨyaganuh, may he be shot in the calf of the leg (probably Coyote's wish directed toward Wolf—mythology); witcaˀɨaruˀʷatsɨ, wound in the calf (or thigh?).

witciˀitsɨ, bird of any small species; the plural, witciˀitsiwɨ, is apparently applied sometimes to all birds collectively (at least to all land birds); witciˀitcikʸanɨ, bird-house, or witciˀitsi kanɨ, bird's house; nest.

witsiˀitsitsɨ, Little Bird (modern pronunciation). Personal name or nickname of a young Chemehuevi girl (o).

wiwavɨ, oil or grease.

wiwˀwingngkuratsɨ, dragonfly.

wiiˀwirah (no etymology). Maria Mountains.

wiwˀwiyatsɨ, species of small brown bird, about the size of the bird called in Spanish *la viejita*.

---

* My notes are unclear, and I have not found a living informant who could clarify the meaning.

wiyaan⁷nikʸaatɨ, Adobe Hanging Like Tears. Place on the Colorado River where there was a Chemehuevi settlement; wiyaan⁷nikʸaatɨtsiwɨ, sing. wiyaan⁷nikʸaatɨtsɨ, people of wiyaan⁷nikʸaatɨ.

wiyavɨ, adobe; also turumpɨ.

wiyaatuʷa (no etymology). Whipple Mountain.

wiyaatuʷanagahuvʷiyavɨ, the Mountain Sheep Song of Whipple Mountain.

yahªigʸapɨtsɨ, parent-in-law; yahªigʸapɨtsigʸaipɨwɨnɨ, my former parents-in-law (said after separation from spouse).

ya⁷a (ya⁷ªi-), died. Said of person, also of eclipse of sun or moon; ya⁷ªiwa⁷ªigʸah, going (away from speaker) to its death; said of waning moon.

yagah, (1) pass between two parallel mountain ranges; (2) a specific placename.

yagagah, crying, weeping, mourning; yagapɨ, "Cry," the Mourning ceremony; yagatɨgaarɨ, pl. yagatɨgaakarɨmɨ, mourner, person who is sponsoring a Cry.

yagahuvʷiyavɨ, Crying Song.

-yaganuh, part of willing formula (usually with -su-, but see under witca-); mamɨsuyaganu panangk punikʸangkuupɨyaganuh, may they (three or more) look up!

yaga´paga´ivʸa. From Mountain Sheep Song. Translated: "will go along crying" (said of the white lamb).

yamasah, pl. yamasaawɨ, raccoon.

yamasaaganivʸa, Raccoon House. Placename.

yampa or yampavɨ, mockingbird.

yampavinʸukʷɨ, Mockingbird Runner. Man's personal name.

yavipayawɨ (from Mohave yavipaya). The Apache.

yavipayaagwatsiwɨ (loosely from Mohave yavipaya ⁷awei). San Carlos Apaches.

yatampɨ, greasewood, creosote bush.

yaarɨ⁷ivʸa, alternate form of ⁷ilyaalyi⁷ivʸa (from the Mohave). Man's personal name.

yawaiya´yawaiyawai (ha!). From Old Bear Women's song (mythology). Untranslated.

yawigʸah, carrying in hand or arms.

yɨ⁷akªitsɨ, disappeared; having disappeared.

yɨvana, autumn; yɨvana⁷ɨwarɨ, autumn rain; yɨvanamɨantsɨ, autumn month; yɨvanawɨ⁷atsɨ, the beginning of autumn.

yɨpatsɨ, fox.

yɨmpɨʔigʸah, quivering, vibrating.

yɨɨpiya, man's sister; yɨɨpiyavɨ, a sister (of a man).

yɨwaʹarukʷaʹituʷaʹ (yɨwa rukʷaʹi). From Deer Song. Translated: "through a valley."

yɨwaavɨ, valley.

yɨwigʸah, three or more sitting down (triplural of karɨgah); yɨwitcɨ, three or more sitters, three or more sitting.

yumigʸah, caving in (said, e.g., of sand or earth).

yuviʸavitcɨ, Pinetree Lying. Walapai Mountains.

yuvimpɨ, pine species.

yuvisavɨ, something dirty and greasy, e.g., a black, greasy pot.

yuvisaavitcɨ, Dirty Greasy (Substance) Lying. Dead Mountains and the range west of Needles which appears to be a continuation of that chain. Also called tuuhʷavitcɨ, Black Lying, but yuvi-saavitcɨ is considered more correct.

yuʔuravatsɨ, small brown bird species; also a mythological female character.

yuwaanʔnikʸaaiyu, tears hanging (being hung) on eyelashes; yu-waanʔnikʸaatɨ, tears suspended on eyelashes; cp. placename, wiyaanʔnikʸaatɨ.

yuwitawɨ, sing. yuwita. Unidentified northern tribe who spoke a language closely akin to Chemehuevi.

INDEX

INDEX

Acorn, 104
Adobe, 87, 88*, 129
Afro-American Folklore, 215
Afternoon, 96
Agave (Mescal Plant), 5, 6, 108, 168-169
Agriculture, 4, 6, 8, 19, 22, 23, 104, 108, 109, 134-135; see Irrigation; Planting
Ainu, 227-229
Alcoholism, 44
Aldebaran, 92
Allegiance, 22
Ambush, see Fighting; Hunting
Animals, 10, 109-118; see also listing for specific animal
Antelope, 177, 180, 226, 251
Antelope Groundsquirrel (Desert Chipmunk), 113, 156
Antlers, 112, 240
Ants, 18, 118, 172, 182
Apache, 4, 15, 38, 73, 74, 75, 79, 105, 133, 144
April, 23
Apron (Woman's), 6, 108, 149, 165
Archery, 159, 184; see Arrows; Bows; Fighting; Hunting
Armor, 100-101, 161, 178, 182, 197-199, 227; see Fighting; Flint; Gila Monster; Mythology (Coyote, Horned Toad, Turtle, Wolf); Rainbow

Stone Shirt, 100, 182, 227
Wrist Protector, 155, 191, 192, 221
Arrows, 5, 107, 159, 167, 184, 189, 195, 200, 201, 240, 250; see Dawn; Fighting; Hunting
Arrowhead, 159, 197; see Flint
Arrowweed, 105, 107, 250, 255
Asparagus, see Indian Asparagus
Astronomy, 89-93
Autumn, 23, 94, 157
Awl, 6, 215, 218
Badger, 113, 172, 203; see Mythology
Badlands, 88, 121
Bands, 6, 22-23, 168, 253
Baskets, 5, 6, 21, 106, 141, 148, 150, 151, 168, 194, 201, 214, 229, 232, 234, 241, 249; see Boats; Food; Material Culture; Rafts
Basket Designs and Motifs (Illustrations), xxvii, 2, 19, 21, 29, 30, 49, 51, 52, 54, 70, 81, 82, 118, 145, 146, 207, 208, 227, 229, 235
Bat, 113, 164, 182-192, 210, 219-221; see Ice Mountain
Familiar, 32, 34, 113, 122
Bathing, 186, 188, 217
Beans, 23, 103, 106, 107, 109, 168

---

* Page numbers appearing in boldface type indicate the page(s) on which the Chemehuevi word for the entry may be found.

337

COLOPHON

Design: Melanie Fisch

Text Type: 11 point on 13, 10 point on 12, and 8 point on 10 Press Roman set on an IBM Magnetic Tape/Selectric Composer

Headings: 11 point Press Roman Italic

Main Headings: 14 and 21 point Andover caps set on an Addressograph-Multigraph Comp Set 500

Book Title: Goudy Extra Bold

Composition: Melanie Fisch

Decorations: Lynn Mathews-Clark

Paper: Warm White 60 lb. Antique Mountie Opaque Offset

Offset Lithography: Rubidoux Printing Co., Riverside, California

MALKI MUSEUM PRESS
MORONGO INDIAN RESERVATION

90414

E
99
C493
L3

LAIRD, CAROBETH
    THE CHEMEHUEVIS.

DATE DUE
